Ian McTaggart-Cowan

Ian McTaggart-Cowan

The LEGACY *of a* PIONEERING BIOLOGIST, EDUCATOR *and* CONSERVATIONIST

RONALD D. JAKIMCHUK,

R. WAYNE CAMPBELL &

DENNIS A. DEMARCHI

HARBOUR PUBLISHING

Harbour Publishing Co. Ltd.
P.O. Box 219, Madeira Park, BC, V0N 2H0
www.harbourpublishing.com

Edited by Betty Keller
Indexed by Stephen Ullstrom
Text design by Mary White
Dustjacket design by Shed Simas
Photos courtesy of Ronald D. Jakimchuk, R. Wayne Campbell and
    Dennis A. Demarchi except where otherwise noted.

 This book was made possible by the Biodiversity Centre for
Wildlife Studies (www.wildlifebc.org).

Printed and bound in Canada

 Canada Council   Conseil des Arts    BRITISH COLUMBIA
for the Arts   du Canada   ARTS COUNCIL
                                                          An agency of the Province of British Columbia

Harbour Publishing acknowledges the support of the Canada Council
for the Arts, which last year invested $157 million to bring the arts to
Canadians throughout the country. We also gratefully acknowledge finan-
cial support from the Government of Canada through the Canada Book
Fund and from the Province of British Columbia through the BC Arts
Council and the Book Publishing Tax Credit.

Cataloguing data available from Library and Archives Canada
978-1-55017-623-0 (cloth)
978-1-55017-625-4 (ebook)

To Xisa—always supportive;
and to my daughter Lyn and son Richard
and to the loving memory of my daughter Patti.
—*Ron Jakimchuk*

To Eileen, Sean and Tessa—
it is a privilege to share my life with you.
—*Wayne Campbell*

To Marilyn Robbins—for continual encouragement;
and to my daughter Diana and son Chris.
—*Dennis Demarchi*

and

In memory of the golden years of biological exploration
and discovery and those who shared the journey.

Contents

Authors Ron Jakimchuk (left), Wayne Campbell and Dennis Demarchi in the foyer of the Beaty Biodiversity Museum on the campus of the University of British Columbia, Vancouver. PHOTO BY CHRIS STINSON, MAY 9, 2013.

Preface

In the spring of 2010, I encountered Ann Schau, Dr. Ian McTaggart-Cowan's daughter, at a choir concert in Victoria. When I asked about her dad, Ann informed me that he would be celebrating his one hundredth birthday on June 25, that there would be a special celebration at Government House to mark the occasion and that I would be invited. A few days later, in thinking about this remarkable man and the impact he had on generations of students and colleagues, I developed an idea for a tribute to his lifelong dedication to zoology. My plan was to publish a supplement dedicated to him and his accomplishments in *Wildlife Afield*, the biannual, peer-reviewed provincial natural history journal. It would be presented to him on the occasion of his centenary.

With this in mind, I invited Wayne Campbell, a board member of the Biodiversity Centre for Wildlife Studies (BCFWS), to lunch to discuss the idea. Wayne had been Ian's friend and colleague for over thirty-five years, and as the senior author had spearheaded the superb four-volume series *The Birds of British Columbia*[1] with Ian as one of the co-authors. Wayne, who is heavily involved in the publication of *Wildlife Afield*, was immediately enthusiastic about my idea and said he would present it to his board for approval. We both felt that this journal was a particularly appropriate outlet in view of Ian's lifelong association with field biology and his leadership in advocating the importance of biodiversity.

In short order, the board approved the project to be done under the auspices of the BCFWS, and the race was on to meet the June birthday deadline. Wayne invited Dennis Demarchi, also a board member, to participate in the birthday publication. The initial concept of the proposed journal issue was to bring together in one place the voluminous and diverse list of Ian's publications supplemented with some biographical material, and at our initial meeting we quickly determined that Ann would be a vital source of information on her father's early and family life.

Subsequently, Wayne and I met with her to explain our goal and seek her assistance. We left that meeting with her support and some information on the early history of the McTaggart-Cowan family and a montage of priceless photographs, many of which appear in this volume. As part of the tribute, we also planned to include submissions from past students, colleagues and friends, in which they would describe memories of their association with Dr. McTaggart-Cowan and have an opportunity to send birthday greetings. We conducted a campaign by telephone and email to solicit input from over a hundred former students and associates.

Work on the project proceeded apace as our meeting with Ann was in late March and the birthday celebration was June 25. However, about two months before his birthday, Dr. McTaggart-Cowan contracted pneumonia and he passed away on April 18. He had been active until a week before his death, visiting Finnerty Gardens at the University of Victoria with Ann. Now the authors had to make a decision regarding the project and its original goal. Much of our preparatory work had been accomplished, and considerable enthusiasm had developed among respondents to our request for memories of their association with Dr. McTaggart-Cowan. Moreover, there was still great value in assembling and preserving the legacy of his publications and other contributions, so we decided to proceed with a more comprehensive documentation of his life and work. And that led to the decision to prepare this book.

For the three authors, there have been many exciting and rewarding side benefits to gathering information and contacting old colleagues, some of whom we had not spoken to for over forty years. There were many delightful reacquaintances and sharing of anecdotes associated with those contacts and our common experiences. Our trip to the University of British Columbia to assemble a list of theses by Dr. McTaggart-Cowan's students was also a noteworthy journey down memory lane. Dennis and I had been students there in the late 1950s and early 1960s, a vigorous time in Dr. McTaggart-Cowan's career as head of the Department of Zoology and his burgeoning influence as an educator and mentor, and Wayne had worked at UBC's Vertebrate Museum in the early 1970s, but we hardly recognized the campus and had to orient carefully to find the biological sciences building! As we peeked into the darkened "Room 100" lecture hall of the Wesbrook Building, a flood of memories of times and lectures there more than fifty years ago enveloped all of us.

With the helpful assistance of Edythe Grant and Margaret Harney in the Zoology Department office, we received keys to the "Theses Room," where a copy of each Department of Zoology thesis was archived. Our goal was to photograph abstracts of all those for which Dr. Cowan had been the supervisor or advisor. We would subsequently summarize, to the degree possible, the principal findings of those studies so they could be preserved and available in this publication. They also reflected Dr. Cowan's intellectual input and interests as well. We had been in that dusty room, poring over theses and photographing abstracts, for some time when I realized that this room had in fact been Dr. McTaggart-Cowan's office when he was head of the Department of Zoology. If those walls could speak, what stories they could tell!

This volume has now become a special tribute to the life and accomplishments of Dr. Ian McTaggart-Cowan. And what a life it has been! Well-lived, productive, innovative, influential, pioneering, seminal are all words that come to mind. However, even in combination, these words seem inadequate to describe this remarkable man because it is difficult to overestimate the breadth and depth of his knowledge as the whole biosphere was his "field" of interest.

Ian McTaggart-Cowan's public persona and record are documented here in various ways. However, much would have been lost if we had not tied it all together to include his scientific contributions along with his life as a colleague, advisor, associate and/or friend. This is the reason for including the informal remembrances and anecdotes in Part II of this tribute. Many of the respondents who provided anecdotes and recollections are themselves now octogenarians, having fulfilled distinguished careers following their academic studies as Ian's students or acquaintances. Their enthusiastic response is testimony to the continuing respect and affection he evokes. We know they will enjoy reading about each other, where their many paths have led, and what they have accomplished.

—Ronald D. Jakimchuk
with R. Wayne Campbell and Dennis A. Demarchi.

Note: In his early years Ian seems to have been undecided about incorporating "McTaggart" into his surname. The UBC calendars prior to 1930–31 show the name as unhyphenated, which followed the spelling of his father's name, but a citation to an article published in the journal *The Murrelet* in 1929[2] shows the hyphen. His graduation photo in the 1932 UBC yearbook (1932)[3] is hyphenated, but the paper he published in the *Journal of Mammalogy* in 1933 (Vol. 14, No. 4, p. 326)[4] is not hyphenated. He used the hyphenated name as author of an article published in *The Canadian Field-Naturalist* in March 1933, but abandoned hyphenation in the same journal in April 1933. It appears that he did not resume the use of the formal hyphenated McTaggart-Cowan in his published works until the 1980s. He employed the hyphenated name in the January 1983 issue of the British North America Philatelic Society's *BNA Topics*. In most cases he used an unhyphenated signature in his role as supervisor of theses and dissertations.

Both forms of the name may be encountered throughout the book. Citations of his publications are presented as published.

Milestones

Ian McTaggart-Cowan (1910–2010)

- 1910 – June 25, born in Edinburgh, Scotland.

- 1927 – Graduated from high school in North Vancouver and met Kenneth Racey.

- 1929 – Published first paper in the peer-reviewed Pacific Northwest journal *The Murrelet*.

- 1930 – Went on first collecting expedition as assistant to Hamilton Mack Laing.

- 1932 – Graduated from the University of British Columbia with an Honours B.A. degree.

- 1935 – Graduated from the University of California, Berkeley, with a Ph.D. degree.

- 1935–40 – Served as assistant curator of biology/assistant director of British Columbia Provincial Museum.

- 1936 – Married Joyce S. Racey on April 21, 1936.

- 1940 – Appointed assistant professor in the Department of Zoology, University of British Columbia.

- 1943 to 1946 – Went on research expeditions to Jasper and Banff national parks.

- 1944 – First master of arts student, Charles David Fowle, completed thesis on sooty grouse.

- 1946 – Appointed Fellow of the Royal Society of Canada.

- 1953 – Appointed head of the Department of Zoology, University of British Columbia.

- 1964 – Appointed dean of the Faculty of Graduate Studies, University of British Columbia.

- 1970 – Named Officer of the Order of Canada.

- 1970 – Awarded the Aldo Leopold Memorial Award by The Wildlife Society.

- 1975 – Retired from University of British Columbia.

- 1979 – Appointed chancellor of University of Victoria.

- 1990–2001 – A co-author of the four volumes of *The Birds of British Columbia.*

- 1991 – Appointed to the Order of British Columbia.

- 2010 – Died in Victoria, BC on April 18.

Part I

LIFE AND CAREER

Ian's birthplace at 40 Great King Street (right doorway), Edinburgh, Scotland, November 18, 2012. PHOTO BY CLODAGH BREEN.

CHAPTER 1

The Early Years

There are many "threads" running through the life and career of Ian McTaggart-Cowan, among them collector, mentor, educator and proponent of ecological and wilderness values. His life was, in fact, a testament to the importance of acquiring knowledge and an understanding of the natural world, then applying that knowledge to preserving environmental values.

The first step in understanding a species is to identify it and to determine what role it occupies in the broad spectrum of environmental interrelationships, and this is where Ian started his quest as a lad, with his collecting and observations in the coniferous forests of Vancouver's North Shore. The impetus for his enthusiasm was his fascination with the natural world and his desire to understand it, and throughout his long life and well into his tenth decade, the word "fascinating" regularly sprang from his lips.

Ian, the young collector, was interested in all of the components of the natural world, from marine and terrestrial fauna to plants. By collecting, he could see similarities and differences—the springboard to understanding the taxonomic and ecological relationships that might not be otherwise obvious. In these early stages of his career, he was a collector of birds and mammals while in later life he collected rhododendrons, alpine plants and stamps as personal hobbies.

In his writings and speeches, it is apparent that from an early age a broad aesthetic sense underpinned his values, but aesthetic sensitivity is often an early motivation for those who ultimately pursue formal biological studies. For example, the beauty of a single butterfly may trigger a desire to learn more about the entire species. A clutch of eggs in a hidden nest may be appreciated as objects of beauty or as a precursor to stimulating other interests; for example, "Why are robin's eggs blue?"

There was nothing in Ian's family background to foretell a life's

Peter McTaggart Cowan holding grandson Ian McTaggart Cowan. Edinburgh, Scotland, circa 1911. PHOTO COURTESY OF ANN SCHAU.

journey in natural history and scientific discovery. His parents were from struggling middle-class Scottish stock. Early records describe his grandfather, Peter McTaggart Cowan, as a civil engineer and his father as a stockbroker.

Ian's father, Garry McTaggart Cowan, and mother, Laura Alice Mackenzie, were married on July 6, 1909, in Edinburgh, and Ian, their first child, was born there on June 25 of the following year. Their second child, Patrick Duncan, was born in Edinburgh on May 31, 1912. A year later Garry was offered a managerial position by a company quarrying limestone on Texada Island, British Columbia, in the Strait of Georgia, and the Cowan family immigrated to Canada, arriving in Montreal via New York City and travelling across the continent by rail. (A third child, Joan, was born soon after their arrival in Canada.) The Vancouver city directories show Garry McTaggart Cowan holding down a succession of jobs, beginning with secretary-treasurer for Pacific Lime Company's Texada operation, followed by positions such as cannery man (1918), Sterling Glove Company (1919), broker with Borcan Resources (1923), manufacturer's agent (1924) and nurseryman (1926 onward). Subsequent city directories indicate a career as a horticulturalist, although according to family recollections he also was employed at Woodward's Department Store in Vancouver in various capacities, including a period as head of the camera department because he was a talented and knowledgeable photographer.

Ian's early years in this country were spent on Nicola Street near English Bay in Vancouver, which may have provided opportunities for outings with his parents to the nearby seashore and Stanley Park. However, in 1919 when he was nine years old, the family moved to a house on Forbes Avenue in North Vancouver and the following year to Jones Avenue, which at that time was on the edge of the settled area of the city. (The site is at the point where Jones is now interrupted by the Upper Levels Highway.) From this location, Ian's parents rented land to establish a dahlia nursery and market garden, and Ian became involved in various aspects of the enterprise, including taking chickens to market.

However, after school and on holidays he would escape to the forests on the lower slopes of nearby Grouse Mountain to set out traplines and observe wildlife. The dedication required to trap secretive small mammals is an indication of the boy's early passion to learn about nature, and although it is unknown whether he established a collection of specimens taken in his traps at this time, he probably made attempts to preserve them. During the course of his woodland explorations he encountered loggers and game wardens, and soon his passion to understand extended even to logging equipment and its operation, and the loggers who befriended the boy were impressed by his eagerness to seek out knowledge.

According to a 1952 newspaper article[5] that was based on an extensive interview with him:

On his twelfth birthday, his mother gave him a .22 calibre rifle, took him to the basement and showed him how to aim at targets set up along the stone foundation. Her shooting experience in the Scottish countryside qualified her as a teacher, and very soon he was hitting nail heads at impressive distances.

The acquisition of a rifle enabled him to expand his wildlife collecting, and in these early years, he collected every species of owl known to occur regularly in the Lower Mainland of British Columbia.

While it may have been mostly Ian's mother who encouraged his interest in natural history, his father had an apparent interest in the subject as well because his written signature "Garry Cowan, 1896" is on the flyleaf of the book *On the Banks of the Amazon* (1891),[6] which became part of Ian's library. When Ian was fourteen years old, he received a book for Christmas entitled *The Drama of the Forests*;[7] in it he wrote "From Daddy." As a youth, Ian also loved the writings of Ernest Thompson Seton, many of which dealt with the habitats and behaviour of wild mammals and birds.

Ian became a member of the Boy Scouts, and when he set out to acquire a naturalist proficiency badge, he met the next important influence in his education: James A. Munro. For many years Munro had supported himself as an orchardist and professional field collector for a handful of North American museums, then in the summer of 1915 he was hired for four months by the British Columbia Provincial Museum to collect birds, mammals and insects in the Okanagan. He was ahead of his contemporaries by including habitat descriptions with his specimens. Then in 1920 he was appointed chief federal migratory bird officer for western Canada (British Columbia, Alberta, Saskatchewan and Manitoba), although after 1933 he concentrated his interests in British Columbia.

In a speech Ian delivered in August 1998 when accepting the Doris Huestis Speirs Award from the Society of Canadian Ornithologists/ Société des ornithologistes du Canada[8] he described how he met Munro:

James A. Munro unknowingly gave me useful advice at a very early stage in my adventures with birds. In 1923 National Parks of Canada offered a book prize to any Boy Scout in Canada who achieved his naturalist badge and submitted a bird diary covering a year of observations. I met the requirements, sent in my diary and in time received a copy of Gordon Hewitt's book *The Conservation of the Wild Life of Canada*.[9] This was my first introduction to wildlife conservation. I still have the volume with its congratulation signed by J.B. Harkin, director of National Parks of Canada. I was impressed. Some days later a letter came from J.A. Munro, federal migratory bird officer. He had read my diary and in a nice way pointed out some mistaken identifications and fine points not covered in my library of one book—Reed's bird guide.[10] I wrote in reply asking more questions and received helpful answers. Of such small kindnesses new directions are born. Twenty-four years later Munro and I co-authored a book on the avifauna of British Columbia.[11]

In his early teens Ian earned his Boy Scout naturalist badge by keeping a year-long diary of birds seen around his North Vancouver home. PHOTO COURTESY OF ANN SCHAU.

Munro was indefatigable in research on the waterfowl of the province, the best in the business at that time. Accompanied by his wife, Olive, he devoted almost every summer to field work in the southern and central interior of the province, followed by many winters at the [Department of] Fisheries research station at Departure Bay, studying marine birds. Although the main focus of his work at the time was waterfowl, his research included the entire assemblage of birds and habitat. His regional studies of provincial wetlands and their birds provide detailed pictures of how they were in the beginning; his research on impacts of fish-eating birds on Pacific salmon,[12] and his species monographs on some diving ducks on their nesting grounds remain essential references.[13] He will be appreciated also for his dogged fights for conservation and the imperative of setting aside habitat for birds. In this area his final success was the declaration of Creston Wildlife Management Area, now dedicated to his memory. I think often of days in the field with him and the research we shared.

During the early 1940s Munro compiled records of the birds in this province mainly supported by the specimens he had collected and his own field notes. With suggestions on format, and editing help from Ian, in 1947 they published an updated account of the book by Allan Brooks and Harry Swarth published in 1925 entitled *A Distributional List of the Birds of British Columbia*.[14] The Munro and Cowan update was entitled *A Review of the Bird Fauna of British Columbia*.[15]

Ian attended North Vancouver High School and graduated in 1927 at the age of seventeen. By then his leadership capabilities were beginning to emerge. He was on the publication committee of the first North Vancouver High School annual as well as assistant business manager for the publication. His personal entry in the annual begins with: "I may be tall, I may be thin, but I'm a blame good fellow for the state I'm in." But the annual also comments on his work ethic, kind disposition and sense of humour and predicts that he was "sure to succeed in his future occupation." As his career attests, the latter comment turned out to be a monumental understatement.

It was during his last year at high school that another pivotal event occurred in his personal and professional life: he attended a lecture sponsored by the Burrard Field Naturalists' Club. The speaker was Kenneth Racey, a mining executive and member of the Vancouver Natural History Society, who gave a talk on the small mammals of the Lower Mainland. The young man must also have impressed Racey, a naturalist par excellence, at this initial meeting as Racey invited him to his home to see his collection of small mammals, and from that moment Racey became an important mentor for the fledgling biologist. Ian quickly became closely involved with the Racey family, accompanying them on many outings and field trips, particularly to their summer home at Alta Lake, which is now included in the Municipality of Whistler. This close association with Kenneth was to continue throughout the remainder of Racey's life.

In 1926–27 Ian served on the publication board of the North Vancouver High School annual as one of the assistant business managers.

There were two other major collectors who indirectly influenced Ian's development and interest in natural history at this time. The first was Allan Cyril Brooks, who lived his first nineteen years in India. He then lived in England and Ontario for short periods; in 1887 he settled on a farm in Chilliwack,[16] although farming for a living interfered with his passion for nature as he was already fully experienced in blowing eggs, collecting butterflies, preparing museum skins and identifying common plants. As a result, he soon left Chilliwack and travelled widely during the next few decades, calling several locations in British Columbia home. He never held an industry, government or university job but made his living painting, collecting and preparing museum specimens, in time becoming a world-famous naturalist and artist. It was his full-colour paintings for Percy A. Taverner's *Birds of Eastern Canada* (1919)[17] followed by *Birds of Western Canada* (1926)[18] that had the most far-reaching effect on Ian McTaggart-Cowan, who received the latter volume as a gift while he was still in high school. This book and *A Distributional List of the Birds of British Columbia* by Allan Brooks and Harry Swarth (1925) were the only comprehensive reference sources at that time for information on British Columbia's birds. Ian's subsequent summer employment and academic pursuits and Allan's busy schedule travelling and painting prevented the development of any kind of relationship, but while their face-to-face meetings were rare, Brooks's work greatly influenced Ian's development as a biologist.

The second collector who had an indirect influence on Ian's interest in natural history was Harry Schelwald Swarth. Harry was born in Chicago and in 1908 joined the Museum of Vertebrate Zoology at the University of California, Berkeley as an assistant. In 1910 he was appointed curator of birds, a position he held until 1927. He spent much of his time in the

Kenneth Racey. It was Ian's friendship with Kenneth Racey, amateur naturalist and collector (and future father-in-law) that helped to foster his interest in specimen preparation. Vancouver, BC, November 27, 1950. PHOTO COURTESY OF ANN SCHAU.

Allan Brooks developed an international reputation as a naturalist and artist. In this photo, Allan is at his easel painting a golden eagle in his studio at Okanagan Landing, BC, circa 1939. PHOTO NO. 18329 COURTESY OF GREATER VERNON MUSEUM & ARCHIVES.

field on collecting trips, and during his early professional career he visited British Columbia and prepared detailed reports on his findings. Four of his classic reports were: *Report on a Collection of Birds and Mammals from Vancouver Island,*[19] *Birds and Mammals of the Stikine River Region of Northern British Columbia and Southeastern Alaska,*[20] *Birds and Mammals of the Skeena River Region of Northern British Columbia*[21] and *Report on a Collection of Birds and Mammals from the Atlin Region, Northern British Columbia.*[22]

By the time Ian completed his undergraduate degree in 1932, he had acquired copies of all four of Swarth's reports, and although he was eager to learn about Swarth's new distributional discoveries, he was more interested in his papers on the systematic status and description of bird species along the Pacific Coast. This stimulated Ian's own work in subspeciation of birds and mammals in British Columbia and later resulted in numerous publications, both his own and those by his students. One of the most influential was written by his graduate student Bristol Foster, who completed a Ph.D. dissertation entitled "The Evolution of the Native Land Mammals of the Queen Charlotte Islands and the Problem of Insularity."[23]

CHAPTER 2

The Student Years

UNIVERSITY OF BRITISH COLUMBIA
AND UNIVERSITY OF CALIFORNIA, BERKELEY

Like many families, the McTaggart-Cowans struggled financially during the Great Depression of the 1930s. One of Ian's contributions to the family larder was to sometimes provide game for the table, usually in the form of deer that he shot on the slopes of Grouse Mountain, although he often took a tram to Lulu Island, just south of Vancouver, to hunt ducks. For these expeditions he wore a coat with special pockets to bring his harvest home; decades later he recounted being told that, if he shot ducks, he would also have to pluck and draw them as well.

Although the family was of modest means—a typical middle-class family of that period—all four children of Garry and Laura McTaggart-Cowan graduated from university and achieved distinction in their careers. Ian's brother, Patrick, earned a degree in mathematics and physics from UBC, then as a Rhodes Scholar received a degree in natural science from Oxford University. He became director of Canada's Meteorological Service and later the first president of Simon Fraser University. Their sister Joan (Zink) became a landscape designer and agriculturist and is locally noted for designing the alpine garden at the Finnerty Gardens at the University of Victoria. The youngest of the siblings, Pamela (Charlesworth), became a highly respected Victoria architect and noted urban visionary. She served on the Provincial Capital Commission for more than twenty years.

In the autumn of 1927, having graduated from North Vancouver High School, Ian enrolled in the honours zoology program at UBC. His transition to university life was undoubtedly facilitated by his prior experience as a field observer and his association with Kenneth Racey, but he was luckier than most students because even his summer jobs provided him with fresh field experiences.

Newgate, BC, with Hamilton Mack Laing:
April 29 to June 2, 1930

In the spring of 1930 Ian was offered a summer field job with the National Museum of Canada and thereby joined the world of serious collectors. Most of the early collectors came from a background in hunting and/or fishing, pursuits that had engaged their interest in the natural world, and from this they had ultimately evolved into keen naturalists and observers. Collecting specimens became just one more step in the process of further biological exploration. There was—and is—both art and science involved in the process. Not only must successful collectors be keen observers of the natural world and its inhabitants, but they must develop skills in specimen preparation, skinning and preservation. They must also provide accurate scientific documentation with detailed field notes pertaining to each specimen including its environment, observed behaviour, and any other aspects of the animal's ecology. Finally, the specimen must be accurately and properly labeled and stored for future study.

Collecting establishes the initial level of biological knowledge for new environments because the presence and distribution of species and the environments they occupy are a fundamental underpinning of ecological understanding. Subsequently, specimens collected for museums provide a basis for taxonomic studies and can act as a baseline for future evaluation of the status of a species or environmental change. For example, in the 1940s and 1950s DDT (dichlorodiphenyltrichloroethane) was considered a safe and effective insecticide to control agricultural pests.[24] However, by the 1960s it was noted that reproduction was being affected in top-level predators, especially fish-eating birds like the osprey,[25] and it was suspected that this was due to eggshell thinning caused by the accumulation of DDT and other toxic chemicals in the food chain. Fortunately, eggshell thinning could be verified by examination of eggshell thickness in museum specimens that pre-dated the agricultural uses of DDT.[26] The insecticide was banned in 1972 although some residual effects are still present in the environment today. Thus, when properly documented with field notes, collections are not an end in themselves but represent an important stage in the process of biological inquiry.

Joseph Grinnell, director of the Museum of Vertebrate Zoology at the University of California,

Ian, a hunter at an early age, packing out a Columbian black-tailed deer from a coastal forest. IMAGE G-03664 COURTESY OF ROYAL BRITISH COLUMBIA MUSEUM, BC ARCHIVES.

Ian McTaggart-Cowan and his brother, Patrick, on a field trip at Clinton, BC, June 1932. PHOTO COURTESY OF ANN SCHAU.

Berkeley, said it well when he wrote that: "our field records will be perhaps the most valuable of all our results . . . You can't tell in advance which observation will prove valuable. Do record them all." Grinnell added:

> It will be observed, then, that our efforts are not merely to accumulate as great a mass of animal remains as possible. On the contrary, we are expending even more time than would be required for the collection of the specimens alone, in rendering what we do as permanently valuable as we know how to the ecologist as well as the systematist. It is quite probable that the facts of distribution, life history and economic status may finally prove to be of more far-reaching value than whatever information is obtainable exclusively from the specimens themselves.[27]

Since the late 1920s the National Museum of Canada had been concentrating its bird and mammal collecting programs in the southern mountainous country of British Columbia from the vicinity of Princeton and east toward the Alberta border, which had not been thoroughly investigated up to this time. This area's proximity to the international boundary elevated the importance of the local vertebrate fauna and their habitats, some of which were very rare in Canada as they were northern extensions of more general distributions south of the border. There was now concern that the fauna of this area should be better represented in national collections.

The Princeton area had been first investigated under the direction of Percy A. Taverner, the National Museum's first ornithologist. In 1927 Taverner was replaced by Rudolph Martin Anderson, a mammalogist from the American Museum of Natural History in New York, and as a result, collecting trips now began to emphasize small mammals.

As the field season for 1930 approached, Anderson hired Hamilton Mack Laing, one of the few independent bird collectors in the country,

Museum technician Michael McNall measuring a series of passerine birds from the British Columbia Provincial Museum ornithology collection. These represent the contributions of at least sixteen early collectors. Victoria, BC, August 1983. PHOTO BY R. WAYNE CAMPBELL.

to explore the area. For this collecting foray, Laing selected the vicinity of Newgate on the banks of the Kootenay River (then the point of entry between British Columbia and Montana), as it was an area not previously visited by collectors. In a letter preserved in the Provincial Archives of British Columbia in Victoria, Anderson wrote to Laing on December 26, 1929:

> There is another factor which enters into the plans. You are now about the only free-lance collector in the West who is competent to do museum collecting and is familiar with the technique, and as an old apostle we want you to help pass on some of the tradition to a disciple. We have a young man in view who has been recommended to me from several different sources. His name is Ian McTaggart-Cowan of North Vancouver, now a third-year student at the University of BC. I met him at Winson's place in Huntingdon last fall, and Kenneth Racey and Allan Brooks spoke highly of him, also Professors Spencer and MacLean Fraser of the department of zoology at the university. They say his forebears were naturalists and he has camped and hunted all his life. Spencer says he is one of the best shots in BC and is a go-getter in the field. I had only a short conversation with him last fall and was much taken by him. I think that Cowan is the real thing and used to bushing it in the West.

Subsequently Ian was hired as Mack Laing's field assistant for the summer, and Laing's wife, Ethel, was hired to cook for the collectors, which allowed them to maximize their effort toward obtaining and preparing museum skins. The story of that summer is recorded in the speech Ian gave when accepting the Doris Huestis Speirs Award in Vancouver in August 1998, when he described Laing as his "mentor in the tasks of field biologist–cum–museum collector." He went on to say:

Ian explored new habitats during his collecting trip with Mack Laing in the open mixed-coniferous forests of southeastern BC. PHOTO BY R. WAYNE CAMPBELL.

Hamilton Mack Laing holding a great horned owl along with two sooty (blue) grouse collected on Juniper Mountain in the Ashnola River Valley on October 7, 1928. IMAGE G-03658 COURTESY OF ROYAL BRITISH COLUMBIA MUSEUM, BC ARCHIVES.

I was instructed to join Laing in Newgate as soon as possible after my university term. It took two and a half days to travel from Victoria to the village of Newgate in the Kootenay valley near the Montana border. The journey included a day on the Kettle Valley Railroad, overnight on a paddle-wheel steamer down Kootenay Lake, more train travel from Kootenay Landing to Fernie. There I slept and caught a small gas-electric car that ran daily from Fernie to Rexford, Montana, with a stop at Newgate. Mack had driven up in his new 1930 Chevrolet van accompanied by his equally new wife, Ethel. They had a comfortable field camp on the river bank by the bridge so we had easy access to both sides of the river. It was an exciting month. I already knew a fair amount about collecting and preparing specimens, but Mack was a master of these arts and I learned a lot from him. We added much new information on mammals of the region. Bird highlights were Williamson's sapsucker and pygmy nuthatch nesting in open stands of western larch and ponderosa pine; horned larks, McCown's longspurs and sharp-tailed grouse on the extensive grasslands of the Tobacco Plains. [28] I understand all are gone today. [29]

Ian kept a journal of that trip in the summer of 1930, and many years later that journal was among some copies of his field notes that he gave to Wayne Campbell for future use. A few entries extracted verbatim from that first journal show the breadth of his interest in natural history. Note that the sighting of a species never seen before is always an exciting event for a biologist, and Ian often identified his "first time" sightings by underlining the entry.

April 29: Arrived at Newgate, BC & made camp.

May 6: Hot sunny day. <u>Saw first Lewis woodpecker</u>. Mr. Sadler shot large male badger 5 miles NW of Newgate and gave it to me—30 lbs [T. t. neglecta].

Skull smashed to atomic pieces, very fat & in good condition. No badger east of Kootenay.

May 12: Bright day. Loon Lake, 6 horned grebes, 3 coots, 2 Holboell [Red-necked] grebes, 1 pied-billed grebe, Sora. Mr. Laing shot 2 blackbirds with much brown. I shot a ♀ blackbird. Found mallards nest, 8 eggs. I set 20 small traps, and Mr. Laing 17. No flying squirrels in traps. I took ♂ ad. ground squirrel. Caught turtle and frog.

May 23: Went up Gold Creek. Found flying squirrel's nest, 3½ feet off ground in a hollow bur in a small fir, ♀ and 3 small young taken. Nest made of black "Old Man's beard" moss. ♀ stomach full of same. Drove a ♂ flying squirrel from hole in stump and shot him. Rocky Mt. jays, [gray jay] olive-sided flycatcher and Townsend's warblers seen. Townsend's singing like black-throated gray. Bear sign examined, contained vegetation such as grass and lupine.

May 25: Skinned badger in morning. Stomach contained ♀ and 3 young ground squirrels. Young ones had been bitten in back of head and swallowed whole. Old one torn into 5 or 6 pieces and eaten in chunks.

During their thirty-five-day National Museum of Canada expedition in the Newgate area that spring, Mack Laing and Ian McTaggart-Cowan prepared about four hundred museum skins, most of which were small mammals. Many of the specimen records, along with incidental observations, filled large gaps in the provincial distribution for at least thirty species of birds and mammals. Some more notable bird records were a pair of territorial Cooper's hawks collected (eastward range extension), horned lark (first confirmed provincial breeding record for "dusky" horned lark *Eremophila alpestris merrilli*), McCown's longspur (second provincial and first interior record) and upland sandpiper (first record for the southern interior).

Jasper and Banff National Parks, Alberta: June 3 to September 15, 1930

After spending just over a month in the field with Ian McTaggart-Cowan, Mack Laing knew that this twenty-year-old was special. He considered him "a born naturalist—not one of those biologists made in college and interested only in the cheque his Ph.D. will pull in for him." It was fortunate that Laing had so much confidence in his assistant because Laing's next instructions from Ottawa were to report immediately to Jasper, Alberta, which meant leaving his wife and his car in the young man's care. In his 1998 speech to the Society of Canadian Ornithologists/Société des ornithologistes du Canada Ian described those events:

On 30 May a telegram from Ottawa instructed Laing to report immediately to Jasper, Alberta, where he was to serve as the [first] resident naturalist at Jasper Park Lodge. He caught the next train, leaving me his new car, his bride and the field camp, with instructions to get the outfit to Jasper as soon as possible. Mack was a trusting soul—as was Ethel. She did not drive and had a fear of heights, and we had lots of both; but she was good company and closed her eyes in the scary places. We all survived the adventure as good friends. On the roads of 1930 it took two days to drive to Edmonton and another two and a half days to negotiate the rain-slicked gumbo track 250 miles from Edmonton to Jasper—an average speed about 7 miles per hour.

His journal notes more succinctly:

June 2: Left Newgate 2.30. Arrived Cranbrook 11.00 [a.m.]. Left 1.30 [p.m.] arrived Radium Hotsprings 5.30 [p.m.] and stayed there because Mrs. Laing is ill.

Ian was now left on his own to collect and investigate the fauna in two national parks, Jasper and Banff. He was responsible for his own logistics, determining significant collecting sites and preparing all specimens.

The rest of that summer was devoted to the mammals of Jasper with some bird highlights.[30] During three weeks when I was alone in the Tonquin alplands, my senses were sharpened by the knowledge that I was the first person to occupy the cabin since the warden was killed the previous autumn by a sow grizzly with cubs. The bears were still in the valley! On the alpine slopes I flushed a timberline [Brewer's] sparrow [*Spizella breweri taverneri*] from her nest in a dwarfed spruce.[31] This was many hundreds of miles south and east of its type locality and nearest known location, Atlin—a major range extension. Exciting stuff! Another surprise was a nesting willow ptarmigan, also a southerly record. (A Columbian ground squirrel ate the chicks.) But it was the golden-crowned sparrows that were unforgettable. Their plaintive three-note song greeted each dawn and closed each day. Just recalling, I can see the great sweep of alpine meadows to Amethyst Lake and the towering Ramparts beyond.[32]

Excerpts from Ian's field notes for the Jasper expedition follow:

June 6: Arrived at Jasper on good road. Saw many mountain sheep and deer. A ram ran 30 miles per hour in front of the car for 100 yards.

June 9: Went to Warden Bryant's station at Snaring and made camp. Very windy.

June 16: Left Snaring at 8.15, party, Mr. Bryant, Kathleen Bryant, Sid Williams, myself and 3 horses. Rained at 9 AM and off and on the rest of the day. Stopped for lunch at Jacques Creek. Saw yellow dryas, small pink phlox, 10 mountain goat, 2 flocks of mountain sheep. Arrived at camp at 3 PM put up tents and set out 15 traps. G-crowned kinglets, hermit thrush, robins, T. solitaire, chickadee.

July 19: Rain. Skinned all day.

July 28: Went down highway to Mile 30. Shot 2 year old male beaver in Athabasca River, swam for it. Decidedly cold. Spent morning skinning crossbills.

August 25: Fine AM. Rain PM. Took hike to town for matches and grub. Back by 12 PM; 2 hours out, 2 ½ hours in. Took 2 chipmunks near 40 mile creek. These are different to ones at higher altitude, as they have more brown in the dark stripes and a redder tail and a different shade in the sides. Saw pileated woodpecker, Tonsend's [sic] solitaire, Cooper's hawk.

Tofino, Port Alberni and Comox, British Columbia with Kenneth Racey: May 4 to June 27, 1931

In the spring of 1931 Kenneth Racey invited Ian on a collecting trip to the unexplored west coast of Vancouver Island. Racey was taking the summer off to recover from an illness, and as he had always wanted to visit the remote fishing and logging outpost of Tofino, this seemed like the perfect opportunity. At that time the tiny community was only accessible via the steamer *Princess Maquinna,* which they boarded in Port Alberni on May 3. They arrived at Tofino later the same day, and because Tofino had no comfortable motels or catered trailer camps in those days, they set up base camp near the high-tide line and early the next morning started collecting birds on the mud flats. Later that morning they walked into town to check on a source of supplies and the availability of a boat in order to plan the rest of their expedition. For the next thirty-four days their fieldwork would be conducted under the most basic conditions of wilderness camping and travel by foot and small boat. Risk-taking became a daily event. For the most part they simply ignored the possibility of accidents, unpredictable weather, stormy seas and encounters with animals.

Collecting by trapping and shooting, they secured specimens from a variety of terrestrial habitats, occasionally visiting offshore islands for seabirds and rock-frequenting shorebirds. They made two visits to Bare (Cleland) Island about fourteen kilometres northwest of Tofino; it is low, rocky, shrubby, and only 7.7 hectares in size, but it supports a breeding population of at least six thousand pairs of seabirds of nine different species of which five thousand pairs were Leach's storm-petrels.[33] The other species include fork-tailed storm-petrel, black oystercatcher, glaucous-winged gull, common murre,[34] pigeon guillemot and Cassin's auklet. This was Ian's first visit to a seabird colony, and it was where he saw his first

Cleland (Bare) Island. In 1971 this low, rocky island became BC's first ecological reserve. PHOTO BY R. WAYNE CAMPBELL.

Brandt's cormorant, Hudsonian curlew (whimbrel), wandering tattler, northern (red-necked) phalarope, rhinoceros auklet and tufted puffin.

The following are selected excerpts that have been transferred verbatim from Ian's 1931 field journal. Note that even in his field notes he held his mentor in such high regard that he always called him "Mr. Racey."

May 4: Morning. Worked mud flats east of camp. Shorebirds not common, gulls very wild. Afternoon: crossed to Meares Island in boat & took gulls & sandpipers; Hudsonian curlew.

May 12: Skinned specimens all morning. Mr. Guppy brought us round a 16 ft flat bottom skiff in place of the leaky old tub the other old crook had passed off on us. In afternoon rowed round to Tofino & brought back a load of mail & supplies. Saw several cormorants but none with crests.

May 16: Skinned our catch of yesterday and cleaned up the cabin in the morning. In the afternoon Mr Racey went into Tofino while I set out a line of traps down the road. Judging by the sign I should say that this country was a washout so far as small mammals are concerned.

May 17: Traps held 2 peromyscus [deer mouse] and one Norway rat. The woods & beaches are simply overrun with these rats.

May 22: Took another trip to Bare Island. The sea was very calm & landing was easy. We noticed that the Glauc. W. gulls were spread out more over the higher rocks & were present in greater numbers than on the previous trip. About 300 to 400 being present. The pigeon guillemots were very active & showed signs of sexual excitement pursuing one another with wings upraised

15

over the back & tail spread out parallel with the ground, all the time emitting their peculiar hissing squeak. About 150 were present.

May 29: Skinned all day.

June 2: Dug clams in the morning then went to traps at Chesterman's. Took one Peromyscus.

June 7: Boat [the steamer *Princess Maquinna*] left Tofino at 6 AM. Good weather until about noon then it started to blow & was quite cloudy & rough by the time we reached Alberni. In afternoon picked up the car & ran out to Beaver Cr. Here we camped with Mr. Noel Cott. [They remained in this area north of Alberni until June 26, working the watersheds of Beaver and Cherry creeks and Stamp River.]

June 13: Rain all day. Took an old male weasel in a trap on Stamp River baited with a mouse. 2 peromyscus in other traps. In afternoon the weather seemed to clear so set out some more raccoon traps on the island in the Somass River.

June 17: Mr Racey took 10 Vaux swifts out of a large flight that came over camp in the morning. These swifts were feeding on green aphids.

June 20: In the morning we packed a light outfit & leaving Port Alberni at 9: 15 we drove over to Nanaimo. We proceeded up the Nanaimo Lake road & up the south fork to the construction site where we left the car. We then hiked 10 miles up the Nanaimo S. Fork, crossed Boulder Cr. & then followed Jump Cr. to a cabin on the right of the trail before reaching Paterson Lake. Here we spent the night.

Rediscovery of the now-endangered Vancouver Island marmot was a highlight of Ian's fieldwork with Kenneth Racey in the summer of 1931. PHOTO BY JOHN DEAL.

One rationale for the collecting expedition in the summer of 1931 was for the forty-nine-year-old Kenneth Racey to recover from an illness, but he had enough stamina and motivation to backpack at least ten miles through rough steep terrain to the subalpine area close to the top of Green Mountain. However, for him this was the highlight of the whole expedition as the two men were searching for "whistlers," otherwise known as Vancouver Island marmots, which had not been reported for two decades.

June 22: at 3 o'clock it stopped raining and stayed fine till almost noon . . . we went along the mountainside . . . and shot 6 [sic]whistlers. The whistlers taken consisted of 2 ad. ♀ 2 ad. ♂ 1 juv ♀ & 2 juv. ♂ all were very dark especially the adult animals which were almost black on the neck. The whistlers seemed to be living on the roots of lupine, the leaves & roots of an Alpine dandelion & and the leaves of the big white-flowered parsnip. All 3 of us observed 3 Clarks' crows [Clark's nutcrackers] at close range flying overhead. No possible doubt as to their identity. We skinned the whistlers & hustled down the mt arriving at the cabin at 5: 30.

June 26: Packed everything into car & said good bye to Beaver Creek. At 4 o'clock we pulled into [Mack and Ethel] Laings at Comox. We made camp in their garage and had dinner with them. Set out a line of mouse traps. [Ian's enthusiasm was still unquenchable, and he had the audacity to set a trapline on Laing's property, ignoring the fact that Laing was a well-known professional collector and one of his mentors.]

June 27: Mouse traps [set the previous evening] held 2 Peromyscus. After breakfast we ran over to Kye Bay to set coon traps but found the place all settled up and no sign of raccoon. Saw kingfishers & rough winged swallows, also cliff swallows. In the evening Mr. Racey shot a nighthawk. Saw a quail's [California quail] nest with 14 eggs & the old bird covering every one of them looked more like a pancake than a Quail.

The following day they left Comox at 11: 30 a.m. and drove to Nanaimo where they caught the boat for Vancouver. However, Ian's adventures with Kenneth Racey were not yet over for that summer.

Chezacut with the Racey Family: July 23 to August 21, 1931

A few weeks after returning from Vancouver Island, Kenneth Racey, though still recovering from an illness, set off on another collecting trip, this time with his family and Ian to the south Okanagan where they "camped and collected in the pocket desert . . . where white-tailed jack-rabbits, burrowing owls and sage thrashers provided fascination. Then north to the biologically unexplored regions of the western Chilcotin."[35] Their destination in the Chilcotin was Chezacut, a small ranching settlement located about two hundred kilometres west of Williams Lake. Racey was aware that the native grasslands in this part of the central Cariboo had not been investigated by collectors, although he knew that F.M. Shillaker, a naturalist and amateur botanist, lived in the region. (Some of Shillaker's plants are housed in the Beaty Biodiversity Museum at UBC.) James Munro, conducting waterfowl investigations in the Cariboo during the late 1930s and early 1940s, also came into contact with Shillaker, and in the latter part of the 1930s Ian encouraged Shillaker to record birds. As a result, between 1939 and 1943, he kept notes on migrants, and Munro used these in his provincial account for northern pintail[36] and later by Cowan and Munro in their *A Review of the Bird Fauna of British Columbia* (1947).

The Chilcotin plateau was a new habitat for Ian, though it was one he would visit again during his tenure at UBC. Selected excerpts, transferred verbatim from his field notes, follow:

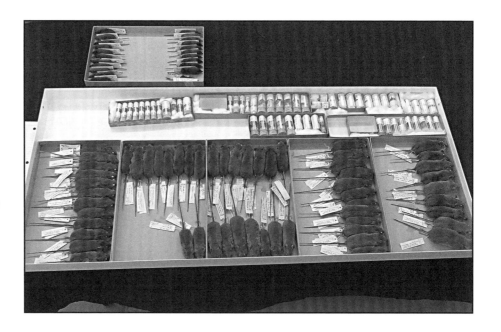

There were few mammal specimens from the western Chilcotin region of BC in museums when Ian and the Raceys visited in the summer of 1931.[37] PHOTO BY RONALD D. JAKIMCHUK, BEATY BIODIVERSITY MUSEUM, VANCOUVER, BC, MAY 9, 2013.

July 23: Arrived at Chezacut Lake at about 6 in the evening & set up the small tent had supper & retired for the night. Mr. Racey set out 6 mouse traps & had a navigator shrew by dark. 3 pelicans were feeding on the lake.

July 24: Spent the morning setting up camp. Pitched the big tent etc. etc. In the afternoon Mr Racey and I launched the dugout canoe & went across the lake to the south shore. I set out a short line of mouse traps & two muskrat traps. Saw Bohemian waxwing. . .

July 26: Skinned nearly all day. . . In the afternoon we had a heavy thunderstorm that took about two hours to pass over—after which Mrs. Racey, Joyce & I went fishing catching 23 fine Rainbow trout in the mouth of the stream.

July 29: . . . On the way down [the lake] in the morning Alan [Racey] & I found a Holboel's [red-necked] grebe nest containing two eggs. . . I spent the afternoon skinning & the evening canoeing on the lake.

Aug 3: Started the day by going over to the spruce woods with Joyce [Racey]. The mouse traps held 2 [illegible] and two peromyscus. While setting a mouse trap a small weasel came out from under a stump and was promptly added to the bag.

Aug 4: Went over to the spruce woods before breakfast with Mr & Mrs Racey.

Aug 8: Joyce & I went over to the spruce woods before breakfast on the way seeing 2 herons. The traps held 2 voles, 2 cinereus shrew & 5 peromyscus. In the afternoon Mrs Racey, Joyce & I went several miles down the river through very dead jack pine country. Found an occupied pack rat nest in an outcropping of rock.

Aug 11: About noon it thundered for a little & after the storm a large flight of black swifts, nighthawks & 3 violet-green swallows came over the camp. I took 6 black swifts retrieving 5 of them.

Aug 17: In the afternoon we drove over to the Shillakers, on the way over we jumped two Sandhill Cranes in the middle of the road.

Aug 26: Packed up & pulled out. Had lunch at Redstone.

On this trip they prepared a series of small mammals, especially heather vole (*Phenacomys intermedius*), western jumping mouse (*Zapus princeps*) and northern bog lemming (*Synaptomys borealis*). They collected few birds, and although Ian was fascinated with the shape, pattern and colour of birds' eggs, they didn't collect any. Recalling this trip in later years Ian said:

> For me it was a summer immersed in new habitats and new birds in companionship of a happy family. To this day as I write about canyon wrens, black swifts, American white pelicans or water thrushes, scenes from that summer guide my hand.[38]

The UBC Biological Discussion Club

In his second year at UBC Ian joined the UBC biological discussion club, which welcomed both graduate and undergraduate students as members and invited professors to present papers and give talks on biological topics. In 1953, 21 years after his graduation from UBC, Ian was invited to speak to the club, now as a professor of zoology at his alma mater. However, unlike most of his fellow undergraduates, Ian was already a published author and experienced naturalist when he joined the club, so as well as becoming an executive member, he was a frequent speaker. In 1929, when he was secretary-treasurer, he presented his first paper, "Fauna of the Mount Whistler Region." The following year he became president and spoke on "Mammals on the Campus." In 1931, while still president, he gave a talk called "A Naturalist in the Canadian Rockies," and in the spring term presented lantern slides on "Banff and Jasper National Parks." In 1932 (his graduating year), he held the position of curator and presented a talk on "Big Game in BC." Presentation of papers and talks before a peer group starting at such a young age undoubtedly provided valuable experience in Ian's future career as a lecturer and public speaker. Interestingly, even in his talks to the biological discussion club, he illustrated the points he wished to make with specimens from his fieldwork and personal anecdotes. For example, in his talk on big game, he told how the moose he studied had spent much of their time in summer in lakes, changing their diet from woody plants to lily pads, which allowed them to avoid the annoying biting insects. This approach,

Ian was fascinated by the social behaviour of this colonial mammal and in retirement regretted that he had not found a graduate student to unravel some of the Yellow-bellied Marmot's complex natural history.
PHOTO BY R. WAYNE CAMPBELL.

using props and stories to generate interest, would become a trademark during his entire speaking career. The topics he chose for his talks to the club also foreshadowed the papers that he would subsequently publish. While still a student at UBC he published three papers on mammals; the first, on the yellow-bellied marmot, appeared in *The Murrelet*[39] in 1929. The other two were published in *The Canadian Field-Naturalist.*[40]

Ian did not graduate from UBC until the spring of 1932, having taken five years instead of four to attain his B.A. The university's calendar for that year, which listed all students by faculty, gave his status as "Conditioned Undergraduate" in the Faculty of Arts and Science for the fourth year. This designation was for "students proceeding to a degree with defects in their standing which do not prevent their entering a higher year under the regulations governing 'Examination and Advancement' of the Faculty in which they are registered."[41] Ian had, in fact, been deficient in a required undergraduate course, organic chemistry, a well-known stumbling block for students in the Department of Zoology. Later in his career as a professor, he was very sympathetic toward students with similar difficulties and provided encouragement and well-timed advice to continue their education in zoology. However, another reason for extending his undergraduate years was his heavy involvement with field surveys in the summer of 1930 with Mack Laing, which took him from the university well before the end of April and kept him away until the third week in September. This five-month hiatus shortened his academic year and likely resulted in a reduced course load, which had to be made up in a fifth year.

The University of California, Berkeley: 1932–35

Ian McTaggart-Cowan graduated with an honours B.A. degree from UBC in 1932, by which time he had already initiated correspondence with Dr. Joseph Grinnell at the University of California, Berkeley regarding graduate studies. In his speech of acceptance for the Doris Huestis Speirs Award in 1998, he explained his reasons for wanting to enroll there:

Ornithology in British Columbia before 1940 drew much of its impetus and direction from the south rather than from eastern Canada, in particular, from the Museum of Vertebrate Zoology (MVZ) at the University of California, Berkeley, which had become one of the world's leading centres of research in ornithology. Joseph Grinnell was founding director of the Museum and over a 30-year period [had] shaped its philosophy and direction. He was a remarkable man, with a prodigious capacity for work, in office and field. Early in his career he helped found the journal *The Condor* and was its editor until his death in 1939. He pioneered the concept of environment and avifauna as inseparable and was a founder of vertebrate ecology in North America. He also emphasized in ornithology and mammalogy the need for a substantial series of specimens and the use of statistical methods in the analysis of geographic variation. By precept, he gave force to his conviction

Joseph Grinnell (1877–1939), field biologist and zoologist, is credited with introducing the "Grinnell System," a method of recording detailed field observations of wildlife. He served as director of the Museum of Vertebrate Zoology at Berkeley from 1908 to 1939. PHOTO BY G. ELWOOD HOOVER, DECEMBER 1930. IMAGE NO. 8421 COURTESY OF UNIVERSITY OF CALIFORNIA MUSEUM OF VERTEBRATE ZOOLOGY.

that field research in ornithology required active participation by senior scientists because only that contact could bring from the field the detailed perception of each species of bird and its special niche. A technician could secure and preserve specimens, but that was only a small part of what a research expedition should yield. The end result of research was publication, meticulously crafted. If you did not analyze your data and publish it, you had failed. We could relearn his philosophy. Government files are full of reports of work half-done, unanalyzed, never exposed to peer review, an uncatalogued record of wasted talent.

As one of his graduate students, I can attest that he read every word of my Ph.D. thesis in my presence and discussed it, a sentence at a time. He had a concise and precise way of expressing every nuance. He was a gentle and persuasive mentor, devoted to his students and their success. He saved more than one of us from financial crises during the later days of the Great Depression. All who worked with him learned much more than a passion for birds and their study. His philosophy and example gave ornithology new direction and new goals.

As early as 1908, the MVZ had turned its attention to north-western areas of North America, with expeditions to islands off southeastern Alaska. Subsequent expeditions studied birds and mammals along the Stikine River in 1919,[42] the Skeena River in 1921,[43] and Atlin in 1924[44] and made important contributions to the understanding of birds in British Columbia. They established the MVZ as a major contributor to knowledge of bird faunas and their distribution in northwestern North America. Harry S. Swarth, a former doctoral student with Grinnell,

One Deer Species from Two

The following is an abridgement of findings in Ian's doctoral dissertation that resulted in mule deer (*Odocoileus hemionus*) and black-tailed deer (*O. columbianus*) being reclassified as subspecies, *O. h. hemionus* and *O. h. columbianus*, respectively.

This study of variation and systematic alignment was based on 602 specimens of deer from western North America. The variation existing in characters of body size, body color, ear, form and colour of tail, dermal glands, antlers and skull was analyzed. These findings have led to re-characterization of races already described, with certain revisions in nomenclature and in range concept; also to the naming of two heretofore unrecognized races of *Odocoileus hemionus*.

Extensive hybridization takes place in the feral state between *Odocoileus hemionus* and *O. columbianus*, using these names in the earlier, specific sense. The remaining offspring are completely fertile and in the first generation they display many characters which are blends of the parental characters. The conclusion reached is that there is but a single geographically variable species of black-tailed deer, rather than two or more as recognized heretofore.

Insular isolation in deer results in reduction of bodily size. Within the race *columbianus* there are several different populations. The coastal group seems to be living under conditions of semi-insularism and to owe the inferior bodily size of its members to factors involved in true insularity.

The genus *Odocoileus* exhibits, within its component species and races, certain general trends correlated directly with environment. The northern races exceed the southern races in size, and they display a greater degree of sexual dimorphism, chiefly as regards body size. The inland races have length of ear and metatarsal gland reduced from north to south, the coastal races the converse. Form and color of tail, size of rump patch, hairiness of ear, length of pelage and intensity of pigmentation all exhibit correlation with environment. Size of skull is closely associated with bodily size, so that in general its measurements increase toward the north. Skull characters seem to vary in different fashion from external characters and to give rise to sudden "new characters" more frequently—characters without environmental correlation. External characters at the same time tend to merge continuously, with close environmental correlation.

was scientist-in-charge of these expeditions. Years later he relived for me his summers in the north and his concepts of the dynamics of bird and mammal distribution there.

Ian McTaggart-Cowan's early record of publishing and mentorships with some of the finest field naturalists of the era provided an invaluable background for his Ph.D. studies under the legendary Joseph Grinnell, who appointed him head teaching fellow. And Grinnell, with his strong background in collecting and preparation of museum specimens, was the ideal mentor for this young, keen and energetic student. They were kindred spirits on the voyage of biological discovery, spirits whose intellectual curiosity encompassed all and varied biological topics and organisms. Evidence of the close relationship between the two men: after Ian broke his leg while home in BC during the summer of 1933 and could not afford to continue his studies, Grinnell sent him money with the admonition not to repay it but in the future to help some other needy student.

During his studies in California, Ian published six articles on topics ranging from woodchucks (*Marmota monax*)[45] to the hibernation of bats (*Lasionycteris noctivagans*)[46] and pathological skin growths in deer,[47] as well as two articles on new races of deer. And during the same year that he was awarded his Ph.D., he published another article on the distribution of the white-footed mouse (*Peromyscus maniculatus sitkensis*).[48] This astonishing pace of publication would continue for the next seventy years.

He completed his studies and received his Ph.D. in the spring of 1935. His dissertation was entitled "Distribution and Variation in Deer (genus *Odocoileus*) of the Pacific Coastal Region of North America." It was subsequently published in a 101-page article in the journal *California Fish and Game*.[49]

Two of the subspecies of the genus *Odocoileus hemionus* studied by Cowan. The left photo shows the narrow black-tipped tail and large white rump patch of *O. h. hemionus* (mule deer). The darker black bushy tail and smaller rump patch is characteristic of *O. h. columbianus* (Columbian black-tailed deer).

PHOTOS BY MARK NYHOF (L.) AND R. WAYNE CAMPBELL (R.).

CHAPTER 3

The British Columbia Provincial Museum

JULY 1935 TO JULY 1940

I n July 1935 Ian McTaggart-Cowan joined the staff of the British
Columbia Provincial Museum, which had been established in 1886 (and
became the Royal BC Museum in 1987). In his speech to the Society of
Canadian Ornithologists/Société des ornithologistes du Canada in 1998
he explained that:

> The new museum was dedicated to preserving specimens to illustrate all
> aspects of flora and fauna, native cultures and history of the province. This
> marked the first recognition by the province of wildlife as an important
> component of natural resources. It was a momentous turning point.
>
> Through its first half-century the museum staff consisted of the
> director and one assistant, supported by a secretary. Temporary assistants
> were hired for fieldwork in summers. John Fannin, a well-known naturalist,
> was a happy choice as the first director. Although financial resources were
> meagre, he immediately set about making a faunal inventory. The first
> publication of the new Museum was *A Check List of British Columbia Birds*,
> prepared by Fannin.[51]
>
> [On Fannin's retirement in February 1904] Francis Kermode took the
> reins. As director he was active and ingenious in building the museum's collec-
> tions, despite a meagre budget. Expeditions were undertaken in 1913 to 1916
> to explore biological resources as far afield as Lillooet, the Okanagan Valley
> and Atlin.[52] Among summer assistants, the name of J.A. Munro appeared first in
> 1915 when he was hired for four months to collect birds, mammals and insects
> in the Okanagan. His brief report on the field season is notable for habitat
> descriptions.[53] He was ahead of his contemporaries in his understanding of

Francis Kermode was the second director of the BC Provincial Museum (now Royal BC Museum) and served in that capacity for 36 years between 1904 and 1940. It was during his tenure that Ian McTaggart-Cowan was hired as the museum's first assistant curator of biology in 1935.
IMAGE A-06434 COURTESY OF THE ROYAL BC MUSEUM, BC ARCHIVES. PHOTO CIRCA 1910.

the essential relationship between birds and their habitats. Budget cuts in 1917 put a stop to field programs, and for 18 years the museum's bird and mammal collections languished and curatorial responsibility was neglected.

Institutional collectors from outside Canada were central in creating and furnishing an environment for bird study in British Columbia. Samuel Rhoads was a pioneer. He made an ambitious expedition in 1892 to study and collect specimens of birds of northwestern Washington and southern British Columbia for the Philadelphia Academy of Natural Sciences. From May to September he collected at carefully chosen locations across the southern and central regions of the province, beginning at Victoria and ending at Field. His report on the summer's work makes fascinating reading more than a century later.[54] Thumbnail sketches of the terrain around each of his collecting sites are evocative; his brief analyses of faunistic elements of the regions visited are concise and accurate. Rhoads is someone I wish I had known.[55]

In 1935 Francis Kermode, who served as director of the British Columbia Provincial Museum from 1904 to 1940, hired Ian to be the museum's "assistant (and only) biologist." His annual salary at this point at the height of the Depression years "was $1,500, less income tax and pension deductions, and [Ian] was glad to have it. The alternatives were not pretty, as the social safety net was almost nonexistent." Ian continued:

The museum's collections of birds and mammals were in a sorry state from lack of curatorial care. There were no current catalogues, and in general the opportunities for progress were unlimited. The situation in government also was ripe for change. A previous government had opposed support for higher education and had starved the university. Several leading university faculty joined the ranks of the Opposition, and in the next election the government was defeated. Three faculty members became ministers and a new philosophy prevailed. Education, energy and enthusiasm were rewarded and good ideas encouraged. It was a great place to start a career.

We reintroduced exploratory field work, filling blanks on the biological map at Quesnel, Ootsa and Eutsuk Lake, Kootenay and Revelstoke national parks. Each area produced its surprises. By far the most exciting was that of May–July 1938 when Pat Martin and I made the first study of birds and mammals in the Peace River region of BC. It was our first adventure with a spring migration that is taken for granted by our eastern colleagues. We were out before dawn every day, fascinated by the torrent of birds from the Mississippi flyway that daily filled the trees and wetlands; many birds I had never seen before. The urgency of that migration was gripping—every day we saw new species, they all seemed in a hurry. In two months we added 10 new birds to the provincial list.[56]

[**Note:** The new species were Franklin's gull, blue-headed vireo, Philadelphia vireo, Cape May warbler, bay-breasted warbler, black-and-white warbler, Connecticut warbler, Le Conte's sparrow, Nelson's sharp-tailed sparrow and common grackle. The publication of the new list initiated the British Columbia Provincial Museum's Occasional Paper series.[57]

From the beginning the Provincial Museum had a special place for birds. After Fannin's distributional list of birds—307 species and subspecies—Kermode produced an updated list of 139 species and subspecies.[58] In 1925 Allan Brooks and Harry Swarth collaborated on a more elaborate and insightful [document, which they titled] *A Distributional List of the Birds of British Columbia.*[59] This followed the style and pattern established by Grinnell. In five introductory pages it presented four bioclimatic life zones of the province, based on the Merriam concept, with a coloured map. The book treated 409 species and subspecies. Twenty-two years later J.A. Munro and I collaborated to produce *A Review of the Bird Fauna of British Columbia.*[60] This broke new ground in recognizing 13

The series of savannah sparrow specimens used in determining the distribution of subspecies in BC.
PHOTO BY R. WAYNE CAMPBELL.

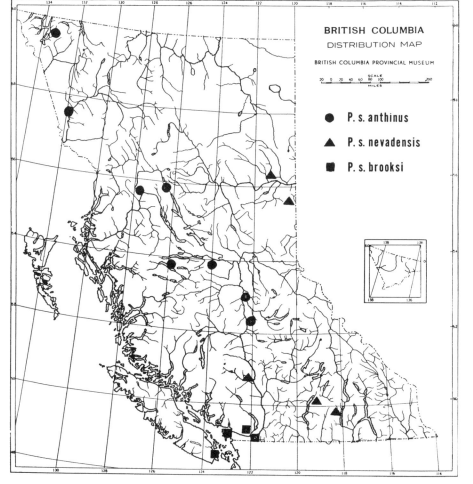

Distribution of three subspecies of savannah sparrow in BC in the mid-1940s from analysis of museum specimens. REPRODUCED, WITH PERMISSION, FROM THE ROYAL BRITISH COLUMBIA MUSEUM.

biotic areas based upon vegetation and occurrence of birds and mammals in them. Data on distribution were based exclusively on specimen evidence, covering 491 species and subspecies, with key dates and places.[61, 62]

Okanagan Valley, Ten Mile Lake, Ootsa Lake, Eutsuk Lake and Indianpoint Lake: June 18 to August 13, 1936

In June 1936 Ian undertook his first major, and longest—57 days—collecting trip for the museum, accompanied by his new wife, Joyce, the daughter of Kenneth Racey. They were a good match, both being seasoned collectors and campers, having accompanied Joyce's father on numerous family excursions and collecting trips prior to their marriage on April 21, 1936. In 1998, looking back on that day, Ian said:

> Sixty-two years ago the Raceys welcomed me to their family as son-in-law. Even young men sometimes make inspired decisions, and this was certainly my best. Joyce and I—at first just us, but later with a son and daughter—have roamed the world, and in our homeland have camped over much of the province from the heathered margins of alpine lakes and the teeming life of Cariboo marshes to the sphagnum bogs of northern islands, always savouring wild places and seeking to understand their creatures.[63]

Ian and Joyce wasted very little time travelling between major collecting areas on this first trip for the museum. They spent ten days in the Okanagan Valley, nine days in the vicinity of Ten Mile Lake north of Quesnel,

Joyce and Ian McTaggart-Cowan raised a family consisting of son, Garry Ian, and daughter, Ann (Schau). When Joyce died in 2002, Ian referred to the loss as "like losing my right arm," for in addition to their marriage, they were collaborators in a shared lifetime of biological discovery. PHOTO BY J. MARY TAYLOR, SAANICH, BC.

twenty-three days around Ootsa and Eutsuk lakes and twelve days with the McCabes at Indianpoint Lake, east of Quesnel.[64] As kindred spirits, the newlyweds endured the rustic conditions of camping in inclement weather, slippery roads and annoying mosquitoes and black flies as well as long hours preparing specimens. Although Ian received a stipend from the museum for travel expenses, the meagre allotment barely covered food for one person, let alone two, so on occasion "they ate a few grouse" before preparing the skins. By the end of the trip they had prepared more than 135 bird and mammal specimens for at least 48 different species, most of them noteworthy additions to the Provincial Museum's collections.

The following are selected excerpts, transcribed verbatim, from Ian's field notes on this inaugural trip for the museum:

June 18: Vancouver–Merritt.

June 21: Camped at 17 Mile Creek–Anarchist Mountain [South Okanagan Valley]. Traps: 1 badger, 5 peromyscus [deer mouse], 2 microtus mordax [long-tailed vole]. The country is so overrun with perys and citellus [ground squirrel] I could catch no perognathus [Great Basin pocket mouse]. Redstarts, pewees, robins & Williamson's sapsuckers extremely abundant. Crossbills & evening grosbeaks nesting. These two species come to water once a day—in the early morning. The mourning doves come once a day—at dusk. Saw a poor-will & 20± nighthawks. Heard a horned owl. Shot an eptesicus [big brown bat].

June 25: Went in to White Lake in the broiling sun & hunted for sage thrashers & Brewers sparrows getting ad ♂ & ♀ & 2 juv of the former & 4 ♂ & 1 ♀ of latter. Also took a sharp-tailed grouse. Brewer's sparrows as common as Vespers. Sage thrashers are just beginning second nests.

June 30: Set up camp at 10 Mile Lake [Quesnel]. Rained torrents all afternoon & evening.

July 5: 10 Mile Lake—Slight rain—mostly warm—mosquitos bad. Took warbling vireo & magnolias [warbler], junco & a hermit thrush. Our one ruffed grouse is still drumming. Young crows & thrush are just out of nest, also R-cr [Ruby-crowned] kinglets. Have seen no calliope hummers or sapsuckers, both were so common 4 years ago.

July 9: Enroute Quesnel–Vanderhoof. Country very uninteresting, miles of jack pine or aspen. Aspens badly denuded by a brown moth. Have seen thrushes eating it but no other birds.

July 10: Enroute Vanderhoof–Ootsa Lake. . . Between Francois [and] Ootsa [lakes] is grassy plains—a most interesting stretch of country; rolling uplands with clumps of aspen in gullies.

Collectors and Cats Reveal Least Weasel's Presence

The least weasel is the smallest of carnivores with a body barely twenty centimetres (eight inches) long. It is inconspicuous, rarely seen, and is known to occur in British Columbia from less than twenty records.[65] Most specimens originate from collectors and cat-killed animals. On June 26, 1936, Ian trapped one at Ootsa Lake, which was preserved as specimen #1687 in the Royal British Columbia Museum, a species new to their collection. There were only two earlier records, both specimens in the National Museum of Canada that had been collected by John Shelford in Wistaria on the north side of Ootsa Lake in 1932 and 1935.

July 22: Ootsa Lake. Settled into cabin again. Found pack rats [bushy-tailed woodrat] in old house & set traps; picked up rabbit skull, caught a Thamnophis sirtalis [common gartersnake].

July 26: Took a ♂ Mustela rixosa [least weasel] a new provincial record. Rain & high wind.

July 28: Ootsa Lake—still raining. [Took] ♂ Sorex cinereus [common shrew] ♂ Peromyscus; mice very scarce this year. After breakfast took a run up to Shelfords about 6 mi west of Wistaria on the Nadina road. John Shelford tells me he found a least weasel in the meadow & trapped another last winter. Sent both to R.M.A. [R.M. Anderson at National Museum of Canada]. Has taken neosorex [water shrew] in his muskrat traps.

Aug 1: Left Ootsa this morning, saw large porcupine on road near Grassy Plains. Lunch at Vanderhoof. Supper in Quesnel. Camped beside 4 mile creek on Barkerville road.

Aug 2: Indianpoint Lake. Came in here from Quesnel today.

Aug 13: [left Indianpoint Lake]

The reason for the twelve-day stopover at Indianpoint Lake was as much business as the pleasure of visiting with Tom and Elinor McCabe. Seventy years later Ian recalled:

Tom McCabe—tall, athletic, impulsive, quick of mind as of temper (more often directed at malfunctioning equipment than at people)—will forever stride through my memory. Badly beaten up by his years as an artillery officer in Europe during the 1914 war, he and Elinor retired to Bowron Lake and then Indianpoint Lake to rebuild his health in the quiet but demanding wilderness environment. Their home was seven miles by trail from the nearest

Access to Thomas and Elinor McCabe's house at Indianpoint Lake was along a seven-mile trail from the nearest road. The McCabes spent most summers in this two-storey wilderness log house and, in winter, lived in Berkeley, California, to be close to the Museum of Vertebrate Zoology.[37] FROM DICKINSON, J.C. 1953. "REPORT ON THE MCCABE COLLECTION OF BRITISH COLUMBIA BIRDS."

road, and everything the house required arrived on Tom's back. They built a beautiful two-storey log house and lived there adventurously for several years. Elinor was the source of Tom's new interest in the natural world as he regained his physical and philosophical stamina. His collections of data and specimens at and from Indianpoint Lake[66] led to contacts with specialists at MVZ [Museum of Vertebrate Zoology, Berkeley] where he was provided with an office and encouragement. The McCabes established a winter home in Berkeley and for many years were migrants between California in winter and field camps or Indianpoint Lake in summer.

Between 1933 and 1939 the McCabes explored the distribution of birds and mammals along the middle BC coast. Joyce and I shared some of their adventures among the islands, five of us squeezed into MV *Seabird*, owned and skippered by Pat Martin, the first marine bird specialist on our coast. Tom died too young—of a heart attack, not surprisingly—but his contributions were many, well beyond the evidence of his bibliography.[67]

CHAPTER 4
Teaching at the University of British Columbia

In July 1940, after four productive years at the BC Provincial Museum and a promotion to assistant director, Ian accepted a post as assistant professor of zoology at UBC. He soon became the driving force behind the establishment of a comprehensive biological curriculum. As well as teaching courses in embryology and comparative anatomy, he designed and taught new courses in the biology of vertebrates and wildlife management that were not available at that time elsewhere in Canada. His teaching week was five and a half days and his classes were crowded, but with all those students to keep him on his toes, his life was busy and interesting.

However, as World War II continued, many of the younger faculty members went into the forces while at the same time the size of the student body increased, and as a result, Ian's teaching assignments became a crushing load. As he told the *UBC Alumni Chronicle* in 1990:

> It was an absolutely mad time during the war. We had no master's degree programs prior, and suddenly we had crash programs for pre-meds. We had a special lab attached to the chemistry building. I held classes in embryology and also comparative anatomy. I taught from 8 a.m. to 10 p.m. every day for two years. The students did pre-med in two years.

By the time Ian began teaching at UBC the once gangly youth had developed into a tall man, imposing in both physical stature and intellect. He was also noted for his charisma and energy. Many students remember him striding across the campus—a man eager to engage in his daily activities. His daughter Ann once remarked that he would "bounce out of bed in the early morning hours" to start his day. Ian had learned how much work

Some Memories of Family Life

At almost the same time that Ian took up his appointment at UBC, he and Joyce became parents for the first time. Garry Ian McTaggart-Cowan was born on July 9, 1940 and their daughter Ann on January 21, 1944. In 2010, Ann wrote the following reminiscence of her childhood:

> My brother and I, as children do, lived in our own little worlds but were also delighted participants in a variety of wildlife adventures—caring for owls in the attic, feeding fawns in the basement, canoeing on interior lakes, trail riding in the mountains, sorting through marine treasures brought up in small dredges, vying for the position of assistant on one of Dad's early TV shows. (Garry won that contest!)
>
> My recollections of early family life also include holidays featuring *Tuchi*, our 20-foot clinker-built boat. The inboard Jeep engine was responsible for a few burns on bare legs! I learned all about walking barefoot on heaving decks, putting out the bumpers and tying up at docks properly. We used her mostly around the Gulf Islands. Dad would leave work at UBC and take off from Horseshoe Bay to run across Georgia Strait to Saturna, quite the trip. August was our holiday month—days of sparkling sun on the sea, picking blackberries for Mum's famous Symes pies (baked in the old wood stove), listening to Dad's harmonica around campfires, rowing while my brother fished, sitting on cliffs above the surf targeting the bobbing kelp with Dad's old .22 rifle.

Both Garry and Ann attended UBC, where Garry was well known for his sense of humour and fondness for practical jokes. In spite of his father's importance and reputation, he was determined to take his own approach to research and follow his own path; consequently, he achieved both an M.Sc. and a Ph.D. degree from the Institute of Fisheries at UBC, studying the morphology and systematic relationships of sculpins (*Cottidae*).[68] He then developed an academic career as a faculty member in the Department of Biology at Memorial University in St. John's, Newfoundland.

Upon his arrival at Memorial in 1968, Garry began working closely with the Fisheries Research Board of Canada and published papers on the life history, reproduction and population dynamics of fishes as well as economic issues related to Canadian fisheries. Like his father, he was admired as an excellent lecturer and teacher; he was promoted to associate professor in 1976. From 1972 to 1988 he held a joint appointment at the Marine Sciences Research Laboratory in Logy Bay.[69]

Ann Schau graduated from UBC in 1965 with majors in biology and microbiology. From 1969 to 1999 she and her husband, Mikkel Schau, lived in eastern Canada, first in Hamilton, Ontario, where Mikkel completed post-doctoral studies in geology. In 1971 they moved to Ottawa where Ann completed a bachelor's degree in music at Carleton University followed by a master's degree (music) in 1984. After 1975 she was a seasonal sessional lecturer in music and held a private teaching practice. Ann and her husband now live in Ian and Joyce's former residence in Saanich, BC.

Garry McTaggart-Cowan as a Ph.D. graduate in 1968. Soon after convocation, Garry joined the faculty in the Department of Biology at Memorial University in Newfoundland as an assistant professor and in 1976 was promoted to associate professor. COURTESY OF UNIVERSITY OF BRITISH COLUMBIA ARCHIVES, PHOTO 5.1-581-1.

one could accomplish in the hours before the rest of the world was awake. It is, in fact, remarkable how many of his initiatives he was able to accomplish in an academic environment, which can be as politically challenging as any other endeavor. To achieve the successes he did, he combined his intelligence with charm, passion, skill and, on occasion, toughness; the recollections of his colleagues and former students indicate that he was a consummate master of advancing his views and personal agenda as well as those of the university.

Peter Ommundsen, who was a student at UBC from 1960 to 1967 recalled Ian McTaggart-Cowan as:

… a celebrity on campus, and his legendary status was reinforced by his personal demeanor and great self-confidence. He always appeared poised and well dressed. He sometimes wore what appeared to be a fine custom-tailored white lab coat that the students referred to as his "silk" lab coat. He reminded me of Basil Rathbone's portrayal of Sherlock Holmes: brisk purposeful stride, rapid speech, fast-thinking, decisive and with an encyclopedic knowledge of seemingly everything. The students held him in awe, and always addressed him as "Dr. Cowan." But despite his commanding stature, he was respectful of others, no matter what their background or education.

Year after year he gave a twice-weekly, later thrice-weekly 11:30 a.m. lecture to several hundred first-year zoology students, inspiring generations with his wit and stories of his wilderness adventures. He said that the technique was to "grab their attention with a prop," meaning an intriguing specimen borrowed from the museum. His lectures attracted students from other sections of the course taught by less able professors, and standing room only was commonplace. The student course evaluation book of 1964–65 stated that a course with Ian was "an enjoyable and rewarding experience," and ranked him "among the few professors who received no criticism whatsoever." Ian's showmanship in the university setting differed from the more reserved persona evident in his various television documentaries.

The introductory zoology lecture was given in a large theatre at the university hospital. Students entered the lecture hall from the main floor, but Ian travelled through a basement passage that allowed him to enter at stage level. I recall seeing him on many occasions striding across the campus to the freshman zoology lecture, often with a zoological specimen in hand. Certain other professors who taught in that hall lacked his sense of theatre and simply used the main entrance, jostling in with the student crowd.

Ian expected the best of everyone, consistent with the university motto "Tuum Est," which means "It is your duty" or "It's up to you." Procrastination was unacceptable. In this context the undergraduate wildlife conservation course required a lengthy field report from a trip to the Sinlahekin Wildlife Area, Washington State, but no submission deadline was given to the students. Several weeks after the trip, Ian entered the classroom to give his morning lecture and announced that he would accept no further submissions. A wave of horror engulfed the class, and a queue of students formed

Several times a week, Ian gave the introductory zoology course in an amphitheatre-like room in the Wesbrook Building, which seated 325 first-year students. He always entered through a side door in order to arrive with a touch of drama before his class. COURTESY OF UNIVERSITY OF BRITISH COLUMBIA ARCHIVES, MAY 26, 1976, PHOTO 41.1/1402. PHOTO BY JOHN MORRIS.

after the lecture to ask for an extension of the deadline. He contemplated this request and finally declared, "All right. But the reports must be on my desk by 8:00 tomorrow morning." Needless to say, many students spent a sleepless night with a flurry of phone calls cross-checking field data.

This lesson was not lost. In a subsequent graduate course, Ian assigned a report on the first day of class and did not specify a submission deadline. He opened the next class by stating, "Today each student will report the results of the investigations assigned last week." I was asked to begin as I was sitting immediately to Ian's right at the conference table. Most of the students were new to the university and unfamiliar with Ian's style. As I began my report, I could overhear panicked whispering and paper shuffling by other students, who would have nothing to contribute. But they, too, learned not to procrastinate.

Peter Ommundsen also recalled that in 1966:

On one occasion, Ian sent the entire wildlife class to Victoria to prepare a critique of the provincial Fish and Wildlife Branch headquarters operation. The understanding with branch officials was that students would be assigned to various divisions and that Ian would assemble the student critiques into a formal document that would be shared with the branch. I was assigned to scrutinize the director's office, at the time occupied by James Hatter, who was a good sport about the intrusion. I recall walking through the headquarters building and seeing students rummaging through filing cabinets as startled employees looked on.

We returned to Vancouver and submitted our analyses but heard nothing more of the document, despite Ian having promised us copies. The student

Ian learned early that using props in lectures was more than entertainment and humour. The antlers, horns, skulls and hides of elk, caribou, mountain goats, bears and wolves aroused the interest of students and visually demonstrated what he was describing in words.
COURTESY OF UNIVERSITY OF BRITISH COLUMBIA ARCHIVES. IMAGE 1.1-19357.

rumour network suggested that the document content was sufficiently harsh that Ian quietly jettisoned the project. No sense antagonizing a major employer!

For Ian, teaching was always a priority and he believed that teaching did not start and end in the classroom. When time permitted, he would leave his administrative office five to ten minutes early with an armful or sometimes a cartful of props for his lecture. During the short trek across campus he frequently caught the attention of passing students, and some of the more curious stopped him to ask what he had. In a conversation with Wayne Campbell in October 1991, he described how one morning he had been stopped by an interested student.

The student said, "That looks like a sabre-toothed tiger skull [Ian's favorite prop]."

Ian replied, "You're right. Are you a biology student?"

"No, I'm in engineering."

Then the teaching began and Ian asked if the student could identify the other large skull.

"Looks like a walrus with those tusks," the student said.

For the next few minutes Ian explained why the skull belonged to a hippopotamus and the adaptations it had needed to survive where it lived. The student skipped his scheduled lecture and attended Ian's class on the skeletal system. Many years later, Ian was informed that a very successful civil engineer had bequeathed a large sum of money to the university, still recalling the enlightening few minutes he had shared with "the professor."

Ian had one peculiarity for which he soon became famous: whenever a student was presenting during a seminar or whenever a guest lecturer was speaking, he would close his eyes and appear to be sleeping. Yet as soon as the speaker ceased, he would be able to summarize everything that had been said or ask questions that demonstrated his complete grasp of the lecture's content. One of those disconcerted by this habit was Miklos Udvardy.

The Hungarian biologist and biogeographer Miklos D.F. Udvardy had arrived at the Zoology Department at UBC in 1952 to lecture in comparative anatomy and ornithology. Ian, who became department head the following year, also expected that Udvardy's experience and research interests would fill a gap in knowledge on the distribution of animals in the province, especially as it related to the biogeography of restricted populations, endemic species and subspecies on offshore islands and in deep mountain valleys.[73]

By the early 1960s Ian was encouraging faculty to become more involved in the community through extension lectures, workshops and field trips, and he asked Miklos to give an evening public lecture to local naturalists on biogeography using study skins from the Vertebrate Museum

The Evolution of the UBC Wildlife Curriculum, 1941–1966

This list of UBC course offerings is based largely on a summary by Peter Ommundsen:

In 1941 the UBC Department of Zoology employed three faculty members: Wilbert Clemens, professor and department head; George Spencer, associate professor; and Ian McTaggart-Cowan, assistant professor. The department offered twelve courses. Clemens taught general zoology, invertebrate zoology and fish biology, Spencer taught entomology and histology and Cowan taught four courses: Comparative Vertebrate Anatomy, Vertebrate Embryology, Biology of the Vertebrates, and Advanced Vertebrate Zoology. Textbooks for the Biology of the Vertebrates course were *Birds and Their Attributes* (Allen)[70] and *American Mammals* (Hamilton).[71]

Cowan relinquished the embryology course in 1948, and in 1953 when Cowan became department head and began teaching the large introductory zoology class, Miklos Udvardy took over the vertebrate anatomy course. The last year that Cowan taught Biology of the Vertebrates was the 1962 summer session, and Jim Bendell had been teaching the course for some years prior to that. The course was transferred to J. Mary Taylor in the mid-1960s.

The first wildlife management course was introduced in the 1943–44 session a graduate course entitled Economic Vertebrate Zoology, using Aldo Leopold's *Game Management* as a text.[72] This course replaced Advanced Vertebrate Zoology and for the 1948–49 session was re-titled Wildlife Management.

In the 1949–50 session the wildlife program included the undergraduate course Principles of Wildlife Biology and Conservation, given by Cowan, and Biology and Management of Upland and Farm Game, given by James Hatter. The graduate wildlife courses were Biology and Management of Waterfowl (Hatter) and Biology and Management of Forest and Wilderness Game (Cowan).

In 1958–59 this curriculum was replaced by graduate courses in wildlife conservation (Cowan), mammalogy (Cowan), and ornithology (Udvardy). In 1960 the wildlife course was moved back to the undergraduate level, then increased in length in 1961 from one term to two, and transferred to Jim Bendell in the mid-1960s when Cowan became dean. A graduate course, Problems in Wildlife Management (Cowan), was added in 1963. The mammalogy course was transferred from Cowan to John Eisenberg in 1963 and to Dean Fisher in 1964.

teaching collection as examples of variation. Wayne Campbell recalls that the lab room was packed as Miklos started his lecture, but he soon noticed that Ian had lost interest and was sitting in a "deep trance." As Miklos continued his lecture, he picked up the nearby stuffed specimen of a double-crested cormorant to use as a pointer when explaining some of the examples he had drawn on the blackboard.

However, about thirty minutes into the lecture Miklos was asked about the difference between deer mice on Vancouver Island and in other parts of British Columbia. Could they be different species? It was a difficult question for an ornithologist, but Ian heard the question and from his seeming "state of estivation" woke up and answered it with verve. Then after the lecture he discreetly reminded Miklos that museum specimens were to be respected and should not be used as pointers.

The Zoology Museum

Ian had been employed as an assistant professor at UBC for less than two years when he and the zoology department hit the front page of the student newspaper, the *Ubyssey*, on February 18, 1941, under the headline PROFESSOR IDENTIFIES BEASTIE: [74]

> The queer animal recently found living on the banks of the Fraser [River] and apparently a mystery to authorities is a specimen well-known to science, according to Dr. McT. Cowan of the Zoology Department.
>
> "The animal is a common inhabitant of South America and is raised on two or three farms in the neighbourhood," stated the Doctor. It probably escaped and was living on the willows lining the river. A resident saw tracks in the sand and set a trap for the supposed raccoon. Much to Dr. McT. Cowan's disappointment the animal's skull was crushed when the department received it.
>
> At present the skeleton is drying in the laboratory, waiting to be cleaned by the new system of letting tiny beetles gnaw the flesh from the bones. It is three feet long, with webbed hind feet, claw-like forepaws and a broad

In February 1941 Ian was challenged to identify a mystery mammal that had been trapped on the bank of the Fraser River below the campus. He identified it as a nutria (*Myocastor coypus*), a large rodent native to South America, that had escaped from a local fur farm. PHOTO BY R. WAYNE CAMPBELL.

beaver-like tail. Long red incisors mark it as a typical rodent. After mounting, it will form a valuable addition to the zoology collection of the University.

"In South America the coypu or nutria is as important as the beaver is in Canada," stated Dr. McT. Cowan. "Its nostrils are set high in the muzzle to facilitate breathing while in the water, much the same as our marine animals."

And so the mystery of the strange visitor is explained.

As the newspaper predicted, the nutria was headed for a display case in the university museum, and three days later the paper's page 3 headline read: UNPAID WORKERS FOR SCIENCE.

Unknown to the majority of students, a colony of cannibals gorged themselves on the reeking carcasses in the fetid atmosphere under Applied Science 1000. This is done with the full knowledge of Dr. Ian McTaggart-Cowan of the Zoology Department.

The reason he condones such a gruesome pastime beneath the feet of unsuspecting scholars is that the savages are only one-half inches long, being dermestid beetles kept for the purpose of cleaning skeletons before mounting. So these pleasant little animals chew happily away in their heated tin pen under the light of a large 100 watt lamp, placed there to keep them warm and to facilitate their munching. At the present time they are busy with a cat skeleton, and a foul odour permeates the air around the pen.

"That smell isn't nearly as bad as the one that accompanied the old system of maceration, which simply meant rotting in water," said Dr. Cowan, smiling at my wry face. "Those little fellows do quite as neat a job and don't take as long."

He explained that in a week they would finish with the cat and would start on the next patient, the coypu, or South American beaver, brought into the department last week. At present the coypu hangs by the tail pathetically awaiting her turn with the flesh merchants.

The dermestid beetle is a native of BC, but the ones used by the department were brought from California recently. They do not require much care, their homes consisting of a wad of cotton batting. To ensure greatest activity, however, they must live in a saturated atmosphere kept at 86 degrees Fahrenheit.

Anyway, having seen this branch of the Zoology Department, we feel that if Professor [Frederic] Wood knew the oppressive odour that exists below his English lecture room, he would not complain so bitterly of the "smelly sophomores" he teaches. They are perfume compared to the effluvia in the cellar.

The osteology units in many museums raise dermestid beetles to clean flesh from the skeletons of specimens. In this photo, individual specimens have been isolated in separate chambers. PHOTO BY JOHN J. OSOSKY, SMITHSONIAN INSTITUTION, WASHINGTON, DC.

In 1942, less than a year after the newspaper brought him to the attention of the university body, Ian took on the job of curator of the university museum in addition to his teaching duties. At that time it was housed in a crowded space in the library building and consisted of about 1,700 specimens from North and South America and the South Pacific islands. It was staffed by student volunteers and open for four hours daily. Ian initiated a program to expand the facilities and increase the collections by encouraging contributions from students. Within a year he had arranged for more storage to be constructed, gathered additional materials from students, reorganized overcrowded exhibits and initiated the development of an interpretive program. In 1949 the museum was moved to a large space on the fourth floor of the biological sciences building and greatly expanded with the addition of the private collections of Kenneth Racey, Walter S. Maguire and J. Wynne as well as H.R. MacMillan's exotic bird collection.

Ian frequently received telephone calls at his office from friends or members of the public asking him to identify a "mystery bird" that was not in their bird books. One day in 1958 he got a call from his dentist saying he had just discovered a large white bird with a pink head in his Point Grey garden. Ian was perplexed and could not identify it even after the dentist explained that the wingspan was over six feet, the back was brown and the belly pure white. And, he said, it had pinkish-red splotches on its head!

The dentist was so convincing in his description that Ian readjusted his daily agenda and drove the short distance to the Point Grey garden. When he got there, he found an adult Laysan albatross with a pink head, a pelagic species that is rarely seen within sight of land! He later learned that biologists Karl Kenyon and Dale Rice were conducting homing experiments on the species and had captured 18 birds on a nesting colony on Midway Island, an atoll in the North Pacific. They had banded and colour-marked them and then released them from points around the Pacific Ocean, including Whidbey Island in nearby Washington state.

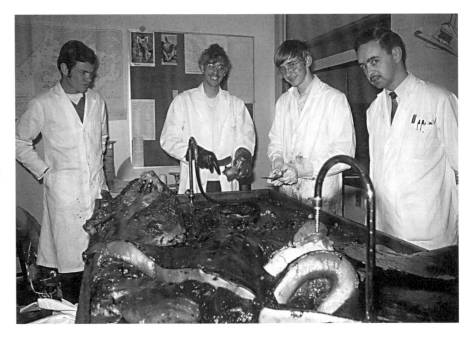

Preserving the skeleton of a beaked whale required two days of flensing followed by several days of slow boiling under a fume hood. From the left: volunteers Kenneth Summers, Jim Biggar and Richard Jerema are watched by UBC staff member Allan Handley during the process. PHOTO BY R. WAYNE CAMPBELL, DECEMBER 1, 1970.

Ian's only comment when he recounted the story to Wayne Campbell was: "Never be surprised where birds show up—they have wings."

Ian was delighted when in 1970 a rare specimen of Stejneger's beaked whale (*Mesoplodon stejnegeri*) was donated to the museum—in the flesh. Although widely distributed in deep pelagic waters, beaked whales (*Ziphiidae*), characterized by their long beaks, are one of the least known groups of mammals. As most of the current knowledge comes from stranded individuals, Ian had made a special effort to encourage volunteers to save the bones of beached animals and arrange to get them to a major museum.

The flensing process for this one was started on a Friday night and

Who Laid a Penguin? Gender and Parents of Egg Still a Mystery[75]

Something was rotten in Stanley Park—a baby penguin who never saw the light of day.

Ever since an egg appeared in the park's penguin pool early in August, Vancouverites have been waiting with bated breath for the event that would put their city on the map.

Unfortunately, however, the egg refused to hatch, and after an extended incubation period it was transported to the University Biology lab for Dr. Ian McTaggart-Cowan to examine. He opened it, and therein lay a tail joined to a penguin.

"This bird, even though he was never born, is surrounded in mystery. For one thing, he was laid at the wrong time of the year according to the penguin's calendar. Also, the chances against Stanley Park's penguins breeding so soon after being transported from their natural habitat were great," said Dr. McTaggart-Cowan.

The most mysterious factor in the bird's appearance is that nobody yet knows who his parents are. The penguin that was incubating the egg had no obvious mate, and no one could tell whether it was a male or a female. At the same time, two others were pretending to incubate an egg, taking turns sitting in a hatching position all day and passing it back and forth at night.

It seems that all penguins, male and female, have an irresistible urge to hatch an egg. Under normal circumstances, the mother and father take turns during the incubation period, passing the egg from one to the other once a day.

When an egg has been laid in a captive colony, the other penguins are aware of it and gather in a circle about the proud poppa or momma (not even the penguins can tell). When the time comes to change shifts, the egg often disappears in the crowd: and this may have been the case in the park's colony. It is possible that the penguin who was incubating the egg had no legal claim to it at all but had stolen it from the pair who had refused to let it become public that they had lost their offspring and so continued the pretense of hatching it.

When the egg didn't hatch, Dr. Ian McTaggart-Cowan was asked to examine it. He opened it with a drill, in order to preserve the shell, and found a perfectly formed baby penguin inside. It had apparently died one or two days before it would have hatched.

The cause of the death cannot be determined, but there are several possible explanations. Dr. Cowan found that the shell was unusually thick. It is possible that because of this the young bird did not receive a sufficient supply of fresh air. Or it may have been that he wasn't strong enough to crack the tough shell.

Whatever the case, the mystery remains. Was the bird that was incubating the egg male or female? And if it was a female, had she laid the egg or stolen it?

We will never know.

—*Ubyssey*, October 7, 1955

continued through the weekend into Sunday afternoon when it was time for the boiling stage to begin. For this a large vat had been borrowed from another faculty and placed under a fume hood, and Ian arranged to have the solution topped up during the evening by the janitor. Alas, the hood was designed for the preparation of small skeletons, not the oily flesh of a whale, and it was far too small to vent the steam and associated odours.

Of course, the technicians cleaning the bones did not notice the smell, but on Monday morning Ian was inundated with telephone calls from staff and faculty. The nauseating, oily smell had entered the ventilation system and permeated the entire building. Some comments he received both in jest and seriousness were: "It smells worse than a beach at low tide," "My lunch tastes like my office smells," "The building stinks" and "Now you know why I went into botany." Ian apologized for the "malfunction" of the fume hood and promised to have it repaired immediately. Several weeks later he had his prized specimen catalogued and added to the museum collection, but the fume hood remained unchanged, ready for the next specimen. Decades later several faculty and staff members from that time remarked that they could still "vividly recall the stench."

During his tenure at UBC, Ian maintained the association of the Vertebrate Museum with the Department of Zoology as a centre for research and educational support for students and faculty. The museum was later renamed the Cowan Vertebrate Museum. Today it is housed as

Volunteers Bruce Macdonald (foreground) and Brad Watts help reorganize the large grey wolf collection in the Vertebrate Museum at UBC, Vancouver, BC. PHOTO BY R. WAYNE CAMPBELL, VANCOUVER, BC, MAY 20, 1971.

a separate collection known as the Cowan Tetrapod Collection in the Beaty Biodiversity Museum at UBC and consists of over 45,000 specimens of mammals, birds (including eggs), amphibians and reptiles.

Judgment Trumps Rules

After he became head of the Department of Zoology in 1953, Ian was able to demonstrate that the wisest use of authority is the use of good judgment to supersede rules that jeopardize a higher goal. While in his ascending career, he had developed the skill of asserting his goals within the expanding zoology department in the relatively young and growing university, and by a combination of charm, logic and assertiveness, he had bent, broken or circumvented rules that threatened to sidetrack worthy students. He saw the best in people and was quick to use his influence to help students bypass academic hurdles, apparently unchallenged by other faculty members. As he wanted them to succeed and he recognized the value of a gentle boost along the way, he developed a reputation for leniency toward students who encountered academic obstacles, such as failing grades in languages, statistics or chemistry. His generosity and empathy has been attributed to his own difficulties with chemistry; his subsequent success in life despite this early setback had apparently taught him that talent should be cultivated rather than thwarted by "red tape."

Two examples of Ian's intervention on behalf of his students are provided by Dave Spalding and Alton Harestad, both of whom continued on to graduate studies and successful careers. (These are representative examples and do not reflect the entirety of Ian's concern for his many students; many of the submissions in Part II - Memories comment on Ian's readiness to assist students even after their graduation.) Dave Spalding's recollection is typical:

> During my first year of graduate studies I enrolled in, and failed, Chemistry 205. When I returned to UBC a couple of years later I again took Chemistry 205, determined to pass this required subject. To my chagrin, and despite my good intentions and hard work, I failed again. When Dr. Cowan heard of my dilemma, he contacted an acquaintance in Chemistry and my mark was moved the necessary point or two upwards, an act of kindness for which I have always been grateful.

Alton Harestad recalled:

> I spent the spring and early summer of 1972 studying the behaviour of northern sea lions at a bachelor colony near McInnes Island on the central coast of British Columbia. At my M.Sc. supervisory committee meeting in the fall, the issue of the academic requirement for a second language was raised. My field was ecology and behaviour and that meant learning German. Dr. Dean Fisher, my supervisor, had put trepidation into my heart; he took

German for his second language and still sometimes woke up in a sweat after dreaming about his language exams from decades before. I did not look forward to this challenge. When the issue of the academic requirement for a second language was raised, Dr. Cowan (one of my committee members) quickly responded: "I don't think a second language is needed in this case. Most of the relevant scientific literature in Alton's field is in English and by the time he graduates the rest will be translated." The committee agreed. Thank you, Dr. Cowan!

Educating the Public

In the mid-1950s, decades before science programs became popular, Ian pioneered the use of television as a medium to educate the public about conservation and the wonders of the natural world. His first series, *Fur and Feathers,* was a weekly fifteen-minute show for small children in which he brought live animals, both domesticated and wild, to the studio and provided facts about them by responding to the children's questions. The show began airing on July 6, 1955, to a CBC-Vancouver audience, but Ian's innate communication skills transferred so readily to the medium of television that the show was an immediate hit, and it was soon picked up by the network and broadcast nationally. The final show aired on June 25, 1956, but by this time Ian was already preparing his next series, *The Living Sea.* These half-hour programs began airing on July 7, 1957, with "The Cradle of Life" episode, which explored the origin of the earth and its oceans. While both *Fur and Feathers* and *The Living Sea* were shown in black and white and lacked sophisticated graphics, Ian was such an effective and stimulating host that they were well received by a diverse audience. *The Living Sea* ran until October 13, 1957 then resumed in early January 1958, ending on March 30, but the whole series was filmed and rebroadcast in 1962.

In 1959 he began hosting a CBC series called *The Web of Life,* which used footage shot by Robert Reid in Uganda, the southern US, the Caribbean, the Arctic and the Gulf of Mexico as well as in BC. These shows, which began as a twenty-six-week series and added two more seasons to end in September 1963, concerned animal life as close as the viewers' own backyards and issues as foreign as the problems in animal husbandry in East Africa. One of the shows in this series won an award for educational television films at an international festival, and selected episodes were purchased by Granada Television to show to British television audiences. For many of the contributors to this book, *The Web of Life* series was their first exposure to Ian McTaggart-Cowan and his explorations of nature.

Ian also appeared in a 1982 film opposing the use of leg-hold traps.

Affiliations

Ian's academic abilities were recognized very early in his career at UBC—for example, his appointment as a fellow of the Royal Society of Canada at just thirty-six years of age. However, although his primary focus in these early years remained with the university, as his public activities and reputation developed, he became involved in a great variety of organizations beyond it, expanding his advisory roles into resource management and environmental advocacy. His participation in so many activities outside of his responsibilities as a teacher and professor required an enormous commitment of time and energy, but according to his colleagues, he was always prepared for meetings and provided both leadership and inspiration to his fellow participants. Although he rose early and worked late, he was very fit and had a healthy lifestyle, and he seems to have developed a personal means of energy conservation by his renowned ability to appear to be asleep during a presentation while remaining perfectly aware of its content.

Some of his most significant affiliations during his years as professor and then after 1953 as department head are listed alphabetically below.

- Chairman of the board of the Arctic Institute of North America (1955). Headquartered at the University of Calgary, this non-profit organization's mandate is the study of the North American and circumpolar Arctic through the natural and social sciences.

- British Columbia Resources Council. Ian was a member from 1949 to 1960 and one-time chair.

- Member of the Fisheries Research Board of Canada (1954–65). The primary federal research organization on aquatic science and fisheries (previously known as the Biological Board of Canada), the FRB opened a permanent biological station at Nanaimo in 1908 that each summer utilized volunteers from Canadian universities.

- Vice-president of the International Union for the Conservation of Nature. Founded in 1948, it is the world's first global environmental organization and the largest professional global conservation network.

- Board member of the Museum of Vancouver (1959–62). The Art, Historical and Scientific Association, which was established in 1894, gave its collections to the City of Vancouver in 1903, and two years later they found a home at the Carnegie Library at Main and Hastings. In 1968 the collections were moved to the newly completed Centennial Museum and planetarium in Vanier Park. Ian's timely commitment to serve was instrumental in the transition to the new site.

- Founding member and first chairman of the advisory committee on wildlife research of the National Research Council of Canada (1955–62). This government of Canada agency promotes and funds scientific research and development.

- President of The Wildlife Society (1955). This is a large international organization that serves the professional community of scientists, managers, educators, technicians, planners and others who are active in the study, management and conservation of wildlife and their habitats.

- Member on the select committee on national parks of the United States Department of the Interior. The United States National Park Service was established as a federal agency in 1916 to manage national parks, monuments and historical lands.

- Chair of the special committee on grizzly bear conservation of the United States National Research Council (1973–74). Organized in 1916, this council elects members with distinguished achievements in original research in a variety of disciplines to provide scientific advice pro bono on matters of increasing national significance.

CHAPTER 5
Research and Mentoring

Like most young professors, Ian had to firmly establish his research interests early in his career at UBC, both to secure funding sources and for the development of his professional reputation. Although there was little competition in the field of wildlife biology in Canada in the early 1940s, between 1940 and 1946 he focussed his personal research on the large mammals in Canada's national parks, and he produced several reports with recommendations for managing big game.[77] At the same time he continued his remarkable publishing pace by completing papers he had started while at the Provincial Museum[78] and authoring new titles on natural history and distribution,[79] including a major monograph on the ecological relationships of the food of the Columbian black-tailed deer.[80] During this period his first graduate students, David Fowle[81] and James Hatter,[82] were also conducting research in British Columbia.

In the summer of 1943 Ian resumed the explorations in Banff and Jasper National Parks that he had begun in 1930, but this time he was accompanied by the legendary mountain guide Jimmy Simpson. And just as he had received academic mentorship from Kenneth Racey, Mack Laing and Joseph Grinnell, he now received mentorship in back country travel from Simpson. The young ecologist and the seasoned mountain man got on well immediately and developed a relationship of mutual respect. Ian learned a great deal from Jimmy about travel in the back country and the state of bighorn sheep and mountain goat populations in the parks, which was a principal goal of their four-month-long survey. Moreover, Jimmy's influence endured throughout Ian's lifetime, and in later years he would speak fondly and at length about those weeks in the wilderness with the famous mountain man.

Jimmy provided Ian with one of the most astonishing and amusing sights a field man could envision. In Jimmy's words:

I took Professor Cowan up to the gap in the range, past two big bunches of sheep as I went up, saw a lone ram on the top of a hill above timberline, of course, sneaked up on him with Dr. Cowan behind me and jumped on his back. He went out from under me like a cablegram going over to the old country for more money.[84]

In Ian's words:

Jim looked at me with a mischievous look in his eye and then catfooted up to this sheep and jumped on its back and grabbed it around the neck. The old fellow staggered to his feet and threw Jim to the ground all covered with sheep hair and then dashed off a few yards and turned back to figure out what was going on.[85]

Jimmy Simpson, legendary mountain man, guided Ian on a four-month field trip through Banff and Jasper national parks in 1943. Jimmy was famous for having bagged the "Simpson" ram, a Rocky Mountain bighorn sheep in 1920; it stood as the Boone and Crockett Club number one record for many years. PHOTO COURTESY OF WHYTE MUSEUM OF THE CANADIAN ROCKIES (V577/II.D./PA/2).

Ian's influence on Jimmy was reciprocal as Jimmy became more engaged in the study. Interestingly, even in these early years, Ian considered himself primarily an educator, a description he would echo many times over the years when commenting on his career. His teaching role was clearly demonstrated when he was collecting wolf scats for subsequent analysis of the wolves' food habits. Since Jimmy preferred to walk ahead of his horse, he would be the first to encounter them, and Ian happily reported that "I felt that it was almost my ultimate triumph as an educator when I found the wolf scats hanging from the low branch of a tree where I could pick them off without even getting off my horse." Ian also recounted how Jimmy, a hunter and guide, was bemused by Ian's hunting priorities, once commenting, "I can't figure you out, Ian. You stalk a goat to hell and back, shoot him, and all you bring back are the bones and guts."[86]

Ian still maintained a journal during his time afield, but his documentation was now more formal and included autopsy and survey sheets for later analysis. Later he would summarize all his information for the trip under each species. His passion for natural history, however, had not diminished as the following extracts from his diaries in Jasper National Park in 1946 indicate:

May 9: Frank Bryant showed us a coyote den. It was at the base of a low hill & overlooked a series of beaver ponds. We dug for about 2 hours until we convinced ourselves that the den was unoccupied.

May 10: At Moberly Flats took a male fox [red] in coyote sets at an elk carcass. Smell violent & quite skunk-like. Stomach contained about 1½ cupfuls of elk carrion.

May 13: Rose at 6 and went to our coyote traps. One set had been disturbed by a black bear and one by a horse or some other large animal. At 9 AM left by horse for Buffalo Prairie accompanied by Frank Bryant. Rode to the wolf den & found it unoccupied. Scats [5]: 3 elk, 1 horse, 1 sheep [Rocky

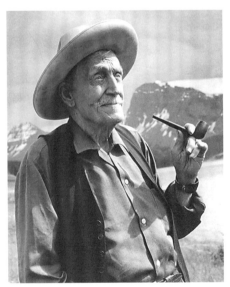

In 1968 Jimmy Simpson celebrated his 91st birthday at his lodge, Num-Ti-Jah, at Bow Lake in Banff National Park, Alberta. PHOTO BY DR. JOHN D. BIRRELL.

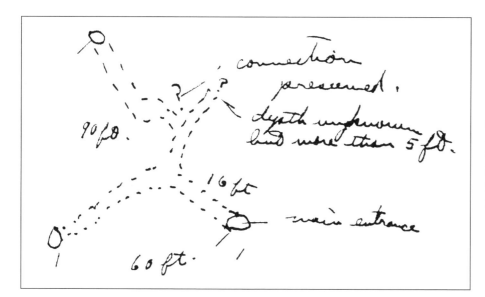

Ian McTaggart-Cowan's field sketch of a coyote den in Jasper National Park on May 4, 1946. Three entrances were available in the sixty-by-ninety-foot site, and while the final depth of the tunnels was unknown, they were more than five feet in length.

Mountain bighorn]. Then to Wabaso Lake & back home by 7 PM. A long day for a first day in the saddle & I can feel it in many places.

May 24: On trail to Dorothy Lakes saw marten sign. Contents of scats as follows. 6 scats Phenacomys [heather vole], 2 scats Clethrionomys [southern red-backed vole], 4 scats Peromyscus [deer mouse], 1 scat mouse fur and elk hair, 1 scat rabbit, 1 mouse, either Perry or Phenac. [Ian's shorthand for the genera Peromyscus and Phenacomys]

May 29: Found 3 newly hatched killdeer chicks at Lake Edith today.

June 5: Climbed to [bald eagle] nest, one chick just about a month old & the size of a chicken, gray down & contour feathers just coming in. Nest composed of sticks with a two-inch layer of grass on top. Only food remains. Hind foot of a black bear & feathers of a flicker [northern].

June 11: Office work all day.

June 14: Citellus [Spermophilus] columbianus [Columbian ground squirrel] colonies on Signal Mt, Emigrants Peak, Jasper Park. Numerous here at timberline.

July 16: Oreamnos [mountain goat] at Wolverine Pass, 6 ad, 3 yearl[ings], 3 kids on Mt Gray above Tumbling Glacier.

Taxonomy

Although his duties as department head restricted his participation in fieldwork after 1953, whenever Ian travelled for conferences or while he was on sabbatical, he visited major museums to examine their holdings to find specimens from British Columbia. When he made significant discoveries, he painstakingly researched the origin and authenticity of the specimens and published his findings in scientific journals. These articles illustrate the intellect, passion, inspiration and wisdom he exhibited in his dual role as scientist and educator. The article below, reprinted in its entirety, exemplifies his attention to detail for a single specimen of a male spruce (Franklin's) grouse that he discovered in the Royal Scottish Museum in Edinburgh in 1962.

The Holotype of the Franklin Grouse (*Canachites franklinii*)[87]

Stenhouse (1930, Novitates Zoologicae 35: 270-276)[88] calls attention to the existence in the Royal Scottish Museum, Edinburgh, of a specimen of *Canachites franklinii**, probably the type specimen. I have recently examined the specimen to determine any further details about it.

The specimen is now catalogued as 1930/183 in the museum and bears two labels. One, evidently originally attached to the stand of the bird while it was on display as a mounted specimen, bears no data of significance except the written statement on the reverse "Exhibited Wernerian Society, 20.2.1830." The ink and the position of the red "Type" label of recent origin leads to the suspicion that even this note may have been applied recently. The data upon the museum label were evidently transcribed from the details contained in [David] Douglas' diary, published in 1914. There would, therefore, be grave doubts about the authenticity of this specimen were it not for certain supporting details. In the first place the specimen was originally in the Edinburgh University collection where it is known Douglas' specimens were deposited. More important, however, and apparently unnoticed heretofore, is that it agrees closely with the description by Douglas of the specimen collected by him on the west side of Athabasca Pass (now in British Columbia) upon May 1, 1827.

As described (Douglas, 1914, Journal. London, p. 258),[89] the bird taken was an adult male. It is further stated that: "This being the first I have seen, could not resist the temptation of preserving it, although mutilated in the legs." The specimen in the Royal Scottish Museum has had the right leg shattered just above the foot and the left foot almost removed, apparently by shot. There seems to me, therefore, to be little doubt that the specimen in the Royal Scottish Museum is in fact the one mentioned by Douglas.

Later in his travels, Douglas mentions shooting other specimens in the eastern foothills of the Rocky Mountains, in an area that we now know to be inhabited only by *Canachites canadensis* or by a population showing intermediate characters. No mention is made of any specimens being preserved except for the one above mentioned.

---

* Boag and Schroeder 1992: the spruce grouse, *Dendragapus canadensis*, was formerly known as the Franklin grouse, *Canachites franklinii*; Bank et al. 1998: the spruce grouse, *Falcipennis canadensis* was formerly known as *D. canadensis*.

When Douglas prepared the original description of *Canachites franklinii* (1833, Transactions Linnaean Society of London 16: 139)[90] he included an accurate account of its colour in every detail, except that he remarks in the English, but not in the Latin description, "Tail square . . . black, white at the points." The tail in *franklinii* is almost always completely black, as it is in the specimen here described. It is safe to assume that the statement was based on his memory of the other individuals shot in the foothills and believed by him to be the same as his first specimen. These eastern foothill birds do, in fact, have the tail tip yellowish brown or dirty white. The inadequate description of the female was also no doubt added from memory and without reference to a specimen. Another product of faulty memory is the statement in the original description that the flesh is white, whereas in his diary he records accurately that the flesh was dark.

Although Douglas makes no specific mention of any specimen in his original description, and thus designates no type specimen, his treatment, in prior position, of the male plumage in detail that was not merely extracted from his diary, leaves no doubt that he had a male specimen before him. In my opinion the specimen in question is the one now in the Royal Scottish Museum and, as the only specimen known to have been in the possession of the describer, can be regarded as the holotype. The type locality then becomes Athabasca Pass, British Columbia, on the headwaters of the Canoe River.

—I. McT.Cowan, November 18, 1962.

Mentoring

Despite the fact that Ian's duties as professor—he had become a full professor in 1945 before becoming department head in 1953—diminished his time for involvement in field work, he was able to continue and extend his passion for museology and systematics by his guidance of two keen young naturalists—Charles J. Guiguet and R. Wayne Campbell.

Charles (Charlie) Guiguet was born in Shaunavon, Saskatchewan, and as a youngster collected butterflies and started a personal natural history museum. In the early 1930s he met James Munro who showed him how to properly prepare specimens for collections, and soon he was donating mammal and bird skins to the local museum. His field skills were also noted by R.M. Anderson, chief biologist with the National Museum of Canada (NMC), who recommended that he assist Mack Laing, who was on contract with the NMC, on a collecting expedition in British Columbia in 1936. Charlie remained part of the field team until 1939.

It was during this period that he also met Ian McTaggart-Cowan, and soon he was preparing specimens for the BC Provincial Museum where Ian was then employed. During World War II Charlie served with the RCAF, completing nearly fifty bombing missions; when he returned to BC after the war, he contacted Ian who by then had been on the UBC faculty for six years. At that time Ian had an interest in the Queen Charlotte

Islands [now Haida Gwaii] and their insular forms of birds and small mammals, especially bats, and he invited Charlie to be his assistant on a research trip to the islands. In the late summer of 1946 they spent over a month collecting and preparing specimens from Langara Island south to Rose Harbour. The following are selected excerpts from Ian's field notes:

August 1: Today arrived at [Queen Charlotte City]. Found Dean Fisher, Ed Barraclough as well as Charlie, Muriel and Joanna Guiguet here. Dean tells me 2 Haida hunters in last 10 days shot 81 [harbour] seals.

August 3: In evening Charlie took another Lasionycteris [silver-haired bat] and shot a saw-whet owl.

August 10: Spent part of day swamping trail to Moore Point [Head] & then Charlie set a line along it. In evening Charlie shot a Myotis keenii [Keen's long-eared myotis], the lone bat that we have seen around the cabin daily.

August 23: Charlie took 3 [buff-breasted sandpipers] together and I took 1 with a pectoral [sandpiper]. All in the grass [at Sandspit].

August 30: Charlie came in from Copper River in the early afternoon bringing with him a goose, a [Steller's] jay & a saw-whet owl as the major results of his 3 days down there. Excellent stuff. The most interesting thing is that our pole trapping technique for the owls works.

Ian and Charlie returned to Vancouver with a significant series of Queen Charlotte Islands endemic species and several first records for the islands, for example, a buff-breasted sandpiper.[91] In addition, Charlie had learned Ian's art of "note-taking" and used that model throughout the rest of his career.

By 1948 British Columbia ornithology had lost three stalwart collectors and ornithologists, namely Harry Swarth (d. 1935), Allan Brooks (d. 1946) and Thomas McCabe (d. 1948). Three others, James Munro (d. 1958), Kenneth Racey (d. 1959) and Mack Laing

A Colourful Partridge

Occasionally botanist David Douglas recorded birds and other wildlife in his journal. On May 1, 1827, he wrote:

Mr. E. killed on the height of land a most beautiful partridge, a curious species; small; neck and breast jet black; back of a lighter hue; belly and under the tail grey, mottled with pure white; beak black; above the eye bright scarlet, which it raises on each side of the head, screening the feathers on the crown; resembles a small well-crested domesticated fowl; leaves of *Pinus nigra* in the crop. This is the sort of bird mentioned to me by Mr. McLeod as inhabiting the higher parts of the Peace and Smokey Rivers. This, however, is not as large as described. Perhaps there may two varieties. Said also to be found in Western Caledonia [western Canada]. This being the first I have seen, could not resist the temptation of preserving it, although mutilated in the legs and in any circumstances little chance of being able to carry it, let alone being in a good state. The flesh of the partridge is remarkably tender when new killed, like game that has been killed several days; instead of being white, of darkish cast.

Male spruce (Franklin's) grouse. PHOTO BY R. WAYNE CAMPBELL.

Charles Guiguet preparing a porcupine specimen. September 16, 1938. PHOTO BY HAMILTON MACK LAING, STUIE, BC. IMAGE G-03674 COURTESY OF ROYAL BRITISH COLUMBIA MUSEUM, BC ARCHIVES.

(who died at age 99 in 1982) were by this time too old for active fieldwork. Ian knew that Charlie Guiguet had collected with most of them and that he understood the relevance of museum collections to British Columbia ornithology, so he was pleased to recommend him to Clifford Carl, director of the BC Provincial Museum, to head and curate an ornithology and mammalogy division for the museum. However, this new position required an advanced degree and Charlie had only just graduated from UBC that year with a B.A.; therefore, under Ian's supervision, between May 13 and the end of August 1948, Charlie carried out an ecological study of Goose Island off the central mainland coast of BC, a study that culminated in a master of arts degree from UBC in 1950 and a Provincial Museum occasional paper in 1953.[92]

In the early 1970s the British Columbia Provincial Museum initiated a public lecture series on the natural history of British Columbia to highlight the museum's scientific collections and seasonal fieldwork, and Ian was invited to be the inaugural speaker. The museum auditorium was packed and he presented a fascinating talk on mammals, intermingling the importance of scientific collecting with the life histories of mammals and conservation. At the end of his presentation he answered many questions from the audience, and then it was time for Charlie Guiguet, his former student and now the curator of the museum's Birds and Mammals Division, to thank him.

Charlie was uncomfortable speaking in public and Ian was aware of this. Charlie started off bravely enough, thanking Dr. Cowan "for taking time out of his busy schedule to come to the museum," but he was becoming more and more uncomfortable as he tried to think of what else to say. Then, to save him further embarrassment, Ian stepped down off

Dr. G. Clifford Carl, a marine biologist, joined the British Columbia Provincial Museum in 1940. From 1942 to 1969 he was the museum's director and oversaw a period of growth and the museum's expansion into its present site. IMAGE H-06354 COURTESY OF ROYAL BRITISH COLUMBIA MUSEUM, BC ARCHIVES.

Charlie Guiguet searching for the nesting burrows of rhinoceros auklets on Cleland Island, BC. June 29, 1970. PHOTO BY R. WAYNE CAMPBELL.

the stage, walked up to Charlie, faced the audience, and began extolling the importance of the museum collections and how Charlie had been instrumental in building them. He threw in a few anecdotes about their time together as friends, and everyone went home appreciating Charlie's value to the museum and Ian's graciousness and sensitivity.

In 1980, after 33 years as a civil servant, Charlie Guiguet retired as curator of the Bird and Mammal Division of the Provincial Museum. He had authored close to forty articles, including ten popular museum handbooks on "Birds of British Columbia" and was the co-author of two major works: *Mammals of British Columbia* with Ian McTaggart-Cowan[93] and *A Catalogue of British Columbia Sea-bird Colonies* with Rudolf H. Drent.[94] Charlie Guiguet and Ian McTaggart-Cowan remained good friends until Charlie's death in 1999.

Robert Wayne Campbell was born in Edmonton on October 1, 1941, and moved to Vancouver with his family in 1946 and a year later to Burnaby where he spent much of his youth exploring marshes around Burnaby and Deer lakes. His early enthusiasm for the outdoors had been fostered by his grandfather, who was an ardent fly fisherman, a fishing-licence inspector and conservationist, and later by his father, accompanying him on many hunting and fishing trips. Wayne became absorbed with natural history and through the 1960s accrued a personal collection of about 4,600 catalogued marine and terrestrial mollusc shells, bird's eggs, bird and mammal skulls, bird museum skins and mounted birds. He also prepared a large collection of duck wings that the local rod and gun club used for training new hunters in waterfowl identification. His wildlife library filled two walls of a spare room in the family home.

The initial meetings between Ian McTaggart-Cowan and Robert Wayne Campbell occurred in the early 1960s, and although not auspicious at the time, they ultimately led to a long professional and close personal friendship, which was a constant influence in Wayne's development as a wildlife biologist.

Following high school, Wayne Campbell worked in construction then took jobs as a truck driver, bartender and musician. From 1964 through 1969 he worked from May through September each year as a park naturalist and interpreter in provincial parks on Mitlenatch Island and Wickaninnish Park (now Pacific Rim National Park Reserve). During this period he explored and surveyed numerous offshore islands and banded thousands of seabirds. In 1970 he was offered a position as assistant curator of the Vertebrate Museum in the Department of Zoology at UBC (now the Cowan Tetrapod Collection in the Beaty Biodiversity Museum). Over the next three years he met frequently with Ian, who was by this time dean of Graduate Studies, to discuss new additions to the collections. Ian was also impressed with Wayne's personal collection of catalogued specimens, which was the largest private collection extant in the province at the time. Ian regretted that the era of public collecting was rapidly vanishing.

Although curating the collection and preparing donated animals were Cowan's highest priority for the museum, he supported Wayne's endeavour to make the museum more visible and interactive outside of the university. Wayne served as the BC coordinator for the North American Breeding Bird Survey and for local Christmas bird counts and as chairman of the ornithology section of the Vancouver Natural History Society. He initiated a provincial photo file to document the occurrence of rare vertebrates,[95] the province's first "birders night," which was held at UBC, an annual "Bird of the Year" award and wood duck nest box and bird-banding projects; he also taught introductory birdwatching courses through the museum. Ian also gave him responsibility for the operation of the BC Nest Record Scheme, which had inadequate support to ensure its viability.[96]

During this period Wayne Campbell published more than fifty titles, including three consecutive annual bird reports for Greater Vancouver.[97] Ian frequently reviewed drafts of articles Wayne had written for scientific journals and provided wisdom that helped guide his career. Ian told him that "good writing is hard work, and if I complete a manuscript page a day, it has been a productive twenty-four hours," and he passed along Grinnell's advice that "the legacy of biologists is in their published works. Their other accomplishments fade rapidly into history."

In 1973 Wayne accepted a post at the British Columbia Provincial Museum as curator of higher vertebrates, and he remained in that position until 1992. While at the museum, Wayne authored another 250 titles, which included lead author for the first two volumes of *The Birds of British Columbia*, comprehensive bibliographies on British Columbia herpetology[98] and ornithology[99] and handbooks on amphibians[100] and reptiles.[101] He was a popular speaker and delivered over 1,300 lectures to a

Wayne Campbell (left) is showing part of his oological collection to friends Ken, Bruce and Ian Kennedy in Burnaby, BC, April 1966. At that time egg-collecting was authorized under federal scientific collecting permits.

PHOTO BY DON TIMBRELL, BURNABY, BC.

wide variety of groups. He also served as an expert witness for federal and provincial governments in court cases involving wildlife infractions and as an external examiner on university graduate theses. During this period he attended the University of Victoria to complete the B.Sc. in biology and geography (1976) that he had begun at UBC and followed that with an M.Sc. in forest science from the University of Washington in Seattle (1983). In 2000 Wayne retired from the civil service and co-founded, with his wife Eileen and Michael I. Preston, the non-profit society Biodiversity Centre for Wildlife Studies. Since 2004 he has served on its executive and as associate editor of the Centre's biannual journal *Wildlife Afield.*

Since publishing his first article in 1964, Wayne has authored over 600 titles of which forty are books, mainly on birds but also including amphibians, reptiles and mammals. He initiated and was lead author of the definitive four-volume set *The Birds of British Columbia* (1990–2001)[102] and was senior editor of a series of four popular CD-ROMs on North American waterfowl, owls, birds of prey and bird songs.[103] Recognition for his work includes the Award of Excellence in Biology (now the Ian McTaggart-Cowan Award) from the Association of Professional Biologists of British Columbia (1989), the Lifetime Achievement Award from the Federation of British Columbia Naturalists (now Nature BC) (1991), the Order of British Columbia (1992) and two commemorative medals of Canada.

The End of an Era

Charles Guiguet and Wayne Campbell are typical of the individuals who provided basic information on the distribution and natural history of wildlife species and their habitats during the pioneering era of biological discovery both in this province and across North America. They were explorers, facing many of the problems of access and unknown conditions that have always characterized attempts to describe and document unknown lands. Their collecting reflected the limitations of travel and discovery available at a time when the techniques of remote survey and sensing (including remote photography) were not only unavailable but beyond imagining. However, these collectors who provided the foundation of wildlife knowledge ultimately had an influence far greater than they could ever have imagined.

Although Ian was also an enthusiastic and dedicated practitioner of museum collecting and curation in those early days, he supported the transition from that era of general collecting (including trapping and shooting) to non-lethal types of documenting wildlife distribution and abundance. He was especially keen on initiatives such as those developed by Wayne Campbell to generate a fund of data from the widespread observations of both amateur and professional observers. Among those initiatives is the BC Nest Records Scheme, now in its fifty-ninth year,[104] which is financed and maintained by volunteers. The seminal four-volume work *The Birds of British Columbia* relied heavily on these knowledgeable individuals to provide the voluminous and comprehensive database from large geographic areas. Such a dataset would have been impossible to generate using only a few individuals or by keeping within the scope of short-term government objectives. But another of the more important outcomes of engaging large numbers of participants in data gathering was the increase in public awareness and support for environmental values.

In supporting the transition from general collecting, Ian was also in step with changing societal awareness of the natural environment and a new emphasis on stewardship. This changing emphasis has enlisted a significant component of society against certain types of exploitation of wildlife, particularly the hunting of large carnivores such as grizzly bears and the commercial harvesting of whales. Although funding for habitat protection and acquisition has often originated with sport-hunting and fishing organizations both in Canada and the United States, there is now widespread support for initiatives to protect and preserve species and their habitats, ranging from establishing parks and ecological reserves to outright acquisition of habitat.

CHAPTER 6

The Dean of Graduate Studies

During the late 1950s and early 1960s Ian McTaggart-Cowan had acted for short periods as assistant dean of Arts and Sciences and assistant dean of the Faculty of Science, but 1964 marked the beginning of an expanded role for him with his appointment as dean of Graduate Studies, a position he would hold until his retirement in 1975. His responsibilities in this post included academic leadership, maintenance of standards, admissions, degree requirements and coordination of all aspects of graduate programs in all faculties. In addition to his administrative and academic responsibilities, he also took on a senior role in overall university administration and governance. While he had been a member of the university senate since 1951, now he began serving as chair of various senate committees and developed a close working relationship with the president of the university. During his tenure as dean, the university experienced a period of explosive growth and reconstruction, and he spearheaded a review and revision of the functions of the Faculty of Graduate Studies and then, as chair of the senate library committee, oversaw the expansion of the growing library.

To accomplish all this, he changed his management style. Geoffrey G.E. Scudder, who joined the Department of Zoology in 1958 and became head of the department in 1975, noted that:

> When Ian was head of the Department of Zoology, he held very few official faculty meetings and was not encumbered by graduate student representatives at those meetings. He made most departmental decisions, delegating few tasks to other faculty members, although he always made decisions that were beneficial to the reputation of the Zoology Department during this time of rapid expansion. As a result, the department had very good standing in the Faculty of Science. However, when he became dean of the Faculty of Graduate Studies, he hand-picked his associate deans and assigned them

specific tasks, delegating much of the running of the faculty to them. He thus operated very differently than when he was head of the Zoology Department.

Meanwhile, even following his appointment as dean of Graduate Studies and his acceptance of the demanding responsibilities the job entailed, Ian was still intent on building a national reputation for academic excellence and research in UBC's Zoology Department, and as a result he continued to attract many top zoologists to join the department. These included Dennis Chitty (population ecology), David Suzuki (genetics) and Geoffrey Scudder (entomology). He also maintained some teaching activities and continued to fulfill an important role as a supervisor and mentor of graduate students. He supervised at least 122 undergraduate and graduate students who benefited both from his own vast experience and knowledge of the field and his understanding of their personal financial hardships.

At the same time he was still keeping a watchful eye for students who showed promise. Wayne Campbell recalls being assisted by Ian during his reticent journey into academia:

> After graduating from high school, I had been more interested in collecting birds' eggs, banding birds and wading marshes in Burnaby Lake than pursuing a university education, but Robert D. Harris of the Canadian Wildlife Service in Vancouver encouraged me to enroll at UBC. I failed first-year math (calculus and statistics) and decided that I was not ready (or adequately educated) for a commitment to university life. Besides, I was having too much fun in the field with new discoveries and experiences.
>
> Subsequently, in 1971 while I was working at the Vertebrate Museum at UBC, Dr. Rudolf Drent (a new faculty member) also encouraged me to start a Bachelor's degree. I told him about my failure with the required introductory math course. Rudi apparently discussed this issue with Ian, and a week later, out of the blue, a professor from the math department visited the museum and mentioned that he was teaching the first-year math course and strongly suggested I take it! Later I learned that Ian had made a timely telephone call to a friend in the math department who agreed to help me get past this hurdle. That support and encouragement eventually led to a master's degree.

During the period when Ian was serving as dean of Graduate Studies, his zoology graduates were achieving distinction in fields that encompass the whole diverse spectrum of biological investigation from systematics and zoogeography to general ecology, population dynamics, wildlife biology and behaviour. Ian was also able to extend the ethics of conservation and resource use through his students as they entered careers in government and academic institutions. Many of them became pivotal in advancing the cause of conservation and preservation of protected areas and parks in British Columbia and elsewhere. During one period in the 1960s the

Bristol Foster (right) and Charles Guiguet on Cleland Island, BC's first ecological reserve, June 29, 1970. Both were Ian's students in the 1950s and 1960s. PHOTO BY R. WAYNE CAMPBELL.

directors of wildlife in every province of Canada were former students of Ian McTaggart-Cowan! Other students and associates became involved in the emerging profession of environmental consulting, developing methodologies for assessing impacts on wildlife and their habitats and establishing mitigation strategies for various types of human activities that have negative environmental effects.

New Affiliations

In addition to his new duties at the university, during the late 1960s and early 1970s, Ian took on a number of new responsibilities in the larger world. Among them were memberships and chairmanships in the following organizations:

- Chair of the Academic Board for Higher Education/Academic Council of British Columbia (1974–76). This board was established in 1964 to coordinate academic, technical and career programs in community colleges and to monitor admissions and transfer arrangements between colleges, institutes and universities. Its major achievement was to enable students from community colleges to transfer full course credits to continuing their education at a major university. It was abolished in 1983.

- Member of the Arctic Environment Council (1974–76).

- President of the Biological Council of Canada (1966–68). This was a body formed to improve biological research and teaching in Canada.

- Board member, Environment Protection Board (1973–76). This board was formed as an independent body to assess impacts of proposed Arctic pipelines.[105] The EPB participated in the Berger Inquiry, which conducted Canada's first major environmental and social review.

- Founding director of the Nature Trust of British Columbia (1971). This non-profit organization is dedicated to land conservation in BC. Ian served as a director until 2002 and was director emeritus until his death in 2010.

A Crowded Lifestyle

As a result of his new affiliations and duties as dean of Graduate Studies, during these years Ian seemed to be everywhere—an environmental review meeting at BC Hydro in Vancouver, meetings on the proposed Mackenzie Valley pipeline in Calgary, meetings of the Environmental Protection Board in Winnipeg, environmental hearings in Yellowknife and Whitehorse and attendance at an International Caribou Symposium in Fairbanks, Alaska. These activities were in addition to his teaching, supervision of graduate students and administrative duties.

Frequently it fell to Joyce McTaggart-Cowan to pick Ian up at the airport on his return from meetings, lectures, Habitat Conservation Trust Fund field trips and other professional commitments, and she could often be encountered patiently reading in the waiting area at Vancouver International Airport. On one occasion Wayne Campbell noted that she carried not one but two pocket books with her. She was apparently prepared for a lengthy wait for Ian due to flight cancellations and missed flights as his meetings had run overtime. With no cell phones at this time, there was nothing for her to do but wait.

Joyce had been Ian's partner in the field at the start of their marriage, and in later years she became a supporter and a skilled adjunct to his biological activities as an assistant, associate or social convener—whatever was needed. Dennis Demarchi met her for the first time when she accompanied Ian on a wildlife management class field trip to the Sinlahekin Wildlife Area in Washington State, just over the border from Osoyoos, BC. It was March 1965 and Ian's lab assistant, graduate student Fred Zwickel, led the outing. Dennis remembers:

A classmate and I sat at the front of the bus right behind Ian and Joyce, hoping that pearls of wisdom would be flowing from him, but Ian immediately closed his eyes, while Joyce constantly watched for birds and other wildlife. When she saw something of interest, she would tell Ian who would then stand up and tell the class what they could see. The rest of the class thought that Ian was the great observer; my friend and I knew he was getting his information from his spouse.

However, over their long marriage, due to Ian's ever-growing list of responsibilities and frequent absences, Joyce had learned to develop her own interests. She enjoyed quilting, gardening, travelling and birdwatching. Until Ian's retirement years when the Cowans hired a cleaning lady, Joyce did most of the domestic chores, including shopping for groceries; occasionally Wayne's wife, Eileen, would meet her in Peppers, the local grocery store in Cadboro Bay, and conversation would soon develop. Eileen recalls:

> Joyce was strongly family oriented, but she was always eager to learn about other people's families and rarely discussed her own—except for grand-children. When talking to wives with husbands who were busy like Ian, she advised them to make sure they developed and retained their own identity and accomplished things that were meaningful to them. Otherwise, she said, you will grow old feeling unfulfilled as a person.

Joyce was sometimes called on to deal with unusual problems when Ian was away. One Saturday evening in September 1972 Wayne Campbell stopped by Ian's home on the university campus to drop off material relating to the bird survey report he was preparing for the Environmental Protection Board (EPB) regarding the Mackenzie Valley Pipeline hearings. Although Wayne knew that Ian was in Winnipeg for the weekend at an EPB board meeting, he had been assured that Joyce would be home. But when he arrived at the back door, in order to knock on the door he had to step over the fresh carcass of a cougar. Joyce explained that the animal had been shot in the Fraser Valley and delivered to her by conservation officers.

However, on Monday morning when Wayne arrived at the UBC Cowan Vertebrate Museum, where he was the curator, he found that the cougar had been deposited in a freezer; all its measurements had been taken and

Ian and Joyce picnicking on the beach on Mayne Island, BC, near their cabin, July 12, 1969. When they were outdoors relaxing, their binoculars were always close at hand. PHOTO BY J. MARY TAYLOR.

the animal had been sexed (it was a young male). Later Ian told Wayne that Joyce had taken all of this information as she knew Ian would want the skeleton and that measurements should be taken when the carcass was fresh.

One afternoon in October 1972 Ian dropped into the UBC Vertebrate Museum shortly after returning from a meeting of the EPB in Winnipeg. Wayne could see that he was very tired but that he wanted to hear about the latest local bird discoveries, discuss the significance of the recently published annual bird reports for the Vancouver area and, of course, be brought up to date on recent additions to the museum collections. It was his "down time."

As he had previously sent Wayne to the Arctic to conduct research for the bird component of the environmental assessment for the pipeline and Wayne was in the middle of preparing his reports,[106] Wayne asked him how the meeting had gone. "It was challenging and frustrating," Ian said. "For the first time we invited some non-wildlife government people to attend and it took almost an hour of posturing before we got down to business." At the end of the day, however, the results had been encouraging. The attendees seemed to be satisfied with progress. Then just before Ian left the museum to deal with "an internal faculty issue," he commented:

> It is easy to impress a person when you know that you know more than they do. The key is timing—don't impress them too often. Be a good listener and hear what someone has to say. I discovered early that I never learned much when I was talking.

Not all of the encounters involving the EPB were positive. On one occasion, Dr. Frank Banfield, a member of a panel of the proponent consultants at the Berger Inquiry, was asked to comment on a series of colour maps prepared by the EPB's staff that depicted wildlife values along the proposed pipeline route. In a somewhat disparaging tone Banfield commented that they were "pretty." At a subsequent break in the hearing, Ron Jakimchuk encountered Ian who was absolutely seething with anger over the dismissive remark.

> I had never seen him display anger as his usual demeanor was to be calm and relaxed, although I had heard that he was quite adept at counter-attacking critics. I do not know if Banfield was unfortunate enough to personally feel the sting of Cowan's rebuke on that occasion.

Ian was not at ease discussing personal issues, and often used a pretext to initiate such discussions. One evening Wayne received a telephone call from him to say that a barred owl was at his bird feeder, probably catching rats. Wayne went over to see the owl, but as Joyce was away visiting a friend, he ended up having a rare discussion on a variety of Ian's personal concerns. Toward the end of the evening, Ian mentioned that Joyce was having difficulty driving her car, which had a standard shift. He said that he was going to buy her a new one with an automatic transmission. Since Wayne had recently discussed getting a used car for his wife, Eileen, he asked Ian what price he was asking for Joyce's Honda Civic. Ian replied, "Probably $2,000." However, when Ian discussed this with Joyce, she convinced him that since Wayne and Eileen had a growing family, a more reasonable price was $1,500. Robert McTaggart-Cowan, Ian's grandson, recalled that Joyce managed the household finances and knew what it took to raise a family.

During the initial visit with Ian, Wayne never did see or hear the barred owl!

Speaking Engagements

Ian had been ambitious from an early age. Undoubtedly his solitary pursuits of trapping and exploring in the forest during his teen years established his self-reliance, and his energy and immense curiosity endeared him to his superb mentors. They in turn fostered his growth as a naturalist and imbued him with the confidence that enhanced his future roles as an educator and administrator. At the same time, he was developing a political sense, which, combined with his personal charm, enhanced his influence among his peers as well as the wider public.

Mentoring a New Generation of McTaggart-Cowans

In 1972, after Garry McTaggart-Cowan and his wife, Virginia, divorced, Virginia brought their children, Mariana and Robert, to Vancouver to live with Ian and Joyce for a year. Mariana, then nine, and Robert, seven, were enrolled in school at Point Grey. It was a crucial time in their lives for the children to be separated from their father, but the support given by their grandparents brought them the stability they needed.

The children remembered Joyce as a disciplinarian, a perfectionist about the way the household was run and about appearances and manners. She was always teaching her grandchildren, whether it was in playing games like Scrabble or just reading. But Ian was the one who contributed most to their early learning, giving them the structure they needed to pursue their education. Although he was now dean of Graduate Studies and constantly in demand as a speaker and committee head, he would always make time to spend with the children. Mariana would come to meet him every day at five in the afternoon on University Boulevard, and the two would walk home together, both talking about their days. She remembers him as her earliest mentor, friend and hero. Ian's story about Joseph Grinnell helping him when he had no money to return to university at Berkeley resonated with her, and once she was in a position to help others, she began working with several charities in Halifax, Nova Scotia. Her brother Robert was always determined to please his grandfather and remembers working especially hard at his studies so as not to disappoint him. Today he credits his grandfather for his success as an anesthesiologist.

After their year with Ian and Joyce, the children moved back to Newfoundland to live with their father, but they still spent alternate summers with their grandparents in Vancouver and on Mayne Island. The family property and cottage on Mayne is now owned by Robert.

Ray Halladay, director of the BC Wildlife Branch (left), Ian and the Honorable Moe Sihota, BC Minister of Environment at the announcement of the formal designation of the Creston Valley marshes as a wetland of international significance, September 1993. PHOTO BY R. WAYNE CAMPBELL, CRESTON, BC.

Teaching had provided him with opportunities for achieving both altruistic goals and personal recognition, and during his teaching years he developed a well-deserved reputation as a scientist as well as a public persona as a conservationist, though he could never have been described as an environmental activist. Instead, he came to occupy the role of an éminence grise—an advocate of wilderness values and environmental concerns but not in the activist sense, and he often took the middle ground on controversial issues regarding the policies of government and industry. But while he was often disdainful of governmental bureaucracy, being prominent but a non-activist also opened many opportunities for appointment to a myriad of government-sponsored committees and non-governmental conservation bodies in his later years. Again his role was that of statesman rather than the activist demanding change and action.

In spite of his continuing interest in the Department of Zoology, after he became dean of Graduate Studies, his focus was inevitably redirected from research to developing a public ethic and awareness of resource use, allocation and protection of the natural world. Fortunately, his association with graduate students and their work kept him at the "cutting edge" of new findings in biology. As a result, he was able to influence public debate and environmental policy not only from his teaching position and through his research but also through his public persona as a speaker and the host of the first television series pertaining to natural history. He delivered many talks outside the classroom, engaging audiences as diverse as hunting and fishing groups, naturalist clubs, garden clubs and philatelic societies. Through his speeches and writings, he raised public understanding of the value of wilderness and wildlife and the need to protect those values.

Anyone who heard Ian speak in public can attest to his great skill as a communicator. Whether he was delivering a formal lecture or a speech to a lay group, his combination of enthusiasm, knowledge and delivery ignited his audiences' interest in the topic at hand. He connected with them in a persuasive manner, always with the goal to inspire their interest and to educate them. This ability swayed many students into the study of zoology and influenced other audiences to support his message of conservation and protection of wildlife and their habitats. His trademarks included a quick wit, a ready smile and a prop or two supplemented with an apparently encyclopedic knowledge of his topic. Flawless delivery was combined with apt metaphors, concrete examples, personal anecdotes and minimal use of jargon.

His unique abilities meant a steadily increasing demand for addresses to the general public. He delivered the following speech at the Thirteenth Annual Convention of the British Columbia Wildlife Federation held at the Royal Towers Hotel in New Westminster, May 7–10, 1969. By this time he had been lecturing and writing on environmental limits and population control for much of the decade, but this speech came at a time of growing environmental awareness. Rachel Carson's *Silent Spring*[107] had been published seven years earlier, the previous year had seen the publication of Paul Ehrlich's bestseller *The Population Bomb*,[108] and Garrett Hardin's widely cited *Science* magazine article "The Tragedy of the Commons"[109] had been published just five months earlier. His speech, which he titled "Wild Values for the Future: Wild Land and the Sportsmen's Federation," is still valid more than four decades later.

> I was fascinated by the address I listened to from your executive director, and I think that what I have to say will probably dovetail very nicely with what he has already told you. But I want to cast the net a little wider to begin with. I will come back home towards the end of my address. There is not a person in the room today unaware that the world falls into two very large camps—the so-called developed nations and the underdeveloped or "emerging" nations. There are great contrasts between these two camps, other than their gross national product: the use of energy by the two groups, the state of their technology, the appetite for resources as the source of economic gain, and—of particular interest to many of us here—the attitudes towards space and wild lands as a source of recreational enjoyment.
>
> There are fascinating contrasts too in the way in which problems are attacked. We, the developed nations, have been so successful with our science-based society that we approach almost every problem with the assumption that it must have a technical solution. The opposite culture will resort instead to spiritism in one form or another. One might say that the seer, the witch doctor or his counterpart looks like the appropriate expert in that culture. I must say that there are times when it seems to me that our land use planning is still in the witch doctor state.

Today in our culture the most serious problems that confront us to an increasing degree come into the category in which we can write "no technical solution present or likely." These problems are basically those of human attitude that arise from misunderstanding. In these the role of the expert is to expose the alternatives—and experts are hard to identify. I would like to spend the next few minutes with you this morning exploring some of these "no technical solution" problems. Because of our mutual interest in the wild land resource, I will confine myself to those problems that we refer to as the problems of the "common resources." Under this category we group the large collection of attributes of the world that we almost instinctively regard as common property: air, water, sea, space, public parks and open area recreation such as hunting, fishing, nature study, etc.

More than a century ago a mathematician, W.F. Lloyd,[111] referred to the "tragedy of the commons," and he used this term "commons" to refer to common resources. He depicted it this way: we acquired our attitude toward the common resources through centuries during which war, poaching, accident and disease kept the populations of both man and beast well below capacity. There are certain flaws in the details of his picture, but in essence it is as valid today as it was then. The day of reckoning comes when these forces of control—starvation, disease, etc.—are no longer operating. Thus, when about a century ago technological man tackled the vital problem of who dies when and of what and successfully attacked for the first time the problems of death and established death control as one of our paramount technologies, the rules were no longer valid. Let me cite some examples.

In East Africa I worked for a while in Masai land. The Masai herdsmen swept into this country from the head of the Nile several centuries ago, driving their herds with them. They have a passionate devotion to the commons—common range. Their wealth is their cattle. We are all interested in increasing our wealth. They are interested in increasing their cattle. So then, each Masai herdsman has to decide annually—should I or should I not add some more cattle to my herd? The answer is obvious. If he does, the value to him is the unit value of the number of animals he adds. The cost to the whole organism is divided between everybody, so of course it's a plus value, and if he's a rational herdsman, he will add those more cattle. But that same conclusion is being reached by all of them, and the end product is ruin.

You can fly north from Entebbe, Uganda, over parts of Chad into the Sudan, and as you look down on a clear day from your comfortable jet aircraft, you can see an extraordinary sight—completely circular deserts, one after the other, separated by a few miles. In the centre of those deserts is the bore-hole well, drilled by French engineers in the confirmed opinion that they were benefiting the people of this country. Each of these wells became a place where you could keep cattle. The deserts are two cow-hikes across. Cattle have to come back to the well every day, so they graze out and they graze back. No people there now. The bore-holes are unused. I think you get my point. Each individual, and it can be said also of each discrete group, advances headlong, pursuing his or its own best interest in a society that

In the 21st century, commercial overfishing is having a major impact on the ecology of global marine environments. Factory ships like these facilitate the over-harvest of marine resources. In addition to the impact on fish stocks, some forms of commercial fishing are having a significant impact on marine mammals and birds through by-catch. PHOTO BY R. WAYNE CAMPBELL.

believes in complete freedom of the common resources. Freedom of this sort in the commons brings ruin to all.

Education is one hope to counteract the rational tendency to do the wrong thing. But this again must be constantly refreshed. Each generation demands new relevance. Thus, another of our tasks today is to keep education relevant and in line with the headlong pace of change. Let me look at some other examples.

The freedom of the seas. We trumpet this as one of the things we really believe in: the right to go and fish in the sea wherever we want to. The sea has inexhaustible resources, we are told over and over again.[112] I wish it did. The tunas that are fished when they are young on the coast of California spawn off the south coast of Japan and in the Philippine Islands. It is the same stock, and it is fished around the whole ocean. Why should a Japanese fisherman restrict his catch? Logically he shouldn't. This is his resource as he sees it over there. The Californian sees it as his resource over here.

The Atlantic salmon is in desperate straits. There was something between—my figures are inexact—3 and 5 million taken last year by the pelagic fishery of Davis Straits and in the waters off southern Greenland. The fact that they were available at sea was only discovered three or four years ago. These are the same salmon that are swimming up the Miramichi River or swimming up the famous rivers of Scotland. Their numbers are dwindling in many of the famous rivers of the North Atlantic. Persistence of this idea that the freedom of the commons is a divine right can lead to the destruction of the Atlantic salmon as a viable resource species. The great whales have been brought to the verge of extinction. The greatest of all, the blue whale, is down to less than 1,000 individuals in the whole world as a result of this same attitude.

We in this part of the Pacific know very well that you cannot exercise the freedom of the commons. So what do we do? We try to divide it up.

We establish a twelve-mile fishing limit, point to point, and exclude other nationals from it. But even then we are not doing enough. So we start talking about licence limitations. These are nibblings at the edge of a devastating basic human attitude. These moves just make the commons a little less common. And we are going to come to it again when we exclude commercial fishing entirely from the Strait of Georgia. Already we have size limits and limits on numbers of salmon that may be taken by the sports fisherman. What will be the next step?

Long ago we learned that the fur animals could not be managed on a come-and-get-them basis—the "commons" attitude. So we established registered trap lines. This involved a decision to recognize trapping as a commercial venture exclusively. There are very large parts of the United States in which trapping is a sport, and it takes hundreds of people into the field weekly to run their small trap lines. They don't catch very much but they enjoy their outings, and it is one of the ways in which you can enjoy the winter season in pursuit of an identifiable goal.

One answer is more parks, bigger parks. I have read with the greatest of interest the report of your parks committee, and I certainly endorse it. But even with more parks, you still have to distribute use, and you cannot do this under a common resource approach. I'm sure every one of you regards it as your absolute and inalienable privilege to roll up to Banff National Park and say, "I'm coming in." The day is not far hence when you will see a sign on the road, "Sorry. Park Full." After all, you make reservations to go to the opera. You make reservations to go to the symphony. You make reservations to do all kinds of things that you regard as choice. You are going to be making reservations to do some of the things that you now regard as your inalienable right. I'll come back to that again.

How to distribute access to very fragile wilderness resources is a very vexing problem. These resources, once they are destroyed, cannot be rebuilt. A destroyed wilderness will never again be a wilderness. Stephen Spur quite properly points out that you can reconstruct something that most people wouldn't detect as spurious. You can start with a devastated piece of country and over a period of fifty years you can put it back to look something like its primitive state, and a lot of people will regard it as wilderness. But this is not the point. How are you going to assign access to these very rare resources if you have to remove them from the commons under the constant pressure of numbers? Are you going to assign them by merit as a reward for civic virtue? This is the way it is done in a large part of the world. Are you going to do it by lottery? Is there going to be a quota, first come first served?

Some years ago I had the interesting experience of visiting Haleakala National Park on the Island of Maui in Hawaii—some of you may have been there. I made a reservation a month in advance for the use of one of the three cabins on the floor of the crater. It's a huge crater, one of the largest in the world, and there is an absolutely fascinating experience of high quality recreation being made available under a democratic system. I requested and I got a reservation. On the appointed day I parked my car at the top of the

Bottom trawlers are unselective in their catch and cause significant disturbance to ocean-bottom habitats. PHOTO BY R. WAYNE CAMPBELL.

hill by the watchtower—the watching area where anybody can go and gaze at the magnificence of this gigantic crater, watch the sunset or the sunrise or what you will. I hiked with my wife and family seven miles down into the crater in the pouring rain. I came to a very attractive cabin, secreted in a little cul-de-sac in the great, sloping sides of the crater. The cabin was equipped with bed, bedding, mattresses, kitchen utensils and dining utensils. We carried our own food and clothes. We used it. We cleaned it and left it the next day. As we left, we could see our replacement party coming over the rim of the crater seven miles away. And that's as close as we got to them.

The silence of the night in that crater is something that I'll remember to my dying day. You could cut it. It was absolute. Not the sound of a cricket or anything. The parks people had made narrow, beautifully designed trails [with] small, discreet sign-posts made out of local rock with signs bearing appropriate notices of unique plants and other natural features. [There] is a sign-post on the road to what lies ahead of us if high quality wild land recreation is to be maintained in some of our finest parks.

Let me turn next to pollution. This is another aspect of the destruction of the space that you and I are so extremely interested in for wild land recreation. This is not a question of removing but of adding to the commons. Sewage, chemicals, radioactive products, hot-water wastes, poisonous fumes, foul odours, noise (such as snowmobiles, trail bikes, power saws, hovercraft, supersonic aircraft), distasteful objects—all these class as pollution.

A rational man again finds that his share of the cost of the wastes he discharges into the commons is less than the cost of purifying them because he's sharing his cost with everybody, and the advantage is all to him. So the rational man will certainly pollute. Since this is true for everyone, we are locked into a system of fouling our own nests as long as rational free enterprise exists without restriction. Redress of this problem finds alternative users demanding removal of sectors of the commons from that state and transferring back to the contaminator the cost of his pollution. This is what you see going on about you in a very small way today.

Let me just briefly sketch a few scenarios. In July 1968 a man out in the Point Grey area was troubled with bugs on his rhododendrons. He applied to the Department of Agriculture for information as to what he should do about this particular kind of weevil and sent them a sample. He got word back: dieldrin or DDT. These were the only alternatives given. So, even though he knew better, he got out the dieldrin and put it in his duster. He chose a still day so there would be no wind and he started to dust his rhododendrons. And then he paused because it was a hot day and looked. Half a block down, he could see this dust rising into the sky. He called his wife to have a look. Do you wonder that the stuff is blowing out all over the world?*

Raw, untreated sewage from the city of Victoria, dumped directly into the ocean at Clover Point, has altered the marine ecosystem as well as such human recreations as swimming, kelp and shellfish gathering, exploring tide pools and fishing. PHOTO BY R. WAYNE CAMPBELL.

---

* The example of the man in Point Grey dusting his rhododendrons sounds suspiciously as if it was Ian himself admitting that some things are best learned by personal experience and how easy it is to fall into bad practices with good intentions.

Let me go to the next example. Hovering over the Antarctic icecap is a helicopter. In it [are] the pilot and a biologist. The biologist is Dr. William Sladen from Johns Hopkins University, and he is one of the world's experts on Antarctic penguins.[113] He is returning for the eighth successive year to one of the remote breeding colonies. He has been increasingly puzzled that there are so few young being hatched and reared by these colonies. So this time he takes a series of eggs for sampling. He analyzes them. DDT—in the Antarctic.[114]

A biologist leaves a village in Anaktuvuk Pass in northern Alaska. He is an insect man, but he is interested in stream populations. He collects a lot of insects out of a little stream which runs down to the Bering Sea. There is a very strange combination of insects, and he's puzzled so he puts them through for analysis. The same answer. DDT.

The biologist whose responsibility it is to analyse the purity of foods in cans will tell you that not infrequently canned tuna taken off the Pacific Coast of North America is contaminated with DDT. So far it hasn't reached the level where it is considered harmful to humans. But it's there. It is impossible today to get uncontaminated food anywhere in the world. I don't care whether you are in the highest Arctic or the farthest out Antarctic. All this is the fallout, the results of aerial spraying and dusting and domestic spraying and dusting, for a very large portion of what is supposed to come down goes up. We think of fall-out only in radiation products. That is not so. The weather meteorologists in the Canadian Arctic who are responsible for snow sampling have been amazed to find that over the last ten years the lead content in the Arctic snow has increased over 300 percent. This is fallout from tetra ethyl lead entering the atmosphere in automobile exhaust.[115]

Clear Lake midges. Dr. Alden Miller, University of California ornithologist, had a summer cottage on Clear Lake in Lake County, California. Clear Lake is known for its midge problem. They don't bite, but there are tens of quintillions of them in the spring and early summer, and they're just a damned nuisance. So they brought in aircraft to spray the area where the midges were hatching, and it made life bearable for the people that were there. They sprayed at a very low level of DDT, known not to be toxic to the birds and fishes. The next spring when Alden Miller went up to open his summer camp, he found the beach littered with dead grebes. He couldn't understand this. They looked healthy enough. He had them analyzed. DDT poisoning.[116]

So he got some of the University of California biologists on the job. The DDT that had fallen into the water had settled on the bottom. There it had been absorbed by the microscopic organisms that form the basic element in the chain of food resources in the lake. The midge larvae had been eating these food organisms and stock-piling the DDT. Each little organism had its own quota, and this was steadily transferred to the midge larvae that ate them. Then as the midges came up and down in their daily migrations, the fish were living on them, and each fish took the little quota that was in the midge larvae and stockpiled it in its liver. Then came the grebes and ate the fish, and after eating a hundred or so fishes, they had a lethal dose of DDT. This is what we call food-chain contamination, and it is one of the things that is most desperately concerning us.

Enough about that. You get the idea. Pollution is a consequence of density, human density and technology. We are still living in very large measure by the old rule-of-thumb [that] flowing water purifies itself in about ten miles.[118] This was fine in frontier days when you could put your biffy out over the water and use that as your sewage disposal system. But it's no good anymore. There is too much sewage. We know that, but I was appalled at a conference in Victoria a year ago to hear a civil engineer from the University of Manitoba refer to the rivers as the cleansers of the nation. The morality of an act is a function of the state of the system. One doesn't know whether fouling a stream or killing a muskox or burning a shrub patch is harming others until you know a lot about the system.[119] It may not matter at all. The laws of our society follow the pattern of ancient ethics and are often poorly suited to governing a complex, crowded, rapidly changing technological world. In such a world it is impossible to spell out all the conditions that may be involved in—say, dumping raw sewage into a river, burning garbage in our backyard, using aircraft to spread DDT over a forest to kill spruce budworm or taking off into the farthest and quietest corners of a national park on a snowmobile. Thus since we can't have a major law to control each situation, we have administrative law [that is] administered by departments of government that are supposed to keep a sensitive watch on the system, and they do this to the best of their ability. This system has two problems. It demands a detailed understanding of the consequences of actions before decisions on the morality of such actions can be judged. It also demands an ingenious and sensitive feedback system to ensure that the custodians remain honest and up-to-date and that administrative law is not capricious.

Let us look at one more phase of our attitude toward the common resources, and this one I maintain is central to all others. I quote Garrett Hardin:[17]

> If each human family were dependent only on its own resources (as it once was), if the children of improvident parents starved to death or died of accident (as they once did), and if these consequences brought their own punishment to the germ line—there would be little or no public interest in controlling the headlong breeding of people.
>
> We are dedicated to a world in which we protect each other—and it is a good dedication. None of us would change it. But we breed as if the world was infinite, and yet it cannot be. There is an increasing urgency to identify Mankind's goals for himself. What are our goals as men? Are our goals to cram this world with as many people as it will hold? I can tell you approximately what it will be like. It will mean 1,600 calories per person per day, and that will give you just enough to stay alive but not enough to get very excited about anything anytime, so that will be a self-correcting problem, as you can see.

Now I seriously doubt that this is what we are about. But few people have really sat down and thought about what their goals are as people. What are our collective goals? We are all so busy doing our own thing that we don't think about the larger issues, and we are not geared to look after the larger issues. If there is a flood, some of us rally around and help tidy up the mud, or if there is a disaster, we send the Red Cross. We have our ways of looking after the short-term emergencies—dramatic things—but not these long-term insidious things that eat away at the quality of our lives as people. To couple the concept of freedom-to-breed with our own ideal that everyone born has an equal right to the common resources is to lock all of us into a tragic course because—and make no mistake—it's the resources of the world that we are talking about. Today we can head off all over the world in search of new things. A few hours will take you anywhere. We have just as much interest today in the presence of elephants and lions and tigers and so on in other parts of the world as we have in antelope, buffalo and muskox in Canada. We can go and see them when our ship comes in and we decide to take that trip of all trips. These are international concerns, and there are international agencies now expressing our interests, such as the International Union for Conservation of Nature and the World Wildlife Fund and so on.

Certainly we have a primary responsibility to manage our own common resources well because we do this not only for ourselves. We do this as custodians for Canadians as yet unborn, Canadians in other provinces, and for many that come from other shores to share in the interesting world in which we live. Many people now realize this, but it is not reflected in some of our laws, our bureaucratic legislation, our economic attitudes or some of our religious ideas. One of our favorite answers to this disparate problem is conscience. Relying on science can't work. If I tell a man, "Look! You shouldn't do that. And if you do it, I'll hold you up to ridicule," he gets two messages: I shouldn't do it and I know it, but if I don't do it, I'll suffer the

In northeastern BC, wood bison (*Bison bison athabascae*) and other large mammals along highways and gravel back roads are an increasing attraction to tourists and photographers travelling between the province, the northern territories and Alaska. PHOTO BY R. WAYNE CAMPBELL.

consequences of not doing it because I won't get these extra advantages that I seek for myself, while the world has to share in the problems that I create. Then he gets the other message in the deep, dark hours of the night: really what this fellow was saying to me was "If you are stupid enough to follow your conscience and not do it while the other fellows are going ahead and doing it, I will hold you up as a dolt." So conscience can't work. This isn't enough.

The bank bandit is a man with a distorted idea of common resources, and we have developed very fixed attitudes towards this kind of person. I would suggest that there isn't all that much difference. It is just a question of immediacy. So the answer is that the concept of common resources in all its aspects is tolerable only under conditions of low density, and we are doing our very best to increase our density. We breed with frightening enthusiasm, and if we are not doing that fast enough, we import people from elsewhere, and we persuade ourselves that this will improve our standards of living. I've yet to see a convincing argument that more people in Canada will necessarily lead to a better life for all.

We are told that "the state has no place in the nation's bedrooms."[120] Okay. Maybe it hasn't. But don't let me hear you howling when the product of your fun and games turns up in the schoolroom or when your competition for resources is not quite as effective as it was. We are told that the fishing on the Fraser River bars here is not as good now as it used to be. Well, how many more people are sharing it? You must be prepared for steady abandonment of one after the other of your cherished freedoms in the commons if you continue to encourage increase in human numbers. We have accepted the change from the food gathering culture to farms, pastures and leased ranges. We resent the fences that these bring onto our former hunting grounds, but they are an inevitable consequence of numbers.

How far have we come in our attitudes toward the consequences of numbers in environmental pollution? Are we determined now that we must no longer discharge sewage into our rivers and lakes? No, we're not. We are still arguing about authorizing major new sewage pollution of the Fraser River in the cause of suburban development. My answer is that, if you can't afford to treat the sewage, you can't afford to develop the area. And that's the only answer. I'm quite sure that within the next four or five years this will be accepted as the general answer.

We must count the cost of further increases in population in all its detail. We must be prepared to be told that we can't freely use DDT and some other of our broad spectrum life-destroying chemicals. I'm looking forward to the day—and I don't think it will be too far away—when Canada will ban the use of DDT and some of the other more ecologically dangerous insecticides.[121] It has already been banned in one or two states of the Union, and there is an interesting citizen's group in the United States that systematically challenges state governments to show the proper cause for the use of—or permitting the use of—these powerful insecticides.

Numbers of people, of course, alter the environment. This is expected and part of an expanding society, but many of the changes are unnecessary.

They result from thoughtlessness, ignorance or apathy. Others are intolerable for their long-term damage to the environment in which man must live. It was [Aldo] Leopold (1887–1948) who in 1925 said that generally speaking it is not timber and certainly not agriculture that is decimating the wilderness areas of our land, but rather the desire to attract tourists.[124] The events of the forty years since this was written have firmly established its truth. It could be well expanded, I am sure, to apply to the pressure of our own numbers. We can witness this even in our national and provincial parks. We are fortunate in British Columbia. We have vast reserves of land not yet ruined by insensitive, ill-advised use. We do have time, but not all that much time, and the rate of change and particularly the rate of change on the accessible areas—the areas that you and I can reach in a long weekend or a week—is frighteningly rapid.

The wild land story of Canada is perhaps a prototype or the evolution of an idea in democracy. A century has passed since we saw this as just a romantic dream of poets, and now wild land is a legal social entity, moved along its course by the gathering strength of popular demand. The proponents of wild land use sought no economic gains themselves. The most powerful motives for the maintenance of wild land opportunities are still ethical, romantic and cultural, and not economic. But we now see these things that we treasure threatened by the sheer numbers of those who would enjoy them. We here are fortunate in having time left to us and the opportunity for profiting from the trial and error experiments of others, but the time grows short, and we must be ingenious and devoted. We will have to turn our thought very quickly now to pleasure in the commons. I mean this in a variety of ways—things that you have never thought about perhaps—smoking in confined public places, for example. There are far more people who don't smoke than smoke, and yet those of us who don't smoke have to put up with this contamination all the time. The right to make noise in quiet places, to advertise grossly on highways, and to go to any park when you wish. These things are on the way out. Hunting and fishing that is accessible will be leased or controlled.

And I would like to refer for a moment to one of the problems that I know your own Fish and Wildlife Branch has been considering for years: the harvest of small, choice crops—such as bighorn sheep—from a small population. Now you can say this is a common resource. Come one, come all—but just make it one weekend. This is a first-rate way to destroy the quality of the experience. But it is more difficult and requires more tolerance to do it in a quality way by a lottery or some other way to decide that a low density experience is going to be had by those who want to use this resource. This has been pioneered by others [so] we know the problems, and we also know the way out. I am quite sure that deterioration of the quality of this kind of harvest is either going to close down the harvest entirely or it will turn us to some other better way of maintaining quality.

Every new curtailment of the commons is a curtailment of someone's personal liberty. The lake you and I used to enjoy is now on someone's ranch.

You used to fish the little creek as the spirit moved you all year round, and you got the little trout. They were good. You can't anymore. My favorite camping spot is now a motel site. We oppose, we shout about rights and freedom, but the ultimate freedom in an increasing population in this sense is the freedom to destroy, to bring universal ruin. Hegel has said, "Freedom is really the recognition of necessity."[126] The most important aspect of necessity today is to recognize the necessity of abandoning the freedom to breed. There are no technical solutions that are going to rescue us from the ultimate miseries of over-population. And long before that time comes, the quality of things that you and I enjoy are going to be gone.

I don't like to leave you with a negative attitude. What then should be our plan of action in the certainty of greater increase of population before man comes to appreciate the necessity of controlling his numbers? These five ideas I would like to leave with you.

1. We should question the validity of our attitude that more people inevitably mean a better way of life for Canadians and an augmented ability for Canadians to help feed the world's hungry and homeless. We're a food surplus country, and this is one of the things we really can do. Can we do it as well when there are 40 million Canadians as when there are 20 million?

2. We should work to change our attitudes toward family size. Two is the magic number.

3. Support the work of your organization to reduce the destructive impact of our society on its environment—pollution in all its forms.

4. When numbers clearly show that the concept of complete freedom of access to the common resources must be abandoned, try to

During the 1960s Still Creek in Burnaby, BC—seen here in February 1970—served as a dumping area for industrial wastes and surface water from paved parking lots at nearby shopping malls. A local environmental group formed in 1969, the Society Promoting Environmental Conservation, started a campaign to reduce the contaminants entering the creek as it flows into Burnaby Lake, an important urban marsh. Within a few years, polluting effluents were greatly reduced. PHOTO BY R. WAYNE CAMPBELL.

maintain a sensible enough point of view to recognize the impending damage before it takes place. It takes so long to rebuild it—if it's rebuildable.

5. When this change in attitude is necessary, play an active part in studying the alternative ways in which new, controlled uses can be planned so that you can continue to maintain a quality recreational experience.

I was discussing this interesting problem with two of my colleagues, one from the School of Community and Regional Planning at the University and the other the director of our Resource Sciences Centre, and we came to the conclusion that the greatest lack in wild land recreational planning today was a lack of an identifiable client. If you are going to build a building, you have got to build it for a client, and he's going to present you with specifications. Here then is the most important mission for the sportsman's federation and also in its larger context of a union with all the like-minded people that is developing so well today. These groups should establish themselves as the recognizable voice of the clients. To do so will require a well-considered and broadly framed set of principles that go beyond our own immediate personal interests in day-to-day fishing and hunting. It will require mature and balanced judgment appropriate to the importance and responsibility of the task. It will also mean the courage and resources to fight hard when this seems necessary.

Canada has no Sierra Club. It has no Izaak Walton League. It has no Wilderness Society. It has no Association of the Garden Clubs of America. And I could go on naming eight or ten more of these. These are the voices of the client in the United States, and we don't have them. Our National Provincial Parks Association is foundering for lack of support. There is a serious void in the private corporate voice of citizens for wild land values. Your government organizations can strive to move forward, but they can only go as fast as the public will go with them. The voice of the client is the most important element to help them do this and also to give them some ideas that they are not going to get by themselves. It seems to me that you have already secured a good hold on this task in the last two or three years, and I urge you to carry on, and I offer you my most enthusiastic support in one of the most important tasks you could undertake.

—Ian McTaggart-Cowan, May 1969

The Sierra Club—Over a Century of Protecting Nature

Founded in 1892 by preservationist John Muir, the Sierra Club is one of the oldest and most influential environmental groups in North America. After 1963, it was active in a variety of environmental issues in Canada, mainly through its United States–based chapters. However, a Canadian office was formally opened in 1989, and three years later this non-profit organization had a national presence in this country. Today the Sierra Club has five chapters across Canada, from Vancouver Island to Cape Breton Island, focussing on pollution, biodiversity, energy and sustainability issues.[127]

CHAPTER 7
The Retirement Years

Ian McTaggart-Cowan retired as dean of Graduate Studies at UBC in 1975, and the following year he and Joyce moved to Ten Mile Point in Saanich, outside of Victoria. Here he planned to garden and collect stamps, interspersing these activities with trips to the family cottage on Mayne Island. He and Joyce also began accepting invitations from Sven-Olof Lindblad's Special Expeditions (now Lindblad Expeditions) to act as naturalist/hosts aboard ecotourism cruises. The company became famous for using small ships to take passengers on marine-focussed voyages along the West Coast.

However, Ian and Joyce were back at UBC for convocation on June 3, 1977, where Ian was awarded the title and degree of Doctor of Science *honoris causa*, reflecting both the scope of his various roles at the university and the high esteem in which he was held by his alma mater. UBC president Douglas T. Kenny, in presenting him to the chancellor for the award, reviewed his career and then said:

> Through a turbulent decade of startling growth and reconstruction he led that Faculty [of Graduate Studies] with consummate skill; its present stability and reputation have emerged in large part from his uncompromising insistence on high standards and his wise understanding of academic complexities. His wide experience made him a charter member of the Academic Board of British Columbia in 1963 and in 1969 he became chairman. For many years the senate of the University looked to him for advice. Despite his considerable administrative responsibilities, he has retained his reputation as a prominent scientist and constantly his knowledge and his presence have been sought by provincial and national professional institutions. Above all, Ian Cowan has been and remains a superb teacher and a strikingly successful interpreter of the world of science to the lay public. A Fellow of the Royal Society, he was named an

Officer of the Order of Canada in 1970 and has won honorary degrees from the Universities of Alberta and Waterloo. Mr. Chancellor, because, with the utmost versatility and grace, he has devoted his life, with singular success, to this university, this province, and this country, I present to you for the degree Doctor of Science, *honoris causa,* Ian McTaggart-Cowan.[128]

As it turned out, in the case of Ian McTaggart-Cowan, the word retirement reflected only a change in direction rather than a withdrawal, and he turned to several brand new roles with undiminished energy. In 1979, at the age of sixty-nine, he was appointed chancellor of the University of Victoria for a five-year term. The University Act of British Columbia requires all universities to have a chancellor as head of the university, and although the chancellor's most familiar public role is conferring degrees at convocation, the person in this role has overall responsibilities for all functions of the university, including chairing convocation and conferring degrees, but also serving on both the board of governors and the senate.

At the same time Ian was also still in great demand as a speaker. Inevitably he was out of touch with much of the new information in natural history and research and had to rely increasingly on his early reputation as a biologist. He became everyone's professor—knowledgeable, charming, influential, and a fabled achiever. His early reputation as a zoologist had given way to a reputation as a renowned educator at all levels of academic life.

His 1976 foreword to Tommy Walker's book *Spatsizi*[129] is typical of his published work at this time. It addresses wilderness aesthetic values and chronicles the historical developments that have encroached upon wilderness environments often by a series of seemingly small increments that collectively become significant. In it he pays tribute to Walker's success in achieving protection for the Spatsizi Plateau Wilderness Provincial Park after a long campaign, and he stresses the importance of individual initiative in conservation efforts.

Foreword to the Book *Spatsizi*[130]

Most Canadians are southerners, living close to our boundary with the United States where climate, landscape and agricultural land have encouraged the development of our cities, our transportation systems and our extraordinarily productive food producing industry. Our history is one of subduing the wilderness, of finding in that great land all the marketable products that can be woven into the comfortable and varied lifestyles that we enjoy. With an efficiency that can only be marvelled at, we have completely changed the face of perhaps a third of our country. To most Canadians the hinterlands, the vast northern tundras, the endless spruce forests that lie between the tundra and the farms and ranches, the vast tumult of mountain peaks, shadowed valleys, sweeping alplands and montane forests that are the far west of

Canada, are seen primarily as unused land, waiting for someone to find in it deposits of minerals or petroleum, a place where a river can be dammed, a market for the trees—anything that will justify "developing" it.

From the first landing of the Europeans on both coasts intrepid men, trappers, traders and prospectors have been pushing their way into these wilderness areas until there can be few corners, no matter how remote, that have not been seen by someone. Most of them were unlettered men and they left scant record of what they saw. Among the western mountains they found a sparse population of Indian people living as part of the land and completely dependent upon their skill in extracting from its plants and wildlife the food, clothing and shelter for survival. Along with the moose, caribou and sheep they prospered or perished as natural forces dictated. They had no backup of an organized society to retreat to or to call on for help.

Then came the aircraft and the bush pilot, and in four decades there were no more places that could not be quickly reached, no more villages or even nomadic families of Indians that were not influenced. Hunters, fishermen, the technological prospector, foresters, biologists, geologists and engineers reached the remote vastness of what had been almost untouched wilderness. And the roads came, from cart track to truck roads to improved highway: the trucks and cars and campers, the litter and garbage and disturbance, the man-set fires and the rivers clouded with mine washings. We have been so engrossed with the processes of development, each community, each company, each individual entrepreneur pursuing what seemed to best suit immediate objectives, that the collective results were overlooked. Little by little we have chopped away at the large remote areas that not only typify the mountainous areas of Canada but are essential to the survival of some of the magnificent wildlife species that occur only there, the Osborn caribou, Stone's sheep, mountain goat, grizzly and wolverine, along with their more widely distributed, more people tolerant associates, the black bear and moose.

The remote homestead has been very much part of our history. Hundreds of families have chosen lives at the fringes of access to communities, where they were in close contact with unspoiled country. These were people who valued solitude, the opportunity to live without the constraints that accompany numbers of people. To them life was best when they could cut their own firewood, take wild meat for the table and furs for some cash income, clear land for their gardens and pastures, enjoy the tranquility as well as the hazards of close contact with wild land, wild animals and a very unpredictable climate. The sharp contrasts of such a life were what they sought. We have had some eloquent chroniclers of this lifestyle. Theodora Stanwell-Fletcher,

Ian signing the honorary degree registry with UBC president Douglas T. Kenny on June 3, 1977. COURTESY OF UNIVERSITY OF BRITISH COLUMBIA ARCHIVES. PHOTO 35.1/62-5.

Spatsizi Plateau Wilderness Park, one of the largest parks in Canada, is not accessible by road. It encompasses 695,102 hectares of alpine tundra, spruce-willow birch and boreal spruce forests. The area was protected as a provincial park on December 3, 1975. PHOTO BY GAIL ROSS. COURTESY OF BRITISH COLUMBIA PARKS, VICTORIA, BC. IMAGE 0279-00HQLD0004.

R.M. Patterson, Rich Hobson, Eric Collier and Andy Russell are names known to thousands who, despite lives linked primarily with cities, have a strong love for wildland and wild creatures.

Spatsizi is a worthy addition to these other chronicles of a lifestyle that is growing difficult to elect. Those of us who have known Tommy and Marion Walker, their devotion to the wilderness and their determination to live their lives in it despite early disasters that would have broken the spirit of most of us, have keenly anticipated this account. It is a timely and fascinating chronicle of a period of British Columbia history told with candour and sensitivity. Theirs is an unpretentious account of life beyond the end of the road told with an affection for those they knew. But *Spatsizi* is much more than that. Tommy and Marion have actively sought wilderness. They were prepared to abandon their treasured spot in the Bella Coola valley when the road came, and by one of the greatest wilderness horse-treks of recent years to reach out for a place to make a new start. This they found at Cold Fish Lake in the heart of the Spatsizi wilderness, south of the Stikine River in northern British Columbia. Here the primitive wildlife populations were virtually unaltered. They could not have foretold how short a period they would have before development intruded again.

The Walkers' love for the Spatsizi grew into a full-blown campaign to save it and the magnificent ecosystem it represented from total destruction. Tommy was the licensed big game guide in this 3,000-square-mile region. He made his living introducing his clients to the magnificent wildlife and the unparalleled scenery of the area. His missionary zeal was contagious, and few of those who traveled and hunted with him returned home unchanged. They became a fraternity of ardent conservationists.

Tommy and Marion have had a dream for their country and for the small group of Indian friends who lived there with hardship before they arrived.

In March 1994 the population of woodland caribou in Spatsizi Plateau Wilderness Park was estimated at over twenty-six thousand animals.
PHOTO BY R. WAYNE CAMPBELL.

They have conceived the Spatsizi as a Wilderness Reserve dedicated to the maintenance of the unique biological system of land, plants, animals and people. It would be a place to learn about how such a system marked a place to come to enjoy but leave unspoiled. They have worked with devotion and determination to bring this dream to reality. A few of us have had the privilege of working with them on their mission. It was the Walkers who provided the steady pressure, by films, by photographic presentations, by letters and personal exhortation. As a road moved up one boundary and a railroad up another the Stone's sheep, caribou, goats and grizzlies decreased in numbers, and it seemed for a time that there was little hope.

Then in 1975 the wisdom of the proposal achieved recognition. An ecological reserve and a provincial park now protect the Spatsizi. There could be no better time for the publication of this volume. Through Tommy and Marion's account we can share the experience of two intrepid, adventurous and very sensitive people, follow the evolution of their concerns with what our society was doing to its treasure spots. We can draw heart from the example they have given of what two people can do to change the bureaucratic affairs.

—Ian McTaggart-Cowan, August 1976

The Birds of British Columbia

In the conclusion to the lecture Ian was required to give when accepting the Doris Huestis Speirs Award from the Society of Canadian Ornithologists/ Société des ornithologistes du Canada in August 1998, he spoke about the problems in bird management that are unique to British Columbia:

Wildlife management is based on research to discover the nature of the problems, followed by attempts to alleviate them. We seldom can manage bird

When Ian found his first robin nest as a lad, he was intrigued that a brown bird with a red breast would lay immaculate turquoise eggs. Over the rest of his life, this fascination continued. Even as a scientist, he appreciated that some of nature's secrets are best left to the imagination. PHOTO BY VI AND JOHN LAMBIE.

In the 1950s and 1960s there was a significant decline in populations of some raptorial birds attributed to DDT contamination. Most susceptible were fish-eating species like osprey. PHOTO BY R. WAYNE CAMPBELL.

The Ashnola River. Riparian habitats along rivers are favourite collecting sites for birds and small mammals. PHOTO BY R. WAYNE CAMPBELL.

Part of the attraction of collecting birds in remote areas is the chance of finding a species new to a region or documenting a range extension. In Jasper National Park Ian spotted a well-camouflaged willow ptarmigan on her nest; this was a significant southern range extension. PHOTO BY R. WAYNE CAMPBELL.

Lewis's woodpecker breeds in open ponderosa pine/Douglas-fir woodlands across the southern interior of British Columbia. PHOTO BY MARK NYHOF.

Clark's nutcracker (Clark's crow), typically a southern interior species, is a very rare find west of the Coast Mountains in British Columbia. Ian's sighting was the third record for Vancouver Island. PHOTO BY R. WAYNE CAMPBELL.

California quail, an introduced species in British Columbia, is an uncommon local resident on southern Vancouver Island, becoming even less abundant northward along the east coast to Campbell River. A nest with eggs discovered by Ian in 1931 at Comox was the most northerly breeding record for the island at that time. PHOTO BY R. WAYNE CAMPBELL.

Ian described his first red-necked grebe nest as "Nest in the lily pads & about 5 feet across. Built entirely of water lily leaves & stems with a few muddy roots in the middle." The light-coloured egg in the photo is newly laid.

PHOTO OF A SIMILAR NEST BY LINDA M. VAN DAMME.

During a field trip with Kenneth Racey in 1931 in the western Chilcotin, Ian saw his first American white pelican.[37]
PHOTO BY R. WAYNE CAMPBELL, STUM LAKE, BC, MAY 25, 1993.

In summer, moose often feed on pond-lilies in wetlands but change to a diet of woody plants in autumn and winter.
PHOTO BY R. WAYNE CAMPBELL.

Atlin, on the eastern shore of Atlin Lake in northwestern British Columbia, was founded in the late 1800s as a result of the quest for gold. In the early 1920s it began to draw tourists as well as museum collectors like Harry Swarth, who during his 131-day stay there recorded 121 species of birds and 21 species of mammals.
PHOTO BY R. WAYNE CAMPBELL.

The hoary marmot, which is associated with subalpine and alpine habitats throughout the province, is one of the twenty-seven species of mammals in Spatsizi Plateau Wilderness Provincial Park. PHOTO BY MARK NYHOF.

In the late spring and early summer of 1938 Ian McTaggart-Cowan and Patrick Martin spent 57 days investigating the vertebrate fauna of the Peace River area, still one of the least known ornithological regions in the province. They recorded 168 species of birds, 10 of which were new to the provincial list. PHOTO BY R. WAYNE CAMPBELL.

Because of its restricted distribution in British Columbia, the sage thrasher was a target species for early collectors visiting the Okanagan Valley. The family Ian collected on June 25, 1936, was the earliest date recorded for fledged young in the province, suggesting that egg laying could have started as early as May 26. PHOTO BY R. WAYNE CAMPBELL.

Wayne Campbell (top) and Barbara Jackson have started to process a beaked whale (*Mesoplodon* sp.) that washed ashore on Wreck Beach in Florencia Bay on the west coast of Vancouver Island in August 1969. PHOTO BY PEG WHITTINGTON.

In the early 1970s the dramatic decline in the grizzly bear population in the area around Yellowstone Park was attributed to the closure of garbage dumps.[76] In 1975 the species was formally listed as threatened under the Endangered Species Act. For two years during this controversial period Ian chaired a committee to provide solutions to stem the decline. PHOTO BY R. WAYNE CAMPBELL.

In 1940 Ian McTaggart-Cowan proposed recognizing seven subspecies of North American bighorn sheep (l.) and three subspecies of Dall's sheep (r.). This was the most important treatise on North American mountain sheep at the time.[83] The photos show a Rocky Mountain bighorn sheep (l.) and a Stone's (thinhorn) sheep (r.). PHOTOS BY R. WAYNE CAMPBELL.

Maligne Lake, Jasper National Park, Alberta. PHOTO BY DOUG LEIGHTON.

While conducting surveys in Jasper National Park in the summer of 1946, Ian recognized that Columbian ground squirrels were ecologically important as prey for such species as golden eagles and coyotes. PHOTO BY R. WAYNE CAMPBELL.

There is growing concern among many professional zoologists that museum holdings are being neglected with the cessation of active collecting programs. Properly catalogued specimens, such as this series of pigeon guillemots, are invaluable in moult studies and detecting changes in environmental contaminants in fish-eating species. PHOTO BY DENNIS A. DEMARCHI.

Banding birds, such as this golden-crowned sparrow captured in a mist net, and searching marshes for bird nests delayed Wayne's post-secondary education until several professors at UBC encouraged him to attend university. PHOTO BY R. WAYNE CAMPBELL, BURNABY, BC, NOVEMBER 1964.

In 2005, 319,400 fresh-water angling licences were sold in British Columbia, resulting in four million angler-days of activity and $480 million in spending by anglers.[110]
PHOTO BY DENNIS A. DEMARCHI.

In the late 1950s prior to DDT spraying to control insects at Clear Lake, California, the breeding population of *Aechmophorus* grebes (now known as two species—western grebe and Clark's grebe,[117] pictured) was greater than 1,000 pairs. Following aerial chemical application, only 30 nests were found in 1960 and 16 nests in 1961. By 2000 the colony had recovered to about half its pre-DDT population size. This example was discussed in Rachel Carson's *Silent Spring*.
PHOTO BY IAN JAMES.

Between 1950 and 1965 the nesting population of peregrine falcons in North America (and elsewhere) showed an unprecedented crash in numbers. It was determined soon after that DDT contributed to eggshell thinning, which in turn affected productivity.[122] By the late 1980s, following the ban on DDT, the population started to rebound.[123] PHOTO BY R. WAYNE CAMPBELL.

Most of the 1,406 sq. km of Kootenay National Park, one of the four contiguous Rocky Mountain parks straddling the provinces of Alberta and British Columbia, is preserved as wilderness.[125] PHOTO BY LARRY HALVERSON, OCTOBER 31, 2011.

In the summer of 1980 Wayne Campbell led a Provincial Museum collecting expedition into the Chilkat Pass area of extreme northwestern BC. Museum technicians (left to right: Phil Nott, Michael C.E. McNall and Christopher D. Shepard) prepare ptarmigan specimens. PHOTO BY R. WAYNE CAMPBELL, NEAR STANLEY CREEK, BC, AUGUST 2, 1980.

During his retirement Ian spent many years as a ship's naturalist for various cruise lines that travelled from Alaska to Mexico. Here, he is using a natural seat on a chunk of ice on the Stikine Flats, Alaska. PHOTO COURTESY OF ANN SCHAU.

Ian always enjoyed trips to the Okanagan Valley where he was assured of seeing the familiar California quail. PHOTO BY ALAN D. WILSON.

Jasper National Park. As a 19-year old student, Ian had the privileged opportunity to visit Canada's Rocky Mountain parks, an opportunity that led to a lifetime interest in research and conservation of the nation's wildlife resources. PHOTO BY DOUGLAS LEIGHTON, JASPER NATIONAL PARK, AB.

species in the wild; usually the best we can do is find out which of humanity's ineptitudes caused the problems and design means to manage people more effectively. Where birds migrate between one nation and another, the necessary action may be out of reach of any one country. International action is imperative. The Migratory Birds Convention of 1916 was a new dimension in international relations and completely changed relationships between people and birds in North America. It was negotiated in response to a request from the provinces (and states), which explains its restricted application. When I first became aware of such things, the concern for birds somewhat resembled fisheries today. The "important" ones were those you could eat or ship to market for a price—ducks, geese, swans and cranes. Even the 1916 Convention gave no protection to eagles, hawks, owls or corvids, and there was a price on the heads of all of these. Protection of non-migratory species, including all raptors, crows, jays, magpies and many marine species, remained the responsibility of the provinces and came later. Ratification of the convention by Canada set in motion the appointment of migratory bird protection officers. . . From that small beginning, the Canadian Wildlife Service emerged as a major force in research and conservation of migratory birds in British Columbia.

In the 1920s and 1930s British Columbia still behaved like a game keeper on a Scottish grouse moor. Its fauna consisted of good and bad creatures. A species seen as a sporting target and eatable was "good"; all those that sometimes killed a "good" bird or ate its eggs were "bad"; all else were of little importance unless they ate our crops, when they too were "bad." The chosen means of controlling the "bad" species was offering a bounty or promoting "shoots" with prizes as rewards. At one time or another all the "bad" species had a price on their heads, a distinction they shared with coyotes, wolves and cougars. My first bio-political campaign was to expose the futility and fraud

At least 515 species of birds occur in BC, more than in any other Canadian province or territory. This province also supports most of the world's population of such species as the burrow-nesting Cassin's auklet, which nests on offshore islands. PHOTO BY R. WAYNE CAMPBELL.

of the bounty system. It took ten years to accomplish this. J.R. Dymond at the University of Toronto was a fellow-campaigner.

Nostalgia of European expatriates led early in the century to attempts to add to our native fauna some 13 species of birds from Europe or the United States.[133] All but a very few failed. Far more harmful to native birds of the province was the introduction of raccoons and Norway rats to 21 islands important to nesting sea birds. In the 1940s a cluster of relatively small, precipitous islands off northern Vancouver Island received raccoons and minks as unauthorized transplants by a local trapper. Even more disastrous was the liberation on Queen Charlotte Islands of raccoons from Vancouver Island; this was done at the request of some resident sportsmen on Graham Island. Indigenous otter, marten and weasel had been no problem to the myriad murrelets, auklets, puffins, murres and petrels that came ashore to nest on the small, well-isolated islands of the archipelago. But the raccoons spread throughout the islands and pose serious threats to survival of some seabird species. Norway rats probably arrived as stowaways and have been equally destructive to some colonies. We now face the expensive and possibly futile task of trying to eliminate them from areas of greatest concern.

With its complex array of ecosystems and habitats, British Columbia has a more varied avifauna than any other province in Canada.[134] We are surrounded by birds that have been tested beyond our imagining. The slate was swept almost clean by glacial ice intrusions, the latest one still melting today. They met the supreme challenges of climatic change but are now confronted by a new arsenal of hazards of human design. The objective of most conservation measures seems to be to stop the clock, and this we cannot do. We desperately need the wisdom to detect problems of our making as distinct from those that are steps in global processes—when to intercede and when just to watch and record. For nigh on 200 years we have been altering or eliminating habitats. We already have lost two or three species and reduced another 50 species and subspecies to the point of serious concern for their survival. Today almost every year some new vagrant bird from eastern Siberia or from the south causes excitement among the life-listers. Is this flow of "vagrants" an artifact of more and better observers? Or is there an increasing trend to malfunction among migrant birds today? Or is the increasing complexity of new chemicals loose in the environment causing more migrating birds to miscue? I suspect both factors contribute. Even a long life is but an instant in biological time, but it is long enough to see worrisome deterioration in our fauna and its habitats. I finish [this speech] as I started with words of wisdom from [Aldo] Leopold: "The first principle of intelligent tinkering is to save all the parts." Tinkering can be inadvertent as well as purposeful. Both are equally final.[135]

By the early 1970s, Ian considered that it was time to begin updating his 1947 book *A Review of the Bird Fauna of British Columbia*.[11] He felt that Wayne Campbell had the necessary enthusiasm, publication record, innovative ideas and commitment to spearhead the project. He told Wayne he

could not be actively involved at the outset because of his heavy commitments as dean of Graduate Studies.

Ian, looking back on that period, remembered that:

At the time I was totally immersed in university duties, and thoughts of a new
bird summary for BC were put aside – by me but not by Wayne. On becoming
a biologists at the [Provincial] Museum in 1973, he embarked upon the many
tasks that had to precede the writing of a new book. Bibliographic research,[137]
surveys of seabird nesting colonies,[138] field studies in blank areas,[139] and
building the British Columbia nest record scheme,[140] and mustering many
thousands of occurrence records into a database occupied fourteen years of
intense activity. Along the way, he gained the confidence and cooperation of
many thousands of amateur bird enthusiasts from all parts of the province as
cooperators in the new venture.

By then 40 years had elapsed since publication of "Munro and Cowan."
With support by the Royal British Columbia Museum and Canadian Wildlife
Service, writing began. The six authors agreed that the many knowledgeable observers across the province with their excellent optical equipment
and cameras made well-documented observations acceptable evidence of
occurrence.[141]

Wayne Campbell had, in fact, already begun work on the project in the
mid-1960s by searching for specimen records in North American museums
and records in published and unpublished literature. Later the databases
he established would be complemented with the observations of thousands of reliable amateur birdwatchers; in fact, before the four volumes of
The Birds of British Columbia were complete, over seven thousand amateur

Over eighty percent of all species of
birds found in BC are protected by
the Migratory Birds Convention Act
of 1916, which is administered by
the federal government. Groups such
as hawks, owls, eagles and corvids
remain the responsibility of the
provincial government. PHOTO BY MARK
NYHOF.

Ian McTaggart-Cowan holding a glaucous-winged gull chick with the bird's rear end pointed in a safe direction. Chain Islets, BC, July 1989. PHOTO BY R. WAYNE CAMPBELL.

birdwatchers and naturalists had contributed their personal observations of birds in British Columbia. Ian kept in frequent touch with Wayne throughout the next decade, but fieldwork to generate new data for the bird books was a high priority, and it was Wayne who led the museum collecting expeditions to the Tatshenshini-Alsek River region, along the Haines Highway, the Atlin vicinity in the northwest and Kotcho Lake[142] in the remote northeast of the province. He also coordinated and directed a survey of seabird nesting colonies along the entire British Columbia coast and freshwater colonial-nesting birds in the interior.

While Ian had picked up some bird-banding skills on waterfowl in the Cariboo-Chilcotin region of south central British Columbia in the 1940s, he had no experience tagging marine birds at nesting colonies. During a photo shoot for the first volume of *The Birds of British Columbia* on seabird islands off Victoria in July 1989, Wayne had the occasion to save him an embarrassing trip to the cleaners by reminding him of the "jet" excretion of feces by marine birds when they are handled. Wayne recalled:

The mistake I had made when banding my first of tens of thousands of young glaucous-winged gulls was to pick up the chick, hold it close to my body where it was secure and apply the band. I only did this once as the nauseating stench of liquid droppings along my clothes lasted the rest of the trip. In the accompanying photo, Ian is being warned to hold the gull chick with its rear end pointed in a safe direction away from his body. Not long after he picked up the young bird, it excreted explosively, and the professor with a sheepish grin seemed grateful for the timely advice.

The preparation of this mammoth publishing project drew on a wide range of resource persons. Dennis Demarchi, who had spent thirty-five years with the Ministry of Environment's wildlife branch as the provincial habitat inventory specialist, was one of them. Early in his career while working in the East Kootenay area with surficial geologists, soil scientists, vegetation ecologists and climatologists, he had begun to develop the provincial-scale concept that became known as the ecoregions of British Columbia. This classification system has proven valuable for protected area strategies and wildlife conservation biologists working throughout this province. In 1988 when it became common knowledge in the Ministry of the Environment that the first two volumes of *The Birds of British Columbia* were in their final stages of preparation, Dennis recalled that:

> In 1988, Andrew Harcombe came to me (we were both working for the Ministry of Environment at the time) with concerns that the outdated "terrestrial biotic areas map" that Munro and Cowan had used in their 1947 publication, *A Review of the Bird Fauna of British Columbia*, was going to be reproduced as the background ecological reference for the updated provincial bird books. Realizing the importance of associating birds with habitats we wanted to promote incorporating the newly developed British Columbia ecoregion classification that I had developed into their publication. During a scheduled lecture by Dr. Cowan in Victoria, a meeting was arranged and the four of us met in Wayne's office in the curatorial tower of the BC Provincial Museum. Both Wayne and Ian quickly confirmed that the addition of such a comprehensive ecological reference in the books would not only be unique but for the first time the distribution, occurrence, abundance and life history of birds in the province could be linked directly to habitats.

The first and second volumes of *The Birds of British Columbia* were published in 1990 by the Royal British Columbia Museum. The first volume covered non-passerines from loons through waterfowl, while

In 1983 the Friends of the Royal British Columbia Museum sponsored a collecting expedition to a remote area of the Tatshenshini-Alsek region of northwestern BC, an area previously unexplored by biologists.
PHOTO BY R. WAYNE CAMPBELL.

the second covered diurnal birds of prey through woodpeckers. In November 1990 at the book launch held in Victoria to celebrate the completion of the first two volumes, Ian presented Wayne with a unique volume pulled from his personal library as he knew that Wayne also treasured historical books of the Pacific Northwest. In the letter enclosed with his gift he wrote:

November 9, 1990

Dear Wayne,

Between 1877 and 1886 the Signal Service of the US Army fostered a series of studies of coastal Alaska. The naturalists who studied the birds, mammals and fish of the region were L.M. Turner and E.W. Nelson. The latter went on to become chief of the US Bureau of Biological Survey.

Both Turner and Nelson's reports of their studies appeared as separate volumes in 1886. Unknown to most people a small printing of their reports were combined with two other short studies and published in a single volume as US Senate Document vol. 8.

I found a copy of this rare volume while I was rummaging in a used book shop in San Francisco in 1934 and bought it even though I could not afford the price asked. It was probably about $7.50!

I have enjoyed it for 46 years and am delighted that it will find an appreciative environment in your hands. I hope you enjoy it as much as I have and for at least as long.

Recently the binding is getting tired with the passage of time. The split calf leather has become brittle. If the museum conservators or the archives people can put you on to where it can be repaired or replaced I would like to have it done for you.

It has been a pleasure working with you on volumes 1 and 2 of this fascinating book and I look forward to the adventures with volumes 3 and 4 of the *Birds of BC.*

All the best

In 1992 Wayne Campbell was seconded to the British Columbia Ministry of Environment as a research scientist to complete the final two volumes of *The Birds of British Columbia.* To facilitate this move, Ian provided a letter of recommendation on October 5, 1991:

To Whom It May Concern,

It is a pleasure to respond to a request from R. Wayne Campbell to provide him with a testimonial letter.

I have known Wayne for more than twenty years. Our earliest close association began in 1969 when, as head of the Department of Zoology at the University of British Columbia, I hired him to curate the collections of the Museum of Vertebrate Zoology there. He was already a knowledgeable vertebrate zoologist with a broad competence in the amphibia, reptilia and mammals on top of his major expertise in ornithology. As curator he introduced a number of innovative ideas that have proven themselves over time. His duties included working with the students in vertebrate zoology laboratories. Here he demonstrated skill in communicating information and in encouraging the enthusiasms of students.

At the [Provincial] Museum he not only fulfilled the usual curatorial duties but his unusual energy and enthusiasm led to his greatly expanding the role to make the Provincial Museum the primary source of information on the birds of British Columbia. He made himself available to several other Departments of Government who had need of expertise in birds for environmental, educational, forensic or other reasons. His early experience in teaching and public education had led to skill in presenting biological information to audiences of all ages. He has been a highly popular speaker in the schools throughout the Province as well as a frequent contributor to adult audiences on a variety of topics centered on birds, the management of renewable resources and related environmental issues. His presentations are well planned, skillfully delivered and interesting to listen to. He has been given several awards for the excellence of his public presentations.

Wayne has become the most widely known ornithologist in the Province and his advice is frequently sought by professional colleagues across Canada. His honours include election to membership by the two most prestigious ornithological societies in North America.

For almost ten years he and I have been associated in planning a new definitive work on the Birds of British Columbia. This task is now well started

The four-volume set of *The Birds of British Columbia* was the first major publication to incorporate Dennis Demarchi's ecoregions of BC land classification system. PHOTO BY MARY JEAN COMFORT, WHITE KNIGHT PEAK, EAST OF CANAL FLATS, BC, AUGUST 1977.

with the publication of the first two volumes of what will be a four-volume set. Wayne has been the leading spirit among the six authors. The approximately five thousand naturalists in BC who have contributed their data to the books have done so almost entirely in response to the trust they placed in Wayne and their liking for him.

After some twenty years devoted to what is now the Royal British Columbia Museum, Wayne has decided to seek other opportunities to use his expertise and energy.

I have been most impressed by his ability to relate his knowledge to the interests of other professionals in the allied fields of natural resources and to work effectively with them. I can recommend him without reservation as a man of the highest integrity who will bring to any task he undertakes thoughtfulness, enthusiasm, ingenuity and a capacity for hard work.

—Ian McTaggart-Cowan

During regular meetings of the authors at Ian's home in Saanich for the completion of the final two volumes of *The Birds of British Columbia*, Joyce McTaggart-Cowan was always there with tea and cookies and cakes, delivering them (with "seconds") throughout the deliberations, some of

The authors of the original two volumes of *The Birds of British Columbia*. Standing from left: Neil K. Dawe, Gary W. Kaiser and John M. Cooper. Sitting from left: R. Wayne Campbell, Ian McTaggart-Cowan and Michael C.E. McNall. VICTORIA, BC, OCTOBER 22, 1986.

which lasted several hours. In the early years she often baked the cookies, though later as her health began to decline, this became too demanding and the baked goods were replaced with packaged goodies to accompany hot beverages. Joyce was also there whenever Wayne and Ian met in his Saanich home for business or personal reasons, and if they talked for more than half an hour, there would be tea and cookies offered. She had an incredible sense of timing as to when a tea break was necessary so that the "recharging period" could result in fresh discussions. (Wayne is convinced she performed this service hundreds of times in her life.)

Volume three of *The Birds of British Columbia* was published in 1997 by UBC Press; it covered passerines from flycatchers through vireos. In August 1998 Ian, speaking to the Society of Canadian Ornithologists/ Société des ornithologistes du Canada, told them proudly:

> The first three volumes of the new book are history, and volume four is in the final stages. So easy to glide over the thousands of hours with a computer screen as sole companion [that is] reflected in that last sentence!*
>
> A most interesting part of the experience was the appreciation we all gained of the role of amateur birders in this massive task. Several thousand cooperators contributed data, often giving access to years of notes documenting their observations of birds in various parts of the province. More than 20 of them made time to review every species account to make certain it reflected their own experience. Some half-dozen volunteered to draft accounts of species with which they had special familiarity. This contributed importantly to the quality of the book. At the same time it strengthened relationships within the community of bird enthusiasts at a time when united action toward conservation has never been more necessary. The amateurs provide most of the eyes and ears of the team. Compiling such a book is a grinding task, and not one I would commend to my friends as a great way to spend your retirement.

Volume four of *The Birds of British Columbia* was released by UBC Press in 2001; it covered wood warblers through old world sparrows.

A Lively Retirement

Ian's long post-retirement included an additional thirty-five years of volunteering, elder statesmanship, activism, mentorship and inspiration to new generations of biologists. During this time he maintained his lifelong interest in natural history, including publishing work on various zoological and conservation topics well into his early nineties. His voluntary

Over seven thousand birdwatchers and naturalists contributed their personal observations of birds to the four-volume set of *The Birds of British Columbia* (1990–2001). Chris Siddle, a major contributor with over seventy thousand sightings and hundreds of nest records, was motivated by Ian's 1939 publication on vertebrates of the Peace River to update the bird fauna of that region through 1999.[143] PHOTO BY R. WAYNE CAMPBELL.

---

* Ian was already well into his eighties when the third volume was underway, and without secretarial resources to draw upon, he had learned computer skills in order to contribute to this major undertaking.

activities mainly focussed on the protection and acquisition of habitat. Some of his affiliations at this time were:

- Chair of the British Columbia Habitat Conservation Fund (HCF) (now British Columbia Habitat Conservation Trust Foundation [HCTF]) (1966–1999). With funding obtained from a surcharge on angling, hunting, trapping and guiding license fees, the HCTF invests in projects that maintain and enhance the health and biological diversity of British Columbia's fish and wildlife and their habitats. Ian was the inaugural chair of the public advisory board of the HCF from 1981 to 1995.

- Chair of the Canadian Committee on Whales and Whaling (1978). This committee was a member of the International Whaling Commission (IWC) to provide scientifically based recommendations on commercial whaling in Canadian territory. Canada banned commercial whaling in Canadian waters in 1972 and withdrew from the IWC in 1982 in protest over the issue of a complete moratorium on commercial whaling.

- Chair of the Canadian Environmental Advisory Council (1975–1979).

- Board member of the Friends of the Royal British Columbia Museum/ Friends of the Royal British Columbia Museum Foundation (1991). The Friends organization was established to build membership and coordinate support activities on behalf of the Museum. In 2005 the "Friends" became the "Foundation" whose principal activities are operation of the Royal Museum Shop, collection of donations, bequests and endowments and supporting Museum projects.

A Continuing Pursuit of Excellence

In all his endeavors Ian was both competitive and in constant pursuit of excellence. His experience and aesthetic sense provided the basis for charting his own accomplishments and sharing them with his compatriots—not unlike his role as an educator and mentor of students in his earlier life. His aesthetic sensibility was especially evident in his gardens, which included a large collection of rhododendrons and a smaller, but cherished, collection of genetic dwarf coniferous trees. He also won the top prize in the Vancouver Island Rock and Alpine Garden Society so many times that he was asked to stop entering in order to give other members a chance to win—the ultimate accolade! As well, he was extremely generous with gifts of plants to other gardeners. Ron Jakimchuk, who also gardens with enthusiasm, says:

I have a nice collection of Chinese ground orchids (*Pleione spp.*), which are semi-hardy in Victoria. When Ian came for a tour of my garden, I was surprised to learn that he was the original source of these orchids to the only

Golden Anniversary

Dennis Demarchi recalls sharing a table with Joyce McTaggart-Cowan at a BC Wildlife Branch managers banquet in Victoria in 1988:

We had made a lot of small talk when I noticed the gold pendant that she was wearing. It looked like a Bill Reid design and I asked her about it. She said that Ian had gone down to the carving shed on the UBC campus and asked Reid if he would get one of his apprentices to make a pendant for his wife for their wedding anniversary. Subsequently Ian learned that Bill Reid himself had created the pendant.

Ian and Joyce had marked their 50th wedding anniversary in April 1986, an event that was attended by most members of the Racey and Cowan families.

commercial supplier in Canada! Later I received a few specimens from his collection as gifts.

As the accompanying article reprinted from the *Vancouver Island Rock and Alpine Garden Society (VIRAGS) Newsletter* of March 1990[144] reveals, he was also generous in sharing his gardening insights and knowledge with his colleagues. He also managed to weave an ecological theme into his instructions to potential exhibitors by advising them to "read up" on their plants and to use substrates for their potted specimens that reflect their natural environment.

The Day before the Show

There [is] a lot of fun to be had in presenting some of your special alpine, rock, or dwarf woodland plants in our annual spring show. [Here are] a few ideas on preparing your treasures so that they will look their best. While it is the plant you are presenting, and you will certainly select the best specimen to represent your efforts, setting and presentation are important. Clean faces and hands, party clothes, and shiny shoes are all part of going to the party.

There are three elements to readying your plants for the show: the container, the plant, and the dressing.

Containers: You will have seen many types of pots and other plant containers in use at alpine shows. There are elegant handmade containers of false tufa, pots of cement, tubs of tree sections, clay pots of an array of sizes and styles but today black plastic pots outnumber all others. With a few exceptions black plastic pots in which your plants may have come from the nursery garden are not considered appropriate for the show bench,

The annual spring show of the Vancouver Island Rock and Alpine Garden Society in Victoria, BC, includes displays and submissions of individual plants for adjudication. Saanich, BC, April 12, 2013. PHOTO BY R. WAYNE CAMPBELL.

but if you have a fine plant growing comfortably in a half gallon black plastic, no problem. The shunned half gallon will nest neatly into a 7 inch green plastic azalea pot. A scruffy one gallon black pot will be unrecognizable inside a nine inch standard clay pot with ground bark or moist peat filling the space between them. A suitable top dressing will complete the disguise and provide you with an elegantly presented specimen. All pots must be scrupulously clean. I start with brushing off the soil or sand and complete the job with a quick wash. Some judges are fussy and even look at the bottom of the pot!

One of the problems with our standard plastic pots is that they deteriorate in the sun and go brittle. Then when you pick them up by the top edge they break or a piece comes away. Show time is no time to be repotting a

The Lohbrunner Trophy, named for the late Dr. Ed Lohbrunner, an internationally known nurseryman from Victoria, is awarded annually. Ian received this award in 1985. PHOTO BY R. WAYNE CAMPBELL.

Gardening Awards

The following list of awards summarizes Ian's accomplishments as a gardener—yet another avocation in his wide spectrum of personal passions.

- The **Lohbrunner Trophy** was initiated in 1960 and is awarded annually "For the Best Woodland Garden Plant." Ian was the recipient in 1985.

- The **V.I.H.A. Challenge Cup,** established in 1928, is for the best "Rock Garden Display." Between 1989 and 1997 Ian received this award seven times and in two of those years, 1991 and 1992, he shared it with his wife, Joyce.

- The **Will and Marjorie Pemberton Trophy**, first awarded in 1955, is "For the Best Species of Rhododendron." Ian received it in 1992.

- The **Christensen Trophy,** established in 1997, is for an exhibit of the "Rarest Plant." Ian was the recipient in 1997.

- The **Alan Brooks Morkill Trophy** is awarded "For Best Native (North American) Plant." It was first awarded in 1997; Ian received it in 1999.

- The **Madge Hamilton Trophy** is an annual award, started in 1997, "For the Best Sempervivum or Jovibarba." Ian was the recipient three consecutive years, 1999 to 2001. This was his last award, at ninety-two years old!

- The **Hugh Preece Trophy**, initiated in 1968, is for "The Best Pan of Dwarf Bulbs or Corms Suitable for the Rock Garden." It was awarded to Ian in 2000.

beautiful plant in abundant bloom. The solution? Take a pair of pliers, or I use a pair of sturdy tin snips, and break away the top inch or so of the broken pot until the broken edge is about at the soil line. Slip your pot into a new one of the same size, top dress to cover the broken edge and all is well.

Clay pots have a snob appeal as well as real advantages for growing some alpines, but they can be troublesome to prepare for the show. They grow algae and embryo mosses on their damp outer surfaces and inside the rim. Often, too, salts from the soil or from fertilizers fed to the plant will crystallize out on the surface of your pot. Some 10% hydrochloric acid, a pad of steel wool and rubber gloves will help you solve the problem. Wearing the gloves, use the steel wool to apply the acid to the area. In most cases the white crust comes off easily. The green algal scum can also be removed with the steel wool but no acid is needed.

Next the plant: The objective of grooming your plant is to remove all dead leaves, flowers, seed heads, twigs and debris. Victoria gardens are blessed with lots of the last, the flowers from oaks, maples and arbutus: flowers and needles from firs, and what have you, that have burrowed into the recesses of your plant.

Cleaning your plants can be tedious if you are impatient but it gives you a face to face close up look at your plants from which you can learn many details. Place your subject at a convenient height, a small turntable or Lazy Susan can be useful, and go to work with a pair of medium 6-inch forceps and sharp-pointed scissors. If you enjoy counting things, try on the needles as you extract them one by one. There are few shortcuts: tip off the old top dressing and with it much of the loose debris. If the needles are dry, try floating them off. Getting the fir needles out of tight buns of some pygmy conifers is beyond my patience and I keep all these coniferous treasures in a cold frame covered with metal fly netting whenever the fibreglass top is off, as it is all summer. I must admit that there is some grooming tasks that are not pure fun. Snipping last year's flowers one at a time from a large *Cassiope* or removing the clinging dead leaves of sturdy *Primula marginata* is a bit of a chore but the plants look so much better after the tidying that it is worth the effort. If you have tried to groom your *Primulas* the night before the show you will develop a firm resolve that henceforth you will do it in January, before the new leaves are in the way.

Top dressing: Can be the creative part of preparing a plant for the show bench. If you are in a hurry, forestry sand or fine water-washed gravel of ¼ inch or less makes a tidy and attractive topping for many alpines, as will ground bark mulch or peat for plants of woodland and fen. However, it is interesting to use a top dressing that suggests the natural habitat of the plant. You can collect shale, limestone chips and crushed slate of a variety of colours as you explore the back roads of the island as well as rock chippings of different sizes and colours, small bark chips and so on. Then read up on the habitat of your plant and top dress accordingly. Most alpine and rock plants occur in a variety of local settings and you can choose one that suits you. In [one] parlour show was a charming

Richard Fleet, a mechanical foreman in the plumbing and pipefitting trade, first met Ian in the late 1990s through their mutual interest in stamp collecting. Like Ian, he won gold medals with displays of his revenue stamps; his collection was the third to be published by the British North America Philatelic Society (BNAPS). The first two books published on revenue stamps were by Ian McTaggart-Cowan. PHOTO COURTESY OF RICHARD FLEET.

Pinus pumila dressed with its own needles—what could be more appropriate? Mate your knowledge with your imagination but avoid a contrived appearance. You will be surprised how much more delight you will get from your plants as an outcome of the detailed concern you have given them in those days before the show.

The Quest for Gold

Richard Fleet, a director in the British North America Philatelic Society (BNAPS), met Ian in the late 1990s through their mutual interest in stamp collecting. He contributed the following account of their association and friendship:

Ian began collecting stamps as a young boy. While other boys of his age were collecting stamps of the world, he was only interested in stamps of wildlife, and not surprisingly, he said his favourite stamps were the stamps of birds. His serious collecting didn't begin until much later in his life. He was attending a conference in Vancouver and, having some time left on his lunch break, decided to browse in Eaton's department store. Passing by the philatelic kiosk, he was drawn to a set of odd stamps under the glass counter. The proprietor, Fred Eaton—no relation to the store's namesake—was only too glad to tell him all about this set of British Columbia Law Stamps, their inception in 1879, the companies that had printed them over the next one hundred years, and the number of irregular varieties that had resulted during the printing process. With a smile on his face, Ian left the store with the set of stamps in his breast pocket. This was the beginning of a passion that would carry through to the end of his life.

It is probably best to mention at this point that the collecting of revenue stamps is only popular amongst a minority of collectors. Revenue stamps were used to show that a tax or a service was paid, for example the testing of a set of weigh scales or a gas meter by a federal inspector or, as in the case of the British Columbia Laws, a legal fee or fees that had to be paid. They were considered the poor cousins of the postage stamps in the philatelic community and were mostly referred to as "B.O.B." (back of the book). If you had some of these stamps in your collection and didn't know what to do with them, you would place them in the back of your album, hence the name.

The law stamps and their uses captivated Ian, and over the next few years he obtained a substantial collection of them. He was fortunate to obtain a letter of introduction from the registrar in Victoria explaining that he was a philatelist and historian, and with letter in hand he had an open invitation to visit the numerous courthouses in British Columbia to inspect their files to examine the law stamps affixed to the old documents. He quite often made these trips with his wife, Joyce, to help him in his search, and boasted of the fact that she had made most of their significant discoveries.

Not surprisingly, it wasn't long before Ian was the foremost authority on BC Law Stamps, writing articles for philatelic publications and giving lectures, and he was only too happy to give slide presentations on his collection to the local stamps clubs. With his renewed interest in stamp collecting, he also became a member of the British North America Philatelic Society, for which he acted as editor for the revenue study group. He also exhibited his collection in various stamp exhibitions.

Ian had received all kinds of acknowledgement for his collecting interest except for one: he had never obtained a gold medal for his collection in a stamp exhibition. He had received several vermeil awards medals (vermeil is a "small gold," the second-highest award), but not the gold that he so coveted.

Although I had met Ian on several occasions, they were no more than glancing meetings. We knew what each other collected and had passed a few words on the subject, but nothing more. It was not until the fall of 2000 that I really got to know him. A National Philatelic Exhibition had been held in Victoria with philatelists attending from across Canada and the United States. I had exhibited my Bill Stamp collection, also a revenue collection, and won a gold medal.

I saw Ian inspecting my exhibit and went up and introduced myself. "Is this your exhibit?" he enquired. "Yes," I said. "It's marvelous, it's really marvelous," he exclaimed. A compliment from such a notable philatelist as Ian was not to be taken lightly. He then said that he had wanted to do something with his BC Law collection and that although he had exhibited it a number of times, he had only been able to obtain a vermeil. I told him that I had seen his collection and that I believed he had gold-medal material, that it just needed to be presented differently and that I was sure he would be able to obtain a gold medal. I then told him that if he should ever decide to rework his exhibit, I would only be too happy to help. I didn't know that at that moment it was to be the beginning of a great friendship.

It was several months later that we would begin working on his exhibit. He would phone me every couple of weeks to remind me that he hadn't forgotten about my offer and that he was "putting his bird books [*The Birds of British Columbia*] to bed" as he wanted to get them out of the way before we began. I would go over to his house several nights a week, look over his material and discuss how he should present it. He had said with a very serious look on his face that he had been a teacher most of his life, but now I was the teacher and he was the student, and he asked what he needed to do to get that gold medal. He was really serious.

My visits began with studying the stamps to be exhibited and examining the pages he had produced, followed by a tea break and some friendly conversation. But it wasn't long before the studying of stamps was outweighed by the friendly visits and conversation and a real friendship developed. Ian was a great storyteller and I was a great listener and many a pleasant evening was spent looking at stamps and telling stories.

It took over a year of work to produce Ian's exhibit and as it was nearing its end, I suggested that we attend the Edmonton National Stamp Exhibition to be held at the West Edmonton Mall that March. We had planned the week's excursion and arrived a day early to allow for registering and entering his exhibit. The next day the show began. We were just entering the show when a gentleman in a wheelchair rode up to Ian, blocking his entrance to the show, and exclaimed in a loud voice, "I know you! You're Ian McTaggart-Cowan. I attended one of your lectures in Edinburgh." Ian was totally taken aback and delighted. That was just the beginning of a great weekend.

The awards were posted the next day and to Ian's delight and my relief, as I had promised him, his exhibit had won gold. At the banquet and awards ceremony, he went up to the podium with a big smile on his face to receive his medal. He had no sooner returned to his seat when he was called again, this time to receive the Grand Award for best exhibit in the show. Upon returning to his seat, he was again called forward to receive the Best British North American Material Award, and then again for the Best Revenue Exhibit, and again for the Best Research Award. As he got up, he exclaimed, "This is getting embarrassing," but we didn't believe a word of it, and he had a grin on him from ear to ear. Ian had gone to Edmonton to win a gold, and he had taken the show by storm!

When we returned to our room later that evening, Ian was very restless, so I suggested we walk down to the mall and get a cup of tea. We walked the West Edmonton Mall into the wee hours of the morning because it was only then that he could finally settle down from all the excitement of the evening. When we finally did return to our room to get some sleep, I could hear him across the room in the dark chuckling to himself. Of all my memories, that is my favourite of Ian: chuckling to himself in the dark.

That wasn't Ian's only gold, for upon returning to Victoria, he immediately began working on his exhibit of Yukon Mining and Law Stamps of which he had a substantial collection. Looking through his material, I suggested that after showing his Yukon stamps, he might do an exhibit of his Alberta

With encouragement and advice from fellow stamp collector Richard Fleet, Ian prepared two displays of his revenue and law stamp collection of the Yukon (left) and BC (right). Both presentations won gold medals at national stamp exhibitions and were published by the British North America Philatelic Society as *The Law Stamps of the Yukon, 1902–1971*[145] in 2004 and *The Law Stamps of British Columbia and Their Uses, 1879–1984*[146] in 2005.

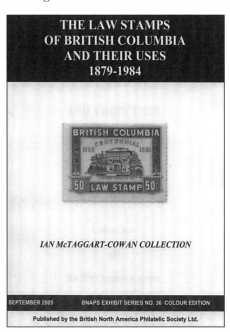

Law Stamps. With a grim expression on his face he said, "I only have three frames of that material and I need five for gold." A frame is sixteen pages of material and a total of eighty pages is required to be eligible for a gold medal. I laughed at his comment and explained, "Ian, I think you've got gold fever." A big grin appeared across his face and he began laughing. He said, "I think you're right." We did a good deal of joking and laughing. This was a hobby that we both loved and enjoyed.

Ian won his gold medal for the Yukon exhibit and BNAPS published both his BC Laws and Yukon exhibits as part of their Exhibit Series. The books are done as a record of outstanding collections of British North American material to be used as reference books and guides for future collectors.

Ian's next exhibit, dealing with Federal Revenue Stamps, did not receive the acknowledgment that his previous two exhibits had received but was instead criticized by the judges, and he was only awarded with a vermeil—not an insignificant award in itself but it was not a gold. Ian was furious. "Those #%#%#% judges, they don't know what they were looking at," he exclaimed. I received several of these phone calls over the next couple of weeks and realized something had to be done. Not only was this nonproductive, but his calls were becoming tiresome. This was a side of Ian's personality that I hadn't seen before. I had no idea up to this point how competitive he was and that he was definitely not a good loser. I had heard the adage that "a good loser is a loser," and I was definitely beginning to believe it.

I contacted one of the judges and asked if he could visit Ian and make some suggestions about the changes he would have to make on his exhibit. The meeting took place, the changes were made, and when next he entered his exhibit, it was awarded the gold medal that it so deserved. But this gold was not received with the enthusiasm that the other medals had brought. He merely explained that the judges didn't know what they were doing, and they should have given him the medal to start with.

Ian then started to put together his exhibit on the hunting and fishing stamps of Canada but failing eyesight prevented him from completing it. I could not understand how someone who had devoted his life to wildlife could be such an avid hunter, and I told him so, but he explained that he attributed his longevity to having a freezer stocked full of venison.

I miss Ian. I miss the evenings in his study looking at stamps, listening to his stories, and the joking and the laughing. He was a lot of fun to be with and the time we spent together was just doing that. His quest for gold brought us together and resulted in a golden friendship.

The Final Years

Even while Ian was immersed in his gardening and stamp collecting in his final decades, his world was marred by the loss of family. His son died on January 15, 1997. Garry Ian McTaggart-Cowan, who had graduated with a Ph.D. from UBC in 1968, was a faculty member in the Department of

Biology at Memorial University of Newfoundland. He co-authored several papers with his father, including one on the naming of a new species of chiton in 1977.[147] He was the father of a daughter, Mariana, and a son, Robert. Garry was fifty-six years old when he died.

On October 11, 1997, Ian's brother, Patrick Duncan McTaggart-Cowan died; he was 85. After serving in World War II as chief meteorologist with the Royal Air Force Ferry Command, Patrick had taken a post with the Meteorological Service of Canada, becoming director in 1959. In 1963 he became the first president of the new Simon Fraser University in Burnaby and followed that in 1968 with the post of executive director of the Science Council of Canada. He retired in 1975 and became an Officer in the Order of Canada in 1979.

Joyce McTaggart-Cowan's health began to decline in the late 1990s, and Ian took on more of the household chores. Despite her declining health, Joyce continued her unswerving support of Ian; although she appeared less often in public, Dennis Demarchi recalls seeing her standing in a reception line at a government house event honouring Ian in 2000. On Friday, November 29, 2002, she passed away peacefully at home surrounded by family; she was ninety years old. Joyce and Ian had been married for sixty-six years.

Ian suffered a major stroke on June 19, 2002, but recovered over the ensuing months.

During his decades of residence in Saanich, BC, Ian trapped hundreds of introduced eastern grey squirrels. Friends with cameras and binoculars were given a gift of a squirrel tail as an excellent dust remover for lenses.

PHOTO BY R. WAYNE CAMPBELL.

Squirrel Tails Make Good Dusters

One day in 1999 when I was visiting Ian at his home on Ten Mile Point in Victoria, I noticed that a metal "Havahart" trap had been set on the ground immediately below several birdfeeders in the front yard. It was, of course, partially hidden by shrubs, reminiscent of the approach of a seasoned trapper. Once inside his house, I had to query Ian on his setup. Without hesitation he told me proudly that he was trapping introduced eastern grey squirrels (*Sciurus carolinensis*), and for the next ten minutes he talked about the animal's natural history and potential competitive threat to native squirrels. I didn't know, for instance, that the origin of the squirrels was three animals brought to Vancouver Island from Ontario and that they had escaped in the late 1960s in the Metchosin area. He also knew that they were now being reported from "up Island" and would eventually reach Campbell River and beyond. He then went on to tell me the squirrels ate too many sunflower seeds in his birdfeeders, his bulbs and the buds of his prized rhododendrons. "Besides," he said, "Did you know squirrel tails make excellent lens cleaners?" Apparently that year seven of his friends received squirrel tails for their cameras! I was one of them! (He gave some of the carcasses to museums, others to youngsters interested in taxidermy and a few to teaching collections.)

—R. Wayne Campbell

Ian remained active throughout his final decade, gardening, stamp collecting and sitting on committees and boards where his long experience made him an invaluable member. He regularly attended concerts of the Sidney Classical Orchestra and the Via Choralis chamber choir where both his daughter, Ann, and Ron Jakimchuk were members. On one occasion, Ron's partner Xisa sat next to Ian during the concert, and prior to the performance and during the intermission they enjoyed a conversation on various topics. At one point she asked him when he was going to write a book on his remarkable life. He replied, "That's a job for someone else." Ron recalls that "When Xisa told me of their conversation, the thought of any involvement in such an endeavor never even entered my mind. I never dreamed that a few years later the job would engage me and my colleagues, Wayne Campbell and Dennis Demarchi."

Ian never lacked for companionship, as former students and colleagues and family members visited regularly. Ron Jakimchuk recalls one of his visits with Ian in these later years:

A month before his death on April 18, 2010, Ian McTaggart-Cowan maintained his passion for learning by visiting the site of the assembly and articulation of a blue whale skeleton that was in progress in Victoria, BC. PHOTO BY JOANNE THOMSON.

> A few years ago he was a dinner guest at my home, and I was looking forward to the evening and the visit. I had prepared a large filet of my sport-caught chinook salmon on the barbeque. A few minutes before serving the fish, Ian's daughter Ann took me aside and said, "Don't give him too much as his appetite isn't what it used to be." I followed Ann's request and put a small portion on Ian's plate with the comment that I hoped he would enjoy it. To my mortification he said that he wasn't sure there was enough on his plate to taste! I flushed with embarrassment, and my ears still turn red when remembering that moment. I had donned the mantle of a miserly host with an honoured guest! Needless to say, I quickly added a suitable quantity from the large filet I had and the balance of the dinner and evening went well.

As Ian approached his 100th birthday, his daughter, Ann Schau, wrote:

> This past Tuesday, March 30, 2010, my father, Ian McTaggart-Cowan, visited the blue whale reconstruction in downtown Victoria. His friend, Margaret Fisher, had a grandson working on the project and she arranged for a private tour. He was fascinated—and moved—as he always is by the myriad manifestations of the natural world. That appreciation, shared with my mother, Joyce, is one of the legacies passed on to the family.

In early April Ian visited the Finnerty Gardens at the University of Victoria with Ann. Some weeks after that he contracted pneumonia. He died on April 18, about two months before his 100th birthday, which he would have celebrated on June 25, 2010.

Full Circle

Ian's century-long lifespan contributed both to the breadth and depth of his influence. It is noteworthy that many of his former students are now retired after distinguished careers that germinated in Ian's classrooms, seminars or thesis discussions. Some have passed away, others are now octogenarians, but many remain engaged in post-retirement interests in wildlife biology and conservation. There are also young, energetic participants in environmental organizations who only recently "discovered" Dr. Cowan in his role as a leader devoted to protection of habitats and other environmental values. His living legacy resides in the continuity of ethics, attitudes and wisdom passed along to these new generations of students, taught or influenced by the teaching and mentoring of Ian's original students. In turn, new generations will form a succession embracing the values and knowledge passed on.

A second measure of Ian's living legacy resides in the institutions he fostered, participated in and helped lead, institutions that today continue the work of habitat protection, providing a voice for wilderness values and other conservation initiatives. The International Union for the Conservation of Nature, British Columbia Habitat Conservation Trust Foundation, International Whaling Commission and Nature Trust of British Columbia are just a few examples of organizations that have benefited from his participation and counsel. He played similar roles in academic institutions, both as a working participant in various committees and councils and in his role as chancellor of the University of Victoria for six years.

Ian's written works, documented in Part III, are his third legacy. Science is a continuous process of discovery, testing and refinement, new findings regularly supplanting old discoveries or elaborating on them. However, scientific progress depends on a sound base on which to lay the foundation for future discovery, and Ian's pioneering work in various fields of zoology continues to provide a valuable baseline to assess the current status of a species against the historical or to provide insights for additional research. This third legacy includes the biological collections that document the fauna of British Columbia, collections that have been pivotal in establishing the early distribution, abundance and taxonomy of British Columbia birds and mammals. Many of the specimens he collected so long ago now reside as the Cowan Tetrapod Collection in the Beaty Biodiversity Museum at the University of British Columbia. This museum was one of his favorite places as he believed that properly documented specimens represent the starting point of an ecological understanding. One of his last excursions was to view the completed reconstruction of a blue whale skeleton just before it was shipped from Victoria for exhibit in the Beaty Biodiversity Museum at UBC.

The reminiscences submitted by friends, colleagues and former students for Part II of this book attest to the personal qualities that Ian possessed and the respect he received from those whose lives he touched. They are no less significant than the lengthy list of honours and awards he received at various mileposts in his life.

Memories of a Daughter: Ann Schau

[Dad's] old harmonica resurfaced a few years ago. I arrived down at his place near Ten Mile Point in Victoria to hear familiar strains issuing from the living room. He had found the old Hohner Echo in a drawer and was busy getting his lip back. The process took a few months, but that well-known persistence paid off. He plays fairly regularly—tunes from his memory—with great rhythm and expression. I should know, being the musician in the family! Recently I took up the Anglo concertina (squee-zebox) and took it with me on some visits. Dad was very supportive and encouraging. He tolerated about ten minutes of my efforts before his hand drifted over to the side table where he kept his harmonica on hand. His version of "Redwing" was far superior to mine! He was a square dance caller when we were young and had a particular fondness for reels and jigs. The instrument keeping him company in his old age is the same one, he said, that he played, alone by the campfire, as a twenty-year-old in the mountains near Jasper. When the old harmonica developed an unrespon-sive reed, I arranged for a visit to the local music store and there Dad was delighted to find, in a drawer full of harmonicas, another Hohner Echo, still being manufactured and presented in the same box as eighty years ago!

In the Victoria house that Dad shared with my mother for more than twenty-five years are more objects—domestic, professional, received and created—that connect him (and the rest of the family) to the past: the little wooden bowl that he carved and polished and presented to Mum on a special occasion, and the framed photograph of her on the shores of Whiskey Cove under a beautiful sunset, a souvenir of years of yachting with friends Tom and Margaret Denny. Dad was a good photographer, taking after his father perhaps. He was also a creative gardener, a trait definitely acquired during his growing up. My grandfather Cowan for several years grew acres of dahlias on Vancouver's North Shore. Dad was his helper as well as companion and labourer in my grandmother's market garden.

Over his lifetime Dad acquired a fine collection of rhododendrons and rock garden plants. Every few days we would go into the garden to visit his collection of miniature evergreens—mostly conifers—kept in pots in a sheltered area of the property. At one time these plants and others were part of Dad's award-winning exhibits at the Vancouver Island Rock and Alpine Society shows. Professional awards, of course, are numerous and displayed in his study. More important to him than all these tangible items were the visits from colleagues, former students and old friends. In our conversations over tea, we both agreed that this is one of the great bene-fits of the teaching profession—the enduring connection with students and co-workers.

In retirement, Ian McTaggart-Cowan could often be found in his garden tending his prize-winning rhododendrons and alpine plants. In this photo, he is standing next to a clump of the autumn-blooming Nerine. Saanich, BC, October 1990.
PHOTO BY R. WAYNE CAMPBELL.

Ian McTaggart-Cowan's daughter, Ann, in the rhododendron garden of Ian and Joyce's former home in Victoria, March 2012, where Ann and her husband, Mikkel, now reside.
PHOTO BY RONALD D. JAKIMCHUK.

It is evident that throughout his life Ian had a very strong aesthetic response to the natural world. In this regard he led a charmed life, being able to experience so many pristine or near pristine wilderness areas and habitats rich in wildlife, and his love and concern for such areas carried through in his efforts to preserve them and their values. It is impossible to quantify his part in preserving specific areas, but with his considerable reputation and credentials, he was a highly effective advocate for environmental values at both provincial and federal levels of government. Future generations may not know the history of the biology of this province, but they will be able to enjoy the results of efforts by Ian and a host of others in the conservation movement, which made such areas possible.

Ian showed by his own example that it is possible to be productive and enjoy a rich and enjoyable life in the process. His was a life not only well lived but a shining example of good citizenship. A man can be defined by his times, his abilities, the opportunities he makes and what he makes of opportunities. Ian McTaggart-Cowan was an inspiration and leader by any of these measures.

Throughout his life, Ian McTaggart-Cowan was fascinated with and marvelled at patterns in nature whether on a lined chiton, a leopard frog, a raccoon or the eggs of a spotted sandpiper. PHOTO BY MARK NYHOF.

A Lifetime Practitioner

FIELD EXCURSIONS FROM THE NOTES
OF IAN MCTAGGART-COWAN

The term "professional" is generally reserved for those who actively engage in their area of training and expertise. However, the implication is that learning does not end with achieving a degree but continues with the application of that knowledge. In turn, experience serves to generate a depth and breadth of knowledge that enhances understanding and fosters new areas of competence.

Ian McTaggart-Cowan continued his practice of biology throughout a diverse career and recreational activities and over a period of retirement that spanned thirty-five years. During his years as a young collector, museum biologist, university professor and retired zoologist, he cherished his time afield, but as his professional career evolved, opportunities for field time were diminished, and by the late 1950s administrative responsibilities had replaced his precious collecting time.

Experiential learning, which is currently fashionable, is not new, but was practiced decades ago by Ian and his colleagues. It was an important aspect of wildlife biology from the 1930s to the early 1960s in that it was primarily field-based. During that period Ian and other naturalists spent much time in the field observing wildlife under natural conditions, noting behaviour and habitat, and collecting representative specimens, and those early studies provided the ecological framework on which later in-depth studies on ecosystem processes could be designed.

Technology has had a profound influence on wildlife studies, enabling acquisition of remote data that were previously impossible to obtain, ranging from documenting wildlife movements to monitoring physiology. However, dependence on technology alone foregoes the intimate contact with wildlife and connection to the land that Ian so passionately expressed and shared with students, colleagues and the public.

In addition to his major early expeditions, Ian embarked on numerous other field trips, sometimes to visit his graduate students or lead a classroom field excursion or take sabbatical leave or evaluate habitats for protection. His contact with students in the field, noting their observations and insights gave him new perspectives. Apart from demonstrating that acquisition of knowledge is an ongoing process, this also established that learning at its best is a reciprocal process—he provided advice and direction to his students, and they provided him with new information and a continuing window on the natural world. His regular retreats to the family cottage on Mayne Island produced thousands of bird records that he and his wife, Joyce, logged. He also kept track of deer numbers and their diet during each visit.

After retirement he lectured as a ship's naturalist on coastal cruises in British Columbia and international cruises with various travel companies, thereby extending his own experiences as an observer and educator to new audiences of recreational tourists. He was also a periodic guest on H.R. MacMillan's yacht, *Marijean*, on cruises along the BC coast and south as far as Mexico and Costa Rica, which expanded his knowledge of pelagic as well as coastal wildlife.

The following is a chronological list of some collecting, research and personal field trips that Ian recorded in his field diaries between 1930 and 1987. Details for each trip have been extracted from copies of Ian's field notes that he gave to R. Wayne Campbell.

Undergraduate Student (University of British Columbia)

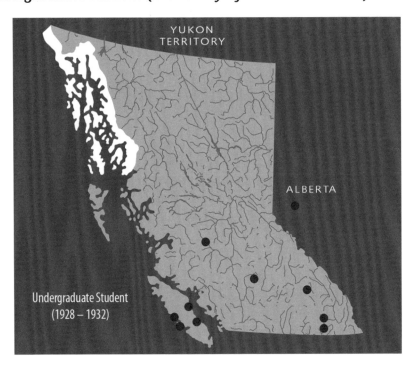

1930 – April 29 to June 2 (Loon Lake, Meadow Creek, Newgate and Gold Creek with H.M. Laing); **June 6 to August 14** (Jacques Pass, Maligne River, Pyramid Lake and Snaring in Jasper National Park) and **August 16 to September 15** (Boom Lake and Cascade Mountain in Banff National Park).

1931 – May 4 to June 27 (Tofino, Cleland Island, Port Alberni and Comox on Vancouver Island with Kenneth Racey) and **July 23 to August 16** (Chezacut with Kenneth Racey family).

British Columbia Provincial Museum Biologist

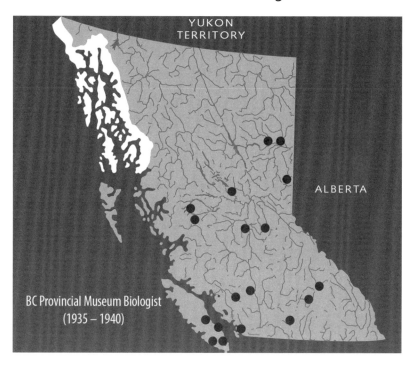

1935 – September 8 (Thetis Lake); **September 18** (Victoria to Mill Bay); **September 27** (Island View Beach); **October 5** (Victoria to Jordan River); **October 10** (Esquimalt Lagoon to Weir Beach); **October 14** (Island View Beach); **October 18** (Victoria); **October 19 to 21** (Malahat at Mile 17 of the Trans-Canada Highway); **October 25** (Becher Bay and Pedder Bay); **November 11 to 16** (Ionian [Iona] Island and Lulu Island with K. and S. Racey); **December 4** (Victoria to Sooke) and **December 27 to January 1, 1936** (Alta Lake with K. Racey family).

1936 – February 23 (Lake Hill to Lost [Blenkinsop] Lake); **February 29** (Island View Beach); **June 18 to August 13** (Okanagan Valley, Quesnel, Vanderhoof, Eutsuk Lake, Ootsa Lake, Wistaria and Indianpoint Lake; with Joyce McTaggart-Cowan); **October 13** (Victoria-Quarantine Lake) and **November 6** (Weirs Beach-Witty's Lagoon with J.A. Munro).

1937 – June 23 to July 24 (Monashee Pass-Mount Revelstoke with K. Racey) and **November 3 to 7** (Texas Creek in Lillooet district).

1938 – May 5 to June 19 (Tupper Creek, Swan Lake, Fort St. John and Charlie Lake with P.W. Martin) and **September 9 to 11** and **20 to 22** (Mount Arrowsmith).

1939 – July 30 (Victoria) and **August 17** (Canoe Cove-Wise Island).

Professor of Zoology (University of British Columbia)

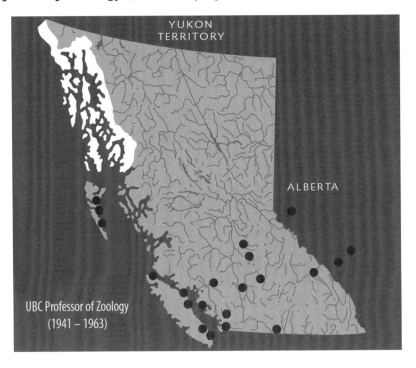

1941 – May 21 to 25 (Osoyoos Lake); **June 5 to 11** (Lac du Bois) and **August 4 to September 3** (Alta Lake).

1942 – August 31 to September 9 (Alta Lake) and **November 5 to 7** (Indian River).

1943 – October 1 (Lulu Island).

1943 – April 15 to 22, July 27 to August 31 and **September 1 to 13** (Athabasca River, Miette Valley and Pobokton Creek in Jasper National Park); **April 23 to 30, June 1 to 22** and **July 2 to 26** (Bow Valley, Cascade River and Lake Louise in Banff National Park, AB) and **June 23 to 30** (Radium Hot Springs).

1944 – August 12 to September 3 (Alta Lake).

1945/46 – May and December; 1945: July; and 1946: May and June (Alta Lake).

1945 – February 18 (Vancouver); **April 7 to 8** (Texada Island) and **May 2 to 11** (Jasper National Park).

1946 – May 6 to June 30 (Jasper National Park); **July 1 to 3, 7 to 20** (Banff National Park with Joyce McTaggart-Cowan, Garry and Ann); **July 4** (Field); **July 5** (Radium); **July 31 to September 3** (combined sea and land trip to Queen Charlotte Islands) and **October 6** (Burnaby Lake).

1947 – January 6 (Vancouver with J. Tener); **October 11** and **16** (North Arm Fraser River) and **October 27, November 18, 23, December 6** and **26** (Point Grey, Vancouver).

1948 – January 6 (Lulu Island with C.J. Guiguet and A. Brooks); **January 7** and **March 24** (North Arm Fraser River); **May 15 to 18** (Ashcroft-Clinton-Williams Lake); **July 1 to August 20** (waterfowl brood surveys and banding in Cariboo-Chilcotin region with Allan Brooks Jr., David Calls, J. Cunningham, R. Yorke Edwards, Jim Hatter, Leo Jobin, James A. Munro, Webster Ranson and John S. Tener) and **August 21 to 25** (Lac du Bois).

1949 – July 4 to August 9 (waterfowl brood surveys and banding in the Cariboo region with Walter H. Cottle, Lawson G. Sugden and Alistair McLean).

1950 – August 12 to 24 (Mohun Lake-Cowichan Lake).

1951 – May 22 to June 3 (Port Clements, Queen Charlotte City and Tlell, Queen Charlotte Islands).

1955 – May 2 to September 8 (summer field camp at Westwick Lake [Cariboo] with graduate students Mary F. Jackson, Nancy M. McCallister and M. Timothy Myres).

1958 – March 28 (Vancouver).

1961 – June 19 to 22 (Hotsprings Island).

1962 – March 5 to 12 (aboard yacht *Marijean* around Tres Marias [Islas Marías], Mexico with H.R. MacMillan).

1963 – May 17 to 24 (aboard boat from Vancouver to Port Neville and Bull Harbour with his son Garry McTaggart Cowan).

Dean of Graduate Studies (University of British Columbia)

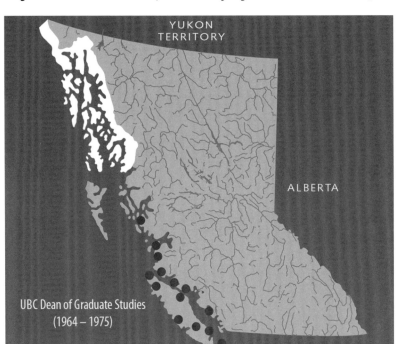

1964 – July 8 to 24 (aboard boat from Campbell River to Port Neville, Bull Harbour and adjacent mainland islands and inlets).

1965 – July 8 to 26 (aboard boat from Sointula to Calvert Island south through Gulf Islands to Gabriola Island).

1966 – June 18 to 20 (aboard MV *Ehkali* from Vancouver to San Juan Islands, Washington state).

1967 – July 15 to 30 (aboard boat from Port Hardy to northwestern Vancouver Island south from Winter Harbour to Tofino Inlet with Joyce McTaggart-Cowan).

1973 – April 20 to 22 (aboard MV *Daphne Isle* to Telegraph Bay and Kuper Island).

1974 – May 18 to 19 (aboard MV *Daphne Isle* at Squirrel Cove, Cortes Island); **June 22** (Green Mountain, Vancouver Island, with D.C. Heard and J. Evans); **June 29 to 30** (aboard MV *Daphne Isle* from Maple Bay to Thormanby Islands); and **July 1 to 17** (aboard MV *Daphne Isle* from Cortes Island to Bella Bella and Princess Royal Island and return with Joyce McTaggart-Cowan).

Retired Zoologist

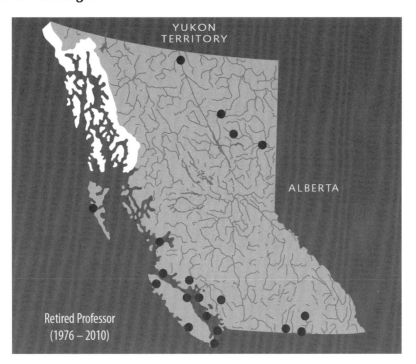

Retired Professor
(1976 – 2010)

1977 – August 8 to September 5 (aboard MV *Daphne Isle* from Campbell River, Knight Inlet, Malaspina Inlet, Lasqueti Island and Salt Spring Island with Joyce McTaggart-Cowan).

1979 – June 4 to July 4 (aboard MV *Daphne Isle* from Cadboro Bay in Saanich to Bamfield, along west coast of Vancouver Island to Barkley Sound, Hotsprings Cove, Winter Harbour, Bull Harbour, south to Quadra Island and Mayne Island).

1980 – March 27 to April 11 (aboard cruise ship from San Diego to islands in Gulf of California, Mexico); **April 18 to 20** (aboard MV *Daphne Isle* from Sidney Spit to Bedwell Harbour and Prevost Island); **May 16 to 18** (Rock Creek, Grand Forks and Castlegar) and **June 27 to 30** (aboard MV *Daphne Isle* to Telegraph Cove, Reid Island, Mayne Island and Pender Island).

1981 – September 10 to 13 (aboard MV *Daphne Isle* to Salt Spring Island, Discovery Island, De Courcy Island and Valdes Island).

1982 – January 9 (Cattle Point, Victoria); **April 8 to 10** (aboard MV *Daphne Isle* to Portland Island, Mayne Island and Java Islets) and **August 22 to September 12** (aboard MV *Daphne Isle* to Newcastle Island, Lasqueti Island, Cortes Island and Echo Bay with Joyce McTaggart-Cowan).

1983 – January 9 to 24 (aboard cruise ship from San Diego to islands in Gulf of California, Mexico) and **June 15 to July 5** (aboard MV *Daphne Isle* from Newcastle Island to Bull Harbour, Bella Bella and return to Cortes Island with Joyce McTaggart-Cowan).

1984 – February 19 to March 14 (aboard cruise ship from San Diego to islands in Gulf of California, Mexico, with Joyce McTaggart-Cowan).

1985 – June 23 (Marble Island).

1986 – July 29 to 31 (by air from Fort St. John to Pink Mountain, Halfway River, Prophet River, Muskwa River, Liard River and Sikanni Chief River with J. Elliott, J. Walker and R. Silver); **August 5 to 14** (aboard MV *Daphne Isle* to Secret Cove, Princess Louisa Inlet, Nelson Island, Pender Harbour, Lasqueti Island and Gabriola Island with Joyce McTaggart-Cowan) and **December 16 to 24** (aboard cruise ship from San Diego to islands in Gulf of California, Mexico).

During summer trips along the coast of southern BC, Ian often encountered small numbers of nonbreeding surf scoters. PHOTO BY ALAN D. WILSON.

Part II

MEMORIES

CHAPTER 8

Celebrating One Hundred Years with One Hundred Memories

The following stories and recollections are largely from former students at UBC but also include respondents from many different walks of life and the wives of two of Ian's students who have passed away. As will be readily seen, there is a great and delightful variety within these recollections. They are not only about Dr. Cowan but reflect their own past and mutual journeys within their cohort.

Long before the advent of the global positioning system (GPS) or satellite downloadable radio-collar signals and before laptop computers were dreamt of—never mind envisioned for field application—we, the young, keen and lean neophyte biologists entered the field with little more than notebooks, pencils and binoculars with which to do our work. There was no Gore-Tex rain gear, lightweight down outerwear or motel accommodations to give us comfort. We "broke in" heavy boots, sweated in rubber rain gear and sharpened our observational skills instead of relying on what is now a vast array of electronic-based wildlife research technologies.

We were highly enthusiastic about the prospects of our dream careers and embarking on a voyage of discovery in a province and country where breaking new ground was a given. We canoed and walked in our quest to identify, locate and quantify wildlife resources. We were thrilled at the chance to survey from airplanes, able to see more area in a day than a month of walking. There was so much that was new that we could accomplish but a fraction of our goals. We found things and saw things that few were privileged to observe, many of them not in the textbooks we studied in university. We were on the cusp not only of new knowledge but of new disciplines emerging from the traditional practice of wildlife biology. We thought we had the best jobs in the world. And we did.

The people listed below in alphabetical order agreed to share some of their favourite recollections.

Ralor (Ray) Blendle Addison
B.Sc. (1963, Zoology), M.Sc. (1965, Zoology), Ph.D. (1970, Zoology), UBC

Ray spent his career in government resource-management programs, starting as a research scientist studying moose and caribou in Ontario in 1968, then moving back to BC in 1974 to participate in the development of resource policies and legislation for the Ministry of Forests. Between 1974 and retirement in 2000, his professional positions spanned those of a resource policy analyst, several section manager appointments and director of the Integrated Land Management Branch, which with reorganization became the Range, Recreation and Forest Practices Branch. Following retirement, Ray contracted his services back to government for seven years as a specialist in forest policy development, emphasizing projects that would bring best-available information to bear on resource management decisions.

Ray Addison enjoying a bright winter day in 2008 at Iron Mine Bay in East Sooke Park, BC, with companion Winston, the schnauzer. PHOTO BY ROBYN ADDISON.

My introduction to Ian Cowan was in 1962 when I transferred into fourth-year zoology at UBC after completing the first three years of a science degree at the University of Victoria. He taught two of my courses, and that was the stimulus I needed to go on to graduate studies. I liked his emphasis on using knowledge, new and old, to improve resource management, and I knew immediately that was what I wanted to do with my career. In the autumn of 1963, I began my master's program with Ian's advice and support and, very important to a graduate student, funding that he seemed to attract in buckets. His influence wasn't limited to science; when I needed a technician to assist on the project, he recommended Robyn Richardson, the daughter of long-time friends and neighbours. In 1965 he gave the toast to the bride at our wedding.

Both my master's and doctoral research straddled the boundary between zoology and animal nutrition and included faculty from both science and agriculture on my committee. As well as Ian, Harold Norden and Alex Wood were key members.

Bryan Allen
B.Sc. (1969, Zoology and Geography), UBC

Ray Addison inspecting telemetry equipment used in a moose research project, Wine Lake, northwestern Ontario, 1972. PHOTO BY RAY ADDISON.

Bryan is a retired fisheries biologist and educator. During his undergraduate years he worked as a summer research technician on Babine Lake sockeye studies under the direction of Dr. David Narver. This experience led to a thirty-one-year fisheries career with the Canadian Department of Fisheries (now Fisheries and Oceans Canada) where he worked on projects that included salmon distribution, salmonid habitat inventory, Pacific herring and abalone and feasibility studies for the construction of the Kitimat federal salmon hatchery. In 1979 he joined the Salmonid Enhancement Program as one of the first four community advisors, working with community groups that included school children, municipal leaders and fish and game groups.

He planned and guided the first British Columbia Corrections Branch salmon hatchery on the Alouette River. He has been acknowledged for his fisheries work, but his special award was the British Columbia Wildlife Federation Ted Barsby Trophy as conservationist of the year in 2000; this award was previously presented to Ian McTaggart-Cowan.

In 1968, as an undergraduate at UBC, I had the good fortune to see the generous side of Dr. McTaggart-Cowan. I had just been elected president of the UBC Rod and Gun Club. We were struggling to increase our membership, but somehow we always fell far behind the Varsity Outdoors Club. Maybe it was because they had women and we didn't!

The suggestion was made that, if we could host a lunch-hour discussion on hunting or wildlife, perhaps we could recruit more members. "Why not ask Dr. McTaggart-Cowan, the dean of the Faculty of Graduate Studies," someone suggested. As president, of course, I was delegated to approach the dean. While I knew of McTaggart-Cowan's reputation as a scholar and teacher, I had not had any personal experience with him. But I did know that he was an important personage in the university and must have better things to do than take time to help out a bunch of mere undergrads. I had my directions, however, and with a large degree of temerity I entered his outer office to face the first hurdle—the secretary. After explaining in a halting manner that I wished to see the dean with a very special request, I was surprised to find myself allowed access to the inner sanctum.

Dr. McTaggart-Cowan shook my hand and before I had a chance to put my request forward, he made me feel at ease by asking what year I was in,

Bryan Allen holding a basket star near Port Hardy, summer 2005. PHOTO BY GERRY SCOTT.

Ian in his office as Head of the Department of Zoology. His legacy includes nearly a century of influencing the lives and careers of hundreds of individuals. COURTESY OF UNIVERSITY OF BRITISH COLUMBIA ARCHIVES, PHOTO 1.1-3071.

Ian's UBC wildlife management course field trip to Washington State, south of Osoyoos, BC, in 1963 with his students. Ian, in wool sweater, is peering at a beaver food cache in a frozen lake. PHOTO BY PETER OMMUNDSEN.

which courses I was taking and what my future goals were. It was then that I pitched the idea of a luncheon speaker for our club. "How many members do you have?" he asked. I explained only twenty, but we hoped to attract more. "I see," he said. "Then why don't we try this . . . book the main lecture theatre in the Biological Sciences building and have your members put the word out that I will be giving a lecture on bighorn sheep." WOW! What an offer!

And it got even better. The lecture hall was packed, and it was a lecture to remember—"The Mating Habits of the Rocky Mountain Bighorn Sheep." For an hour we listened fascinated as the dean described the foreplay and the follow-through that it took to make a lamb. No one left before the end of his presentation. And the result for our recruiting for the Rod and Gun Club was two more members, though we still didn't have any girls! But I have always remembered Dr. McTaggart-Cowan's willingness to take the time to try to help out a bunch of lowly undergrads. In my view he showed his real greatness at that moment.

Percy John Bandy
B.A. (Hons.) (1952, Zoology), M.A. (1955, Zoology), Ph.D. (1965, Zoology), UBC

John Bandy, born August 13, 1927, passed away on August 1, 2010, at the age of eighty-two. The following account was written by his wife, Helen Bandy. She was born August 18, 1932 and passed away June 14, 2014.

John was appointed biologist with the British Columbia Game Commission in Vancouver in 1958 and regional biologist in Nanaimo in 1960. After graduating with his Ph.D., and until his office was moved to Victoria in

John Bandy with captive black-tailed deer at the University of British Columbia research facility. PHOTO BY JOHN ROBERTSON, 1957.

1971, John was an adjunct professor at UBC. He also served as head of the wildlife research division for the British Columbia Fish and Wildlife Branch at UBC during this period. As well, he spent some time as a research fellow at Cambridge University in England.

John published several research papers and was noted for his work on lung disease in Rocky Mountain bighorn sheep.[149] Noteworthy positions he held included president of the British Columbia Waterfowl Society, which operates the George C. Reifel Migratory Bird Sanctuary; member of the Canada Land Inventory Committee and advisor to the deputy minister of British Columbia Native Land Claims and Treaties.

As early as 1948 Dr. Ian McTaggart-Cowan had become known across Canada for his expertise in zoology. Thus, in 1950 when John was attending the Ontario Agricultural College in Guelph, and Dr. Hoar came to speak to the students and mentioned the wildlife management program at UBC, John decided to leave Guelph and transfer to UBC. He worked under Dr. Cowan for both his undergraduate and graduate degrees. John admired the charisma, excitement, dedication and knowledge that Dr. Cowan brought to both his public speaking and his university lectures.

Once early in John's career, he and I [Helen] were visiting Joy and Glen Smith in Cranbrook. At the same time the highly respected Dr. Cowan was coming to Cranbrook, and Glen invited him to dinner. Joy, of course, was trying to impress the great man with a wonderful meal. However, by mistake she doubled the spices in an already spicy meat sauce. We had a hilarious hot, choking, tearful dinner. John with his Mexican background loved it, while the rest of us spluttered away. Dr. Cowan was always the polite gentleman, so after the meal he praised and thanked Joy for such a delicious dinner.

John and Helen Bandy with a captive deer fawn at UBC experimental farm at Oyster River in 1956.

John started his Ph.D. at the State College of Washington at Pullman under Dr. H. Buechner, but in 1956 he left Pullman to complete his Ph.D. on black-tailed deer physiology under Dr. Cowan. Fawns were captured from four subspecies of black-tailed deer and housed at the Oyster River Farm on Vancouver Island. I was employed as a laboratory technician for the research program and discovered that Sitka deer fawns had sickle cells. A paper by Dr. Cowan was subsequently published about this phenomenon.[150] Dr. Cowan visited the farm regularly, and on one occasion he was determined to collect a bat specimen from those that inhabited the house. We all sat on the porch with fishnets poised ready to catch a bat. However, not a single bat was captured by the well-known professor and his prodigies. It was interesting to note that Dr. Cowan had the most remarkable eyesight and could spot and identify birds and mammals long before anyone else could see them. No student ever dared contradict his identification because usually they were unable to spot the specimen.

One endearing characteristic of Dr. Cowan was that he kept in touch with his ex-students throughout their careers. Ian and Joyce welcomed many students into their house on the University Endowment Lands, and Joyce was always a cheerful, friendly hostess. For many summers Garry, their son, worked as an assistant in John's research laboratory. In later years we always saw Joyce and Ian as they volunteered at the annual University of Victoria plant sale. Ian was most knowledgeable about rhododendrons and was welcomed as an expert on local native plants.

There is no way to adequately explain the influence that Dr. Ian McTaggart-Cowan had on John's career. Without his mentorship, John would probably have spent his entire career unsuccessfully farming in Ontario. Instead, he had an extremely gratifying and successful career as a research biologist in British Columbia.

William (Bill) D. Barkley
B.Sc. (Hons.) (1964, Zoology), M.A. (1972, Adult Education), UBC

Bill worked for the Canadian Wildlife Service for ten years after university graduation in the area of interpretation and managed a 2,500-acre marsh near Midland, Ontario. With the support of David Munro, he opened the first wildlife centre there. While employed with the Canadian Wildlife Service, Bill was allowed to return to UBC and take a degree in adult education. He pursued his interest in vertebrate biology with a thesis on a "game" that was based on the struggle between the ranchers and their land use practices related to Rocky Mountain bighorn sheep in the East Kootenay region of British Columbia.[151]

While in Midland, Bill worked for Yorke Edwards and later followed him to the British Columbia Provincial Museum (later named the Royal British Columbia Museum); he became the director after Yorke retired in 1984. Bill retired in 2001 and established an active consulting business with projects in Nova Scotia, Newfoundland, Labrador and Yukon Territory. At

Inspired by Dr. Cowan's undergraduate zoology and ecology lectures, Bill Barkley completed his undergraduate degree at UBC with Ian as his supervisor and went on to work in nature interpretation and museology. PHOTO BY EILEEN C. CAMPBELL.

present he sits on the board of the Canadian Museum for Human Rights in Winnipeg.

Dr. Cowan supervised Bill's B.A. (Hons.) degree on deer physiology.

The story about Ian McTaggart-Cowan I recall occurred when I was in the final stages of my honours bachelor's degree. Ian was my advisor and I was working with a drug called Trilafon that was used quite extensively in psychiatry on humans. We were intending to use it to keep deer calm because, whenever we tried to take the animals' heart rate, the deer became too excited, which resulted in an elevated reading. I started injecting the deer, but Dr. Cowan did not think I was giving a large enough dose, so he increased the dosage, injecting it himself. Unfortunately, the deer died and fell on Dr. Cowan, breaking his ribs. As he was being carted off in the ambulance he told the two of us standing there, "Do an autopsy on the deer and have it butchered and sent to the campus hospital."

Like many students I was fortunate to have taken Dr. Cowan's Zoology 105 course. Later I heard a lecture he gave on ecology and made up my mind I wanted to go into that field of study. I have never for a minute regretted my choice.

Tom Beck

Tom pioneered environmental protection and management in the Canadian petroleum industry. He worked for a Canadian oil company for twenty years before moving to the French company Elf Oil Exploration and Production Ltd. to pursue a more aggressive conservation policy by the oil industry in Canada. From 1980 to 1982 he was director of environmental and social affairs for Petro Canada. He was a founder of the Alberta Wilderness Association, governor of the Arctic Institute, and member and then chairman of the Canadian Environmental Advisory Council from 1978 to 1987. Tom served the Inuvialuit of the western Canadian Arctic as commissioner of the Mackenzie Delta-Beaufort Sea Land Use Planning Commission and then as chair of the Environmental Impact Screening Committee for the western Arctic (Inuvialuit) Claims Settlement Area.

In 1989 Tom received an honorary LL.D degree from the University of Calgary, and in 2010 he was presented with the Alberta Wilderness Association's Wilderness and Wildlife Defenders Award.

Tom Beck during a fly-fishing trip, Livingston River, AB, 2010. PHOTO BY MIKE STURK.

Over a period of time, I noticed a number of outstanding individuals in the scientific/wildlife field in Canada and the United States. Names like Geist, Stirling and Mair—among many others—kept popping up. Eventually it became obvious there was a common denominator—namely Ian McTaggart-Cowan. I believe that at one time most of the key people in western United States wildlife agencies and many of the prominent authorities in Canada were members of the "Cowan Corps." Watching Ian in action professionally

Tom Beck and his wife Shirley with Ian (on the right) on a deer hunt in the foothills of Alberta. PHOTO BY JOYCE MCTAGGART-COWAN, NOVEMBER 1978.

on the (Northern) Environmental Protection Board and (USA) National Audubon Society and being involved with him on various initiatives, including the Arctic Land Use Research Committee and the Canadian Environmental Advisory Council, I can attest to the high standards, inspiration, leadership and continuing influence he provided to so many.

Personally, Shirley and I came to know Ian and Joyce as close friends. That friendship included fun-filled fall hunting trips to our cabin in the Alberta foothills. As the accompanying photos show, and thanks to Ian's marksmanship, Ian and Joyce always went home with a good supply of wild protein. On one occasion Ian's 30.06 was pressed into action with his customary standing shot at a rapidly moving mature mule deer buck. The deer continued in high gear although Ian felt sure it was hit. I examined the poplars between Ian's stance and the deer track and found his shot went through one of them. Sure enough, we found the expired deer about three hundred yards away—testimony to Ian's accuracy and preference for 180 grain bullets!

On another occasion we set out for the day with fresh snow for tracking. Having spent the morning climbing a few steep hills, we were ready for the sandwiches Shirley and Joyce had sent with us. We built a fire and while boiling up some tea and toasting our sandwiches, we began reminiscing about our home country of Scotland. Ian talked about the hypothermic winter he and Joyce spent in Edinburgh when he studied there. We discussed how the cold damp draft would penetrate between the sandstones in the walls and how much of a challenge it sometimes was to even be warm in bed and how lucky we were to be in Canada! Then we had a good chuckle—at ourselves—when we realized we were sitting in a foot of snow, below zero, with a north wind blowing and considered it a "grand day to be outdoors."

Ian and Joyce had been making the annual trek to the foothills for several years when after supper one evening I asked him how many deer of each species (mule and white-tailed) he would estimate per square mile in the area. He responded by asking how many males of each species had been taken in the previous hunting season. I gave him the numbers and he soon presented me with his figures (I still have his calculations). Prior to asking the question, I had written down my best guess based on close personal observation. We were within one or two points of each other—Ian's figures being more reliable, I am sure.

Suffice it to say, Ian was a paragon, an outstanding Canadian and a cherished friend.

James F. Bendell

B.A. (Hons.) (1950, Biology), University of Toronto; Ph.D. (1954, Zoology), UBC

Jim Bendell netting caterpillars in a jack pine forest at Gogama, ON, June 2007. PHOTO BY LEAH BENDELL.

Jim retired as professor emeritus from the Faculty of Forestry and the Department of Zoology at the University of Toronto in 1995.

From 1946 through the summers to 1949 he was a research assistant to C. David Fowle at the Wildlife Research Station in Algonquin Park, Ontario. He then followed an academic course, completing his Ph.D. at the University of British Columbia. Afterwards, Jim was a professor and researcher at Queen's University, UBC and the University of Toronto. He spent a sabbatical year at the Edward Grey Institute of Field Ornithology (Oxford University) with David Lack, the Nature Conservancy (Edinburgh, Scotland) with Adam Watson, and another year as staff mammalogist with the Canadian Wildlife Service.

Jim is the founding president of the Canadian Society of Environmental Biologists and the founding president of the Federation of British Columbia Naturalists (now Nature BC). He was a director of the George C. Reifel Migratory Bird Sanctuary operated by the British Columbia Waterfowl Society and is an officer and member of many scientific societies and environmental groups such as the Mississippi Valley Field Naturalists and the committee for the Rattray Marsh Conservation Area in Mississauga, Ontario.

Jim has published many scientific papers and has written material for, or contributed information to, numerous books. He shared the Wildlife Society's Publications Award for Outstanding Monograph for 2005 with colleague Fred C. Zwickel.[152]

Drs. Cowan and Jim Adams supervised Jim's Ph.D. dissertation on the life history and population dynamics of the sooty grouse. Work continues on the factors that affect density and distribution of sooty, ruffed and spruce grouse and the snowshoe hare.

My few words can but touch upon Ian McTaggart-Cowan's life and contributions. His outstanding achievements are demonstrated in love of family, excellence in teaching, scholarship and administration, publication, and guidance and inspiration of students. He achieved appointments to high office in universities and as a scientific advisor to governments. His example is manifest in many followers including myself. He stressed good teaching and the inclusion of all who wanted to learn.

Ian was a close friend of mine for some twenty years as a graduate student, associate professor and colleague. Our time together began in 1950 and extended into the period of explosive growth of the university after the Hitler war. Many of his graduate students were once soldiers, sailors or airmen. They came from all over the world and after graduation returned and became educators in their homelands. Dr. Cowan and UBC offered excellence in science in the field of vertebrate taxonomy and ecology in the traditions of Joseph Grinnell and Aldo Leopold. As a graduate supervisor, Ian reflected the UBC motto: *Tuum Est*, which I translate as "It's up to you." "There is the animal, make something of it. I give my full support."

This is the species approach and we worked on vertebrates from shrews to walrus, from grouse to ducks. One outcome was a wealth of new data and publications on little-known species and the development of new questions for research. Many students followed this route and have made or are making successful careers and worthy contributions. At one time students wanted more individual attention, and he began meeting with individuals at 7:00 a.m.

As chairman of the Department of Zoology, he was confident, open and saw what needed to be done. He appointed staff and let them get on with it. With staff and in committee, he listened carefully and gave support. Where change was necessary, he adapted or complied with new needs—for example, wildlife biology became vertebrate zoology. The rapid expansion of the student population demanded increases in staff and space, and there was never enough of either. New staff brought freshness but also different priorities and values. Inevitably, there was rivalry and tension, but with Ian's tact, ability and firm convictions, the department was kept on track. He and a few others built the world-leading foundation in zoology and ecology that UBC is today.

Some of the quick wit and sage advice Dr. Cowan gave to students and faculty remain vivid in my memory:

Optimism: On a field trip to a remote part of Vancouver Island where old logging roads ran everywhere and we became lost, he said, "We are not lost. We have not crossed any ocean."

Knowledge: To a severe critic from a grey stone and towered university of Britain: "You don't know what you are talking about."

Loyalty: On discussing potential staff: "I want a Canadian."

Evaluation: "A wasted life."

Morality: "Better to be hanged a lion than a lamb. Confession is good for the soul but bad for the reputation."

Priorities: "Better a book than a bottle."

Consolation: "Hindsight is better than foresight by a damn sight."

Advice: "What said and how said are equally important. The inarticulate are not followed."

I am very glad to have known Ian and been his friend. Very few can claim such a long and well-spent life.

Arthur T. (Tom) Bergerud

B.Sc. (1959, Wildlife Management), Oregon State College; M.Sc. (1961, Wildlife Management), University of Wisconsin; Ph.D. (1969, Zoology), UBC

Tom is retired and farming on Salt Spring Island, BC, with some two hundred chickens and seven sheep. He continues to write and is presently preparing a peer-reviewed paper based on thirty-six years of data, entitled, "The persistence and extirpation of caribou in Pukaskwa National Park from wolf predation" as well as a book on the herbivores of the Slate Islands, ON, on the north shore of Lake Superior, 1974–2006.

Dr. Cowan supervised Tom's Ph.D. dissertation on caribou demography.

Tom Bergerud enjoying a marine fishing trip off Salt Spring Island, BC, January 2, 2004. PHOTO COURTESY OF RYDER BERGERUD.

There were three turning points in my career. The first occurred in 1967. I had resigned my chief biologist position in Newfoundland as I was upset with the lack of funding and the fact that the government was going to flood the beautiful wilderness lakes in the interior to generate hydro power. The day after I resigned I went to press—a full-page article appeared in the *Evening Telegram* titled "Rape in the Name of Progress." The government was furious, and I had to steal back to my office at night to get my books. It was "Come Home Year" in Newfoundland, but I was leaving—off to UBC at age thirty-seven in the hopes of doing a Ph.D. with Dr. Dennis Chitty. I had ten years of cyclic ptarmigan data that I thought fit his theory on population regulation (known later as the Chitty Hypothesis). Upon arrival I told him my hopes, but he replied he did not agree with a thesis where the data had been gathered a priori to a hypothesis and the conclusions assigned a posteriori to fit a hypothesis. He said I must return to Newfoundland and gather more data with a better scientific method. I told him I had burned my bridges there, and he replied burning one's bridges was a luxury few could afford. There would be no ptarmigan thesis.

Then I went to Dean Cowan with my study of ten years of the demography of the Newfoundland caribou. He asked me to show him the data. I worked all summer and presented him with a booklet of statistics of all my data in tabular form. I heard nothing. It appeared that I was not going to be allowed to proceed. I was in Dr. Chitty's office one day when he answered the phone and replied only in single syllables: "Yes . . . yes . . . yes." He put down the phone and said I was accepted for a thesis on caribou demography. It had been Dean Cowan calling.

The second turning point was my oral defence of my caribou thesis. I could not answer the genetics questions. My knowledge was at the Mendelian level; I wasn't familiar with the DNA helix, and I did not know who Watson and Crick were. I was failing and my mind began to shut down. I could not even answer questions on caribou. Dean Cowan told me to leave the room. I paced the hall thinking it was over—age thirty-nine and no Ph.D. I was asked to return to the committee room. As I entered, Dean Cowan said, "Tom, you passed." My thesis, without change, went straight to the *Wildlife Monographs* series[153] with Dean Cowan and his former student Dr. David Klein as the guest editors. In 1983 it was published in a more popular format in *Scientific American.*[154]

The third turning point in my career came in 1974 when I submitted a paper to *The Journal of Wildlife Management.*[155] I argued that caribou in North America had not declined because of a lack of lichens resulting from their destruction by burning or overgrazing but rather from overhunting and predation, primarily by wolves. At that time Paul Errington's view that predation[156] was *not* regulatory was widely held by a generation of biologists, which had included me. Several biologists in British Columbia got wind of my submission and were extremely upset. They planned to call for my paper's rejection and, if that failed, to write a rebuttal. There was no need; it was rejected. I asked the editor for a second set of reviewers and he graciously gave my paper another chance. Weeks later the second review arrived and the paper was accepted. Dean Ian McTaggart-Cowan and Dr. Douglas Pimlott said in their reviews that "they did not know if Bergerud was correct, but there were some data in the paper."

In that same year (1974), because of the predation controversy, Heather Butler and I bought the largest boat that would fit on our truck and set sail for a cluster of islands way out in Lake Superior. We were going to test the lichen/predation rival hypotheses with work on islands and on the adjacent mainland in Pukaskwa National Park. This time I was going to be taught the scientific method by Dean Cowan and Dr. Dennis Chitty, including experimental and control populations. Further, Drs. Cowan and Chitty had always preached the dictum of long research studies.

From this island/mainland study of thirty years duration, we have published only one peer-reviewed paper,[157] but our paper was discussed and shown in graphic form in Charles Krebs' 2009 bestselling ecology text book.[158] I hope this research using "crucial testing" of two hypotheses that predict different outcomes is a credit to the scientific method as I was taught by Dr. Chitty and Dean Cowan at UBC.

My mentor will always be Dean Ian McTaggart-Cowan. He is the father of wildlife management in Canada and walks with Aldo Leopold and Charles Elton. We celebrate his lifetime of ethical, respected leadership giving us good science. I owe him all.

Donald (Don) A. Blood

B.Sc. (1959, Zoology), M.Sc. (1961, Zoology), UBC

Don is a retired wildlife biologist. Following employment with the Canadian Wildlife Service, Saskatchewan Department of Natural Resources and the British Columbia Fish and Wildlife Branch, Don established a wildlife resource consulting company in 1974 (D. Blood and Associates Ltd.).

For the following twenty-eight years he carried out assessments of industrial impacts on wildlife throughout western Canada. Don attributes his success in those positions in large measure to training and stimulation received from Ian McTaggart-Cowan.

Dr. Cowan supervised Don's M.Sc. thesis on California bighorn sheep.

Don Blood, a retired wildlife biologist, still enjoys observing animals. PHOTO BY BRIAN BLOOD, LANTZVILLE, BC, MAY 10, 2014.

My first awareness of Dr. Cowan was when, in grade 12, I was reviewing the 1955–56 UBC course catalogue and noted that he was head of the Zoology Department and taught courses in wildlife biology and game management. Being a keen hunter, this was for me! I took at least four courses given by Cowan: Introductory Zoology, Biology of the Vertebrates, Wildlife Management and a graduate course in mammalogy.

I soon realized, too, that Dr. Cowan was widely known and had influence that could open doors for students like me. In 1958 I arrived in Regina for a summer job to be greeted by the director of wildlife, Ernie Paynter, with, "You must know McTaggart-Cowan—what a fine fellow." The next summer I went to Newfoundland and on arrival in St. John's, the director there, Captain Walters, said, "So you are from UBC. You must know McTaggart-Cowan. What a great speaker he is."

Dr. Cowan agreed to my wish to study the Ashnola California bighorn sheep herd for my M.Sc. research topic. As my supervisor, he was instrumental in the success of that work in several ways:

- Providing financial support such as the R.J. Pop scholarship. (Cowan knew R.J., the Granville Street furrier in Vancouver.)

- Putting me in touch with information sources like the British Columbia Game Commission (then on Burrard Street in downtown Vancouver) where Jim Hatter and Ernie Taylor provided maps and advice. He also put me in touch with Hamilton (Mack) Laing, who had collected Ashnola sheep for the National Museum of Canada back in 1928.

- Providing his field notes from Ashnola bighorn counts for 1950 through 1955. (Yes, he had been there, done that!)

- Arranging for my use of Herb Clark's cabin as a base for my Ashnola work.

- Lending me his personal scope-sighted rifle to collect sheep and deer specimens. My open-sighted 30-30 wasn't accurate enough.

- Demonstrating post-mortem examination of sheep entrails when I arrived from the field unannounced and got him away from important business. He rolled up his sleeves and showed me minuscule abomasal (stomach) worms that I would never have found on my own.

Thanks to Dr. Cowan's encouragement, advice and support, I was able to obtain my M.Sc. at age twenty-three. Following his recommendation, I published three peer-reviewed papers from my thesis, which acknowledged his support. When I announced suddenly that I was not going to pursue a Ph.D., Dr. Cowan was immediately on the phone to the Canadian Wildlife Service in Ottawa to find a job for me. Shortly thereafter, a position materialized in Edmonton, the start of a lifetime career in wildlife science. If not for encountering Ian McTaggart-Cowan in my early years, my career would undoubtedly have followed a far less rewarding path.

I was always in such awe of him that I could never call him by his first name. Well, I guess it is never too late. God bless you, Ian!

Lynne Bonner

Diploma (1975, Natural Resource Management), Lethbridge Community College; B.Sc. (1981, Wildlife Management), University of Alaska, Fairbanks

Lynne is fortunate to have done fieldwork in fish and wildlife projects throughout British Columbia with the BC Ministry of Environment as well as in Alaska while working for the Alaska Department of Fish and Game. She also spent four years with the Sport Fishing Institute in Washington, DC, creating their Artificial Reef Development Center before returning to British Columbia to work again with the provincial Ministry of Environment. She has worked on developing provincial standards for applying wildlife habitat ratings to ecosystem mapping and, more recently, on provincial state of the environment reporting. Lynne currently works with the Habitat Conservation Trust Foundation as manager of Biological and Evaluation Services.

Lynne Bonner at Sunset Point, Cox Bay, Vancouver Island, BC. December 12, 2006. PHOTO BY ALEXANDRA BONNER.

I first met Dr. Cowan in 1988 when I started working as a biologist for the Habitat Conservation Fund (HCF) (now the Habitat Conservation Trust Foundation). At the time he was chair of the HCF Public Advisory Board with Dr. Bert Brink the vice-chair. Dr. Cowan presided over the board as each year they reviewed 120 or more proposals for funding from every region of the province.

His wide knowledge and experience of wildlife and their habitats in British Columbia guided the HCF board's review of hundreds of fish and wildlife enhancement projects. He was able to comment astutely on everything from a moose to a vole and on habitats from the grasslands of the Rocky Mountain Trench to seabird nesting sites on the windswept islands of Haida Gwaii (formerly Queen Charlotte Islands). The board meetings were punctuated by Dr. Cowan's stories of his experiences around the province, sometimes going back to the 1930s and always regaled in stunning detail.

When I first met him at HCF, he was approaching ninety years. It was not unusual that, after several hours of debating the merits of so many enhancement projects, he would quietly close his eyes and give every appearance of having nodded off. But in the middle of some debate over the merits of a

From left to right, Ian McTaggart-Cowan, Nancy Anderson and Lynne Bonner bird-watching at Pickering Hills, East Kootenay, BC, during a Habitat Conservation Trust Fund field trip. PHOTO BY DENNIS A. DEMARCHI, MAY 14, 1990.

prescribed burning proposal, he would suddenly voice a cogent remark that quickly brought the discussion forward to a reasonable resolution.

I remember his sense of humour at a post–board meeting dinner at a Prince George restaurant. We were discussing meat-eating versus vegetarianism while indulging in one of the best prime rib meals I've ever had. I commented on the First Nations' concept of respect for the animals they hunted and fished, so with a twinkle in his eye Dr. Cowan raised his glass to mine and we toasted the cow that had given its life for our dinner that evening.

Dr. Cowan was the first chair when HCF was established in 1981, and he continued in that role for nearly twenty years as the organization evolved into the non-profit Habitat Conservation Trust Foundation. He brought the thoughtful, science-based approach to fish and wildlife management that is his legacy to the organization today.

Andrew A. Bryant
B.E.S. (1984, Ecology), University of Waterloo; M.E.Des. (1990, Environmental Science), University of Calgary; Ph.D. (1998, Biology), University of Victoria

Andrew is an independent consultant who specializes in conservation biology and endangered species management. In the past he worked in the field on red-shouldered hawks (Ontario), burrowing owls (BC and Washington), hibernating bats (BC), old-growth forest songbirds (BC), Eurasian water-milfoil (Quebec), grizzly bears (BC), rare butterflies (Ontario), thread-leaved sundew (Nova Scotia), Geoffroy's spider monkeys (Costa Rica) and the Atiu kingfisher (Cook Islands). From 1987 through 2008 he was primarily focussed on the conservation of Vancouver Island marmots. He lives with his wife Heather in Powell River where he enjoys playing with his cat, camera and computers.

Andrew Bryant holding the first Vancouver Island marmot captured on "P" Mountain in the Nanaimo River watershed, June 3, 2000. PHOTO BY ANDREW GARDNER.

I was never a student of Dr. McTaggart-Cowan. Specifically I never sat in any of his classrooms so cannot relate any humorous stories about this or that particular lecture or field day or memorable supervisory committee meetings. But perhaps I was Ian's student in a more meaningful way. Without his work I would be far less knowledgeable about British Columbia and far less excited about the practice of field biology.

My favourite story about him concerns his early involvement with Vancouver Island marmots. After collecting a few marmots in 1931 with Kenneth Racey and finding a few more on Mount Arrowsmith in 1938, Ian promoted the first ever field study of this species[159] after he became associated with UBC in 1940. At the time handheld global positioning system (GPS) units had not been invented, and topographic maps were not very accurate, so the 1931 specimens had been catalogued as being obtained from "Green Mountain." The fun part came when Doug Heard invited his supervisor for a day in the field in 1973 to see what his graduate student was up to. "My word, I'd been there before," is what Ian told me in 1987. "I recognized that cliff . . . that's where we cooked the deer." In fact, the true location of the marmot find was the well-known Haley Lake bowl, which is one of few sites with long-term records and about eight kilometres from Green Mountain.

Ian later reviewed my Ph.D. dissertation[160] with generous use of red pen. Some of his remarks were nice. "I think this is a solid piece of work, based on an amazing amount of fieldwork and a daunting amount of computer hours." But some remarks were not so complimentary: "I really didn't like the way you calculated survival rates . . . you need to account for variable trapping effort." After ten years I view his critique rather differently. What Ian taught me—and so many others—is that passion and pursuit of "getting it right" is an appropriate road to follow—even if you don't get it right the first time.

I can think of only a few people who have led so successfully by example. Ian knew that wild marmots continue to occur at Haley Bowl and Green Mountain and a number of additional sites. That fact, and indeed many other things, represents a spectacular lifetime achievement. Bravo, Ian.

Joseph (Joe) Edward Bryant

B.A. (Hons.) (1951, Zoology), M.A. (1955, Zoology), UBC; L.L.B. (1987), University of Ottawa

Joe Bryant spent about 30 years working for the Canadian Wildlife Service in northern and eastern Canada and retired in 1964. Later he attended the University of Ottawa and received a law degree in 1986.
PHOTO BY HANS FOERSTEL, OTTAWA, ON, SPRING 2010.

Joe started post-university work as a provincial field biologist in northern Manitoba in 1951, using research there for a master's degree in 1955. Further work as a field biologist for the Canadian Wildlife Service (CWS) took him and his family to the western Arctic and southern Ontario. In between those assignments, he worked several years for the Northwest Territories government as superintendent of game, based at Fort Smith, Northwest Territories. A year's sabbatical at the University of Edinburgh in Scotland led to responsibility for the Lands and Enforcement programs of the CWS in eastern Canada and subsequently as regional director, CWS

East, then regional director, Ontario, and finally director of research and interpretation at CWS headquarters in Hull, Quebec. Upon retirement, he became involved in a number of local and national non-government organization volunteer activities, mainly in the fields of wildlife and public health. Joe and Mary have greatly appreciated the long-standing interest and friendship of Ian and Joyce Cowan.

Dr. Cowan supervised Joe's M.A. thesis on moose.

Ian McTaggart-Cowan, eighty years ago: In the summer of 1930 Ian was hired by the then National Museum of Canada (NMC) to collect vertebrate specimens in the western National Parks. He arrived in Jasper on June 9 and was assigned to park warden Frank Bryant (my father) for assistance in getting around (that is, by auto, horseback, canoe or on foot). Bryant was based at "Snaring Cabin," a short distance from the bridge that spans the Athabasca River and about twelve miles northeast of the town of Jasper. He was thirty and had a background as a farmer and trapper but no scientific training. Ian was nineteen and already an experienced collector. Nevertheless, the two men hit it off right from the start, learning from the other, and they remained friends until my dad's death in 1956.

The following stories are quoted from a letter to my wife and me in 1996 in which Ian wrote about some of his experiences in that summer of 1930.

Ian, the collector of museum specimens: On June 9, the day I arrived at Snaring, your father and I were scouting the Athabasca River not far from your house when we spotted a yearling beaver in one of the sloughs that fed into the river. I wanted beaver for specimens for the NMC, and since there was no one in sight but your father and me, I shot it with my .22 single shot. The inconsiderate beast headed for the Athabasca just above the bridge, so I stripped off and went after it—and got it. By this time the current had taken me to the bridge, and at the same time a carload of tourists came along and stopped to see what I was doing. I was slowly freezing, hanging onto a bush with one hand and holding the dead beaver out of sight under water with the other. Fortunately, your father persuaded them to move along, and I extracted my lean and chilled frame from the muddy ice water and headed for my clothes. With the temperature of the water, there would have been little visible evidence as to whether I was [male] or [female] anyway, but I didn't want them to see my dead beaver! It was #94 in my year's catalogue.

That trip with Frank . . . over Jacques Pass and on to Swiftwater Creek was fascinating to me. I was 19 at the time and had not previously been in the field in the Rockies. The pack horses that carried us—or rather our gear—were wearing the first diamond hitches I had seen. As I recall, the purpose of the trip was to pick up the traps left along the Swiftwater and up to Merlin Pass by the poachers your father and another warden had arrested and brought out sometime early the previous winter. At Swiftwater River I found the remains of a wolverine the poachers had taken and brought that out as a

Joe Bryant (top) with Frank McLeod (left) and George Mitchell on a duck banding expedition in 1950. PHOTO BY LAWSON SUGDEN.

specimen for the NMC. Your father had seized the hide and brought it to the park when the arrest was made. It was later reunited with its skull in Ottawa!

Ian, the innovative fisherman: I recall that your mother remarked one day that she hoped I liked "bully beef" because that was about all the protein available to wardens at the time. I asked whether your father ever went fishing for the table. To which the reply was no. I had already seen some good-sized pike in the slough across the road from your house at Snaring and suggested that they were available as a reasonable relief from "bully beef." Your father stated that they were uncatchable, which seemed to me like a reasonable challenge. So when he was off patrolling that morning, I tried my hand with bits of mouse, grasshopper—dead and living—a large moth, a young *Microtus*. I offered them anything I could think of, but no go! However, when your father came home I had four good fat pike gutted, beheaded and ready for the table. I'm sure he suspected foul play to which I would not admit. I put it down to secret skills developed in coastal British Columbia. Truth to tell, upon finding that the beasts would not take any of my baits, I took out a small triple hook I had on a small fishing spoon. That nice little hook fastened to the tip of my rod with a breakaway thread worked like a charm. I got each of them in the lower jaw from below. Tasty they were, too! However, I did not press my luck too far and much bully beef followed!

(Although Ian and his wife visited Jasper and the Bryant family on many subsequent occasions, I doubt that Warden Bryant ever learned what constituted Ian's "secret skills.")

Ian McTaggart-Cowan, the Zoology Professor, 60 years ago: In the autumn of 1949 a dozen or so students, mostly veterans, stayed behind in the lecture room to discuss an aspect of a lecture we had just heard concerning the digestive system of an octopus. We were all rather confused. Just then Dr. Cowan walked by the open door and one of the vets called out to him for help. Without hesitation Dr. Cowan came in and was quickly briefed on our problem. He stepped to the blackboard, sketched the octopus innards and within a very few minutes had explained the system with great clarity. I don't recall that there were any cheers, but the earlier frowns had all turned to smiles of appreciation. The following spring at the final lecture period in a course of comparative vertebrate anatomy, Dr. Cowan undertook to answer any questions the students had submitted in writing. There happened to be a few theology students in the class and one of them had stated that they couldn't accept the theory of evolution, a rather important background in the course. Dr. Cowan replied that he understood their quandary but that he, as a practicing Christian, had no trouble reconciling the bible and evolution. In a very kindly way he said that to him a creator who had arranged the universe in such a way that evolution could proceed over time to do what it appears to have done is a greater creator than one who would take a lump of clay and cast it as a bear, another as an elephant, a man, a woman or a fossil, etc. I don't know if the theology students were swayed but the rest of us admired—and remembered—that explanation.

At a class meeting in the zoology museum, Dr. Cowan told us we should be able to tell furbearers apart by feel. We tried but some of us were not having great success. Mary Jackson came up behind Dr. Cowan and asked him to put his hands behind his back. He played along and Mary placed two pelts in his hands. Within seconds he correctly identified both and we all went back to trying to learn how to do it. That was one of the many "extras" in Ian's courses that would prove so useful in our later roles as field biologists.

Mary Agnes Bryant (née Harrington)
B.A. (Hons.) (1951, Botany and Zoology), UBC

Mary, born March 3, 1919, passed away on April 6, 2011 at the age of ninety-two.

Mary graduated from UBC with a degree in botany and zoology in 1951 and participated in many field studies including assisting husband Joe Bryant (above) with his graduate work. She recalled Ian McTaggart-Cowan deleting botany courses from Joe's curriculum, stating, "You don't need that. You'll have Mary!"

Mary also was mother to two Ph.D. graduates, taught hundreds of aboriginal students in the north and many more hundreds of college students in the south. She received many awards, painted countless canvasses, wrote several books and is a member of the Rick Hansen's Hall of Fame. Mary credited Joyce Cowan with making the encouraging remark, "You go day by day."

Mary Bryant (née Harrington) first met Dr. Cowan in the late 1940s while she was teaching aboriginal students in Aklavik, NWT. He was accompanying his student Ward Stevens during Ward's graduate research on muskrats. PHOTO CIRCA 1945.

In the late 1940s, Mary was out walking with some students on the trail following the riverbank of the Peel Channel of the Mackenzie River when she noticed a figure coming up from the river boats. He was tall and slim with a pale coloured jacket—evidently not a native to the delta. After four years living there she thought she could recognize all the local individuals. With the stranger was Ward Stevens, a student from UBC whom she knew well. When they approached, Mary was introduced by Mr. Stevens to "Dr. Cowan, my boss," and after Mr. Stevens disappeared into the Hudson's Bay Store, she had a lively conversation with Dr. Cowan. He was interested in, well, just about everything. In just a few minutes he had asked her many questions. This wasn't usual with visitors to Aklavik—most wanted to take pictures, be shown the Mission or to meet someone.

Then in 1949 when she was selecting courses for her continued studies at UBC, Mary came across the name Dr. Ian McTaggart-Cowan again. As she walked into her first lecture in comparative vertebrate anatomy, she was greeted by name. "It's Mary Harrington," he said; then he saw Joe Bryant by her side. Not many days after that lecture Dr. Cowan let Mary know that she had chosen a "good friend, indeed, if he's like his dad." Mary profited greatly from her association with Dr. Cowan, both as a teacher and as a friend.

Fred Bunnell at Mount Jilg, south of Chetwynd, BC, October 4, 2004. PHOTO BY R. WAYNE CAMPBELL.

Fred L. Bunnell

B.Sc.F. (Hons.) (1965), UBC; Ph.D. (1973), University of California, Berkeley

Fred studied forestry and wildlife biology in British Columbia, Switzerland and the United States, including Berkeley in the 1960s. He has been at UBC for almost forty years where he was a professor in the Faculty of Forestry in forest wildlife. He is now professor emeritus. Fred has served as chair of Forest Renewal British Columbia in conservation biology and is a founding director for the Centre of Applied Conservation Biology. He has published hundreds of scientific articles and reports to government and industry and has received provincial, national and international awards for applied research. Fred has served on provincial, national and international committees dealing with resource management.

We all have people who changed our lives. Cowan changed mine. As a forestry undergrad in 1964 I registered for Cowan's wildlife management course. The course changed my life. Cowan made the understanding of wildlife fascinating. I finished in forestry, but ten years later Cowan and I were co-teaching a graduate seminar on wildlife at UBC. I still like trees, but wildlife has remained fascinating.

Ian helped me to acquire a joint appointment between forestry and the Institute of Animal Resource Ecology. That proved critical in my adaptation to UBC and I am very grateful because I learned a lot from him that I tried to practise later in teaching. His lectures were filled with personal examples that made them wee adventures. He demonstrated that Ph.D. comprehensives and even defences need not follow the stifling approach that terrifies some students. I learned, too, that at boring International Union for Conservation of Nature meetings, it was all right to close your eyes and appear to doze, provided you still listened. I suspect Ian enjoyed startling those who assumed he had dozed off with a perceptive question. I found it was more relaxing to emulate this practice but never became so able a practitioner.

Tom J. Cade

B.A. (1951), University of Alaska, Fairbanks; M.A. (1955), Ph.D. (1957), University of California, Los Angeles

Tom is professor emeritus of zoology at Cornell University and the founder of the Peregrine Fund, a non-profit organization headquartered in Boise, Idaho, that is devoted to the study and conservation of falcons and other birds of prey. His research has involved both fieldwork in various parts of the world, mostly on the ecology of raptors, and laboratory research on the physiological ecology of birds and mammals, mainly to do with water economy and torpidity. For more than forty years he has concentrated on the recovery of endangered raptors, such as the peregrine falcon,[161] aplomado falcon and California condor, employing the techniques of captive propagation and reintroduction.

I met Dr. Cowan at the University of Alaska (UA) in early September 1951. He had come up from UBC to visit the University prior to attending the second Alaska Science Conference to be held in McKinley National Park. After graduating from UA the previous spring, I had just returned to campus from a summer's canoe trip searching for peregrines on the Yukon River. Dr. John Buckley, leader of the Alaska Cooperative Wildlife Research Unit, introduced me to Dr. Cowan and asked me to show him through the university's small museum and collection of bird skins. I was keen to show him a tray of specimens I had collected on Sledge Island, just off the coast of the Seward Peninsula in 1950. His eyes quickly picked out a pair of exotic shorebirds. "These are dotterels," he exclaimed, "but I see they are incorrectly labelled as Mongolian plovers." I was mortified because I knew they were dotterels, but by some quirk of mental transposition I had written the Latin name as *Charadrius mongolus* instead of *C. morinellus* on the specimen label. (Both species are rare Asiatic stragglers to the Alaska coast.[162]) We had a good laugh about it, and he kindly mentioned a similar incident that had occurred to him; but I never forgot that Dr. Cowan saved me from possibly committing an egregious error in my publication on the birds of Sledge Island.

The next day a group of scientists from the university took the train down to McKinley (now Denali) Park to attend the conference. In addition to the paper sessions, there were several field trips into the park. On one occasion I found myself on a full day trip led by none other than Dr. Adolph Murie, the famous park biologist who had studied wolves and Dall's sheep for so many years.[163] Others in the group included Dr. Cowan; Dr. Frank Pitelka from the Museum of Vertebrate Zoology, University of California at Berkeley; Dr. John Buckley; Dr. Robert F. Scott, a waterfowl biologist and pilot with the

Tom Cade with a hybrid gyrfalcon x peregrine falcon and greater sage-grouse.
PHOTO BY KENT CHRISTOPHER, CROOKED CREEK, ID, CIRCA 1990.

United States Fish and Wildlife Service and Dr. Brina Kessel, newly arrived from Cornell University to take up a position as assistant professor at UA, Fairbanks. Our group was headed for Wonder Lake at the far end of the park road from the hotel, but it was a rainy day, and we made slow progress. When we reached the Toklat River, the bridge was washed out, and Murie decided to take us to a nearby field research cabin to wait out the storm. As we were walking from the trucks to the cabin, I spotted a low flying raptor over a distant slope. I put up my binoculars and then shouted, "I think I see a gyrfalcon." Everyone looked through their binoculars. "No," said Pitelka, "it's probably just a marsh hawk." Kessel agreed. No one else offered an opinion, but later Dr. Cowan came up to me and said, "Tom, I think you were right; it was a gyrfalcon." I felt redeemed for having mislabelled the dotterels.

During a prolonged lunch while we were waiting for the weather to clear, our conversation drifted to the subject of collecting and preparing museum specimens. Earlier in the day Murie had shot a couple of willow ptarmigan that were beginning to moult into winter plumage, and we had been admiring their variegated feathering. Someone asked who were the great collectors? Names such as C. Hart Merriam, Joseph Grinnell, Rollo Beck, Alfred M. Bailey and Ira N. Gabrielson were bandied about. Who prepared the best-looking skins? Brina Kessel championed Louis A. Fuertes and George M. Sutton for their ability to restore a "lifelike" appearance to their specimens. How many skins can a good preparator put up in a day's work? Perhaps fifteen to twenty depending on how many large birds are involved. What were the best instruments and materials to use?

At one point Frank Pitelka opined that it was too bad none of us had thought to bring along some skinning equipment as we could then have spent our waiting time making specimens out of the ptarmigan Murie had shot. His comment stimulated Dr. Cowan to say, "You know, I bet I could skin and stuff one of those ptarmigan in twenty minutes using nothing more than my pocket knife and whatever materials are handy." "You're on," Pitelka urged. (I do not remember what the wager was—if there was one.) Cowan took out his knife and proceeded to skin out the ptarmigan in near perfect condition and then stuffed it, as I recall, with some sphagnum moss. He had no needle and thread to sew up the abdominal incision in the skin, but the two sides of the belly feathers lay so close together that one could not tell where the cut was. It had taken less than twenty minutes. Frank Pitelka, no mean preparator himself, was duly impressed—as were we all—and Murie had a perfectly acceptable specimen to add to the park's collection.

Dr. Cowan and I had little contact after that trip, but I have always admired how well he could engage in pure scientific research and also delve into the practical aspects of wildlife management and conservation. He was a Grinnell protege of the first rank.

Robert Wayne Campbell

B.Sc. (1976, Biology and Geography), University of Victoria; M.Sc. (1983, Forest Science), University of Washington, Seattle.

Wayne retired in 2000 having spent most of his professional life as a curator of vertebrates with the Cowan Vertebrate Museum at UBC and Provincial Museum (now Royal British Columbia Museum) in Victoria. He finished the last few years of his career as a senior research scientist with the British Columbia Ministry of Environment in Victoria, completing the four-volume set *The Birds of British Columbia* as senior author.[164]

He is an award-winning writer[165] and has authored, co-authored or contributed chapters to over forty books and has written over 600 scientific papers and articles encompassing birds, amphibians, reptiles, mammals, molluscs and echinoderms. He has been honoured for his work with many awards including the Award of Excellence in Biology (now the Ian McTaggart-Cowan Award) from the Association of Professional Biologists of British Columbia (1989), the Order of British Columbia (1992) and two Commemorative Medals of Canada.

He is co-founder of the non-profit organization Biodiversity Centre for Wildlife Studies (www.wildlifebc.org) and has served as associate editor of its biannual journal *Wildlife Afield* since its inception in 2004.

Wayne Campbell with Northern Pacific rattlesnake at hibernaculum near Penticton, BC. PHOTO BY ALTON S. HARESTAD, APRIL 1983.

First impressions are usually long lasting and can often be life altering. Five quite different events are indelible in my mind from casual meetings with Ian. The first four recollections were brief encounters and all impressed me with his enthusiasm and ability to communicate effectively with people. The fifth resulted in two decades of having the privilege of working closely with Ian on a major provincial bird project. His influence and encouraging support contributed to my career choice as a museum curator and wildlife biologist.

After graduating from high school, I worked for a scaffolding company and in the early 1960s I had to deliver equipment to a new building site on the UBC campus. I had already purchased a copy (for two dollars) of *A Review of the Bird Fauna of British Columbia* by James Munro and Ian McTaggart-Cowan,[166] published in 1947, and I knew that Dr. Cowan had left the Provincial Museum and was a professor in the Department of Zoology. During my lunch break I sneaked into a lecture room that was packed with students sitting everywhere. Soon Dr. Cowan arrived, as did the fire marshal. Students sitting in the aisles were told they had to leave or find another spot. Dr. Cowan suggested that they could perch on the floor around him if they were still interested in his lecture on the human circulatory system. Everyone shifted forward. I was one of them but it was obvious I was not a student in my stained work clothes.

He started his lecture but soon a student had a question. Dr. Cowan could sense the "panic" in the student's note-taking, stopped the lecture, and let the fellow ask him the question. I vividly remember Dr. Cowan asking him if he knew anything about cars. He did, and in the blink of an eye Ian started comparing the circulation of blood in a human body to fluid coolant in a car's engine. Everyone was captivated and I left the lecture realizing this guy could really communicate!

My second recollection, and first meeting, was embarrassing. During my high school years in the late 1950s, I developed a real passion for collecting natural history objects that included a catalogued assortment of bird's eggs, marine molluscs and books. I knew that Dr. Cowan had an interest in malacology and had a large personal collection of marine shells. A few days after that lecture I called his secretary early in the morning and asked if it was possible to meet with Dr. Cowan to help identify some molluscs I had recently collected. I told her I was not a student and that I made daily trips to UBC to deliver building material. To my surprise she said, "Dr. Cowan could see you later in the morning."

I picked up the box of unidentified shells, and raced to UBC. When I arrived, Dr. Cowan was at his desk editing a thesis by Bill Barkley. He got up and said, "What do you have there?" I said, "A box of *shit-ons* I can't identify." He opened the box, paused for a moment and in a courteous manner said, "Oh, you have some beautiful *ki-tons.*" When I got home I was truly embarrassed but realized that my mistake in pronunciation of "chitons" would be kept within the walls of Dr. Cowan's office.

I was grateful to Dr. Cowan that my third memory did not result in a criminal record for me. Like many prairie-born youngsters, I was an avid egg-collector. My family moved to British Columbia when I started grade school, and in my late teens I applied, and received, a federal permit to collect birds, their nests and eggs, for scientific purposes. The first one hundred or so species were easy to find but locating nests with eggs of many of the small passerines was becoming a challenge. While on one of my egg-collecting forays in May 1964, I noticed a female common yellowthroat fly into a patch of sedges in a large wet field that was part of the farm grounds for inmates at Oakalla Prison in Burnaby. It was mid-afternoon and no prisoners were working the fields, so I decided to creep to the spot where I suspected the nest might be. That three hundred yards was an arduous and wet excursion, but I did collect the nest and eggs and immediately returned to my bicycle carefully carrying my prize. Waiting for me were two Royal Canadian Mounted Police cars, each with an officer. I explained what I was doing and, of course, I did not have my permit with me to prove it. In a panic, I asked them to call Dr. Cowan at UBC, and within minutes I was on my way home with a new addition to my egg collection and no criminal record.

Later I learned that Dr. Cowan had told the policemen that I was helping him fill in gaps in the university oology collection and he was very appreciative that I had collected specimens of a very difficult species to find. What Dr. Cowan didn't know was that one of the police officers had taken his introductory zoology course at UBC!

The fourth reminiscence was a delightful tit-for-tat exchange that

Wayne in tree with nest box. From the late 1950s through the 1960s Wayne Campbell (standing on branch) put up over 1,100 wood duck nest boxes from Burnaby and Pitt Meadows to Chilliwack in the lower Fraser Valley. He enlisted cub and scout groups, sportsmen, naturalists, students and land owners to help construct and monitor use of the nest boxes. PHOTO BY JOHN G. SARLES, MCGILLIVRAY SLOUGH, BC, MARCH 2, 1963.

happened four months before I moved from UBC's Vertebrate Museum to the Provincial Museum in Victoria. Each autumn before the semester started at UBC, Ian would drop into the Vertebrate Museum to chat. During one visit I remarked that our collection of some corvids, especially crows and ravens, was poorly represented. I even suggested that it would be useful to have a large series of northwestern crows and American (common) crows to determine the species' transition zone between coastal and interior ranges. As a professor in the Department of Zoology he had contemplated such a project but stated that funding wasn't available for what were considered "garbage" birds.

As we chatted, I mentioned that the raven was my favourite bird. He quickly replied, "Mine, too!" And we started swapping stories. He told me about watching ravens patiently following a pack of wolves hunting big game in Jasper National Park in order to return to the kill later to feed. I rebounded quickly with a story of ravens learning to cover light-sensitive lamps in northern mining camps with their wings in the dead of winter in order to activate them for warmth. Almost before I had finished my account, he told me about a group of ravens in Alaska he had watched working in unison on the edge of an empty forty-five-gallon drum filled with garbage to spill its contents. After twenty-five minutes or so we were out of stories, but our collective experiences confirmed that ravens were long-lived, intelligent and cunning with complex vocal communication. These traits are also prominent in the mythology of the raven in coastal Native cultures. It was also apparent that the adaptable raven could thrive on bare mountain tops as well as marine shores and are clever companions on hunting trips. I can't remember who told the last story, probably Cowan, but as he left the museum to return to his office he mused, "ravens are not as black as they're painted."

My fifth vivid memory would eventually lead to a major reference work on the birds of British Columbia. In the early 1970s, I was on staff at UBC working as a preparator and assistant curator in the Vertebrate Museum in the Department of Zoology. In November 1972 Dr. Cowan invited my wife and me to dinner at his Point Grey home. We enjoyed swapping stories, learning how significant his wife Joyce was in his daily and professional life, and became enthralled with his genuine interest in encouraging and developing young people with an interest in natural history. Towards the end of a fascinating evening Dr. Cowan casually mentioned it was time to update his 1947 bird book and wondered if I might like to help. He certainly knew that I had no university training, but that I had already spent eight years compiling information for such a project and that I had already published over one hundred articles on birds of this province, which was a good "jump-start" to a co-operative project of this kind. We shook hands to cement the deal, and as I was leaving, I remember him saying, "Passion and enthusiasm will get the job done." Little did I realize then that those qualities would be challenged many times over the next two decades!

Harry Carter, seen here at Santa Cruz Island, CA, August 8, 2007, is still conducting seabird surveys along the coast of western North America thirty years later. PHOTO BY PERCY HÉBERT.

Harry R. Carter
B.Sc. (1978, Zoology), UBC; M.Sc. (1985, Zoology), University of Manitoba

Harry is an independent seabird biologist at Carter Biological Consulting (CBC), Victoria, BC. For thirty-nine years he has conducted seabird research, monitoring and surveys as well as conservation, restoration and injury assessments mainly in western North America. He assisted the first survey of British Columbia seabird colonies in 1974 to 1978 by the British Columbia Provincial Museum[167] and conducted early studies and conservation of marbled murrelet and common murre on the west coast of Vancouver Island from 1972 to 1982 during his M.Sc. studies at the University of Manitoba.

He was a biologist at the Point Reyes Bird Observatory on the Farallon Islands, California, between 1983 and 1989, led a state-wide seabird colony survey in California between 1989 and 1991 by Humboldt State University (HSU), co-led a HSU seabird research monitoring and restoration program in California between 1992 and 2003 and has conducted various projects between Baja California and Alaska and in Japan since 2004 through CBC. He was also a member of the United States Fish and Wildlife Service's marbled murrelet recovery team.

Harry has received various awards and commendations and has authored or co-authored over 110 scientific publications and reports.

I did not know Dr. Cowan well on a personal level but was profoundly influenced by him, especially through others whom he had more directly influenced. All of my chief early role models (Charles Guiguet, Wayne Campbell, Spencer Sealy and my father, Harry Carter) had been under Cowan's wing. This story is an example of how his influence has passed from generation to generation.

I first met Cowan at the Guiguet house in 1973; I was then the boyfriend of Guiguet's daughter, Suzanne. In my mind at this time, Guiguet knew everything there was to know about wildlife, but Cowan was so highly revered that it felt like meeting royalty. Yet he was warm and engaging, even to a teenager who had not yet shown much interest in wildlife. The great friendship, mutual respect and storytelling between Cowan and Guiguet were inspiring. They knew everything about everybody who had ever done any wildlife work in British Columbia.

In the summer of 1974, after my first year at the University of Victoria, Guiguet hired me for my first wildlife job in the Bird and Mammal Division at the British Columbia Provincial Museum where I began by preparing skeletons for the collection. Cowan walked in one day and made the rounds to say hello to all staff. He made a face at the strong smell of some dead thing I was boiling on the stove and stated that such work would serve as a strong foundation for a career in wildlife.

After working at the museum for a couple of months, I was sold on wildlife biology, although I still preferred fieldwork over specimen preparations.

Guiguet said, "If you are serious, go to the UBC and study under Cowan." Wayne Campbell agreed. My father did not question my desire to leave UVic to go to UBC once I mentioned Guiguet's recommendation and Cowan's name. During World War II Guiguet and my father had gone through military training together, and after the war my father (who became an orthopaedic surgeon) had been one of Cowan's students when Guiguet was his teaching assistant.

At UBC in the autumn of 1975 I was fortunate to take Cowan's last wildlife management course before he retired. Every lecture was informative and well delivered, and he clearly enjoyed every minute of it with a gleam in his eye and a smile on his face. I looked forward to each lecture and listened intently, even though I was becoming more interested in non-game, specifically seabirds. I had spent the summer of 1975 with Guiguet and Campbell surveying seabird colonies on the west coast of Vancouver Island for the Provincial Museum, with my father as skipper aboard his volunteered boat, MV *Tedmac*. My final project for Cowan's course was the first collation of the seabird colonies of Vancouver Island, based on the 1975 surveys, east coast data provided by Campbell, and the little available literature[168]—a far cry from the course's primary subject matter. Although this was my interest, I did not expect Cowan's reaction. When I picked up my project from his office, he told me that this kind of work was extremely important, not enough of it was being done these days, and that I should continue on with this line of study. Although I ended up having only this one course with Cowan and few personal interactions, this one key moment of support was critical to my continued interest in seabirds. Others at UBC did not encourage my interest in them, reflecting the gap that seabirds then fell into between the better-developed fields of game studies and more theoretical studies. But Cowan understood the need to know more about seabird populations, as did Guiguet and Campbell. Only recently did I find out that Cowan also had been instrumental behind the scenes in encouraging museum interest in nesting seabirds in the late 1970s for *The Birds of British Columbia* project.[16]

Spencer Sealy later became my M.Sc. advisor, primary seabird mentor and lifelong colleague. Cowan, Guiguet, Campbell and Sealy all pursued interests in fieldwork, museum studies and the historical literature, which I also follow.

My story is just one small example of how Cowan's influence has carried on through several generations of biologists over a period of eight decades through an intricate web of connections that is difficult to fully describe because it is so complicated. Even though much work has been done, much remains to be done by future generations to continue Cowan's goals: to describe, study and protect wildlife in British Columbia. Without strong influences from Cowan and those he influenced, my seabird career would never have blossomed. Their vision, training and wisdom have guided me well. I give thanks to Ian for teaching us all.

Along the BC coast when notebooks become full or soggy during fieldwork, one must use whatever is available for recording data. Here, Harry Carter uses a dry cardboard box during a seabird survey, Moore Islands, BC, June 26, 1976. PHOTO BY R. WAYNE CAMPBELL.

Michael (Myke) John Chutter

B.Sc. (1976, Zoology), UBC

Myke is a wildlife biologist working for the British Columbia Ministry of Forests, Lands and Natural Resource Operations in Victoria. Following graduation from UBC in 1976, he spent four years as a wildlife technician for D.A. Blood and Associates in Nanaimo, BC, conducting bird and mammal surveys throughout British Columbia, the Yukon Territory and southern Saskatchewan. In 1981 he joined the provincial wildlife branch in Nanaimo as part of the Integrated Wildlife-Intensive Forestry Research Group conducting deer/forestry research on Vancouver Island. He was transferred to Victoria in 1991, and shortly after that became the provincial bird specialist responsible for coordinating bird management across the province, a position he still holds today.

Myke was responsible for initiating the province-wide ban on lead shot for waterfowl hunting in British Columbia, which later became a national ban. He served as secretary of the steering committee for the final two volumes of *The Birds of British Columbia* and later chaired the national spotted owl recovery team. In 2006 Myke was awarded the Habitat Conservation Trust Fund Silver Award (named for Rod Silver) for exemplary achievement in wildlife conservation.

I had the good fortune to be an undergraduate student in the final wildlife management course that Dr. Cowan taught at UBC. The course was slated to be a weekly three-hour lecture, but at the first class Dr. Cowan announced that he was shortening the time to two hours, regardless of what the head of the Zoology Department said. And then as an afterthought, with a wry smile he added, "Of course, I'm the head of Zoology." This was one of the many things I learned to admire about the man—in spite of his well-known achievements, he never took himself too seriously and was always quick with a joke, including poking fun at himself.

His charm, stature and breadth of experience made for wonderful lectures and the whole class was enthralled. No one dozed off during Ian's lectures. When he couldn't be there to present a lecture, he asked one of his graduate students to fill in, which always added to the depth and breadth of the material, as often they were working on exotic species in faraway lands. If there was ever any doubt in my chosen vocation, this course erased it, and so in no small way he had a major effect on my life as I have been a wildlife biologist ever since.

I still have in my possession a term paper on muskox that I wrote for him in 1975. I thought it was pretty good, but he was a fairly tough taskmaster and always expected the best of himself and thus expected the same of his students. Thus, while I only received seventy-five percent on the paper, I learned to expect more of myself and to push myself harder after that.

Myke Chutter holding a young American white pelican for banding.
PHOTO BY R. WAYNE CAMPBELL, STUM LAKE, BC, JULY 28, 1993.

Our paths crossed again many years later when I became secretary of the steering committee for volumes three and four of *The Birds of British Columbia*. Dr. Cowan was chair of the committee, and even though he was almost ninety, he was able to keep the authors working together to enable a timely completion of the project. During that time I was able to get to know him a bit better and even brought in that paper on muskox to show him; he chuckled and told me that he must have been in a good mood when he marked it as I was lucky to get seventy-five percent! I was constantly impressed at his work ethic, dedication and incessant enthusiasm and amazed at how he could continue to master new tasks including modern computer-based technologies and taking over as "chief cook and bottle washer" after his wife took ill.

Once, when visiting him at his home regarding *The Birds of British Columbia* project, he took me on a tour of his yard where I learned that in addition to all his other talents he was also a world expert on rhododendrons. Virtually every space in his yard had rhododendrons from somewhere on the globe. He knew the names and origins of all of them, when they bloomed, how often, what colour the flower was and when and where he had acquired each one. I learned later that he taught courses on rhododendrons in his "spare time" and also had won almost every conceivable rhododendron award. Was there anything this man wasn't an expert in?

The last time I saw Ian was at a concert at the University of Victoria when he was in his late nineties. He obviously still had an enthusiasm for life and a desire to get out and enjoy it. We exchanged pleasantries as he still recalled who I was even though our paths hadn't crossed for several years.

I was saddened by his passing, overwhelmed by his dedication and contributions to wildlife management, pleased beyond belief that I was fortunate enough to have been able to spend a small amount of my life sharing time with such a great man and amazed in retrospect at what a profound, positive influence he had had on my life.

James T. Cuthbert
B.Sc. (1972, Marine and Terrestrial Ecology), University of Victoria; M.Sc. (1979, Natural Resource Management), UBC

Jim's professional career spans a variety of biological and communication positions in both the public and private sectors. These include field biologist with LGL Limited environmental research associates, the University of Victoria Department of Biology and seasonal and full-time positions as a naturalist with Parks Canada at Pacific Rim and Waterton Lakes national parks. He also served as natural resource management planner for Parks Canada in British Columbia and Alberta. From 1978 to 2004, he was employed with British Columbia Parks where his assignments included regional interpretation and information officer, visitor services officer/manager, extension (communications) officer and facility officer.

While in British Columbia, Jim has served as manager of the Islands

Jim Cuthbert, who studied bald eagle/airplane interactions, was one of Ian's last students. PHOTO BY DENNIS A. DEMARCHI.

Trust Fund (conservancy), national field office director for the Western Canada Wilderness Committee, senior project (conservation) officer for the Land Conservancy of British Columbia and natural science/study tour programmer for Capilano College. Since 2002 he has provided environmental and communications consulting services, including commercial film supervision in parks and protected areas, environmental assessments, integrated storm water management planning and bird surveys. He also served three terms as elected councillor for the District of North Vancouver.

Jim has volunteered on the governing boards of the British Columbia College of Applied Biology and the Association of Professional Biologists of British Columbia.

Dr. Cowan supervised Jim's M.Sc. thesis on bald eagle ecology from 1974 to 1978.

In 1974 Ian and I first met in his spacious dean's office where I outlined my proposed master of science study on bald eagle ecology. I had been working since 1971 as a field biologist for LGL Limited studying bird hazards to aircraft at the Port Hardy Airport on northern Vancouver Island and expanding this research to an M.Sc. thesis seemed a logical progression. I was delighted when Ian agreed to supervise the study.

This marked the beginning of a positive relationship that lasted for many years. Ian not only critiqued my thesis manuscript as it was developed but also made time in his very busy schedule to fly to Port Hardy from Vancouver specifically to meet with me onsite to discuss the study. He demonstrated a keen interest in my work throughout the term of the project. He was pleased to tour the Port Hardy Airport lands and meet the staff. While in the field, he provided numerous helpful suggestions, which I adopted, especially in the area of collecting, recording and analyzing field data. His knowledge of field biology was remarkable.

Ian also touched my life through his excellent and lengthy contribution to the Nature Trust of British Columbia. He has been a true inspiration to me throughout my career and has served as an ideal role model for so many people.

Elmer A. DeBock

B.Sc. (Hons.) (1966, Zoology), UBC; M.Sc. (1970, Biology), University of Alberta

Elmer is retired, having worked most of his professional career on biological studies with mining companies and mineral exploration. Fieldwork included research on the behaviour and winter predation of grey wolves on mountain goats, the population dynamics of the Porcupine caribou herd in northern Yukon Territory and eastern Alaska and incidental studies on caribou. Often this research was done co-operatively with the Alberta Fish and Wildlife Branch, Canadian Wildlife Service and Renewable Resources Consulting Services Ltd.

Elmer DeBock during a trip into the Ogilvie Mountains, Yukon Territory, in early autumn of 1974. PHOTO COURTESY OF AUDIE DEBOCK.

Dr. Cowan was Elmer's supervisor for a B.Sc. thesis on morphometrics of skulls of captive and wild black-tailed deer.

Dr. Cowan's forte was the selection and encouragement of promising and enthusiastic students in their field of choice. In the autumn of 1965 he listened patiently to my problems as a bewildered undergraduate zoology student and deftly guided me into a rewarding career and lifetime in field biology. He suggested that my casual interest in big game behaviour and ecology should be pursued, and part of my introduction was completing a B.Sc. thesis under his direction, examining variations in deer skulls between wild and captive animals.

Looking back at the bewildering number and diversity of interests of students that Dr. Cowan supported and guided, it is easy to understand the great contribution that he and his students have made to the field of zoology.

Dennis A. Demarchi

B.S.A., (1966, Plant Science),UBC, Faculty of Agriculture; M.Sc. (1970, Range Management), University of Idaho, College of Forestry, Range and Wildlife, Moscow

Dennis worked for the British Columbia Ministry of Environment's (MOE) Wildlife Branch as habitat biologist and then as the provincial habitat inventory specialist for thirty-three years. After retirement in 2000, he was self-employed as a part-time habitat consultant, mainly keeping the province's ecoregion classification current.

During his career, he participated in habitat assessment and evaluation projects throughout the province and spearheaded the development of the British Columbia wildlife habitat classification system and the ecoregion classification. For the latter work he was awarded the British Columbia Association of Professional Biologists' Award of Excellence (now called the Ian McTaggart-Cowan Award for Excellence in Biology) and the Shikar Safari Club International's British Columbia Conservation Officer of the Year award. The ecoregion classification was a critical selling point for having the provincial Wildlife Branch involved in the British Columbia's protected areas strategy. Dennis is currently the president of the Biodiversity Centre for Wildlife Studies.

Dennis Demarchi participating in a survey of wetland birds in the Nicola Valley, BC, September 23, 2012, following the annual general meeting of the Biodiversity Centre for Wildlife Studies. PHOTO BY R. WAYNE CAMPBELL.

I first became aware of Dr. Cowan in 1960–61 when I was in high school in Kamloops. I was in Darrell Rye's biology class [one of Cowan's former students] and being a boy from the interior I didn't know much about sea life. I can remember watching Dr. Cowan on television discussing marine animals. In those days, television screens were small in spite of being housed in large consoles, images were not clear, and were in multiple tones of grey, but Dr. Cowan came through clearly and those programs helped me understand the sea life that I was studying in biology class.

In the winter of 1964–65 I took Cowan's Zoology 421 wildlife management class. I remember that he made each lecture and each subject highly interesting, so much so that even parasites were made exciting; he had a passion and spoke with a clarity that few other professors had. The next year Dr. Cowan entertained a wildlife ecologist from Australia and invited Dr. Bert Brink to bring a couple of students to his house to meet and talk with the Australian visitor. I can only vaguely remember the visitor, but I do remember well one of Dr. Cowan's comments. In talking about the marking system at the University of British Columbia, he said, "The top students here can only get eighty-five percent on an exam; if the professor was to take his own exam, he would only get ninety percent. And if Christ were somehow to take that same exam, he would only get ninety-five percent. What are we saving that top 15 percent for?" I guess that's why the best marks I ever got at university were in his class.

In 1988, Wayne Campbell and Dr. Cowan were working on the first two volumes of *The Birds of British Columbia*[16] when Andrew Harcombe came to me (we were both working for MOE at the time) concerned that the authors were thinking of using the "terrestrial biotic regions map" that Munro and Cowan had developed for the 1947 publication, *A Review of the Bird Fauna of British Columbia*,[18] as the background ecological reference for the new book. Andrew wanted me to convince Dr. Cowan and Wayne to use the British Columbia ecoregion classification that I had developed. A meeting was arranged and the four of us met in Wayne's office in the curatorial tower of the BC Provincial Museum. I rolled out my map, not knowing what arguments I would be faced with, but right away we started to discuss various biological aspects of the province and how the ecoregion classification expressed those. It was confirmed quickly and without much discussion that my ecoregion classification should be used in the updated bird books.

When we were walking back to our office after the meeting, Andrew turned to me and said, "What was that all about?" I simply replied, "Mohammed had to go to the Mountain." Ian McTaggart-Cowan has always been that "mountain" for wildlife conservation in British Columbia, and we thank him for making it easier for the rest of us.

Raymond Alexander Demarchi
B.S.A. (1962) and M.S.A. (1965), Faculty of Agriculture, UBC

Ray is a retired provincial wildlife biologist. He was employed by the British Columbia provincial government as a regional wildlife section head in the Kootenay region from 1965 to 1992, as the provincial protected area specialist from 1992 to 1995 and as provincial chief of wildlife from 1995 to 1997. He spent much of his career improving the province's game management and hunting regulations, contributing to the doubling of the province's protected areas with direct involvement in the establishment of the Purcell wilderness area and the northern Rockies wildlife management and protected areas, developing the province's grizzly bear management strategy and contributing to the provincial wildlife harvest standards.

Raymond Demarchi at Saugahatchee Creek in Auburn, Alabama, January 1, 2011. PHOTO BY CAROL HARTWIG.

Raymond Demarchi, camp cook, at a hunting camp on Stanley Creek in the Tatshenshini River valley, BC. PHOTO BY DENNIS A. DEMARCHI, AUGUST 1975.

After leaving government, he and his wife, Carol Hartwig, formed a conservation consulting partnership. Although mostly retired, Ray still maintains an interest in improving the management of the province's hunted cervid populations via selective harvest strategies and remains actively involved in local environmental issues in the Cowichan Valley where he lives.

Dr. Cowan and Dr. Bert Brink were co-supervisors for Ray's thesis on California bighorn sheep in the Ashnola Valley.

I was an academically marginal second-year university student from small town British Columbia (Kamloops, population then: twelve thousand) when I sat down in the biological sciences lecture hall in September 1959 and experienced my first exciting lecture at UBC. There was something very special about the dynamic, entertaining and perfectly clear first class in Zoology 105 being delivered to a packed auditorium by the highly charismatic and obviously highly respected professor with the double-barreled surname. Four years later as a graduate student under the shared direction of Drs. Ian McTaggart-Cowan and Vernon C. "Bert" Brink, I considered myself privileged to have the honour of referring to myself as one of Ian's graduate students. Both Ian and Bert had put their faith in a student who had barely made it through first year (after my first term a student counsellor had told me that I should quit wasting my time and my parents' money and go home) but who had progressed sufficiently from that first zoology lecture to gain the support of two of Canada's premier professors in the fields of zoology and plant science, respectively.

My master's thesis experience was only possible because of the support I received from a number of people. Dr. Cowan, as I still refer to him, was one of the most important. I did not appreciate the politics of academia at the time. As I neared the completion of my master's thesis, however, I realized that without the skillful guidance of both Drs. Cowan and Brink—who worked as a team to steer my practical, field-oriented wildlife and range research program through the academic minefield that was the Department of Zoology at the time—that my goal of becoming a wildlife biologist would never have been achieved.

Over the years since then I have used Ian's approval as a yardstick for my work, particularly with respect to mountain sheep management and research. This continued into my retirement when I worked on a number of BC provincial mountain sheep status reviews with my two sons, Michael and Donald, my brother Dennis and my wife, Carol. It seems almost surreal that all of this began when my thesis proposal and budget, which included provision for the purchase of two horses and pack equipment, was handed back to me by Ian's private secretary stamped: APPROVED: I. McT.-Cowan.

Alexander Dzubin
B.A. (Hons.) (1951, Zoology) and M.A. (1954, Zoology), UBC

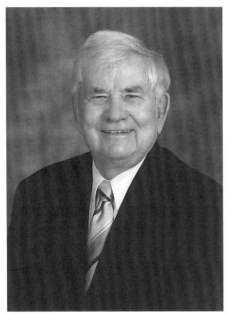

Alex Dzubin in Saskatoon, March 2010. PHOTO BY IPC CANADA PHOTO SERVICE.

Alex is a retired research scientist who was employed by the Canadian Wildlife Service from 1955 to 1989. His lifelong interests included waterfowl population dynamics, demography of lesser snow, Ross's and greater white-fronted geese and the identification of geese using metrics and pigmentation of tail rectrices. He assisted Dr. F. Cooke of Queen's University in banding and mensural studies at Churchill, Manitoba, for twenty-two summers (July) and conducted environmental assessments north of sixty degrees north latitude for ten years.

Alex spent three years (1953, 1954 and 1960) at the University of Wisconsin in Madison. He is the author or co-author of six book chapters or sections and has published twenty-two articles in peer-reviewed journals. His time is still occupied by waterfowl productivity monitoring studies on the Canadian prairies and development of new keys for the National Species Composition Survey. (Species considered include lesser snow, Ross's, Canada and cackling goose.)

Dr. Cowan was Alex's supervisor for his M.A. thesis on waterfowl breeding biology and production in "pothole-agricultural" regions of south-central Manitoba.

The year 1951 was transformative for this naïve student from the Crow's Nest Pass, Alberta. Dr. Ian McTaggart-Cowan had arranged a two-hundred-dollar BC Sugar Refining Company scholarship, found me a room on campus in army hut H-31 and coaxed me to fill out a request for a Canadian student stint at the Delta Waterfowl Research Station in Manitoba. There I had the possibility of a summer working with Dr. H. Albert Hochbaum, its director, who had been one of Aldo Leopold's students. A four-month stipend of six hundred dollars and an opportunity for a master of arts study drew me east of the Rocky Mountains. Painfully I switched loyalties from studying mountain goats and mule deer to mallards and canvasbacks—a "forced juncture" that positively changed my life forever.

Dr. Cowan's clear, inspirational lectures, his insightful advice and well-reasoned arguments attracted me to his Vertebrate Zoology 306 class. This opened a new world with exciting possibilities and a sea change in my employment path. I bought into the promise of making a career out of natural history studies. Sixty years later I have no regrets.

Dr. Cowan set the bar high for his graduate students. He expected logical data, sound interpretation and good science. Implicitly he promised his support, his honesty and integrity and always the inferred hope of a lifetime adventure in the fresh air. He showed a deep respect for all living things as a necessary component of life on this planet.

He was an "old-guard" environmentalist before the new science of computers, models and trends. Everything was interconnected. Though a champion of new ideas, he carried in him the history of the development of wildlife ecology as a scientific discipline in Canada—a West Coast protege of Aldo Leopold, if you will. He was an authentic icon who taught his personal values of self-reliance, high ideals and the need for evidence-based knowledge to several generations of students and budding wildlifers. As a professor, he was a supportive, loyal advisor, mentor and counsellor who touched your very soul with his enthusiasm. He found National Research Council grants and other resources such as scholarships and technical jobs for his students to carry on. He cared.

Dr. Cowan's eternal words of wisdom, I cherish to this day: "Don't sweat the small stuff—like a passing grade in organic chemistry"; "you can't kill a deer under the same tree every year" and "make up your morning kindling before you slip into your sleeping bag."

Fast forward sixty years. My daughter Jean, a birthing recovery–room nurse in Calgary's Foothills Hospital, occasionally works with another Dr. McTaggart-Cowan, an anesthesiologist. Ian's grandson is a great talker, a sound decision-maker and collaborative staff worker. A small world.

Donald S. Eastman
B.Sc. (1962, Zoology), UBC; M.Sc. (1964), University of Aberdeen, Scotland; Ph.D. (1977, Zoology), UBC

Don is a wildlife biologist who worked for thirty-three years in wildlife research for the British Columbia Ministry of Environment. His main research interests included large mammals, endangered species and other aspects of biodiversity conservation. He has served on many wildlife-oriented committees, including the Canadian Biodiversity Strategy.

After retiring from government, he worked as the faculty coordinator for the restoration of natural systems program at the University of Victoria where he is an adjunct associate professor in biology and environmental studies. Throughout his career and currently he has volunteered

Don Eastman in Fairfield (Victoria), BC, February 14, 2011. PHOTO BY DENNIS A. DEMARCHI.

in conservation organizations at local, provincial, national and international levels.

In 1959 I was an undergraduate student at the University of British Columbia when a friend suggested that I audit another section of one of my classes. I was reluctant to do so because my course load was very heavy, but finally I agreed to go. The large lecture room quickly filled to capacity, and when the class began, I knew I was in a special place. The professor spoke clearly and logically with a commanding grasp of the subject. However, what really impressed me was the enthusiasm he communicated, and I quickly realized that I would be attending two sets of classes that term! That course was Zoology 105, and the professor was Ian McTaggart-Cowan.

Since those early student days I enjoyed a long association with Ian, appreciating his naturalist's enthusiasm and curiosity for the natural world and his phenomenal knowledge of wildlife, and I continue to be impressed when I learn about the many dimensions of his impact. I recently read the foreword he wrote in Tommy Walker's book *Spatsizi*, published in 1976,[169] which describes his efforts to protect that wilderness area. Ian clearly articulates the pressures on wilderness, the need for its protection and the importance of individual efforts to save wild places, and Tommy acknowledged the support he received from Ian in his conservation efforts.

Thinking back on my career and those of his many other students, I can only marvel at the remarkable influence he had on the profession of wildlife biology and the discipline of wildlife conservation from provincial to national and international levels. He attracted excellent students and colleagues. All of these people have made and continue to make significant contributions to wildlife conservation. But perhaps Ian's most enduring legacy is the example he provided. He was an excellent scientist, committed

Donald Eastman (right) with John Bandy establishing a vegetation productivity cage for a Rocky Mountain bighorn sheep study. PHOTO BY DENNIS A. DEMARCHI, WIGWAM RIVER FLATS NEAR ELKO, BC, MAY 15, 1967.

to conducting sound science and publishing the results of his work. He recognized the need to communicate to the general public about the importance, beauty and complexity of nature and the need for its protection. He was an articulate and forceful advocate for issues he believed important, such as a science-based approach to conservation. He was committed to public service, and throughout his professional life and well into his retirement years he continued to contribute significantly to many important conservation initiatives. What better role model could one ask for?

John P. Elliott
B.Sc. (1968), University of Alberta; Ph.D. (1975, Zoology), UBC

John is a retired wildlife biologist and civil servant, having worked with the British Columbia Ministry of Environment as fish and wildlife section head for the Peace region based in Fort St. John. He is currently a senior scientist for the Tryon Professional Group focussed on servicing industry operations and developments in northeastern British Columbia, northern Alberta and the adjacent territories.

Dr. Cowan was John's supervisor for his Ph.D. dissertation on prey capture by the African lion.

John Elliott during field research on prey capture of the east African lion in the Ngorongoro Crater, Tanzania.
PHOTO BY JOHN P. ELLIOTT, CIRCA 1970.

Ian McTaggart-Cowan was a fine scientist who helped fellow scientists, students and the general public to understand the functioning of wildlife populations. He encouraged me personally to think beyond the simplistic and to follow the numbers not the herd.

As a young fellow I was impressed how Ian (only in his fifties at that time!) would seem to be soundly asleep during all the graduate seminars, and yet at their conclusion he would snap awake and know and understand everything that had been said. No wonder he lived for nearly one hundred years. I am thankful for his leadership.

Joyce Elliott (née Lanko)
B.Sc. (1960, Zoology), M.Sc. (1962, Zoology), UBC

Joyce was born in Winnipeg and moved to Vancouver in 1943. She attended UBC from 1956 to 1962 and following graduation was employed for a year as a laboratory teacher in the Zoology Department. She then left for Australia and started a Ph.D. program at Monash University in Melbourne; in 1965 she married and started a family. That same year she and her husband, Kevin Elliott, a mechanical engineer and amateur naturalist, started an animal-trap business called Elliott Scientific Equipment. The "Elliott trap" remains today the most commonly used device for trapping small mammals alive in Australia.

I was a late starter studying zoology, having entered university with the expectation of becoming a biochemist. However, after attending Zoology 105 with

Joyce (Lanko) Elliott with a gopher snake at a Department of Zoology display during open house at UBC in early 1959. PHOTO COURTESY OF THE VANCOUVER SUN.

Ron and Jennifer Erickson at Whistler Mountain, BC, circa 2004. PHOTO BY J. SHIKATA.

Ian Cowan, the direction of my life was changed. What a great teacher! Subsequently my thesis on subspecies of *Peromyscus* in Ontario gained me a master's degree.

A wildlife management course with Ian encouraged me to apply for a Ph.D. at Monash University in Melbourne, Australia. My thesis topic was a study of marsupial hair scale samples both in Australia and South America (where there are many marsupials) in order to postulate biogeographical connections between these continents. Unfortunately, marriage and four children prevented completion of this study.

Early in our marriage (1965), my husband Kevin designed and developed a folding, live-catching animal trap, which to date has sold in excess of two hundred thousand units worldwide. Ian's teaching of wildlife principles has helped me to advise our clients on aspects of trapping, animal behaviour and biodiversity.

L. Ron Erickson

B.Sc. (1969, Agriculture), UBC; M.Sc. (1971, Agriculture), Oregon State University

Ron grew up in Salmon Arm, BC, and later pursued a graduate degree in agriculture at Oregon State University. After graduation he worked as an environmental consultant and finished his career as the executive director of the Nature Trust of British Columbia from 1985 to 2001.

My fondest memories of Ian McTaggart-Cowan revolve around our mutual involvement with the Nature Trust of British Columbia. He was appointed to the board of directors in 1977 and continued to serve as a director emeritus until 2010. I was employed by the trust from 1984 until I retired in 2001. The board consisted of a cross-section of prominent business executives and ecologists, and their mandate was to acquire ecologically significant land in British Columbia. One of Ian's keenest interests was to secure a conservation stronghold in the south Okanagan Valley. As a result of the persistence of Ian and his compatriots on the board, Drs. Alastair McLean and Bert Brink, the Trust initiated the south Okanagan critical areas program in 1989, and this resulted in a successful partnership of government and non-government organizations to achieve this ambitious goal. One of their strongest allies in the south Okanagan program was the Habitat Conservation Fund headed by Rod Silver, and on road trips to the south Okanagan, Rod and I used to orchestrate the logistics so that we could travel with Ian and Bert. We looked forward to opening a topic as we started our journey and then listening to two of the most knowledgeable ecologists in the province explain their views. More than once, as we passed through Princeton, Ian and Bert were still discussing a topic that we had introduced in Tsawwassen.

My appreciation of Ian's unique personality increased as I had more opportunities to spend time with him. During the preparation of his contributions to the final volume of *The Birds of British Columbia*, he told me that he frequently got up before dawn so he could get a few hours of writing in before his wife got up. As she expressed more and more concern about the amount of time and energy the project was taking, Ian began setting his clock an hour earlier so he could put in more time without alarming her. When I commented that it sounded like a lot of work, he responded, "It depends on your perspective. I think it's fun."

Once on a drive to the Vancouver Airport, Ian expressed considerable interest in my car and then explained that he was shopping for a newer vehicle. The caveat was that it had to fit into his current budget because he and Joyce were setting aside ten percent of their income for their old age. At the time Ian was in his early eighties!

Early in his career, one of the many papers Ian presented was to a conference in Texas. As a token of their appreciation, the organizers gave Ian an armadillo. A *live* armadillo! A jackknife, the hotel bathtub and the plastic liners for the garbage pails were all the equipment he required to prepare the specimen to bring it back to Vancouver in his luggage. At the time of the storytelling, the specimen was on display at the Vertebrate Museum at the University of British Columbia.

Working for the trust provided me with the opportunity to meet many extraordinary people, but Ian was one of the most exceptional.

Anthony (Tony) John Erskine
B.Sc. (1952, Chemistry), Acadia University; M.A. (1955, Chemistry), Ph.D. (1957, Chemistry), Queen's University; M.A. (1960, Zoology), UBC

Tony Erskine at Scales Pond Provincial Park, PEI, summer 1992.
PHOTO BY JANET ERSKINE.

In 1991 Tony retired from a thirty-one-year career with the Canadian Wildlife Service (CWS), having served as biologist, research scientist and division chief. Between 1991 and 2006, before returning to "civilian life," he was appointed research scientist emeritus to work on projects relevant to CWS such as oversight of the *Maritime Breeding Bird Atlas*,[170] a summary of Canada goose studies in the Atlantic provinces and a review of Maritime shorebird survey data from 1974 to 1998. Tony also contributed to the selected bibliography of CWS work from 1947 to 1997 that accompanied a history written by J.A. Burnett[171] and a summary of ornithological work by CWS and preceding agencies for the period 1918 to 1999 for a Nuttall Society publication.

My contacts with the head of UBC's Department of Zoology were mainly in 1957–60, when I was completing a master of arts degree in zoology there. Dr. Cowan was in Europe when my application reached the department, so acceptance was delayed until he returned two months later. When I reached UBC in September 1957, just another new grad student, he assigned me courses and workspace, noted my need for financial assistance (he arranged a Canadian Industries Limited wildlife fellowship later) and told me to return when I had found a study topic. He was approachable, despite an imposing presence, but always busy; one booked meetings with him several days ahead. A year of "make-up" courses (my Ph.D. was in chemistry) in a new field left me time to find my way around the department.

My regular contacts with Dr. Cowan were mostly at lectures on verte- brate biology the first year and mammalogy the second. He was an impressive lecturer, holding the class's attention throughout, but not always easy for me to follow as British Columbia's geography was at first unfamiliar and because shifts between topics—without explanation—sometimes left me puzzled. In the lab his demonstration of preparing museum specimens—a mouse or small bird completed in fifteen minutes—was amazing to a beginner—even one determined to achieve that skill.

Though still less than fifty years old, Dr. Cowan was among the older faculty in zoology (except for emeriti) and was clearly a leader even among that group of strong personalities. Every month or so I touched base with him regarding my work as I wasn't then assigned to another supervisor. An anecdotal remark in my second year was his assertion that he had collected every species of owl on the British Columbia list within the city limits of North Vancouver before he was sixteen, using a homemade silencer on his gun. Documenting research with collected specimens was basic to wild- life studies in those days. Dr. Cowan also introduced various distinguished guest lecturers to the department, including Drs. Dennis Chitty (Oxford), Frank Pitelka (University of California, Berkeley) and L. von Haartmann (Finland), evidently having many international contacts after ten years with the Department of Zoology.

A year before my (anticipated) thesis completion, I applied for future employment with CWS. Several months later a notice of interviews for CWS positions reached me—in the field three hundred miles from Vancouver— after the interviews were already completed. I phoned Dr. Cowan who understood the situation—though the Civil Service Commission evidently did not—and he said he would try to arrange another interview. This finally happened several months later.

After my second field season Dr. Miklos Udvardy was named head of my thesis committee. He was surprised as he had been on sabbatical for the sixteen months since my first winter at UBC. I hardly met Dr. Cowan that third winter until my (successful) thesis defence in early March 1960. I left the campus with an impression of him as a knowledgeable scientist and an extremely able administrator. I seldom asked him for advice as I had already completed two postgraduate degrees, and I found a suitable thesis topic on my own—on cavity-nesting buffleheads—by discussion with fellow grad students. (This work was later incorporated into a monograph on the species.[172]) I knew he was available for consultation but I didn't encroach on his time needlessly. Our later meetings were brief and inconsequential.

After leaving UBC in March 1960, I joined CWS. Over the next few years I learned that about two-thirds of the scientists then in CWS had earned their first degrees, and often their masters, too, at UBC after Dr. Cowan had come to the Department of Zoology there. In that period, UBC had the only

Tony Erskine's master's thesis was on cavity-nesting buffleheads. Nearly all potential bufflehead nest-sites in trembling aspen parkland were reached with a portable ladder. PHOTO BY JIM WIGGS, WATSON LAKE, BC, MAY 17, 1958.

biology department in Canada with an explicit wildlife focus, and that originated mostly from Dr. Cowan's efforts and personality.

J. Bruce Falls
B.A. (Hons.) (1948), Ph.D. (1953, Zoology), University of Toronto

Bruce is professor emeritus in ecology and evolutionary biology at the University of Toronto. He retired in 1989 after thrity-five years teaching ecology and related subjects, conducting field research and supervising the work of thirty-six graduate students and five post-doctoral fellows. His chief research interests were bird vocalizations and related behaviour, dimorphism in the white-throated sparrow that affects plumage, breeding behaviour and ecology, and populations and behaviour of small mammals in relation to weather and food supply.

He is an author of over one hundred scientific publications in journals and books. He is a fellow of the American Ornithologists' Union, the Animal Behavior Society and the Deutsche Ornithologen-Gesellschaft. Bruce was a post-doctoral fellow at the Bureau of Animal Population in Oxford from 1953 to 1954, a visiting scientist at Commonwealth Scientific and Industrial Research Organization (Canberra) in 1964, UBC (Zoology) in 1973, Rockefeller University (New York) in 1980 and the Edward Grey Institute (Oxford) in 1981 and 1988. He is a past president of the Society of Canadian Ornithologists/Société des ornithologistes du Canada.

Bruce Falls, Toronto, circa 2010. PHOTO BY ANN FALLS.

In 1945 my last posting with the Royal Canadian Air Force was in Calgary and I was given leave, which I used to visit the West Coast for the first time. I had received the outline of a correspondence course in wildlife management based on Aldo Leopold's book *Game Management*[173] and I planned to look up the author of the course at UBC. That's when I met Ian Cowan, an enthusiastic young professor just twelve years my senior. I didn't finish the course but returned to Toronto, where I already had a year at the University of Toronto under my belt, and pursued biology. This eventually led to teaching and research in animal ecology at Toronto.

Ian knew my boss, J.R. Dymond, and both were conservation activists, so he visited us from time to time, and I renewed my acquaintance with him. In 1965 when the Conservation Foundation convened a conference on "Future Environments of North America," Ian was one of the organizers and gave a presentation that was essentially a review of wildlife management. The proceedings were published in 1966,[174] the same year that the Conservation Foundation identified Ian as one of the world's leading animal conservationists. I was impressed with him as a speaker, and when I and others initiated a teach-in on human populations, "Exploding Humanity, the Crisis of Numbers," at the University of Toronto in 1968, we invited him to speak at the closing session. He gave a seven-point outline for Canada's future, emphasizing maintenance of wild environments and calling for restraint in population growth. It was a carefully reasoned argument that was well received by the audience.

I was keen to see Ian receive the Doris Huestis Speirs Award for Outstanding Contributions in Canadian Ornithology from the Society of Canadian Ornithologists/Société des ornithologistes du Canada (SCO). I had previously nominated him for a fellowship in the American Ornithologists' Union, but because of a feeling among some fellows that he was a mammalogist and also because there was an arbitrary cut-off, I passed the material that I had gathered to the SCO and was very pleased when he was honoured at the annual meeting in Vancouver in 1998.[175] He gave a lecture entitled "Moments from the Education of an Ornithologist"[176] mentioning early ornithologists of America, especially BC, who had influenced him. Ian certainly influenced Canadian ornithologists and wildlife biologists. Some, like me, admired him from a distance.

I last saw Ian Cowan about ten years ago when we visited a friend in Victoria. We walked to his house and he took us for a tour of his beautiful garden. We had a rapid course on his large collection of cyclamens. Then we went inside and he showed us proofs of the fourth volume of *The Birds of British Columbia* that had engaged his energy for many months.[177] He was full of the subject and bursting with pride. Although aged about ninety, he was the same enthusiastic Ian that I had met over the years.

Donald (Don) R. Flook

B.S.A. (1949), University of Manitoba; M.S. (1955, Range and Wildlife Management), Utah State Agricultural College; Ph.D. (1967, Zoology), University of Alberta

Don retired in 1984 after thirty-four years with the Canadian Wildlife Service (CWS) as a biologist, research scientist and research manager. He worked as a mammalogist out of Fort Simpson, Northwest Territories, from 1951 to 1955 and as a biologist/research scientist in Edmonton from 1956 to 1969. He transferred to the New Zealand Forest Service on post-doctoral research for two years between 1969 and 1971, at which time he returned to Canada. From then until 1982 he was a research manager for the Eastern and Ontario regions of the CWS in Ottawa and the Pacific and Yukon region in Delta, BC. He completed his career as a secondment to Ottawa to seek consensus for an act to regulate export, import and interprovincial transport of wildlife.

Don, who was born in Winnipeg, had a grandfather and five uncles who hunted, a father who fished and a mother keenly interested in nature. Not knowing he could earn a living studying wildlife, he took his first degree in agriculture, but a summer job assisting Ward Stevens in his study of muskrats on the Mackenzie River Delta crystallized Don's career aspirations. Ward had begun his involvement in that project with a season on the Delta with Dr. Cowan.

Donald Flook warming at a lunchtime fire during an American marten survey, near Hislop Lake, north of Fort Rae, NWT, 1951. PHOTO BY JIM ERASMUS.

After two years at Utah State, Don obtained a job with CWS at Fort Simpson on the Mackenzie River. He spent five years there surveying American marten, beaver and moose populations and, with John Kelsall, engaging in an experimental grey wolf control project to reverse the decline in barren-ground caribou numbers. His next job was advising Parks Canada on wildlife matters in the ten national parks from Manitoba west (excluding Wood Buffalo National Park). When an opportunity for a year of university leave came up, Don spent the winter at UBC taking courses under Dr. Cowan's guidance. By 1960 when his next opportunity for educational leave came up, he had begun an elk research project in the national parks and had settled in Edmonton where Dr. William Fuller, another mentor and former CWS colleague, had joined the faculty of the University of Alberta. Bill agreed to accept Don as a graduate student. Don finished his thesis when Bill was on sabbatical, and Fred Zwickel acted as supervisor and chaired the committee. John Hayward, who served on his committee, had also been Dr. Cowan's graduate student.

In 1969 Ian visited New Zealand on sabbatical, and I was there on secondment from the Canadian Wildlife Service to the New Zealand Forest Service. We arrived about the same time and soon after attended the annual meeting of the New Zealand Ecological Society in Dunedin. News of the growing North American concern for the environment had reached New Zealand, and reporters quickly found Ian and he was quoted at length in the New Zealand press on environmental problems in general. A little later a session of papers on North American elk (known as wapiti in New Zealand) was sponsored by the New Zealand Forest Service and the New Zealand Deer Stalkers Association. It was held at the University of Canterbury in Christchurch. I was one of the speakers and there were two others—Les Batcheler of the New Zealand Forest Service and a Ph.D. candidate who was studying wapiti in Fiordland sponsored by the New Zealand Deer Stalkers' Association. There was a history of animosity between the Deer Stalkers and the Forest Service, which had a mandate under the Noxious Animal Act to exterminate all deer species, which had been introduced; the Forest Service had deer cullers in the field shooting deer as these animals were having such a profound effect on native vegetation.* The Deer Stalkers advocated management of deer, wapiti in particular, because they were prized as trophies. As an impartial international authority, Ian was asked to chair the session. As we would expect, he kept the discussion on track, and I understand that the dialogue was less acrimonious and more objective than had occurred in a long time.

---

* Commercial deer hunting by helicopter for venison export, which was in its early stages in 1969, has done what New Zealand government cullers were unsuccessful in achieving, reducing deer numbers to a level at which native vegetation has markedly improved. Capturing deer to stock deer farms and exporting both venison and antlers removed in the velvet became part of the New Zealand deer industry.

Later during his sabbatical Ian visited Australia. Sure enough, within weeks word crossed the Tasman Sea to New Zealand that right under the noses of the Aussies, Ian had re-discovered a marsupial shrew previously thought to be extirpated. That gave me a feeling of national pride!

J. Bristol Foster

B.A. (Hons.) (1954, Zoology), M.A. (1957, Zoology), University of Toronto; Ph.D. (1963, Zoology), UBC

Bristol is a retired zoologist, professor, administrator and environmentalist.

While studying mosquitoes at the Defence Research Board at Churchill, Manitoba, after university graduation in the mid-1950s, Bristol discovered a large population of the rare eastern heather vole (*Phenacomys ungava*). He returned to the University of Toronto to study the ecology of this rodent, but in 1957, after twenty years of schooling, he decided that a break seemed like a good idea. That year he set off with artist Robert Bateman to travel around the world for eighteen months visiting Africa, southeast Asia and Australia. Along the way they collected scores of mammal specimens for the Royal Ontario Museum.

With wanderlust temporarily satisfied, Bristol enrolled in a Ph.D. program at UBC with Dr. Ian McTaggart-Cowan as his supervisor. Ian suggested that he study the evolution of the unique native mammals on Haida Gwaii (Queen Charlotte Islands). Upon completing a Ph.D. in 1963, Bristol set off with his wife for Nairobi, Kenya, where he taught wildlife ecology at the University of East Africa for five years. He returned to British Columbia in 1968 to accept the position of assistant director of the British Columbia Provincial Museum. (Nobody had held this position since Ian had been assistant director at the end of the 1930s.) Subsequently Bristol became the museum's director. He left the museum in 1974 to lead the province's Ecological Reserves Program,[178] which involved travelling all over the province looking for rare, endangered or representative habitats worthy of protection for research and education. After ten years Bristol left to make television documentaries on natural history topics worldwide and lead natural history expeditions while at the same time volunteering for the boards of various environmental organizations.

Ian was Bristol's supervisor for his Ph.D. dissertation.

During his decade as the first coordinator of the British Columbia Ecological Reserves Unit, Bristol Foster—seen here at Solander Island, BC, May 5, 1976—was instrumental in establishing nearly one hundred ecological reserves to protect representative examples of BC's ecosystems. PHOTO BY R. WAYNE CAMPBELL.

When I arrived at Dr. Cowan's office in 1959 to discuss a Ph.D. topic, I told him that I wanted to work on evolutionary ecology. He recommended concentrating on the native mammals of the Queen Charlotte Islands [now called Haida Gwaii] where he had already been on field trips with Charles Guiguet collecting and analyzing specimens. Cowan joined me and my assistant (the late Mike Bigg) for a week travelling by inflatable boat (he called it a "mobile air mattress"), thoroughly enjoying himself by potting an occasional deer for dinner or cheerfully pushing a heap of dead deer mice to one side to make room for his breakfast. He felt the giant deer mice on the

Bristol Foster and Wayne Campbell (foreground) during a seabird survey on Solander Island, west of Brooks Peninsula, northwestern Vancouver Island, BC. It is a protected 7.7-hectare ecological reserve. PHOTO BY R. WAYNE CAMPBELL, MAY 6, 1976.

smaller Haida Gwaii islands were a relict population left over from earlier times. I determined that these rodents evolved *in situ* as a result of the special ecological characteristics of small islands. Ian stuck with his idea that these were just relicts, but as a significant testimony to his generosity he passed my thesis.

One day he called me into his office to review the first draft. "Bristol, you seem to have trouble with existence." I did not want to admit that I did not know what he meant; I quickly assumed all graduate students have trouble with existence most of the time. But on reading over his corrected draft, I saw that I always spelled *existence* as *existAnce*—hence, the dilemma.

Ian's low-ball wit often sneaked up on you. After a cataract operation he complained how everybody had aged (suddenly all the wrinkles showed).

While I was in Kenya, Ian came to a conference there and set aside a couple of weeks to go on a camping safari with me to Serengeti, Ngorongoro and Amboseli and visit Mount Kenya. At the latter location, we hiked up to the thirteen-thousand-foot level and looked in astonishment at the two-plus-metre-tall *Lobelia* and *Senecio*. His sharp eyes and mind deduced things in a few days that I had missed in my years in East Africa. In the Serengeti he sat safely in the Land Rover, amused, while I jacked up the vehicle from an aardvark hole with a pride of lions watching with keen interest about ten metres away.

Many years ago a famous lecturer was invited to UBC, and Ian, as head of the Department of Zoology, was to introduce him, which he did in his usual eloquent style. But as we were enjoying the stimulating lecture, I noticed that Ian's head was tilting to one side; I could see that he was asleep, and I knew he was to thank the speaker. Unfortunately, I was too far away to give him a nudge and those sitting next to him were too absorbed in the lecture to notice. Ian showed minimal signs of life now and then but generally kept his head down. I felt grateful, having shared a tent with him that he did not snore. Eventually I could see the time of reckoning was fast approaching as the lecturer was winding up his speech. During the loud clapping that ensued Ian sat upright and joined in, then he got up, summarized the talk most eloquently by picking out some of the high points, added witty observations and sat down to further applause! This was not a unique event!

In later years I would drop by for tea with Ian and Joyce and latterly took Ian out for lunch every few months. In the autumn of 2010 we drove out to Sidney to have tea with Muriel Guiguet, a long-time friend. As we drove along, he regaled me with experiences from over seventy years ago—trapping pocket mice and jumping mice in bucket traps one day in the Okanagan Valley then going out that night to mist net three kinds of bats. His distant memory was amazing and prodigious.

Mark A. Fraker
B.A. (1967), M.A. (1969), Indiana University, Bloomington

Mark is a consulting biologist and president of Terramar Environmental Research Ltd. in Sidney, BC. For more than forty years he has conducted research on marine and terrestrial wildlife in the Canadian and Alaskan Arctic and the Pacific Northwest. He has represented Canada and the United States on committees of the International Whaling Commission and has served on advisory groups to the United States National Science Foundation (Polar Programs), the United States National Academy of Sciences and the United States National Marine Fisheries Service.

Throughout much of Mark's career, Ian McTaggart-Cowan has been a mentor and role model.

Mark Fraker researching chipmunks in the Delphine Creek drainage, Purcell Mountains, BC, August 1998.
PHOTO COURTSEY OF MARK FRAKER.

When I arrived at UBC to start graduate studies in the fall of 1968, Ian McTaggart-Cowan was among the first persons I met. He took me to lunch in the rarified atmosphere of the Faculty Club, which was a particular honour for a young graduate student. Unfortunately for me, he had just assumed the position of dean of Graduate Studies, so working under his guidance was not an option. In the 1970s as I developed my research on bowhead and beluga whales, we met on several occasions—he was at that time chairman of the Canadian Committee on Whales and Whaling—and we saw each other occasionally at the biennial conferences on the biology of marine mammals and at the Victoria symphony. Even after I moved to Alaska in 1982, we kept in touch.

When my wife, Donice, and I moved from Alaska to Sidney in 1993, Joyce and Ian became our adoptive aunt and uncle. Donice preceded me by six months, and while she was here on her own, Joyce and Ian invited her to their home for supper and she joined them at the symphony. To avoid having her return late at night to her apartment on the Saanich Peninsula, they insisted that she stay overnight in their guest bedroom. In the morning they prepared her breakfast and off she went to work.

Mark Fraker (left) with Joyce and Ian McTaggart-Cowan at their cabin on Mayne Island, BC. PHOTO BY DONICE HORTON, AUGUST 22, 1998.

On one of their many visits, Donice led Joyce in re-creating a sweater that someone had knit from wool Joyce had purchased in New Zealand. As the two ladies unravelled and washed the yarn, Ian joined in by making stretcher bars around hangers to air-dry it. Then he watched with interest as they charted a sweater customized to a style and size of Joyce's choosing.

Donice and Joyce often had knitting projects to discuss, and on one occasion when they had been on the phone for quite a while, I observed to Ian that in the time the two women had been talking it had stopped raining and the sun had come out. He retorted that "when those two get to talking, whole weather systems move through!" This snappy comeback was typical of his quick wit.

Donice and I frequently visited with Joyce and Ian, and because Donice's birthday is just four days after Ian's, we celebrated the two birthdays together. Ian and I would often talk about gardening or some biological matter. In the late 1990s I was working on taxonomic and distributional problems with small mammals in the Kootenays—chipmunks, red-backed voles and pocket gophers—all of which Ian had collected and studied as early as 1929. We had several discussions about these animals, and his memory of fieldwork conducted almost seventy years earlier was clear.

Ian and I went hunting together just once; it was for fallow deer on James Island in February 2000, when he was eighty-nine. He shot a nice doe but was concerned that his rifle was not shooting exactly as it should. I took it to the range and found that the sights needed adjustment. In October just before his annual trip to Alberta to hunt white-tails, he and I went to the rifle range. He took one shot, which hit the bull's eye, and said, "That's all I need to know." A few days later he had a white-tail hanging.

Early in his career Richard Fyfe, while working in the Vertebrate Museum at UBC, got to know Ian and his father-in-law, Kenneth Racey. PHOTO BY TREVOR ROPER, FORT SASKATCHEWAN, AB, MAY 9, 2014.

Richard William Fyfe

Professional Teaching Certificate (1959), Saskatchewan Department of Education, Regina; B.A. (1961, Zoology), UBC

Richard is a retired Canadian Wildlife Service (CWS) research scientist and environmental consultant. He worked with the CWS toxic chemical unit monitoring the effects of agricultural pesticides on wildlife in western and northern Canada and in Central and South America. In 1970 under the direction of Dr. Ward Stevens he set up the CWS *anatum* peregrine recovery program at the CWS captive breeding facility and remained responsible for the program until his retirement in 1987.

Following retirement he worked fourteen years as an environmental consultant for the Alberta government and co-produced four educational videos. Recognition for his conservation and research include the J.D. Soper Award for contributions to environmental biology, the Fran and Frederick Hamerstrom International Award for significant achievement in the understanding of raptor ecology and natural history from the Raptor Research Foundation, and the Order of Canada. While in the CWS he participated in a number of national and international committees related to birds of prey and served for seven years as chairman of the Working Group on Birds of Prey for the International Union for Conservation of Nature World. He has authored or co-authored over fifty scientific papers and contributed chapters to three books related to raptor management and conservation. He was also involved in community activities and specifically with the Alberta Rural Crime Watch (ARCW). He has received recognition and several awards for his community involvement, which included local and provincial recognition from the Royal Canadian Mounted Police and ARCW, together with federal and provincial medals for community involvement.

Richard took several courses at UBC taught by Ian McTaggart-Cowan, including ornithology and wildlife management.

From the time I was a small boy, perhaps seven or eight years old, I have always been fascinated by birds, and for some reason, specifically birds of prey. This was not a "cool" thing in small town Saskatchewan, and for years I would do my birdwatching under the guise of hunting gophers (Richardson's ground squirrels) or jackrabbits. It was not until my late teens that I made contact with anyone else interested in birds. I wrote a letter to the curator of birds at the National Museum to inquire if there was anywhere I could go to university to learn about birds. He advised me that the only university in Canada where I could get courses related to wildlife was UBC where graduate degrees in wildlife management were offered under Dr. Ian McTaggart-Cowan.

After graduating from high school, I was accepted at UBC, but it wasn't until my second year that I met Dr. Cowan. I had heard that a few students worked as volunteers collecting and preparing specimens for the Department of Zoology, and I went to volunteer my services to prepare study skins. I went to a small room where an elderly gentleman was busy preparing study skins and told him that I had done some taxidermy in my teens and wondered if I could volunteer my services. He said he thought it might be possible but I would have to talk to Dr. Cowan. While I was visiting with the older gentleman (who I later found out was Dr. Cowan's father-in-law, Kenneth Racey), Dr. Cowan came into the room and suggested I contact him another time. I did, and as a result, I was able to spend some spare time doing study skins for the collection.

That changed in my third year as I contracted a parasite, apparently from some animal, and I was only able to complete half of my third-year classes. However, Dr. Cowan allowed me to remain at the university, and I spent a couple of months working alongside Mr. Racey, and to this day I remain appreciative for the opportunity to do volunteer work with him. Although I did not get to know Dr. Cowan other than as a student, I saw him frequently and will always remember him coming into the room where Mr. Racey and I were preparing skins and pointing out things and relating little anecdotes about the specimens. I always felt he enjoyed sharing his knowledge and at the same time liked the opportunity to be "hands on" with the specimens and skins.

I recall being overwhelmed by his knowledge, and I remember his personal enthusiasm about so many things I knew only through my reading.

Although it was not possible for me to return and attend graduate school, I can only hope Dr. Cowan would have been pleased with the results of my work and what I was able to contribute to wildlife conservation through toxic chemical monitoring and endangered species recovery.

Bryan Rodd Gates

B.Sc. (1964, Biology and Zoology), M.Sc. (1968, Zoology), UBC

Bryan is a retired wildlife manager, impact assessment manager and energy project director with the government of British Columbia.

After completing a B.Sc. at UBC in 1964, Bryan moved to Victoria to join the provincial Fish and Wildlife Branch, returning to Vancouver a year later as regional wildlife biologist for the southwestern Mainland. (He succeeded Ernie Taylor in that position.) Bryan's responsibilities extended from Vancouver to Manning Park, the Fraser Canyon as far as the Gang Ranch, the extreme southern Chilcotin, Mount Waddington and the southwest Mainland coast. Together with the Canadian Wildlife Service and Ducks Unlimited Canada, he successfully established several wetland and wildlife reserves in the Fraser River Valley and at the same time continued with wildlife inventory, setting harvest regulations and enhancing habitats.

Bryan took a leave of absence in 1968 to complete his M.Sc. degree at UBC, supervised jointly by Dr. Cowan and Dr. John Bandy. In 1974 he joined the newly established Secretariat to the Environment and Land Use Committee in Victoria and eventually retired, in 1997, from

Bryan Gates at the celebration of Ian McTaggart-Cowan's life, Fairmont Empress Hotel, Victoria, BC, May 4, 2010. PHOTO BY MICHAEL C.E. MCNALL.

the Environmental Assessment Branch of the British Columbia Ministry of Environment. His achievements there included chairing an intergovernmental task force that led to the establishment of the Robson Bight Ecological Reserve (the first marine reserve for killer whales), testifying for the United States Federal Power Commission on the impacts of raising the level of the Ross Reservoir near Hope and flooding more of the Skagit River Valley in British Columbia, heading a task force to draft a management plan for the Cowichan River estuary near Duncan and coordinating government agencies in mitigating the impacts of oil and gas development in northeastern British Columbia.

He is currently enjoying world travel as a tour leader and lecturer/naturalist.

Dr. Cowan was Bryan's co-supervisor for his M.Sc. thesis on food production for Columbian black-tailed deer in certain seral stages of a coast forest.

There are many former UBC students who, like me, remember leaving our English lectures early and racing across campus, hoping to be in time to find a seat in the first-year zoology lectures given by Ian McTaggart-Cowan. If you were late, you sat in the aisle. An overflow crowd squeezed in each week. Even students who were not registered for zoology heard about the teaching skills of this man and attended regularly. That was the nature of his ability to communicate and educate with facts, illustrations and a wealth of knowledge, most of it obtained through his own field explorations. But my admiration for the man had begun even before I started university, with the natural history and biology programs he presented on black-and-white television. He was a pioneer in that field, turning every topic into a fascinating adventure.

I was very fortunate to have Ian as director of my graduate studies. Years earlier he had spent time studying black-tailed deer and offered much advice. His encouragement to me and to every student was a strength that we all appreciated.

During my term as president of the Association of Professional Biologists of British Columbia I was pleased to present Ian with an honorary life membership in the association. For that occasion his faculty mate, Dr. Peter Larkin, had relayed to me an anecdote from Ian's early years at UBC. It seems that upon arrival at his office one morning, Ian received an anonymous report of a dead whale washed up on the beach somewhere below the university. It was thought to be one of the rare beaked whales. Terribly excited, Ian quickly gathered his dissecting kit, flensing knives, a saw, collection bottles, formalin, gloves, notebooks, camera and even his chest waders. He raced down to the shoreline. A long and frantic search around all of Point Grey followed, but to no avail. He decided it was because the tide had risen. He would return later as the tide ebbed. Exhausted, he arrived back at his office to be greeted by a smiling group of colleagues, one of whom was holding a calendar. The date was April 1. There was laughter all around, with Ian getting as big a kick

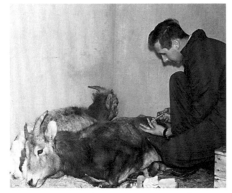

Bryan Gates administering antibiotic treatment to a ewe Rocky Mountain bighorn sheep at UBC during studies of an extensive die-off of East Kootenay bighorns in the mid-1960s.
PHOTO BY P. JOHN BANDY.

out of the prank as the others. And in truth, he probably got the upper hand because no doubt he had collected various biological gems from the beach that day, most of which are probably still in the UBC collection.

I shall never forget one piece of advice he gave me. I had just presented a graduate seminar on the population biology of the enclosed, predator-free, George Reserve deer herd in the United States. Just minutes into my talk, Ian's eyes closed and his head fell. My heart sank as I apparently had put him to sleep with ease. As I ended my technical presentation, replete with facts, figures and graphs, he sat up and immediately commented, questioned and offered suggestive criticism, all of which made it clear that he had heard and digested every word I had said. His final suggestion, however, has stuck with me throughout my career. He ended by saying: "Never get so wrapped up in the accuracy of your technical details that you forget to kick people in their emotional ass." I realized then that I had been so concerned with the minutiae of science that I probably had not hammered home the importance of predation in the control of any wildlife population. Ian's pearl of advice has guided me many times throughout my career.

Then there was the "Great Escape." The janitor of the campus elementary school arrived early one morning to find a large window smashed in. "Damn kids again," he told himself. He found a trail of blood spots in the hallway and then heard footsteps. "I'll get you this time!" Peering into an open classroom, he found himself face-to-face with the big brown eyes of a Rocky Mountain bighorn sheep—a heavy ewe. He backed off and called the RCMP, who in turn called Dr. Cowan. Ian had learned just the day before that two sheep captured for studies of a massive die-off of sheep in the East Kootenay, a study in which I had played an early part, had escaped their pens at the research barns on campus. One had been seen standing up to its belly in the waters off Spanish Banks the day before, but it had escaped back up the cliffs. With the skill and brawn of the police, the schoolroom ewe was soon cornered, hog-tied and returned to its pen. But the other one was still missing!

A day later Ian received a call from the university president. He was concerned about a strange deer-like animal on the lawn of his campus residence. Both embarrassed and perplexed, Ian called John Bandy, wildlife research manager, and suggested that the roundup be completed forthwith and that some assurance be given that a solid lock would be installed at the barns. So, off we went, John and I and others, to the president's home, dart gun and ropes in hand. (Bear in mind that these were the days of experimental wildlife immobilization techniques. Dart guns and tranquilizer drugs were still much of an unknown quantity.) We found the ewe in the backyard, but it soon retreated into thick brush on top of the steep bluffs. As expected, a well-placed dart to the rump didn't even faze the animal. We had to resort to a "surround and lunge" technique. Bruises, scratches and lacerations later (to us as well as to the ewe), we finally had the second animal back in custody. And with no harm done. In fact, the schoolroom ewe gave birth to a healthy lamb just a few weeks later. Ian would recall this incident, especially his exchange with the president, for many years to come.

Finally, Ian's most lasting gift to me began in 1990, many years after graduation. He phoned to ask if I would fill in for him as naturalist/lecturer on a coastal cruise of British Columbia and Alaska. The Smithsonian Institution had chartered the ship and the guests were eager to learn. Needless to say, I jumped at the chance and am glad that I did because I have continued to accept contracts in that same capacity for the past twenty-one years. As a student I had never really thought I would get to see much of the world, but Ian's initial 1990 request has taken me on biological quests to five continents, including Central and South America, six excursions to Africa and a most memorable month in Antarctica. I am immensely thankful to Ian for decades of science, encouragement and generosity.

Valerius Geist
B.A. (1960, Zoology), Ph.D. (1966, Zoology), UBC

Val was born 1938 in the Ukraine and emigrated in 1953 to Canada via Germany. He is professor emeritus of Environmental Science in the Faculty of Environmental Design, University of Calgary, where he was the founding program director of the environmental science program. He also served the graduate faculty as a professor and associate dean until he retired in 1995. Val had a cross appointment with biology, where he taught evolution and ecology to undergraduates in human affairs. In the new faculty Val pioneered an interdisciplinary approach to knowledge and design pertinent to humans in a modern environment. His 1978 book is dedicated to Drs. Cowan and J.B. Cragg.[179] Val continued

Valerius Geist with Rocky Mountain elk. As a respected behavioural ecologist, Val also enjoys recreational hunting. PHOTO BY RON DUBE, SOUTH OF YELLOWSTONE NATIONAL PARK, WY, SEPTEMBER 10, 2006.

with research that centered on policies in wildlife conservation and large mammal biology. He has authored seventeen books, over 120 scientific papers and book chapters, as well as hundreds of popular articles. He also participated in documentary films and contributed articles to many encyclopedias. Val is currently retired, but still active in conservation organizations including the International Union for the Conservation of Nature and the Boone and Crockett Club.

I first heard Dr. Cowan's name from the late Fred Bard, director of the Saskatchewan Museum of Natural History [now Royal Saskatchewan Museum] in Regina from 1947 to 1970. While still living in Germany, I had read a book by a German nobleman, Lothar Graf von Hoensbroech, about his hunting trip in 1939 to the Prophet River in BC where he bagged, among other animals, two great Stone's [mountain sheep] rams. These sheep tickled my interest, and they were the prelude to my first meeting with Dr. Cowan after I came to UBC in 1957 and walked into his office in the Zoology Department.

As an undergraduate I "discovered" feral goats on Saturna Island, in the BC Gulf Islands, and I eventually shot and autopsied three billies and brought the horns back to the university. I placed them in a tub of water so that the skulls might soak prior to boiling and cleaning. I forgot about them until a penetrating stench emanated from that room, and I was told in no uncertain terms to do something about it. I took the skulls, now crawling with maggots, to the basement preparation room in the old biological sciences building. Here I began boiling them but neglected to open the ventilator hood. Within half an hour the building was filled with a penetrating stench, and Dr. Ford, a professor of embryology, arrived at the door to ask me, for heaven's sake, to shut down the operation as there were complaints from every corner of the building. Well, the skulls were not yet ready so I procrastinated, and that brought Dr. Taylor, the head of botany, with a very similar message, followed by our professor of genetics, both gasping for air. Finally, there stood Dr. Cowan. He looked over the situation, opened the ventilation hood, smiled and sat down on a table, legs dangling. "Well, what are you cooking?" he asked. And we had a lovely discussion, and those goat heads and several others are still in the museum that he loved so well. I ultimately studied Stone's sheep because Tommy Walker, guide and outfitter at Coldfish Lake on the Spatsizi Plateau, implored Dr. Cowan to send somebody to study them as a first step in having that vast region declared a wildlife research park.

My tête-à-tête with Dr. Cowan over those stinky goat heads was not the only one. He took me for a visit to his museum, explaining the collection and his taxonomic work, and he also took me on a deer-hunting trip with his son, Garry, to Saturna Island. On the first day Garry shot his first black-tailed buck and got a second one the following day. Dr. Cowan was a very happy, proud father. Every morning when he woke us, the breakfast table was set as if arranged to be photographed. It was beautiful, a real psychological boost to start a fine day.

I had taken along an old, heavy, but very accurate Mossberg .22 calibre target rifle, and on the second afternoon Dr. Cowan took a sharp-shinned hawk for his collection with that rifle with one clean shot. He showed his Scottish heritage when he gleefully told us about trading in an old rifle he had bought for seventy-five dollars and used in his extensive black-tailed deer studies on Vancouver Island. He gave it on consignment to Harkley and Haywood, a wonderful gun shop on Hastings Street in Vancouver, and received $115 for it after they had taken their commission!

Dr. Cowan taught us that there are no silly questions when asked honestly. I was deeply impressed by his tact with students when he answered with a straight face and dignity questions that made others cringe. He had great patience with screwy ideas and guided discussions until they were no longer screwy. He was never afraid of novelty but eager to hear more and place these novelties into perspective.

Dr. Cowan's fine and sensitive grasp of human nature and the drama of life never failed to amaze me. My field research for my Ph.D. dissertation, during which I was literally absent from campus and family for years on end, was not all peaches and cream. And during one trying period he wrote a long letter, not to me, but to my wife. I was moved. For all his sternness and firm demeanor, he had a very astute mind and a soft, warm heart. Down deep he was a shy, sensitive man.

Harold (Hal) John Gibbard
B.A. (1956, Zoology), UBC

Hal is a retired biologist, provincial parks environmental planning supervisor and administrator, mostly for the Ontario Ministry of Natural Resources. In the provincial parks position he supervised and directed the definition of the Ontario Nature Reserve System from the late 1960s to 1976. He is married to another Cowan student, Ann Gibbard (née Heywood).

When I was persuaded to enter university, I found many of the undergrad courses to be rather boring and/or uninteresting or simply a matter of cramming facts into my head for exam purposes—the sort of facts one would look up on the web today. Then I attended lectures by Dr. Ian McTaggart-Cowan and found him interesting, even fascinating at times, and most importantly an inspiring teacher with obvious real experience beyond the ivory tower. It was then that I decided to go into wildlife management.

Several aspects of Dr. Cowan's view of biology stayed with me and were further reinforced by my own working experiences. One of these is that no one should teach at a university without first spending a significant number of years actually applying his knowledge in the field where "the rubber hits the road." The studies and field research normally associated

In retirement Hal Gibbard is a director of the Garry Oak Meadow Preservation Society. PHOTO BY ANN GIBBARD.

with a graduate degree are very limiting in scope. Perhaps going straight from university into a purely research position can be acceptable, but most employment in biology is of a more applied sort and requires a broader knowledge and set of skills to be successful. Dr. Cowan had enough experience to be convincingly knowledgeable to students, other professionals and the general public. He had an ability to communicate well that proved invaluable not only to himself as a good teacher but also as an example for students in environmental management because most problems are really "people problems." If you can see the biological/environmental problem and have scientifically proven it, the solution can almost always be found through changing a human behaviour. Many scientists do not communicate well with the general public, and the more they specialize or become "experts" the less they seem able to connect with the very public whose understandings, biases and beliefs must be changed for the sake of the environmental component that needs attention. The late Yorke Edwards was the only other person who significantly influenced my early professional years.

If you list the students that Dr. Cowan has mentored and plot their distribution throughout the world along with their accomplishments, it would be impressive indeed. His longevity has been a huge benefit to the world.

Douglas Gordon
B.Sc. (1963, Zoology), M.Sc. (1966, Marine Ecology and Oceanography), UBC;
Ph.D. (1970, Fisheries Management and Economics), University of Idaho, Moscow

Doug has more than five decades of experience throughout Canada and the United States with a specialty in fisheries involving interdisciplinary problem solving related to land and natural resource management and development, environmental protection planning and Native issues. His career encompassed positions ranging from research assistant with the Institute of Fisheries at UBC, assistant professor at the University of Idaho and senior consultant with F.F. Slaney & Co. Ltd. He is currently president of Armstrong Resource Management Consultants Ltd.

Douglas Gordon with Chinook salmon caught while conducting fisheries research for the Nisga'a Wylp Syoon fishing lodge in Portland Inlet, 55 km north of Prince Rupert, BC. PHOTO BY KEN BEKCA, CIRCA 1996.

I met Garry Ian McTaggart-Cowan, Ian's son, in the early 1960s when we were both enrolled in Zoology 105 taught by Ian. We became good friends, taking many of the same courses, and both of us became lab instructors during undergraduate and graduate school. We also participated in several field-research initiatives together.

Both Garry and I had a well-developed sense of humour and shared pranks and practical jokes. For example, after Ian became dean of Graduate Studies, he had a pass-key that let him into virtually any facility within the university. Through a process unknown, Garry somehow came into possession of a copy of this key, and this enabled us to access the fisheries museum where a large quantity of 95% ethanol alcohol was stored. Subsequently we developed a recipe for "fisheries punch." Ian also allowed Garry to use the family's Point Grey residence to brew our own beer. Then, with his permission, we expanded into making sake, and this led to our experimenting, with a blind eye from Ian, to "spiking" the sake with the basic ingredient for our punch, ethanol from the fisheries lab.

Then came the day that Dr. Cowan and Norman Wilimovsky, Garry's supervisor in the Institute of Fisheries, agreed that the department needed a research vessel that could be shared. Norman purchased a twenty-eight-foot vessel, which we informally christened the *Big Daddy*, and Ian decided that the boat would be used for a three-week field trip to Vancouver Island. On the trip to relocate the boat to Sidney on the Island, Garry was at the wheel when it hit a deadhead that damaged the outboard motor. He had the dubious pleasure of informing his father. After repairs were made, the boat was returned to Horseshoe Bay.

Early one morning I was walking along the lower hallway of the biological sciences building when I heard bellows from down the hall. It was Ian shouting at me, "Doug! Doug! The @#$&%^ boat has sunk! Do something!" It turned out that, when it had been brought back from the Island, it had been tied at a very exposed part of the dock at Horseshoe Bay where it was subject to strong winds and waves. Unfortunately, since the rear deck had not yet been caulked, its self-bailing design had made it a self-sinker.

Shortly thereafter there was an informal rechristening; by consensus the *Big Daddy* became the *Benthos*, which means bottom dweller. When we informed Ian, we actually saw a slight smile on his face. Several times thereafter the boat lived up to its new name.

Garry was best man at my wedding. The last time I saw him and his father was on July 23, 1994, when they visited our place on Salt Spring Island with Ian's wife, Joyce, and Garry's second wife, Judi. At the time Garry was battling throat cancer; he passed away two and a half years later.

Peter R. Grant
B.A. (Hons.) (1960), Cambridge University, UK; Ph.D. (1964, Zoology), UBC

Together with his wife, Rosemary, whom he met at UBC while a graduate student, Peter has worked on the Galápagos Islands for thirty-eight years studying the ecology and evolution of Darwin's finches. Peter and Rosemary have been recognized for their joint work with several awards: they are fellows of the Royal Society of Canada and Royal Society of London, and they have received the Darwin medal of the Royal Society of London, the Darwin-Wallace medal of the Linnaean Society of London, the International Balzan Prize and the Kyoto Prize. They have authored or co-authored over two hundred scientific articles and written or edited five books. Peter is professor emeritus of zoology at Princeton University, New Jersey.

Peter Grant with a young blue-footed booby. PHOTO BY ROSEMARY GRANT, TRES MARIETAS ISLANDS OFF MEXICO, AUGUST 23, 1962.

Dr. Cowan was Peter's supervisor for the last year of his Ph.D. dissertation on the insular variation of birds on small uninhabited islands off the west coast of Mexico.

Ian McTaggart-Cowan, more than anyone, was responsible for my shift across the Atlantic. I first "met" him on TV. I watched a program in which he stood on Vancouver's gravelly shore and explained some of the fascinations of marine biology. I was impressed. Later while I was working for a downtown Vancouver parking corporation as a summer student, I paid him a visit at UBC on my day off. He was courteous, informative, enthusiastic and encouraging, so when I returned to Britain for my final undergraduate year, I applied for graduate work in his department, and it was his letter (actually a telegram) that told me I had been accepted.

I took two graduate-level courses from him, mammalogy and wildlife management, both of them broadening my horizons. I remember his lectures as being extremely clear, delivered enthusiastically in a forthright style. His enjoyment of the material and boyish enthusiasm were infectious. Then he interceded in my research at two critical points. The first arose when I was searching for a thesis topic and not progressing. One day out of the blue he asked if I would like to study the birds of the Tres Marías Islands off the coast of western Mexico, and without hesitation I said yes. It was an impetuous decision, but a good one. (I have not encouraged my students to follow this route to a Ph.D.!) It turned out that Peter Larkin and Ian had accompanied H.R. MacMillan (of MacMillan, Bloedel and Powell River Limited) to western Mexico to help with identification of the big fish MacMillan caught from his luxury yacht (really a liner!). After two or three such trips Peter and Ian managed to persuade H.R. to support a graduate student's research on the poorly known bird fauna of these scarcely disturbed islands, and I was the lucky beneficiary.

Ian played another critical role by bailing me out of difficulties when my money ran out in Mexico and my supervisor was off somewhere else. This was in the days before email and cell phones. After fieldwork was finished, he helped to steer me through the final year of my Ph.D. studies while my supervisor was away. We wrote one paper together, a faunistic account of the birds of the Tres Marías Islands.[180] Ian laid the foundations with his collection of specimens, to which I added with follow-up studies. And then finally Ian made a crucial phone call that led to a post-doctoral year for me at Yale. I have much to be grateful for from this generous man.

Even at the advanced age of almost one hundred, I can imagine Ian to have been constitutionally almost as vigorous as he was twenty-odd years ago when, on board a tourist boat at Darwin Bay, Genovesa Island (Galápagos), he chatted away with undiminished enthusiasm about all he had seen that day, far from his beloved British Columbia.

Ian McTaggart-Cowan (left) and Charlie Guiguet on a mountain on Vancouver Island, BC, August 29, 1950. PHOTO BY JAMES F. BENDELL.

Muriel Guiguet with Ian McTaggart-Cowan at the Oak Bay Marina restaurant, Oak Bay, BC, August 21, 2008. PHOTO BY J. BRISTOL FOSTER.

Charles Joseph Guiguet
B.A. (1948, Zoology), M.A. (1950, Zoology), UBC

Charles, born September 2, 1915, passed away on March 27, 1999, at the age of eighty-three. The following account was written by his wife, Muriel, and their son, Mark.

Charles was curator of the Birds and Mammals Division at the British Columbia Provincial Museum (now Royal British Columbia Museum) from 1948 to 1980. Early in his career he worked without staff to pioneer the study of birds and mammals in the province while adding significantly to the museum's collections. He published many articles on the higher vertebrates of British Columbia as well as ten museum handbooks in a series titled *The Birds of British Columbia*. He co-authored *The Mammals of British Columbia*[181] with Ian McTaggart-Cowan, and it remained the standard reference for four decades. Like Ian, he encouraged many young people to pursue their interests in natural history and consequently fully supported Wayne Campbell in leading the province's first survey of marine-nesting birds around Vancouver Island and other initiatives.

Dr. Cowan was Charlie's supervisor for an M.A. degree on the ecology of terrestrial mammals on Goose Island,[182] an isolated archipelago off the central coast of British Columbia.

Ian McTaggart-Cowan and Charles Guiguet met in 1945 when Charles and I [his wife] were living in Vancouver and Charles was an undergraduate student in biology at UBC. Ian knew that Charles had been working for Dr. R.M. Anderson of the National Museum of Canada, and he sponsored Charles when he moved to the coast to complete his master's degree. During this time Ian and Charles worked on a number of projects together, one of which was a field-collecting trip to the Queen Charlotte Islands. This was the era of the "scientific collector" and it was an accepted practice to obtain as many specimens as deemed necessary in whatever manner possible. One summer evening Ian, Charles and I were sitting on the veranda of the Queen Charlotte Hotel enjoying the sunset with some of the locals when Ian noticed bats flying close by. With little fanfare Ian and Charles got their shotguns and "dust shot," sauntered to the middle of the street and collected a number of specimens. The locals were intrigued by these fellows who wanted to shoot bats, and UBC's collection was enhanced.

Ian and Charles's professional relationship and friendship grew as they collaborated on new projects, one of which was co-authoring *The Mammals of British Columbia*.

After Charles graduated from UBC with a master of arts degree, he became curator of birds and mammals at the Provincial Museum in Victoria. Ian often stayed with us when he was in town, and he and Charles, of course, went fishing. I laughed the day Ian, who was six feet four inches tall, had to borrow some fishing clothes from Charles, who was five feet seven inches tall. The clothes were a little tight and a little short but nevertheless off they went and enjoyed each other's company as they fished in Oak Bay in the "clinker."

Charles held Ian in the highest regard professionally and enjoyed his friendship. He respected his knowledge and ability in the field, but most importantly, he admired his talent and willingness to share wisdom with students and colleagues.

D. Raymond Halladay

B.S.A. (1965, Agriculture) and M.S.A. (1968, Agriculture), UBC

Ray is a registered professional biologist and the senior environmental scientist with Halladay Environmental Consultants Ltd. He began his professional career as the survey and enforcement biologist with the Canadian Wildlife Service working in Winnipeg in 1968 and 1969. Between 1970 and 1990 he served as the bird management specialist, chief of wildlife, deputy director and, briefly, acting director of the British Columbia Fish and Wildlife Branch. In 1990 he became director of wildlife in the British Columbia Ministry of Environment. He began consulting in 1998.

Ray directed the development of several programs that helped modernize wildlife conservation and management in British Columbia. He worked with others to secure critical habitats through partnerships involving provincial and federal government agencies, local governments, landowners and non-government organizations. Those efforts resulted in successful habitat and land stewardship programs delivered through British Columbia's Pacific Estuary Conservation Program and the Pacific Coast Joint Venture, the latter covering coastal British Columbia, Washington, Oregon and northern California. Ray is a past member of the Wildlife Society, a member of the Association of Professional Biologists of British Columbia and a member of several volunteer groups that work toward the protection and restoration of wetland habitats in the Okanagan Valley. Ian McTaggart-Cowan fostered in Ray recognition of the value of good science, the significance of habitat in sustaining all life, the importance of public support and the need for individual effort to achieve those goals.

The Creston Valley was classified as a wetland of international significance on February 21, 1994. The formal announcement of the establishment of a RAMSAR site here was made at a ceremony involving Ray Halladay (right) and Ian McTaggart-Cowan on September 25, 1993 at the wildlife interpretation centre, Creston, BC.
PHOTO BY R. WAYNE CAMPBELL.

I was an undergraduate student working toward a degree involving biological and agricultural sciences through the Faculty of Agriculture at UBC when I first became aware of Dr. Ian McTaggart-Cowan. Fellow students told me that he was the most interesting and stimulating lecturer in the field of biology. Attending his classes was a must. Unfortunately, I didn't get a chance to join any of his over-subscribed courses until I was working on a second degree. That course was a fourth-year wildlife management class.

A memorable aspect of Dr. Cowan's approach to teaching the seminar class was his habit of appearing to fall asleep during many of the student presentations. The breadth of his knowledge and his uncanny ability to rise

Ray Halladay during his master's thesis research on the bird-hazard problems at the Vancouver International Airport on Sea Island, BC, July 1966.

Alton Harestad on a BC ferry near the old Namu cannery (in background), September 13, 2010. Alton and his wife Kristie had visited family in Bella Coola and were on their way to Fitz Hugh Sound where Alton had worked as a deckhand forty-three years earlier. PHOTO BY KRISTIE STEWART.

from his seeming slumber and involve the presenter fully in question and discussion sessions after each presentation kept every student on his toes. It instilled in me a motivation to know the subject of all seminars well and, in particular, to prepare for my own seminar presentation as fully as possible.

As a student, field biologist, wildlife administrator and consulting biologist I have admired the monumental body of work Dr. McTaggart-Cowan has contributed in the field of biology in British Columbia and internationally, and I still consult and refer to some of those works. I admire his innovative efforts to educate the public about biology and wildlife; I believe he was one of the first to use television for that purpose. I admire, too, his unbridled enthusiasm as a volunteer mentor and leader of a group of publishing scientists and of funding bodies supporting environmental education and research, habitat securement and habitat restoration.

Most of all, I am thankful to Dr. McTaggart-Cowan for instilling in me the desire to seek knowledge and to become a biologist myself.

Alton S. Harestad
B.Sc. (1971, Zoology), M.Sc. (1973, Zoology), Ph.D. (1979, Forestry), UBC

Alton is professor emeritus in the Department of Biological Sciences at Simon Fraser University in Burnaby where he taught courses in vertebrate biology, wildlife biology and environmental science from 1981 to 2009. He was also curator of mammals and herpetology at the British Columbia Provincial Museum in Victoria in 1980 and 1981.

As a registered professional biologist in British Columbia, Alton continues to contribute to conservation and management of wildlife and their habitats through research and as a member of scientific and management committees. Ian McTaggart-Cowan was a member of Alton's M.Sc. thesis committee, taught a graduate course in wildlife management that Alton attended, and over the years encouraged Alton's study and love of mammalogy.

In the early spring of 1975 I was in the Nimpkish Valley doing fieldwork for my Ph.D. project on Columbian black-tailed deer. Along a spur at the end of a logging road on Mount Cain I noticed a raven a little way into the logging slash. When I investigated, I discovered a "wolf" carcass, so I skinned it carefully and took the skull. Back at my lab in Woss logging camp, I removed the flesh and boiled the skull, being mindful not to overcook my prize and weaken the bone. I noted a bullet hole through the skull but it didn't do much damage; the wolf was still a good find.

On my next trip back to UBC, I went to the zoology museum intent on proudly showing Dr. Ian McTaggart-Cowan my "wolf." Delighted with my treasure, I knocked, opened the door and took a step or two into the museum. Dr. Cowan was standing near the desk across the room. "Dr. Cowan, I have a wolf skull I would like you to look at," and I held it up for him to see. Ian looked across the room. "It's a dog, not a wolf." Deflated by his decisiveness, I stood still near the door and asked, "How do you know?" Ian replied, "The face is too narrow and the carnassial teeth are too small." I brought the skull over to him, and he proceeded to point out that wolves have a small orbital angle, large carnassial teeth and inflated auditory bullae. As well, with a twinkle in his eye, he revealed two other pieces of evidence he could see when he had the skull in hand: "The teeth have plaque on them. That's from dog meal. Wolves don't have plaque," and, "Look at the angle of the bullet hole through the skull. It's almost straight down. A wolf would never be shot at this angle." Two things I learned from this teaching moment: as a person, always scrub your teeth, and as a scientist, always look at the evidence—all the evidence.

Frederick (Fred) Eugene Harper

B.Sc. (1963, Zoology), M.Sc. (1969, Plant Science), UBC, Faculty of Agriculture

Fred Harper holding a ring-billed gull chick on Christmas Island, Shuswap Lake, BC, June 24, 1993. PHOTO BY R. WAYNE CAMPBELL.

Fred worked as a district agrologist for the British Columbia Department of Agriculture from 1963 through 1966. After earning his M.Sc. degree in 1969 he was employed as regional wildlife biologist for the British Columbia Fish and Wildlife Branch until 1999 when he retired. He spent nineteen of those years in the Peace River region in Fort St. John, three years in the Okanagan in Penticton, and the final eleven years in the southern interior in Kamloops. He worked on many species of wildlife but primarily on managing public use of game animals and on the conservation of all wildlife and their habitats. He was the first biologist in British Columbia to quantitatively equate grizzly bear densities to various habitat classes.

Ian McTaggart-Cowan inspired my education and my working life more than any other person. From the very first lecture in Zoology 105 through my association with him in graduate school, he was an inspiration. Later during my working life we often met on matters related to a Habitat Conservation Trust Fund project or a Nature Trust of British Columbia project. Again, I was inspired by his insight, his knowledge and his advice.

One particularly memorable event was a meeting of my graduate student committee at my thesis study area in the Ashnola River drainage in southern BC. We had spent the day reviewing my research work and had returned to camp for supper. When it was ready, Dr. Cowan was nowhere in sight, so I went to look for him. I found him sitting on a rock about a half kilometre from camp, overlooking a basin frequently occupied with California bighorn sheep. I suggested we return for supper, but he suggested we just sit and talk for a while. I don't recall what we talked about, but I do remember that it was an enjoyable and philosophical discussion and very inspiring. It was that same evening after we returned to camp and were having a group discussion about my thesis topic that he appeared to fall asleep. Then with no warning, he joined into the conversation, asking some very relevant questions about

Fred Harper at a vegetation plot for research on bighorn sheep/livestock competition on Juniper Slope, Ashnola River, BC, September 1975.
PHOTO BY DENNIS A. DEMARCHI.

Gordon Hartman in the Vanderhoof community hall giving a lecture on salmon in the Nechako River and the implications of the Kemano completion project, May 26, 1990.
PHOTO BY RICHARD TARNOFF.

topics mentioned when I had thought he was sleeping. I learned later that he was renowned for this ability to totally relax, while his brain was still at one hundred percent attention.

Another memorable occasion occurred one day in the early 1980s on a field trip at the south end of Charlie Lake when Ian stated that he had seen a rare songbird at that location back in the 1940s. He asked me if I had ever seen one, and I had to admit that I did not even know what it was, never mind seen one. He then told me: "All you Fish and Game Branch biologists are the same. All you ever think about is game animals. You should broaden your outlook." Well, I did, and I am thankful for it. Again his insight and inspiration was contagious. He was an extraordinarily inspirational person, and I feel very privileged to have known him.

Gordon Frederick Hartman
B.A. (1954, Zoology), M.A. (1956, Zoology), Ph.D. (1964, Zoology), UBC

Gordon Hartman had a varied career in biology working as a fisheries research biologist with the British Columbia government, a professor of zoology at the University of Guelph and a director of wildlife in the Yukon Territory. In his last formal employment he was a scientist with the federal Department of Fisheries and Oceans (DFO) and coordinator of the Carnation Creek watershed project on Vancouver Island.

After retirement from the DFO he completed foreign aid work in Africa on three projects. In 1975–76 he carried out a fisheries baseline study and impact evaluation for the Food and Agriculture Organization of the United Nations for a proposed pulp mill on Lake Malawi. In 1987–88 he managed the completion of a Canadian International Development Agency–funded fisheries education program at Addis Ababa University in Ethiopia. In his third African project (1998–99), he served as project administrator on a World Bank–funded fisheries research and training project at Senga Bay on Lake Malawi. In other post-retirement work Gordon carried out contract studies evaluating fish habitat improvement programs and examining industrial impacts on fish and their habitats.

He has published about ninety-five papers. Most are primary, but many are technical reports for public use on resource management issues. In 1990 he and Charles Scrivener co-authored a DFO bulletin integrating the first seventeen years of results from the Carnation Creek Project, a multi-agency fish and forestry research program.[183] In 2004 he and Tom Northcote wrote parts and edited all of a multi-authored book, *Fishes & Forestry: Worldwide Watershed Interactions and Management.*[184] Gordon is a keen birder and a long-standing member of the Nanaimo Field Naturalists. He lives with his wife, Helen, in Nanaimo, BC.

During the time that I spent at UBC, Dr. Cowan served as professor of zoology, head of the Zoology Department and dean of Graduate Studies.

I had the good fortune to be first an undergraduate and later a graduate student (M.A. and Ph.D.) during his tenure. Because I was in a fisheries program rather than in wildlife, I may have had less contact with him than the many wildlife students to whom he taught courses or provided direction in graduate work. However, to the extent that I was involved as a student in an undergraduate course and a candidate in a graduate program, he was a strong, ever-fair and stimulating teacher. I took Zoology 306 (biology of BC vertebrates) from him. It was one of the most interesting courses that I took at UBC. Indeed, many of us in that course did not like to hear the bell ending the lecture.

Dr. Cowan sat on the graduate committee for both my M.A. and Ph.D. programs. During a committee meeting for my Ph.D., an invertebrate zoology professor very aggressively criticized my experimental work on the competitive interaction of juvenile steelhead and coho salmon. His comments were that I had "inadequate experimental control, not a well-planned research program, and would not really allow one to understand the relationships in the wild." There was, in fact, considerable control in the experiments, at least as much as was possible with the situation. In any case, the criticism went on for a while with little comment from the committee, and I began to fear a major setback in my thesis program. Then Dr. Cowan intervened. He stated that there was valuable and meaningful research on wild animals though much of it did not involve fully controlled conditions. Then he added, "In fact, I cannot imagine doing work on lions and holding them in a glass dome with controlled temperature, humidity, etc." That was the end of criticism of that type. The thesis was completed and two primary publications and one management report came out of it.

Gordon Hartman recording fish-fence data at Loon Creek, BC, during work on Dr. C.C. Lindsey's trout migration study in the summer of 1953. PHOTO BY IRA "ZEKE" WITHLER.

Not all recollections are serious or academic. Three of us—Dick Krejsa, Jack Gee and I—once failed Dr. Cowan. He and a CBC camera team were out on the Chilliwack River filming for his television show *Web of Life*. They set up the cameras to film the three of us collecting fish—fisheries fieldwork. Unfortunately, the water was deep and the current swift where we were to do the sampling. Even so, we put our big seine net into the river to collect fish. As the cameras rolled, the current tore the net away pulling Dick and me into the current where we stumbled over the rocks and eventually crawled back to shore. After a few more sampling episodes with similar results at this "heavy-water" site, Dr. Cowan's team packed up and left. This matter did not come up in any committee meeting, and the film crew told us that Dr. Cowan would not be using the film. However, it was used at the CBC Christmas party!

The last time I saw Dr. Cowan, about four years ago (1996), I told him that even after all these years I still appreciated his Zoology 306 course. I suggested that with a lapse of close to fifty years, such comments could no longer sound like "looking for a good mark." He smiled. "Yes, it would be a little late for that now, wouldn't it?"

I have good memories and great respect for Dr. Cowan. He stood on the top of the mountain.

David Francis Hatler

B.Sc. (1964, Wildlife Management), M.Sc. (1967, Wildlife Management), University of Alaska; Ph.D. (1976, Zoology), UBC

David is a practicing wildlife biologist with more than thirty-five years of working experience in British Columbia with both government and industry. His government experience includes five years as the province's first regional wildlife biologist in the Skeena region, subsequent involvement on provincial wildlife management committees, and preparation of numerous management strategies, guidelines, plans, technical reviews and wildlife inventory standards. He is currently on the board of directors of the Habitat Conservation Trust Foundation.

Since 1980 he has been the proprietor of a small consulting firm, Wildeor Wildlife Research & Consulting, which has undertaken a long list of wildlife and habitat impact assessment projects and provided mitigation, reclamation and management advice to clients in mining, forestry, hydro and transportation development, back country recreation and trapper education.

He is the lead author of the trapper education manuals currently in use in British Columbia and Alberta and of the recent Royal British Columbia Museum handbook, *Carnivores of British Columbia*,[185] which was dedicated to Ian McTaggart-Cowan, "an extraordinary naturalist, remarkable biologist, wonderful human being, and as good a mentor as anyone could hope for."

Dr. Cowan supervised Dave's Ph.D. dissertation on coastal American mink.

David Hatler filleting a freshly caught lingcod during his Ph.D. research at Tofino, BC, August 28, 1970. PHOTO BY R. WAYNE CAMPBELL.

I'm sure that many of the contributors to this collection of Cowan-related reminiscences will refer to the hugeness of his presence wherever he appeared, his ability to take charge of situations (usually gently) and his gifted understanding of human nature. He recognized that his graduate students were humans first and biologists second. Although he was my leader and mentor for sure, in the eight years I worked under his direction I never felt that I was less than his colleague and friend. Indeed, taking friendship to a higher level, in my case he was also a confidante when that was needed. With those important thoughts transmitted, I will turn to descriptions of three incidents that reflect these qualities.

The first occurred early one fall morning when I was driving off the UBC campus to go hunting. The tall, athletic figure that suddenly loomed up in the headlights turned out to be Ian, then dean of the Faculty of Graduate Studies and by then in his sixties, jogging up Chancellor Boulevard. Although the longevity advice he passed on at the celebration for his ninetieth birthday was to "choose your parents carefully," my observation that day suggests that there was more than just genetics involved.

The second incident involved a difference of opinion, the only one I can remember, and it proved to be a defining moment for me. A conclusion he had reached in consultation on a pending development in a national park was contrary to one I had reached (mostly through youthful idealism), and I questioned him on it. His response did not resonate with me at the time, but came back to me front and centre when I began working in the "real world," and it has been a guiding principle for me throughout my career: "I was asked for my professional opinion, *not* my personal opinion."

And finally there was the time he came to visit me at my graduate study field camp off the west coast of Vancouver Island. After a day in the field, where he impressed me with his keen ear for birds and encyclopedic knowledge of intertidal fauna and flora, we retired to my cabin at a long-abandoned First Nations village site. I had renovated the cabin from a mere shell, and although it was adequate for my purposes (for example, it now had a wall-to-wall roof), it was, shall we say, Spartan. Consistent with that ambiance and my graduate-student status, the meal I began preparing was decidedly not gourmet. Stirring things in the pan, I asked, "How do you like your Spam?" He responded quickly, "Rare . . . and by that I mean not very often."

James (Jim) Hatter
B.A. (1945, Zoology), UBC; Ph.D. (1952, Zoology), Washington State University

James, born on September 23, 1921, passed away on May 19, 2012, at the age of ninety-one.

Jim was the first chief game biologist (1952) hired by the BC Game Commission. He served as the BC Fish and Wildlife Branch's director from 1963 to 1976 and retired in 1979 as wildlife policy advisor to the deputy minister of the BC Ministry of Environment. In retirement, Jim,

James Hatter at the time of his appointment as first director of the British Columbia Fish and Wildlife Branch, Victoria. IMAGE I-25971 COURTESY OF ROYAL BRITISH COLUMBIA MUSEUM, BRITISH COLUMBIA ARCHIVES.

who was married for sixty-one years to Olive, enjoyed travelling with his wife, maintaining his traplines, teaching trapping courses and guiding hunters on the private land portion of Sidney Island. Throughout his career and in retirement he was a strong advocate and teacher of wildlife management in the province. He was a serious hunter, trapper and angler as well as a naturalist. He continued to learn and care about wildlife, the ethics of hunting and the politics of wildlife management until his passing. In his last years he also became an avid gardener and enjoyed going to the opera.

He registered with the Association of Professional Biologists in 2000.

Jim authored two books, *Politically Incorrect*[186] and *Wolves and People*.[187] *Politically Incorrect* includes a list of most of his publications, papers and speeches. Copies are in the collections of the British Columbia Archives. In 2011, with the encouragement of Valerius Geist, Jim self-published his Ph.D. dissertation entitled *Early History and Management of the Moose in Central British Columbia*.

Dr. Cowan was Jim's supervisor for his B.A. (Hons.) thesis and an M.A. thesis that was elevated to a Ph.D. dissertation (at Washington State University) on moose in central British Columbia.

I first met Ian McTaggart-Cowan in 1937 when I was sixteen. He was visiting Dr. Clifford Carl who was the manager of the Lake Cowichan fish hatchery. On his next visit he invited me to accompany him to the Bald Mountain Game Reserve where he was studying the depletion of winter deer browse. I was soon aware that he was an enthusiastic bird and mammal collector. He added much to the British Columbia Provincial Museum's vertebrate collection years before he became a curator.

James Hatter with his party's bag of Canada geese, hunting from a wheelchair at Michell's Farm on the Saanich Peninsula, Vancouver Island, on one of his last hunts, September 17, 2011. Days before his ninety-first birthday, Jim shot three geese with only two rounds. PHOTO BY TERRY VENABLES.

When Cowan learned of my own interest in collecting the occasional less common species, he recommended me for a migratory bird–collecting permit. This was opposed by Jim Munro, the federal migratory bird officer, who felt I was too young. Nevertheless, Dr. Cowan pursued it and I apparently became the youngest person in British Columbia—and possibly in Canada—to have such a permit. In 1941 the collection I had accumulated since 1938 went to the Provincial Museum. It included the specimen of a mountain cottontail from Anarchist Mountain in the southern Okanagan Valley, which was the first record for British Columbia.[188]

In 1943 Dr. Cowan signed a contract with the National Parks Service to carry out game surveys in the Rocky Mountain National Parks, and at the end of my third year at UBC I was fortunate to be hired as his assistant. It was a most welcome change from having to work in a logging camp to earn money for university. It would now be possible for me to get material for a B.A. thesis. Cowan suggested that I should study the food habits of coyotes in Jasper National Park for an undergraduate thesis, for which I collected several coyotes and hundreds of scats.

In my graduating year I was motivated by Dr. Cowan's course on game management, based on *Game Management* by Aldo Leopold,[189] who was considered the founder of scientific game management in North America. Dr. Cowan suggested that an ecological study of the expanding moose population in central British Columbia would meet the requirements for a Ph.D. He was able to obtain funding from the British Columbia Game Commission for fieldwork to begin in the spring of 1946 as well as funds for me to attend Washington State University for a Ph.D. degree in vertebrate zoology. Needless to say, my interest and work in wildlife management, leading up to becoming director of the British Columbia Fish and Wildlife Branch from 1963 to 1976, was mainly due to the early stimulus of Ian McTaggart-Cowan.

Douglas C. Heard

B.Sc. (1973), University of Waterloo; M.Sc. (1978, Zoology), UBC

After graduating with his M.Sc. degree in 1978, Doug worked as the caribou and wolf biologist for the government of the Northwest Territories. In 1992 he moved to Prince George where he worked as a regional wildlife biologist with the provincial government of British Columbia and as adjunct professor in the Ecosystem Science and Management Program at the University of Northern British Columbia. His professional interests focus on how predation on ungulates affects both their behaviour and population dynamics, especially as it applies to sustained yield hunting.

Douglas Heard moose hunting at minus 30°C near the Missinka River, east of Prince George, BC. PHOTO BY MIKE GILLINGHAM, DECEMBER 2007.

Cowan was interested in all aspects of wildlife biology. When he heard that a Nanaimo deer hunter, Ted Barsby, had noticed a Vancouver Island marmot colony at Haley Lake in the autumn of 1972, he realized that the "discovery" presented an opportunity for study. Other than the few weights and lengths

Douglas Heard, the first graduate student to study the Vancouver Island marmot, with a captured marmot at Haley Lake in the Nanaimo River watershed on Vancouver Island, BC, 1974. PHOTO BY DEREK MELTON.

Daryll Hebert with a sockeye salmon on the Babine River, BC, August 2005. PHOTO BY MATTHEW BURR.

that he had published in his mammal book with Charles J. Guiguet,[190] little was known about the endemic mammal, and Ian had long been interested in them. In the spring of 1973 he accepted me as a graduate student and offered me the opportunity to learn more about those marmots. He placed no constraints on what specific aspects of their biology to research, and he fully supported my proposal to study their sociobiology. He simply wanted to learn more about Vancouver Island marmots.

Cowan remarked when I graduated and was about to leave for work with the government of the Northwest Territories that a lot of his students had graduated and gone on to work as government biologists. Many got frustrated with the bureaucracy and eventually gave up and left, but the ones he worried about most were those that gave up and stayed. He probably told this to all of his students.

Daryll M. Hebert
B.Sc. (1965, Zoology/Agriculture), M.Sc. (1967, Zoology/Agriculture), Ph.D. (1971, Zoology/Agriculture), UBC

Daryll is a retired wildlife biologist, having worked with National Parks Canada, Alberta Fish and Wildlife Branch, British Columbia Fish and Wildlife Branch and Alberta Pacific Forest Industries before becoming president of Encompass Strategic Resources Inc.

Dr. Cowan was Daryll's supervisor for his M.Sc. on mountain goats and a Ph.D. on bighorn sheep.

For me, it's been a great fifty-five-year association with Dr. Cowan. In 1955–56 (grade 8), although I didn't really know who Dr. Ian McTaggart-Cowan was, I used to rush home after school on Wednesdays to watch his marine biology program on television. Thus began my training as a wildlife biologist. Subsequently I wrote for his advice regarding courses at UBC. He responded with a full outline. In 1965 I began my M.Sc. program with him as advisor and left for the field in April. I was actually receiving scholarship money and field support to be in the mountains. In June, Gladys, his trusted secretary, phoned to see where I was. She said, "Dr. Cowan likes to hear from his students at least once over the summer." I thought, *Once?* I can handle that. We're going to get along great.

On a sunny July morning in 1966 we were hiking at Paradise Mine in the East Kootenay. While taking a breather in the sunny alpine, Dr. Cowan pointed out a rocky ledge where he had collected a least chipmunk in 1944,[191] a year after I was born.

At a Nature Trust board meeting following my brain surgery, he pointed out that my anesthesiologist was probably his grandson. It's a small world. A few years later I received the Ian McTaggart-Cowan award for proficiency in biology from the Association of Professional Biologists of British Columbia. I couldn't think of a better way to end my career.

Dr. Cowan had an influence on my life for a long time and I couldn't have asked for a better mentor. Throughout my professional career, I followed his lead of finding the best people and giving them the most responsibility. It's worked every time. He has made a magnificent contribution to wildlife biology, education and all the people associated with it.

Manfred Ernst Gustav Hoefs

B.Sc. (1967, Zoology), M.Sc. (1968, Zoology), University of Manitoba; Ph.D. (1975, Zoology), UBC

After graduation, Manfred worked for a year with the Canadian Wildlife Service on a contract for an inventory of the mammals and birds of the newly established Kluane National Park and Reserve, Yukon Territory. After that, he was employed by the Yukon Territorial Government and worked for almost thirty years in capacities ranging from sheep/goat biologist and chief biologist to assistant director, and lastly as head of habitat and species at risk. He interrupted his work in the Yukon to spend a year at the University of Giessen and the government wildlife research station at Bonn in Germany. Since retirement, he has been writing a book and continuing with some contract work.

Dr. Cowan was Manfred's supervisor for his Ph.D. dissertation on ecological investigations of Dall's sheep in Kluane National Park and Reserve.

I started working on my Ph.D. dissertation in 1969 and finally finished it in 1975. I had completed the fieldwork by 1973 but decided to accept a job offer, which delayed completion by at least a year. The reason for starting to work before finishing the degree was financial as I had been a student continuously for more than six years by then, subsisting primarily on student loans and the odd scholarship.

Manfred Hoefs combined botany and zoology on his ecological study of Dall's sheep. Mount Wallace, Kluane National Park, YT, summer 1971.
PHOTO COURTESY OF MANFRED E.G. HOEFS.

I did not have much personal contact with Dr. Cowan, which I have deeply regretted, since I had a very high opinion of him even before I got to UBC. The reason for the lack of contact was the remote location of my study area at Kluane Lake in the Yukon, which at the time—with the Alaska Highway just a gravel road—amounted to a five-to-six-day journey by car from Vancouver. I therefore never returned to UBC until my fieldwork was completed. Also important was that Dr. Cowan went on sabbatical while I was his student. If I remember correctly, he went to Australia or New Zealand and while there, developed medical problems and had to be hospitalized. In any event, I saw him only once during my studies when he came to the Yukon for a three-day visit.

As already mentioned, I held him in high regard because he was always helpful and supportive, and that support started when I applied to him to accept me as a Ph.D. student. I wanted to get into wildlife work, but two potential supervisors at other universities had turned me down, their reason being that my master's thesis was a plant ecological study and they recommended that I should continue with botany. With Dr. Cowan a compromise was worked out because my thesis project had a strong botanical/range-science component where my botanical background could be put to good use. He was also very helpful in securing the substantial financial resources needed for a study in such a remote location; it also included two winters in the field. He also arranged logistical support from the Yukon Game Branch and hired summer students to assist me.

His support and generosity became very apparent when my fieldwork was completed and I returned to UBC to return my equipment and discuss the preparation of my thesis while I was working in the Yukon. I had been given a university pickup truck for my study, and I did not look after it as well as I should have since the nearest repair shop was 160 miles away. In addition, four helpers had also used that vehicle over the three-year period. In any event, I drove the truck onto the ferry in Haines, Alaska, to be shipped down to Vancouver since I was driving my own vehicle back to Vancouver. When I arrived a few days later, I was informed that the vehicle was a wreck, so I expected the worst when I went to my meeting with Dr. Cowan the next day. I had dreams of being presented with a bill for a motor-rebuild or something of that nature, and I had no idea where that money would come from.

Dr. Cowan and I had a very long session the next day about the organization and write-up of my thesis, how to access library help, and a how to obtain copies of scientific publications and other items required to complete the thesis since I would be living and working in Whitehorse, Yukon. At the very end of the meeting, the truck issue came up, and Cowan said something like: "Don't worry about the truck. It has served its purpose since you got your thesis done with it. Nothing else matters."

Maurice Hornocker

B.Sc. (1960), M.Sc. (1962), University of Montana, Missoula; Ph.D. (1968, Zoology), UBC

Maurice started studying mountain lions (cougars) in the central Idaho wilderness in 1964, and since that time he, his students and colleagues have studied the solitary feline in environments throughout western North America. During his career Maurice has also researched numerous species of carnivores, including groundbreaking research on wolverines, though he is best known for his work with wild cats. These include the mountain lion,[192] bobcat, Canada lynx and ocelot in North America, jaguars in Central and South America, leopards in Africa and Asia, and tigers in India and far eastern Russia.[193]

He was the leader of the Cooperative Wildlife Research Unit at the University of Idaho, Moscow, from 1968 to 1985, where he mentored forty graduate students. In 1985 he founded the Hornocker Wildlife Institute and was its director until 2000, when it was merged with the Wildlife Conservation Society (WCS). Maurice was a senior conservationist at WCS until his retirement in 2006. He is widely published in both scientific and popular literature, and his wildlife photographs have been published throughout the world. In 2006 he founded the Selway Institute, a non-profit research and education foundation where he currently serves as director.

Dr. Cowan was Maurice's supervisor for his Ph.D. on mountain lion predation on mule deer and elk in Idaho.

Maurice Hornocker during joint American-Russian Siberian tiger project, Gayvoron, Eastern Russia, 1998. PHOTO BY MARC MORITSCH.

Dr. Cowan's reputation was well established when I entered undergraduate school in the mid-1950s. He was already a living legend to those of us who, as students, aspired to a career in field biology, so I was overjoyed when several years later he enthusiastically accepted me as a doctoral candidate at UBC. This was doubly rewarding because others had discouraged me from undertaking my proposed rigorous mountain lion field project for my doctoral dissertation. He invited me to come to Vancouver in advance of the academic school year to discuss the UBC program. I have never forgotten our first meeting. He was totally positive and enthusiastic about my thesis project and pledged his support at all levels.

Then, after discussing my research and academic schedule, Dr. Cowan announced that we must go directly to a lecture because a prominent professor from eastern Canada was on campus and, according to Dr. Cowan, might have something useful to say. We entered the rapidly filling lecture room, and Dr. Cowan made directly to the front row seats. Shortly after the speaker began, I noted Dr. Cowan's head canted forward. He had fallen asleep! He nodded occasionally but actually napped throughout the talk. Imagine my surprise and amazement when the speaker ended his lecture and Dr. Cowan sprang wide awake and asked the first and very pertinent question that got right to the heart of the speaker's message. He had heard and processed every word!

Maurice Hornocker, who conducted the first major research on cougar in North America, holding a cougar kitten during the study. PHOTO BY GARY KOEHLER, BIG CREEK, IDAHO PRIMITIVE AREA, 1967.

I was to learn later that this was standard procedure for Dr. Cowan, truly one of the most amazing people I've ever known, a true renaissance man in every sense of the word. His contributions are timeless and his influence on our understanding of the natural world will last forever. His infectious enthusiasm carried through to the conclusion of my tenure at UBC and beyond, and that support helped me through some difficult times. I feel so fortunate to have known and worked with him; he played a key role in shaping my career and my life.

Rodger A. Hunter

B.Sc. (Hons.) (1973), M.Sc. (1976), Faculty of Biological Sciences, Brock University; M.P.A. (1988), University of Victoria

Rodger worked for the British Columbia government for over twenty-seven years. He started as an inventory/habitat biologist and coastal specialist with the Ministry of Environment (MOE) then moved to the Treasury Board. He finished his career back at the MOE as an assistant deputy minister. For several years he did a weekly interview series called the "Animal of the Week" on CBC Radio. Rodger received both the Shikar Safari Club International's British Columbia Conservation Officer of the Year Award and the British Columbia Naturalist Award.

Rodger Hunter at his home in the Koksilah Valley south of Duncan, BC, January 22, 2013. PHOTO BY DENNIS A. DEMARCHI.

I worked with the Habitat Conservation Fund (HCF) (now the Habitat Conservation Trust Foundation) while Ian was chair of the board. I had first heard of him when I was a student of the late A.W.F. (Frank) Banfield at Brock University. It was clear in the lecture hall that Frank greatly admired Ian but also regarded him as somewhat of a competitor. Ian, I later learned, regarded Frank as a rather unusual fellow who knew an enormous amount. The one thing they had in common was their love of sophisticated and corny puns. Ian in particular savoured the impact of a pun on his audiences, large or small.

Ian possessed an amazingly active and inquiring mind, and when he was interested in something, that interest ran deep. The HCF flourished as a result. When I started with HCF in 1986, it was already well established under the guidance of Ian and vice chair Dr. Bert Brink, but Ian wasn't satisfied. We are just getting started, he said. We need to create a more transparent and constructive review process. We need to be more accountable. We need to raise our profile. So with Ian's determination and support we went to work on a game plan.

Ian was always there for you. He had a "noblesse oblige" attitude, and it was displayed at its finest when he was in the field. If you were lucky enough to be with him on a field trip, it quickly became evident that not only was he a masterful biologist, but he was there to make natural history come alive for those around him. In fact, the combination of Ian and Bert Brink on an HCF board field trip was like being immersed in an encyclopedia of natural history. And being exposed to Ian's comfortable charisma in the field—his outdoor classroom—instantly transformed new board members into passionate advo-cates of the HCF.

I left HCF in 1988 and was succeeded as head of biology and evalua-tion by Maureen Wayne* who continued working toward the organization's vision for many years. Maureen and Ian had a special relationship. Like Ian, she loved natural history, attended to detail and was committed to HCF. She was also a redhead and as Ian once told me, "I don't exactly know what it is, but I have had very good fortune with redheads." Maureen died of cancer in 2000 at forty-eight years old. I remember how difficult it was, but I spoke at her tribute and several days later Ian called to say, "That was wonderfully done. I am sure that Maureen would be extremely proud. Let's get together for lunch." And I felt myself being lifted from depression. That was Ian.

Ronald (Ron) D. Jakimchuk
B.A. (1962, Zoology), UBC

Ron was the regional coordinator of the Canada Land Inventory for wildlife within the Canadian Wildlife Service from 1964 to 1967. He co-founded Renewable Resources Consulting Services Ltd. (RRCS), working first as a consulting biologist in the company and then as pres-ident from 1967 to 2008. The company maintained offices in Sidney, BC, and Edmonton and for several years in Fairbanks and Anchorage, Alaska. In the late 1960s he developed an experimental lure crop program in Alberta to mitigate damage to grain crops by waterfowl. That program became operational and continues to this date. In 1972 Ron became a founding member and first president of the Alberta Society of Professional Biologists.

After returning to British Columbia in 1977, he joined the Association of Professional Biologists of British Columbia and subsequently served a term as chair of the ethics and discipline committee. For thirty-six years Ron was an active researcher on barren-ground caribou in Yukon Territory, Alaska, Northwest Territories and Ungava and on woodland caribou in British Columbia and mountain caribou in Alberta. RRCS conducted pioneering experimental field studies of disturbance to caribou and birds in northern Canada and Alaska, and carried out studies of a wide range of other Arctic species.

Ron has been a technical advisor on wildlife to several federal envi-ronmental assessment panels and a witness before numerous tribunals, including the Berger Inquiry on the Mackenzie Valley Pipeline. In a 1976 paper to the Alaska Science Conference, he proposed the need for an international management structure for the Porcupine caribou herd, which stimulated discussions that eventually led to an international treaty and joint management protocol for the herd.[194] He has authored thirty

Ron Jakimchuk on a survey of marsh-nesting birds near Tunkwa Lake, BC.
PHOTO BY R. WAYNE CAMPBELL, JUNE 2012.

---

* Maureen Wayne's biography is featured on the HCTF website (www.hctf.ca)

publications, nineteen of which were peer reviewed, and authored or co-authored over 150 reports.

I first entered Dr. Cowan's office in 1958, my first year in the zoology program, at the callow age of 17. The details of that meeting are vague, but I remember feeling very privileged to meet the head of the Department of Zoology whom I had known from his enthralling television series in the mid-1950s.

Around 1962 I asked him to speak to the UBC Rod and Gun Club, which had thirty or forty members at the time. Such was the renown of his speaking skills that the noon-hour talk attracted an overflow audience to the lecture hall in the biological sciences building. This crowd was many times the size of the gun club membership, which was somewhat surprising since the topic concerned big game hunting and a talk on antlers and horns. Dr. Cowan's talk was illustrated with some impressive specimens from the zoology museum. Later he generously gave us the beautiful mounted head of a California bighorn sheep, and it became a mascot in our campus club room.

After graduating, I enrolled in the Faculty of Education for a brief period in 1963, but by mid-October, I decided to return to zoology. With his characteristic generosity, Dr. Cowan enrolled me as a graduate student despite it being six weeks into the term. He placed me in a graduate students' office with Fred Zwickel and Val Geist—and that was another education in itself! In the following decades I crossed paths with Dr. Cowan on numerous occasions and in various locations including conferences, symposia, meetings associated with boards of which he was a member, hearings (the Berger Inquiry hearings and federal environmental assessment panels), and as a result of our common interests in gardening. My contacts with him increased after 1995 as I sang in a chamber choir with his daughter Ann for many years, and Ian attended our choir and orchestral concerts.

Over the years Dr. Cowan made frequent use of the word "fascinating" in conversations about the natural world. His fascination continued over a lifetime in his diverse areas of interest, as reflected in his publications and hobbies. He also shared these fascinations with an infectious enthusiasm and a ready smile to a host of students, associates and the public. Especially interesting were his stories of his early days and adventures with Jimmy Simpson, who was obviously a favourite companion and mentor on many aspects of wrangling and backcountry travel in the national parks of Alberta.

I never formally studied under Dr. Cowan at UBC but was always inspired by him—a sort of academic osmosis. His monumental legacy is not only described in this book, but resides in all that were touched by his leadership, formidable talent and contributions in so many fields.

With fond respect and appreciation.

Stephen R. Johnson

B.Sc. (1966, Game Management), Humboldt State College; M.Sc. (1968, Biology), Kansas State University; Ph.D. (1972, Zoology), UBC

Steve retired in 2009 after a career spanning thirty-five years as a wildlife consultant with LGL Limited. He served as senior vice-president of the company for many years and was instrumental in directing the company's Canadian, American and Russian operations. His project work involved designing and conducting wildlife inventory and monitoring programs in areas of proposed resource development in Arctic and subarctic regions of Alaska, Canada, Greenland, Norway and Russia. Between 1975 and 1994 his job included the initiation of long-term marine and coastal waterfowl mitigation and monitoring programs in the Alaskan and Canadian Beaufort Sea in conjunction with nearshore resource development. After 1995 he helped design protection plans and mitigation and monitoring programs for wildlife in the Beaufort Sea region,[195] in East Siberia and the Okhotsk Sea regions of the Russian Far East. He co-authored two books and wrote over fifty peer-reviewed scientific papers and over one hundred unpublished reports.

Dr. Cowan was Steve's doctoral supervisor for research on thermal adaptation in two introduced species in the family Sturnidae: European starling and crested myna.

Steve Johnson during a trip to Santiago, Chile, 2007. PHOTO BY JEAN JOHNSON.

My tenure at UBC was from 1967 through 1972, though my strongest memories of Ian and Joyce Cowan during that period are not so much related to academics or science but more to the personal exchanges that we had. I remember cheerful gatherings at the Cowan household in Point Grey, usually to celebrate the achievements of Ian's students. I especially remember the evening visits and containers of hot soup brought to me when I was conducting all-night experiments at the old UBC vivarium. But the most cherished memories I have of Ian and Joyce was their commitment and dedication to family—both their own and those of Ian's graduate students and especially to me and my family.

In 1973 after finishing a post-doctoral fellowship at the University of Alaska and before heading off to New Zealand for a two-year teaching stint, I returned to Vancouver after a particularly difficult domestic complication in Alaska. With sole responsibility for two pre-school children, I felt pretty isolated and very discouraged about life in general. Ian learned of my situation and graciously came to my assistance. He kindly offered interim financial support and office space while I reworked my thesis for publication. It was during my regular visits to his office with various drafts of manuscripts that I learned that he and Joyce had taken on some rather significant family responsibilities of their own. Several days each week during the spring and summer of 1973, Ian packed up his briefcase (at the time he was dean of Graduate Studies of the entire University of British Columbia), left his office around noon and walked home to take the afternoon shift of babysitting

Steve Johnson, during fieldwork on St. Lawrence Island, Alaska, summer 1970. PHOTO BY STEPHEN R. JOHNSON.

their two very young grandchildren. As I eventually learned, a complication in the life of one of their own children had put Ian and Joyce in a situation similar to my own. I was greatly impressed and deeply moved that this couple would have taken on the enormous added responsibilities and commitment and rearranged their complicated work and private lives to provide the necessary support for their family.

My own life was greatly enriched by the kindness and understanding of Ian and Joyce Cowan, and the experience of 1973 gave me a much greater appreciation of the depth of good character and level of family commitment of these two excellent people. Ian's accomplishments were great, both professionally and personally, and I'm proud to have been associated with him.

Pat Johnston moved permanently, with her late husband Gerard van Tets, to Australia in 1963. PHOTO BY JANET BRADLY, CANBERRA A.C.T., AUSTRALIA, JUNE 14, 2009.

Patricia (Pat) Anne Johnston

B.Sc. (Hons.) (1961, Zoology), M.Sc. (1964, Zoology), UBC; Advanced Certificate in Public Administration, 1996, Canberra, Australia

Pat was born in Vancouver and lived in the downtown area until 1961. Then she and her mother moved to a tiny house on 10th Avenue where she lived until she married Gerard Frederick (Jerry) van Tets (Ph.D. 1963, UBC); they moved to Australia in 1963. In Australia she worked at the Australian National University, leaving after two years to raise a family of two daughters, Janet and Kit, and a son, Ian. She worked in the Australian Public Service and enjoyed being a volunteer lifeline counsellor and palliative care visitor for many years. Her interest in science has continued throughout her life. Jerry died in 1995 and Pat is now retired.

Dr. Cowan was Patricia's supervisor for her B.Sc. (Hons.) thesis and her M.Sc. thesis on the electrophoresis of blood proteins in deer.

In 1957 I entered UBC from King George High School in downtown Vancouver. My original plan was to become a physician, but it didn't take many science prerequisites to change my mind and remain in the Department of Zoology. Ian was a very busy man with many responsibilities, but he always found time for me. Although I came from a disadvantaged background, he never put me down but constantly encouraged me and enthusiastically expanded my vision of science and the world. Over the years a friendship developed, and I felt very honoured when he agreed to give me away at my wedding to Jerry van Tets in 1963. Although Jerry and I moved to Australia after our marriage, we continued to correspond with Ian, and he and his beloved wife, Joyce, visited us in Australia on two occasions. He also very kindly agreed to be a godfather to our son, Ian, who is named after him. My son, who is also a biologist, enjoyed visiting Ian in his home on Vancouver Island in 2008 and was pleasantly surprised by how healthy and active Ian was for a man of his age. They spent a pleasant hour exchanging stories and walking in Ian's garden. Ian was very special to me and my family, and his influence continues.

Lindsay E. Jones

B.Sc. (1978, Biology), University of Victoria

Lindsay worked for fifteen years with non-profit conservation groups including Ducks Unlimited Canada and the Nature Trust of British Columbia prior to joining the British Columbia government in 1994. Since then, he has been involved in the resolution of many controversial land use issues along the British Columbia coast. This work has included implementation of the sustainable ecosystem management recommendations of the scientific panel for sustainable forest practices in Clayoquot Sound and the development of the ecosystem-based management recommendations and conclusions of the central and north coast land and resource management plans as well as those for Haida Gwaii. As a result of these experiences, he has successfully developed further agreements and protocols involving land and resource shared decision-making with many First Nations on the coast.

Lindsay Jones, Departure Bay, Vancouver Island, BC. PHOTO BY F. WOLTERSON, MARCH 2014.

It must have been in 1975 or 1976 when one day it was announced to the biology students at the University of Victoria that Dr. Ian McTaggart-Cowan would provide a lecture on Friday afternoon. Many of us knew of him and his work, either through his British Columbia Provincial Museum publications or his role as the dean of Graduate Studies at UBC. I recall that many were not that impressed that the lecture was scheduled for 4:30 or 5:00 p.m. on a Friday, well past the time when all conscientious biology students had given up their studies in favour of cold beer at the campus pub.

A couple of us decided to drop in on the talk as it was on the way to the Student Union pub anyway, and I was amazed to find the lecture hall in the Elliott Building almost full. We managed to find seats, and for the next hour and a half we were mesmerized by Dr. Cowan's ability to fascinate us all with his observations on the research that he had either participated in or supervised over a good portion of his career. I particularly remember his observations on the hierarchy of individual members of a wolf pack according to how high the tail was held, and his comments on grizzly bears hunting ground squirrels "like swatting mosquitoes with a sledge hammer." Despite the draw of traditional pursuits on a Friday evening, not one person left the hall until both the lecture and the question period were completed.

I am sure that this is but one small example of Dr. Cowan's ability to engage and inspire all who came in contact with him through his many years of public life. In the early part of my career I benefited from many conversations with him on field trips and at conservation meetings, but probably more important to me is the legacy he created through his association with other biologists. Tom Sterling, Don Benn, Glen Smith and Dennis Demarchi were all students or associates of Dr. Cowan who went on to develop their own distinguished careers in British Columbia and who have served as my mentors throughout my working life.

Chuck Jonkel, co-founder and president of the Great Bear Foundation in the office in Missoula, Montana, circa 1993. PHOTO COURTESY OF CHARLES J. JONKEL.

Charles (Chuck) J. Jonkel

B.Sc. (1957), M.Sc. (1959), University of Montana, Missoula; Ph.D. (1967, Zoology), UBC

Chuck began bear research in 1959, the first year that dart guns were readily available. Three other studies were started that same year by Frank and John Craighead, Art Pearson and Doug Pierson; Jonkel is the last of this group still working on bears fifty-one years later. He has studied black, brown (grizzly) and polar bears and has taught and advised graduate students for many years at the University of Montana.

Chuck Jonkel worked for the Canadian Wildlife Service from 1966 to 1974. He developed the Canadian position on polar bears under the International Union for the Conservation of Nature (IUCN), established European, South American and Asian bear working groups for the IUCN and was the first president of the International Association of Bear Biologists. He also created the International Wildlife Film Festival in 1978, the first-ever, largest and longest-running festival of its type worldwide. He was a co-founder of the Great Bear Foundation and has continually advocated for more honest, educational wildlife films, programs and classes. He has been a persistent critic of mass-media exploitation of wildlife. He conducts school and field classes for thousands of children and adults annually in "the Cowan Way," and he works to promote Native American/First Nations values relative to bears.

Dr. Cowan supervised Chuck Jonkel's Ph.D. dissertation on black bear ecology in Montana.

> Dr. Cowan was a walking inspiration whether in the city, mountains, ocean or wilderness. From the dense forests of Montana/British Columbia, I found my association with Ian and my work on American black bears very rewarding. He enabled my future research on bears and he saw me through tough times at UBC. Because of Dr. Cowan, Montana continued funding my bear project so I put my spruce grouse and moose interests on hold.
>
> I have been ever grateful to Dr. Cowan for the inspiration and effort he brought to building the zoology/wildlife programs at UBC and building UBC itself. It was Dr. Cowan who found and brought excellent faculty from across Canada and the world to UBC. He was the chief architect of lab science, field science and the Ph.D. program there. He was incredible at gathering financial support for the university from industry, the British Columbia outback, all of Canada, the United States and Europe. He was as much at home in a logging camp or on a fishing boat as he was in a Vancouver boardroom or the premier's office. In my view, it was Dr. Cowan who put UBC "on the map." For a decade or more the university had the finest wildlife program anywhere on earth because of him.
>
> Dr. Cowan inspired the following question and answer that was overheard in my Zoology 416 lab at UBC in 1965:
>
> **Q:** Bittern thoughts of this cuckoo lab creeper cross my mind. What is

Willet lower taxes? *Cervus* in any way? This creative gem, written by graduate student Chuck Jonkel, was inspired by Dr. Cowan. Willet (l) and Rocky Mountain elk (r). PHOTOS BY R. WAYNE CAMPBELL.

the porpoise of owl this *D*ama skink? Willet lower taxes? *Cervus* in any way? Guano *montanus* and *Lemmuus* alone!

    A: Chiropt, you *Sorex*! The scaup of this course is to make all buffle-heads and *Bubos* into genus. The *Buteo* this is you. Willet knot tern into rat finches or get scent to the nuthatch by your Family. So, you *Mus* gull the whet from the chat. *Pica* veery good *Anser*, and work like beavers in Order to become *keeni Canadensis*. If otter fallows *Canis* grasp the *princeps*, you canid too.

Deborah (Deb) Kennedy

B.Com. (1976), UBC, Faculty of Commerce and Business Administration

Deb is the development and communications manager for the Nature Trust of British Columbia. With a diversified background in marketing, administration and fundraising, she has enjoyed contributing to the successful operation of a national household paper company and a Vancouver newspaper, along with volunteering for a number of business and non-profit organizations.

Deborah Kennedy at The Nature Trust of British Columbia Burgoyne Bay Acquisition Celebration on Salt Spring Island, BC. PHOTO COURTESY OF JEN MACLELLAN, *GULF ISLANDS DRIFTWOOD* NEWSPAPER, JULY 29, 2012.

Meeting Ian McTaggart-Cowan for the first time was one of those moments when I realized that I was in the presence of someone very special. I had heard so much about him as a senior board member of the Nature Trust of British Columbia, a man who was highly revered for a lifetime of accomplishments. For a relative newcomer to the organization and one with very little science background, I was intimidated. However, the experience was truly inspirational. In this meeting he talked about population dynamics. A conservationist at heart but a realist, he had my attention. With eyes twinkling, he spoke candidly about the point where a species population is too low to survive; no matter how passionate the cause, he was clear that there is a time to say it is over and move on to a situation where you can make a difference. He made me think, and I came to understand that this was Ian the scientist, the educator and the communicator in action. He was thoughtful and incredibly perceptive. His clarity was inspiring.

I also had the pleasure of listening to Ian speak on camera about his experiences outdoors. Here he shared one of those pearls of wisdom profound in its simplicity: "If you spend part of your life alone in the wild, you are changed." He had recognized early in his life the importance of connecting with nature, and it became the foundation for his incredible career and contribution to our world.

Ian was one of the Nature Trust's original life members appointed by the Prime Minister in 1977, and he worked hard to establish the reputation and the conservation legacy that the Trust enjoys today. From conservation accomplishments on the Adams River, now part of the Roderick Haig-Brown Provincial Park, to the magnificent Hoodoos in the Rockies, we owe much of the Nature Trust's success as a leading land conservation organization to his scientific expertise, critical thinking and vision of conservation.

Getting to know Ian was a privilege, one that I will treasure forever.

Ian McTaggart-Cowan, Heather Lemieux (standing) and Winifred Kessler at a British Columbia Habitat Conservation Trust Foundation meeting, Victoria, BC, circa 2006.
PHOTO BY BRIAN SPRINGINOTIC.

Winifred (Wini) B. Kessler
B.A. (1972, Zoology), M.Sc. (Range Management, 1973), University of California, Berkeley; Ph.D. (1978, Range Science), Texas A&M University

Wini retired in 2010 after a thirty-five-year career in wildlife ecology and natural resources management. About half of those years were in faculty positions at the University of Idaho (Moscow), Utah State University (Logan) and the University of Northern British Columbia (Prince George), where she was the founding chair of the forestry program. Her remaining years were in positions with the United States Forest Service, including national wildlife ecologist and most recently as director for the Alaska region. Wini's awards include Texas A&M University Outstanding Alumnus Award (2004), the Wildlife Society Special Service Recognition Award (1999), British Columbia Academic of the Year (1997), University of Idaho Alumni Award for Excellence in Undergraduate Instruction (1982, 1983) and Outstanding Advisor Award (1982). She has been a certified wildlife biologist since 1979 and was named a fellow of the Wildlife Society in 2009.

In retirement, Wini continues an active record of volunteer service in the conservation arena. She has served fifteen years on the board of directors for the British Columbia Habitat Conservation Trust Foundation (HCTF), including two terms as chair, and she has been active in the Wildlife Society throughout her career. She became a professional member of the Boone and Crockett Club in 1993 and has managed their conservation research grants program for most years since then.

When I think of Ian McTaggart-Cowan, what comes to mind is a man in motion. I see a tall, distinguished gentleman in a herringbone blazer and running shoes with a spring in his step and a keen eye for anything of interest around him. The word "spry" best conveys my impression of this extraordinary person that I came to know through our shared membership on the board of the HCTF, never mind that he was well into his eighties at the time of our first meeting. There was no mistaking the boundless energy, sharpness of mind and keen wit that were Ian's special trademarks.

Of course, I had known about Ian McTaggart-Cowan for decades by virtue of my career choice in wildlife ecology. His work was prominent in ecology textbooks, wildlife classes and anything to do with the taxonomic relationships of deer. One of the great pioneers in wildlife ecology, his name had assumed legendary status well before I enrolled in my first zoology class at Berkeley. It was beyond imagining that thirty years later I would have the opportunity to work alongside him in a successful conservation program that in so many ways bears his personal and professional stamp.

The HCTF did not originate with Ian, but his initial and sustained leadership largely accounts for the program's history of success. The mission of the HCTF has always been to invest in projects that maintain and enhance the health and biological diversity of British Columbia's fish, wildlife and habitats so that people can use, enjoy and benefit from these resources. When Dr. Ian McTaggart-Cowan was asked to chair the board, he graciously agreed, and his leadership continued for nineteen years.

In the late 1990s the BC Wildlife Federation appointed me to a seat on the HCTF public advisory board. As my first meeting approached, an enormous box of proposals was delivered to me. Opening it, I momentarily balked at the huge job ahead, reviewing more than three hundred proposals in the scarce time afforded by evenings and weekends. But then I saw the cover letter from the board chair, Dr. Ian McTaggart-Cowan, and experienced an instant change of attitude. This would be a privilege, not a burden! I was privileged to serve with Ian for the years up to his retirement from the board, and special years they were indeed. At each spring meeting he would lead us through discussion of each and every one of those proposals. No matter what the subject, from bighorn sheep to dragonflies to white sturgeon to kids on mudflats, Ian had a keen interest in what was being proposed and who aimed to do it. Even more amazing was the knowledge, usually based on personal experience that he contributed to those diverse discussions. Sometimes he would pull a pertinent research finding from memory, complete with the author, journal title and volume, year of publication and—incredibly—sometimes even the page numbers! Other times he would begin with, "I remember when I made the first sighting of that species back in 1938, the day after we camped on that ledge in a thunderstorm . . ." and we'd again be regaled by his sharp memory and extraordinary grasp of BC's natural history. At the end of his long term as chair he reflected on what BC's hunters, anglers, trappers and guide-outfitters had enabled through the fund. In his words, "Truly no other group in society has demonstrated such dedication to the preservation of wild places and wild creatures of our land." Clearly he felt very good about this program that he had a major hand in shaping.

It was a pleasure and a privilege to serve with Ian on the HCTF board and an even bigger (and daunting) privilege to follow him as chair. I'm extremely grateful to have worked with him and for the opportunity to help carry on a part of his amazing conservation legacy.

David R. Klein
B.Sc. (1951, Wildlife Management), University of Connecticut; M.Sc. (1953, Wildlife Biology), University of Alaska; Ph.D. (1963, Zoology), UBC

Dave is professor emeritus at the University of Alaska in Fairbanks. He was leader of the Alaska Cooperative Wildlife Research Unit from 1962 to 1986 and senior scientist with the Alaska Cooperative Fish and Wildlife Research Unit until his retirement in 1997. His interests are broadly ecological with primary focus on plant-animal relationships at high latitudes and the associated consequences of climate change. He was lead author for a chapter in the 2005 Arctic Climate Impact Assessment (ACIA), *Management and Conservation of Wildlife in a Changing Arctic Environment,*[196] and received the 1999 Wildlife Society Aldo Leopold Award.

Dave was a Fulbright Scholar during 1971 and 1972 at the University of Oslo, Norway, where he lectured on wildlife ecology and environmental philosophy and did research on wild reindeer ecology. Also in 1972 and subsequent years, through his European Fulbright affiliation and the United States AID program, he provided advice on management of the newly established Peneda-Gerês National Park in northern Portugal and on wildlife conservation and fire management throughout Portugal. Dave's subsequent long history of research and associated educational activities on wildlife ecology, the environmental influences of climate change and northern development have been of an international nature and have included work in Canada, Greenland, Norway, Sweden, Finland, Iceland, Denmark, Russia, Portugal and South Africa.

Dr. Cowan supervised Dave's Ph.D. dissertation on how deer respond physiologically to variation in the quality of different ranges.

Ian McTaggart-Cowan was well known through his wildlife publications by many of us in Alaska involved in wildlife investigations and management in the 1950s when Alaska was still a territory. Then a deer biologist based in Petersburg, southeast Alaska, I received a letter from Ian requesting live Sitka deer fawns for the initiation of his study with A.J. Wood of the comparative growth of the three subspecies of the coastal black-tailed deer. Deer population levels were high around Petersburg at that time and several so-called "orphaned" fawns that were picked up by well-meaning but uninformed locals had been turned in to me, the lone deer biologist in all of southeast Alaska at the time. My wife, Arlayne, willingly took on the task of bottle-feeding them, but she had the forethought to ask what we would ultimately do with our increasing number of homeless fawns. Ian's letter offered what seemed an ideal solution to the problem, though the obstacles to getting the fawns, still

Dave Klein on a winter ecology ski tour, Fairbanks, Alaska, March 2010. PHOTO BY NED ROSELL.

Dave Klein on archaeological cave reconnaissance in March 2012 in the White Mountains National Recreation Area, AK. PHOTO BY WILLIAM WALTERS.

only a few days old, from Alaska to Canada seemed overwhelming. Ian dealt with the necessary permitting. Arlayne and I obtained cardboard cartons from a local grocer, one for each fawn, and, in lieu of diapering them, we provided lots of absorptive material in each carton to minimize leakage while the fawns were in transit. Two flights in floatplanes were required before the fawns could be transferred to a larger plane for the flight from Annette Island to Seattle. Ian or his assistants had to drive to Seattle to meet each shipment, but all of the Sitka fawns survived the rigorous international travel and thrived on the high-quality diet they enjoyed during their participation in Ian's nutrition and growth studies of coastal black-tailed deer. My contact and experience with Ian, via the Sitka black-tailed deer fawns, provided a strong impetus for my decision to take educational leave when Alaska achieved statehood in 1959 to move with my young family to Vancouver and enter the Ph.D. program at UBC with Ian as my major advisor.

I was not alone among Alaskan wildlife biologists who sought Ian's guidance as a graduate advisor and mentor during this period of Alaska's transition to statehood. Among this group was Jim Brooks who guided development of the new Alaska Department of Fish and Game and later served as its commissioner. Francis (Bud) Fay's research on the Pacific walrus resulted in the classic monograph in the North American Fauna Series[197] that answered basic questions upon which an international system regulating harvest of Pacific walrus could be based. Robert F. Scott, who did graduate studies at UBC under Ian, rose to be director of the United States National Wildlife Refuge System and went on to work for wildlife conservation in Third World countries through the International Union for Conservation of Nature.

Ian McTaggart-Cowan, through his investigative studies and associated training of students in wildlife ecology, played a major role in the pioneering

Charles J. Krebs at a live-trapping station for small rodents, Kluane Lake, YT, July 2007. PHOTO BY ALICE KENNEY.

For twenty-five years Ernie Kuyt was dedicated to the study of whooping cranes nesting in Wood Buffalo National Park. In this photo, taken on August 13, 1979, he is with an immature, colour-banded whooping crane near the Sass River, NWT.
PHOTO COURTESY ELSIE KUYT.

and advocacy of this relatively new discipline of the biological sciences, gaining broad acceptance and application in the management and conservation of wildlife.

Charles J. Krebs

B.Sc. (1957, Wildlife Management), University of Minnesota; M.A. (1959, Zoology), Ph.D. (1962, Zoology), UBC

Charles is professor emeritus of zoology at the University of British Columbia. He has studied the population and community ecology of vertebrates in the boreal forest and tundra ecosystems of northern Canada for forty-one years, concentrating on voles, lemmings and snowshoe hares. His scientific passion is to carry out large-scale field experiments to test hypotheses about the ecological processes affecting populations and communities in northern Canada. In his spare time he writes ecology textbooks and has recently published *The Ecological World View*[198] and *Ecology*.

Dr. Cowan supervised Charles' M.A. thesis on reindeer in the Mackenzie River Delta and, with Dr. Dennis Chitty, co-supervised his Ph.D. dissertation on the lemming cycle in the Northwest Territories.

Ian Cowan brought me to UBC from Minnesota with the then-magnificent scholarship of six hundred dollars per year to do an M.A. degree. I worked on the Mackenzie Valley reindeer herd, and we published one joint paper from this work.[199] I then asked if I could study the lemming cycle for my Ph.D., and my most vivid memory of him was sitting in his office as he asked me who was the best person in the world in the small rodent field. I said Dennis Chitty at Oxford. He said we should get Dennis over for some lectures and advice to help plan my Ph.D. He got on the phone to the president of Canadian Pacific Airlines and said something to the effect of "Gordon, I have a man in Oxford and I need a ticket to bring him over to UBC to lecture." The next thing I knew Dennis Chitty was coming to UBC to give a series of lectures that culminated in his 1960 classic paper[200] and the offer of a job at UBC from Ian Cowan. Ian was a marvelous supervisor, working from the attitude of "tell me what you want to do and I will find the money." He and Dennis Chitty co-supervised my Ph.D. and launched my career, for which I am most grateful.

Ernie C.M. Kuyt

B.A. (1957, Zoology), UBC; M.A. (1970), University of Saskatchewan

Ernie, born May 3, 1929, passed away on May 21, 2010 at the age of eighty-one.

Ernie, a wildlife biologist, was born in the Netherlands on May 3, 1929, and immigrated to Canada with his family shortly after World War II. His pursuits in the fields of biology and conservation led him to Saskatchewan

Ernie Kuyt with a young male grey wolf at a den site on Duplex Island in the Thelon Game (Wildlife) Sanctuary, NWT, August 4, 1961.
PHOTO COURTESY OF ELSIE KYUT.

where he met and married Elsie Kulyk, with whom he spent an adventurous fifty years. He joined the Canadian Wildlife Service in 1960 and enjoyed a successful career in wildlife conservation, dedicating twenty-five years to working with whooping cranes. His commitment and passion culminated in receiving the Order of Canada.

I was never a good student at UBC. [I was] good as a Thunderbird soccer goalie[201] but decidedly less so at my courses. Although my first two years resulted in first class marks, in my third year I ran into a mental block in organic chemistry, had other problems and failed the year. They finally gave me credit for organic chemistry after my third try—I guess they felt sorry for me.

The course in Zoology 306 that year got me a first class mark; I was enthralled by the brilliant lecturing of Dr. Cowan and Jimmy Hatter. Part of the course involved collecting, labelling and preparation of specimens. Most of the students used mice and sparrows, but that was not good enough for me. I wanted to impress the professors and went after big game. I set a trap for raccoons near Fort Camp [UBC student housing], but it was a house cat that was taken, not the intended quarry. Nevertheless, I prepared the pelt and submitted it as part of the course. Later I heard that the cat from President Norman Mackenzie's residence [next to Fort Camp] was missing. Needless to say, I kept quiet about the incident.

Dr. Cowan inspired me with his lectures and I was fascinated by his knowledge and presentation. He had a great influence on my career selection. Much later in life I learned that he was one of the few biologists or conservationists to receive the Order of Canada. When I received the same award in 1996, I was cognizant that Dr. Cowan had played a major role in my choice of career and subsequent awards.

William (Bill) Alec Low

B.Sc. (Hons.) (1962, Zoology and Botany), Ph.D. (1970, Zoology), UBC

Bill was born and raised in Kamloops, BC. In 1969, just prior to completing his Ph.D. at UBC, Bill moved to Alice Springs in Northern Territory, Australia, where he still resides. He worked there as a research scientist with the Commonwealth Scientific and Industrial Research Organization (CSIRO) for eleven years. Then in 1980 he formed a consulting partnership, Low Ecological Services, which has been involved in environmental management and research projects in central Australia for the past three decades.

Bill Low (right) with Bryan Gates preparing an open house display on deer at UBC, March 1964. PHOTO COURTESY OF BRYAN R. GATES.

My difficulty in writing a short note about Dr. Cowan has been compounded by trying to decide what to write about and then getting it onto paper. Dr. Cowan recognized this problem when I was trying to begin writing my Ph.D. dissertation; he said that he had never seen anyone sit and stare at a blank piece of paper longer than I did. (I like to think that he may have said this to other students as well!)

Dr. Cowan was one of several mentors, including Jack Gregson, Bert Brink, Vladimir Krajina, John Bandy and several zoology and fisheries professors, who had a great impact on me and my development while I was at UBC, but his was the greatest as we had a twelve-year association while I went from undergrad to grad student. Mine eventually became one of the longer Ph.D. candidacies at UBC with nine years of grad school to arrive at a Ph.D.

Dr. Cowan's ability to inspire people was remarkable, but his loyalty to his students was equally outstanding. He stuck by me for all my time at university and long afterwards, including the times I went down wrong research pathways and he called on friendships to provide options for new directions—such

Bill Low overlooking Krichauff Range in Northern Territory, Australia. PHOTO BY HOLGER WOYT, FEBRUARY 2011.

as when I spent too much time looking at too much detail of collared peccary population behaviour and then at the cytology of reproductive activity in the laboratory to explain the behaviour, or when I had to rewrite my thesis, and he found a replacement typewriter to match the antiquated keys that my old typewriter had possessed! And finally while we were both in Australia in 1970, he provided the stimulus to get me over the last hurdle of re-writing a finalized dissertation to satisfy a critical committee. At the time he was on a sabbatical with CSIRO working on honey possums, and I was just starting a new ecosystem dynamics study including the productivity of so-called wild cattle in central Australia. We both achieved success in publications of these ventures, though my success was not as smooth as his!

Over the next forty years whenever I dropped in from over the ocean to visit Ian and Joyce in Vancouver or Victoria, my family and I were always welcomed like family. While Joyce plied us with tea and cookies or cake, Ian would tell me about his latest studies of gastropods or rhododendrons or birds or his Baja consulting or tours or his collection of official stamps and the paper he was to deliver on them at a national conference. He continues to be my mentor, and his presence and thoughts are still with me in my environmental consulting business. When I have to make decisions about people or places or environmental impact and management, I can apply his teachings in the way that he taught us, reflecting the interdependence of nature and people and the ramifications of impacts and seeing beyond the obvious.

Sent with fond memories and thanks for the opportunity to dwell on Dr. Cowan for a few hours again.

Wayne McCrory

B.Sc. (Hons.) (1965, Zoology), UBC

Wayne is a dedicated environmentalist whose career is rooted in his work as a protector of bear habitat and in ensuring that wild areas remain wild and undeveloped. He is proud to have worked with his colleagues at the Valhalla Wilderness Society and others on the establishment of four major provincial protected areas: the Valhalla Mountain Range, the Khutzeymateen Grizzly Bear Sanctuary, the White Grizzly/Goat Range Park and the mid-coast British Columbia rainforest, home of the white phase of the black bear (Kermode or Spirit Bear).

Wayne teaches outdoor bear safety courses and advises film crews for bear documentaries. He is regularly consulted by government agencies at all levels to help develop policies that will reduce bear/human conflicts and make wild areas "safer for people and better for bears." Wayne has published numerous reports on bear ecology and conservation, as well as bear hazard studies and conflict management plans for many parks and communities.

I was a small-town boy starting to work my way through UBC to be an engineer, but in 1963, after a year of schooling, I decided engineering was not

Wayne McCrory examining grizzly bear tracks along the Khutzeymateen River, BC. PHOTO BY ERICA MALLAM, CIRCA 1988.

215

what I wanted to do. So in my third year I decided to switch and take a number of first-year courses to see what else interested me. I was lucky to get into Ian McTaggart-Cowan's Zoology 105 course as it was packed. It was a real eye-opener and what an inspirational teacher he was! His natural enthusiasm made everything interesting from marine molluscs to wildlife parasites. This, plus Botany 105 and range ecology from Dr. Bert Brink (another conservation-oriented teacher) inspired me to drop engineering and study natural sciences. But I did not wish to be a teacher—so what else was there? One day while browsing through the UBC calendar I made an exciting discovery. There was actually a career called wildlife biology, so the next year I registered in honours zoology and signed up for several more of Dr. Cowan's courses.

I needed an honours thesis topic and as soon as Dr. Cowan heard I was interested in studying mountain goats, off the shelf came his proposal to study the speciation of mountain goats. I had the feeling he had been just waiting for some young, eager student to download this onto—and there I was. What a miserable task it was, especially sitting in a stuffy lab room using calipers to painstakingly make some thirty measurements of 165 mountain goat skulls shipped from various natural museums all over the world. And some of them stank.

When the measurements were done, the next year I had to analyze the data and write the thesis. That was even more fun. I had to do a covariance analysis of select skull measurements from different North American subspecies zones to see if there were any significant differences. This was even more challenging because, although I liked math, I knew absolutely nothing about statistics. At the time there appeared to be only one computer on campus, a giant brain that used punch cards. Cowan, by then dean of Graduate Studies, pulled some rank to get a math professor in statistics to take me under his wing and show me how to punch the cards and run the covariance analysis. The math professor was not too happy about my lack of statistical knowledge and gave me a hard time if I made mistakes, but by using this method, we showed that mountain goats did not have separate subspecies.

Periodically I had to report back to Cowan and it took a long time to get an appointment since his ascendancy to the deanship. The long and short was that I did not finish the analysis and the background research until final exam time. Right after exams, thanks to Donald A. Blood, another student of Dr. Cowan's, I escaped academia to do a mountain goat and Rocky Mountain bighorn sheep study for the Canadian Wildlife Service in Jasper National Park. Living in a remote warden's cabin doing wildlife research was a dream come true. But along came the box of mountain goat data and my portable typewriter, and everyone knows the different procrastinations for technical writing. I became a master at avoiding writing up my honour's thesis, and finally Cowan sent me a note that summer to encourage me to get it done.

That summer of hiking, research, photography and dating young belles in Jasper also intervened to delay the write-up. However, by fall, even though I was in hiding in my remote warden's cabin, Cowan, having worked in Jasper

The Kermode bear (*Ursus americanus kermodei*), also known as the spirit bear, is a subspecies of the American black bear living on the central and north coast and adjacent islands of British Columbia. Because of its ghost-like appearance, the spirit bear holds a prominent place in the mythology of First Nations people. PHOTO BY WAYNE McCRORY, PRINCESS ROYAL ISLAND, BC, CIRCA 2006.

National Park and knowing the chief warden, Mickey McGuire, knew how to phone me via the land line strung through the trees along the road. So one day the phone rang and there was Dr. Cowan enthusiastically asking me how it was going. By then I was actually making some progress, but he told me that, in order to get my course credit, I would now have to pay to register for the course at UBC for another year. This I did and finished the thesis by Christmas.

In 1970 Dr. Cowan demonstrated his further enthusiasm for mountain goat speciation by publishing a paper with my name listed as junior author.[202] Of course, he let me know after the publication came out. I found out later that, if you weren't around and available to get something published (as I wasn't), his scientific enthusiasm and dedication led to getting studies being published under joint authorship. This was called "pulling a Cowan."

The other things I remember fondly are the times in my wildlife classes that Dr. Cowan had some of his grad students or another wildlife professor talk about their wildlife research. We learned so much, whether it was Val Geist with his behavioural studies, Chuck Jonkel with black bears or Maurice Hornocker with mountain lions. But it was also Dr. Cowan's nap time and once his student got started, he would put his feet up on the desk at the back of the room and promptly have a siesta. He had a remarkable biological clock, for when the speaker was nearly finished, Dr. Cowan would promptly wake up and thank the speaker for such an interesting presentation. Anyone who placed a bet that he would sleep beyond the end of the graduate student's presentation always lost.

However, it was Dr. Cowan's and Dr. Brink's inclusion of wildlife conservation and protected-areas issues in the curriculum that also had a profound influence on my life's work as a biologist and conservationist. Dr. Cowan's stories of research in the mountain national parks and trying to get the wardens to stop killing predators were also fascinating. One of the things I recall him saying in one of his lectures was that the bulldozer had done more to alter the state of wildlife habitat and wilderness than any other single thing on the planet. This was in the mid-1960s before the word environmentalist was commonly used. It was a year or two later that I found a new logging road bulldozed into one of my favourite mountain valleys in the West Kootenay area where I grew up. It was then that Dr. Cowan's comment about bulldozers struck right to the heart of me, and I sent a letter to BC Parks asking that old-growth forests comprised of six or so mixed conifer species be protected as a provincial park. It never happened. But in 1975 when I learned the Valhalla Range was going to be logged, I remembered Dr. Cowan teaching us the need to protect wildlife habitat and so joined some colleagues to fight for its preservation; eight years later it was saved as a major lakeshore-to-mountaintop provincial park. The rest is history. When I look back nearly half a century later, I realize what an honour it was to have been taught by such an outstanding professor and conservationist as Dr. Cowan as he has directly and indirectly done so much for so many careers and for wildlife conservation in Canada.

William (Bill) Trevor Munro

B.Sc. (1962, Zoology), UBC; M.Sc. (1965), University of Laval, Quebec City

Bill is a retired wildlife biologist living in Victoria, BC. From 1962 to 1969 he worked for the Canadian Wildlife Service based in Quebec City as a field biologist studying migratory birds and their habitats in Quebec. From 1969 to 1974 he was the supervisor of habitat in the eastern region of the Canadian Wildlife Service in Ottawa, responsible for the operation of the habitat assessment, acquisition and management program in eastern Canada. From 1974 to 1992 he held the position of bird and endangered species specialist with the British Columbia Fish and Wildlife Branch in Victoria, providing advice on their management to senior staff and provincial regions. He also represented British Columbia as the authority for the Convention on International Trade in Endangered Species of Wild Fauna and Flora and on the Committee on the Status of Endangered Wildlife in Canada. He chaired the latter committee from 1988 to 1992.

Bill served as deputy director, British Columbia Wildlife Branch, Victoria, from 1992 to 1997; in this role he was responsible for the wildlife program and wildlife branch operations involving staff specialist services in animal management, appeals, licence cancellations/suspensions, regulations, new legislation, commercial activities and policy development.

In 1958, as a seventeen-year-old freshman in biological sciences at UBC, I had occasion to help out at an open house in the Department of Zoology. One of the displays was a full-mount of a magnificent male frigate bird in full breeding condition. Someone from the passing crowd asked me what the throat pouch was for, and I replied in ignorance that it was for storing food.

Bill Munro with his dog Duke during grouse research in the Salmon River Valley between Salmon Arm and Falkland, BC, autumn 1975. PHOTO BY DEANE MUNRO.

Sometime later, when there was no one else around, Dr. Cowan came over to me and gently said, "For your future reference, the pouch is for courtship display and not for food storage." By correcting me in private, he impressed upon me a lesson in human relationships that I have tried to emulate ever since.

Peter D. Ommundsen

B.Sc. (1964, Biology and Zoology), M.Sc. (1967, Zoology), UBC

Peter was employed for thirty-two years with the wildlife and environmental science programs at Selkirk College in Castlegar, BC. Inspired by the teaching skills of Ian McTaggart-Cowan, he promoted innovation in college biology education and received teaching excellence awards from the United States and Canada. Currently retired on Salt Spring Island, he continues to study natural history and coastal marine history, draws ecology cartoons for conservation magazines and volunteers with environmental organizations.

Dr. Cowan was Peter's supervisor for his M.Sc. thesis on the early growth of the Columbian black-tailed deer.

My fascination with natural history began when as a small child I lived near the UBC forest and became especially interested in mammals. This pursuit was enriched by the book *Mammals of British Columbia*[33] co-authored by Ian McTaggart-Cowan. At UBC I was fortunate to have him as my thesis supervisor and as my professor in three wildlife courses. Ian was a talented naturalist and a charismatic teacher. His virtuosity inspired in me a lifelong interest in biology

Peter Ommundsen on Salt Spring Island, BC, March 30, 2012. PHOTO BY ARLENE OMMUNDSEN.

Peter Ommundsen with a golden-mantled ground squirrel. PHOTO BY ARLENE OMMUNDSEN, KOOTENAY LAKE, 1972.

education, and I pursued a career as a community college instructor in wildlife and vertebrate biology. His passion for natural history was contagious, and his enthusiasm is exemplified in a letter he sent me describing his travels in French Polynesia, saying, "I have some shells from Moorea fit to drool over."

Ian usually refrained from drawing attention to the public speaking efforts of others, but an exception occurred following a presentation by a guest speaker, R. Yorke Edwards. Ian told the students, "Finally we have a speaker who didn't just slap something together on the ferry on the way over." Other memorable comments include the following:

On wildlife management: "Wildlife management is ninety-five percent people management."[25]

On books: "I judge a person's interest in their profession by the size of their bookcase."

On children: After some children brought in an elk bone found in the university forest: "Always have time for children; they are the next generation of naturalists."

On churches: "Most people entering a church hang up their brains with their umbrellas."

On geography: "Geographers as a profession can't make up their minds what to study."

Ian's students learned from the example of his professionalism, his legendary work ethic and his high expectations of others. He gave freely of his time and knowledge, he provided a stimulating learning environment, and he worked tirelessly to help students secure financial aid, graduate placements and career opportunities.

William J. (Bill) Otway

Bill, born on June 15, 1935, passed away on October 17, 2010, at the age of seventy-five.

Bill was born in Fort William, Ontario, and moved to British Columbia in 1948. He worked as the executive director of the British Columbia Wildlife Federation (BCWF) for nine years then served as the recreational fisheries advisor/ombudsman for Fisheries and Oceans Canada for the next fifteen years, retiring from that post in 2000.

For over fifty-five years he was an active volunteer for the conservation movement in British Columbia. He was a member of the Fraser panel of the Pacific Salmon Commission for eight years and sat on the original management board of the Pacific Salmon Southern Endowment Fund. He served as chairman of the BCWF Native Affairs Committee and in that capacity was on the federal/provincial treaty negotiations advisory committee. He served on the national board of directors of Ducks Unlimited Canada for over nine years, was provincial chairman for seven years and was an active volunteer in that organization for over thirty-five years.

The late Bill Otway during his tenure as executive director of the British Columbia Wildlife Federation. PHOTO BY CAROL OTWAY.

Bill was awarded life memberships by several fish and game clubs and organizations. He also received awards from other organizations for his conservation and fund-raising efforts. In 2003 he was recognized for his work for the fisheries and for anglers by being awarded one of only five Canadian National Recreational Fisheries Awards. He also served as president of the Family Fishing Society of BC for two years.

I first became aware of, and acquainted with, Dr. Cowan back in the 1950s while attending the annual meeting and convention of the BC Federation of Fish and Game Clubs, the forerunner to the BC Wildlife Federation. Ian was the keynote speaker and he was, as usual, spellbinding. I was a very young buck then and very much impressed with the knowledge and information this man had on wildlife and wildlife management. More importantly, I was really impressed that he could disseminate that information in such a way that all of us simple hunters and fishermen could understand and appreciate what he was saying. I was even more impressed and awed when he stayed around for the balance of the conference and spent his time mixing and talking with delegates such as me and did not confine himself to the upper echelon. He made me feel almost like an equal. He had the courtesy to listen to what I had to say, and as his actions proved over the years, he was interested in what those of us in the field had to say. He respected our love of the outdoors and the wildlife resource and our dedication to better management and a sustainable resource for the future.

Briony Penn

B.A. (1981, Geography), UBC; Ph.D. (1988, Geography), Edinburgh University, Scotland

Briony has been an adjunct assistant professor at the School of Environmental Studies with the University of Victoria. She is an award-winning journalist and educator. She has published many articles in the popular press on natural history as well as several books. She is currently working on a biography of Ian McTaggart-Cowan based on his field journals and his correspondence. She was a broadcaster with CHUM-TV for several years and continues to lecture widely on a variety of topics including "green mapping." Briony is a co-founder of the Land Conservancy of British Columbia and the Garry Oak Meadow Preservation Society. She served as a board member of the Raincoast Conservation Foundation and initiated a coastal sandhill crane research project through the Foundation. A three-year research project was started with graduate student Krista Roessingh, supervised by Dan Smith, Dennis Jelinski and Neville Winchester for her subsequent master's thesis and documentation of breeding cranes on the central coast.[203]

Being born precisely half a century later than Ian, I only had the privilege of knowing him for the last decade of his life after he had retired to his

Briony Penn with red sea urchin on Haida Gwaii (Queen Charlotte Islands), BC, June 2013. PHOTO BY TAVISH CAMPBELL.

beautiful home and garden on Ten Mile Point. I had an opportunity to work with him both as a journalist and as a researcher. I was researching a book on important naturalist/scientists of British Columbia, which had the working title *Beautiful British Columbians.* After an introduction through our mutual friend Bristol Foster, Ian kindly let me interview him. That initial session with Ian stretched into a much longer relationship. I started with short articles in Victoria publications *Focus* and *Monday Magazine.* Later, as a television broadcaster with CHUM, I used the material to do a short documentary on his life, illustrated with the early CBC footage from his television shows.

Researching his biography, I was able to delve much deeper into the significance of his work to Canadian conservation and the extraordinary network of people he worked hard to support. So many of our lives have been enriched by his work, either behind the scenes, in front of the camera or out in the field.

In 2000 Ian was finishing the edit of his contributions to the final volume of *The Birds of British Columbia,* and during one interview he described how he had watched sandhill cranes on Spider Island "running like rabbits" from the lagoon into the forest. Seventy years later I landed on Spider Island and went to the lagoon that Ian had described in such vivid detail. There on the beach was a pair of cranes who ran like rabbits into the forest. And that story tells you everything about Ian: his meticulous memory, his keen observation, his long commitment to the natural world, his welcome attitude to those of us who went into the popularization of science and his enthusiasm to share his knowledge.

Andrew Radvanyi

B.Sc. (1948, Zoology), M.Sc. (1950, Zoology), McMaster University; Ph.D. (1959, Zoology), UBC

Andrew Radvanyi at Edmonton, AB, March 2014. PHOTO COURTESY OF KRISTINE JUNCK.

Before his retirement in 1984 Andrew was a research scientist, having worked his entire career with the Canadian Wildlife Service. After graduating from UBC, he became the first biologist stationed in Aklavik, Northwest Territories, where for two years he studied large and small mammal populations along the coast of the Beaufort Sea, including Herschel Island. He then moved to Edmonton, where he worked with Environment Canada on issues related to national parks. He has published thirty-four reports and peer-reviewed articles, mainly on small mammals.

Dr. Cowan was Andrew's supervisor for his Ph.D. dissertation on the pioneering study of photoperiod rhythms and nocturnal activity in the northern flying squirrel.

As a student I could not have had a better instructor and teacher to see me through those hard years. If I had to repeat them today, I do not think I could. Dr. Cowan provided years of helpful guidance in my Ph.D. research on the northern flying squirrel. It was much appreciated and I am thankful for his guidance.

Laszlo Istvan Retfalvi

B.S.F. (1961, Forestry), M.F. (1965, Wildlife Biology), Faculty of Forestry, UBC

Laszlo retired in 1994 after a twenty-eight-year career in habitat management and ecological assessments with the Canadian Wildlife Service in Edmonton, Ottawa and Delta, British Columbia. In 1965 and 1966 after his graduation from UBC, Laszlo was employed as a park naturalist in Cape Breton Highlands National Park, Nova Scotia. He then worked on national park wildlife problems related to biotic communities and garbage disposal affecting grizzly bears. He also coordinated biological studies on the Mackenzie Highway project in the Northwest Territories. For five years after retiring he worked as a consulting biologist on a number of environmental impact studies.

Laszlo started his M.F. thesis on bald eagle biology on San Juan Island, Washington state, with Dr. Miklos Udvardy (Department of Zoology, UBC), but Dr. Cowan became his official supervisor when Miklos took sabbatical leave partway through Laszlo's research.

Laszlo Retfalvi on Mount Seymour, BC, circa 2003. PHOTO BY G. DONATH.

I have three vivid memories of Dr. Cowan.

I worked three summers with Mr. [Louis] Witt as a museum preparator at UBC, mainly skinning rather than stuffing birds and mammals as Mr. Witt was rather possessive of the specimens and was better at stuffing. At the time Dr. Cowan was head of the Department of Zoology and very keen on building up the UBC Vertebrate Museum's collections, therefore he was a frequent visitor to our basement room to give instructions. In 1959, my first summer there, I served as an "unofficial translator" for Mr. Witt. Dr. Cowan used to speak fast as he was a busy man and had a lot to say, and Mr. Witt quite obligingly nodded at whatever was said to him. Only after Dr. Cowan left did Mr. Witt turn to me and ask, "What did he say?" Dr. Cowan knew, of course, what was going on and he always had a whimsical smile on his face as he spoke. Over the years Mr. Witt's English improved, but he always complained that he had difficulty understanding Dr. Cowan. Maybe it was Ian's (nonexistent) Scottish accent, he said!

From the late 1950s to the late 1960s Ian hired a specimen preparator to give a presence in the Vertebrate Museum at UBC and build up its collections of birds and mammals. Here Louis Witt is preparing a specimen of a long-billed curlew at his tiny workstation in the basement of the zoology building, June 1970. PHOTO BY R. WAYNE CAMPBELL.

I entered graduate school in 1961 under Dr. Miklos Udvardy's tutelage and with Dr. Cowan as an advisor to the Faculty of Forestry from which I graduated. However, Dr. Cowan ended up as my official supervisor because halfway through my studies Dr. Udvardy left on a sabbatical to the University of Hawaii. But there was some difficulty in the minds of the forestry members of my committee with my thesis topic on bald eagles. Dr. Cowan's position was that as long as the Faculty of Forestry offered a wildlife management option, my topic was perfectly acceptable. He finally put an end to the squabble by exhorting them: "What do you want—bald eagles to eat fir needles for it to qualify as a forestry topic?" As it happened, we sort of played a pioneering role in having a master's degree in forestry granted on matters ornithological.

Many years later a seminar was scheduled at the old zoology building. Being one of the conveners and worried that one of our Canadian Wildlife

Service speakers was not yet present at the start, I tried to phone his home in Sidney, BC, to find out whether he had left in time to catch the ferry that morning. Right opposite the small lecture hall there was a phone booth built into the wall, but it was too shallow for me to back up enough to read the telephone directory. Just as I was giving up hope, Dr. Cowan walked by and helped me out of my predicament. Though close to thirty years my senior, he had no difficulty reading the small print.

Ralph Withrow Ritcey

B.A. (1950, Zoology), graduate studies (1953, Zoology), UBC

Ralph is a retired provincial wildlife biologist and an active naturalist. Shortly after his university training in the early 1950s, Ralph worked in Wells Gray Park, BC, studying the biology and ecology of the park's fauna, especially moose and caribou. In 1963 he moved to Kamloops for family reasons and became the regional wildlife biologist with the British Columbia Fish and Wildlife Branch there. He remained in Kamloops after his retirement. He has co-authored several government reports as well as peer-reviewed articles and in 1995 completed a major work on the *Status of the Sharp-tailed Grouse in British Columbia.*[204]

Ralph Ritcey, a retired regional wildlife biologist with the British Columbia Fish and Wildlife Branch.
PHOTO BY KENT WONG.

As a war veteran, I was given economic assistance to further my education and chose biology as my field of study, but two years of undergraduate courses at an eastern college seemed to be leading me nowhere. Then, while working in Trail, BC for the summer, I found a UBC catalogue offering a curriculum destined to lead me towards an exciting and rewarding career in wildlife management.

At UBC I first fell under Dr. Cowan's spell while a student in his third-year course entitled Biology of Vertebrates. His lectures entertained, enlightened, educated and informed students on many aspects of British Columbia's vertebrate fauna. Nowhere in my educational experience, before or since, have I seen such rapt student interest in a lecture series. Zoology students of that era who were entering the field of fisheries management at UBC were led by the brilliant and youthful Peter Larkin. His students were more gifted in the fields of mathematics and chemistry than most wildlife biologists, but they often tended to overlook or failed to attempt to understand the fish they studied. There was a keen rivalry between the two student groups, with fisheries referring to Cowan as "the Great White Father." Perhaps there was more than a bit of jealousy when they tried to belittle our leader.

After UBC I went to work in Wells Gray Park where, directed by Yorke Edwards (another Cowan student), I studied the distribution and ecology of many of the park's wildlife species, especially moose and caribou. Wildlife was abundant in the park with moose to be seen daily in winter from our home in the Hemp Creek Valley. Mule deer, both black and grizzly bears, mountain goats, caribou, timber wolves and coyotes plus a variety of fur-bearing mammals were also present but in smaller numbers. The numbers and species of birds fluctuated seasonally, influenced by food supply, migration patterns and nesting success, but they were always of interest and enjoyment even in the depths of winter.[205]

In 1963 I joined the staff of the British Columbia Fish and Wildlife Branch (BCFWB) in Kamloops as a wildlife biologist. This posting brought many new challenges including the task of informing the public and other resource agencies of the need for wildlife habitat protection measures and for acceptable but effective hunting regulations to protect the wildlife resource. Public speaking on those issues was a problem for me, but one nugget of Cowan advice—"Make sure you are well informed on the subject being discussed"— helped me through many controversial management problems.

Last year my introduction to a biologist from Ontario included the statement that "Ralph was a student of Cowan's." Although those student days happened more than fifty years ago, they made up the most important learning period in my life. Ian's skills of observation, problem analysis and communication were ideal examples of the abilities needed for a successful career in the field of wildlife management. Like many others, I consider myself fortunate to have known him, although emulating him set the bar much too high for me.

Ralph Ritcey during a mountain caribou survey near Goats Peaks, Wells Gray Park, BC. PHOTO BY PATRICK W. MARTIN, SUMMER 1950.

Donald J. Robinson
B.A. (1949, Zoology), M.A. (1951, Zoology), UBC

Don's interest in animals started early with bug collections, raising frogs and salamanders and keeping chickens and ducks. Identifying birds and finding their nests was another enjoyable escapade, and all these experiences were useful for his future career. Upon graduating from UBC in 1951, he joined the British Columbia Game Commission as a game biologist responsible for Vancouver Island and the Queen Charlotte Islands. In 1960 he became the chief game biologist for the province and followed that with the post of assistant director responsible for a wider set of resource issues and administrative duties, all of which changed as the government reacted to the public's new interest in the environment. Finally in 1976 he assumed responsibility for wildlife resources and administration as the director of the Fish and Wildlife Branch of the British Columbia Ministry of Environment. He retired in 1984 and began fifteen years of volunteer involvement in resource management and negotiations concerned with Native affairs.

In all the segments of his fifty-year career, Don was influenced by Ian McTaggart-Cowan, especially regarding his positive reaction to new ideas, processes and attitudes, because Ian believed in good science as the basis for resource decisions supported by public education. He understood that the public needs time to accept new science and associated facts.

It came as a surprise to me that Ian McTaggart-Cowan had a strong competitive nature. After four years of lectures, seminars and group field trips I had perceived him as one who set the agenda and described zoological functions

Don Robinson determining the age of a Columbian black-tailed deer by dentition during a game check with a colleague from the Washington State Game Department, Campbell River, 1956. PHOTO COURTESY OF CAMPBELL RIVER COURIER.

Don Robinson and Muriel Guiguet at the celebration of Ian McTaggart-Cowan's life, Fairmont Empress Hotel, Victoria, BC, May 4, 2010. PHOTO BY BRYAN R. GATES.

beyond critical review. Accompanying him on several field trips to Sayward Forest on Vancouver Island in the early 1950s had confirmed this opinion, so I looked forward to a trip in early May to check several exclosure plots he had established and to experience some low-key birding.

When I picked Dr. Cowan up in Nanaimo, he was accompanied by Dr. Miklos Udvardy, which made for a tight fit in the panel truck as my dog Brant and our gear took up most of the remaining space. But away we went to Sayward. Ian and I slept in the truck with Brant on the floor of the front seat and Miklos outside. In the morning Ian arose and restarted the fire; Miklos kept warm in his sleeping bag while taking sips from a flask. Ian didn't comment and Miklos soon dressed and got ready for breakfast, cooked by Ian.

As we hiked to the first exclosure, Ian began to identify bird species, commenting on their lifestyles. Udvardy quickly began to do the same, except he identified birds by their song. Although territorial singing was in the terminal stages, Udvardy was successful in identifying the greater number of species. Cowan quickly changed our course to more open areas with greater edges, whereas the original path had been through a Douglas-fir plantation with limited visibility. Now the two of them began searching for species rather than simply identifying them along a leisurely route. I became aware of the competition when each of them attempted to have me confirm their identifications, but neither received much support from me because I couldn't identify the birds and I didn't want to show any favouritism. At all times both birders gave great courtesy to each other and this even included me. Fortunately, we soon reached the exclosure plot, which was just as well, as birdwatching was impacting on the competitors.

I often think about this field trip and the behaviour of the senior members. They were courteous, fair, included me in all discussions but were also *very* competitive. My original opinion of Cowan broadened as I realized he was a competitive team player in the field.

Mikkel Schau

B.Sc. (Hons.) (1964, Geology), Ph.D. (1968, Geological Sciences), UBC, Department of Geology

Mikkel has held professional teaching positions in various geological disciplines at McMaster University, University of Manitoba and the Nunatta campus of Arctic College. He also served for twenty-three years as a field officer with the Geological Survey of Canada, mapping in the northeastern Arctic. After retiring, Mikkel acted as a consulting geologist for federal and provincial governments and for private mining and exploration companies in Nunavut, Nunavik (Quebec), Yukon, Ontario, Quebec and British Columbia. He currently consults and prospects in British Columbia. Mikkel is married to Ian McTaggart-Cowan's daughter, Ann.

I have known Ian since I started courting his daughter so many years ago. Of course, he was Dr. Cowan to me back in those days.

Once I was at the Cowan dinner table and began describing a campsite I had run into along Laventie Creek up in the Eutsuk Lake country as a junior assistant for a mining company. It was a long way from anywhere, and the site was old. It had a rock firepit and a rack for tying horses. As I was describing the site, Dr. Cowan added to the description, noting where the dried-out tent poles had been stored! It was one of his old campsites!

Somewhat later Ann and I decided to cast our lot in life together, and I went to discuss this decision with Dr. Cowan. We had a general discussion and he handed me a book and asked me to read it. It was a pamphlet written by Francis Galton in 1872 called *Statistical Inquiries into the Efficacy of Prayer*.[206] I read it and was queried about it on a return visit. We had a long discussion about the scientific method and how it can be applied in so many different ways. Then Ann and I got his well wishes on the nuptials to be!

Geoffrey G.E. Scudder

B.Sc. (Hons.) (1955, Zoology), University of Wales, Aberystwyth; Ph.D. (1958, Entomology), Oxford University

Geoff is a professor emeritus at UBC, having served as head of the Department of Zoology from 1976 to 1991 and interim director of the Centre for Biodiversity Research from 1993 to 1995. He spent his whole career at UBC, other than study leaves at Imperial College, University of London, in 1964–65 and the Wau Ecology Institute, Papua New Guinea, in 1972, plus collecting expeditions over the past fifty-two years to all the world's zoogeographic realms.

He has authored or co-authored over 250 scientific papers and co-edited three books. He is a member of the Order of Canada and a fellow of the Royal Society of Canada. In 1975 he received the gold medal from the Entomological Society of Canada for outstanding contributions to entomology. He is the only UBC faculty member to have received all four of the top awards at the university, namely the Master Teacher Award, the Killam Research Prize, the President's Service Award for Excellence and the UBC Alumni Faculty Citation Award. He happily served with Ian on the board of the Nature Trust of British Columbia.

Geoff Scudder, head of the Department of Zoology at UBC from 1976 to 1991 and now professor emeritus, remains active in retirement still doing research on insects. PHOTO COURTESY OF GEOFF G.E. SCUDDER.

Ian McTaggart-Cowan hired me as an instructor in zoology in 1958, sight unseen. In the autumn of 1957 I was visiting my friend Tony Dixon at Glasgow University when at coffee one morning Alex Hill, another faculty member at the university, showed me an advertisement in the journal *Nature* for a faculty position at UBC. Alex had just returned from a sabbatical year in the Agriculture Canada laboratory on the UBC campus and said he thought I would like Vancouver as it was by the sea, close to mountains and very picturesque, much like Aberystwyth in Wales where I had taken my undergraduate studies. I applied for the UBC position as an assistant professor, but I was hired as an instructor. When I wrote to enquire how long I might expect to spend as an instructor, Ian replied that it should be no more than four years. As it turned out, I spent two years at this level and was promoted to assistant professor on reappointment in 1960. On my arrival at UBC, I was informed by another junior faculty member that Ian had hired me because, being British, I was five hundred dollars cheaper to hire than a competing American. I gather this was correct.

At the same time that I applied for the faculty position at UBC, I also applied to the British government for a deferment from national service in the armed forces. In 1959 deferment was possible if one went into university teaching, but until that time such deferment had only been given for teaching positions in the United Kingdom. My application was supported by a letter I obtained from Ian that stated that my position was mainly teaching with no mention of research. Luckily, I was granted an exemption from national service.

My appointment was effective on July 1, 1958, so I anticipated that I had to be in Vancouver by this date. At that time, UBC did not provide any expenses for relocation, and at twenty-four years old and having just graduated from Oxford University with a doctorate, I had no savings. My wife's savings paid for our travel to Liverpool, but I had to borrow from UBC for the Liverpool to Montreal boat fare and the cross-Canada train fare to Vancouver. Ian was kind enough to arrange this loan, but I had to repay it over the first six months following our arrival. It was only after I had repaid it that I learnt I really had not needed to arrive at UBC until September 1, and that the first two months of my salary could have been banked as a cushion for expenses.

I was hired to teach entomology but nothing had been said about the need to obtain outside grants for the support of research and graduate students. Ian provided seventy dollars for entomology teaching expenses and said I could use any spare dollars for my research. I spent the first two months at UBC collecting insects and making microscope slides for the introductory entomology course. I also started to amalgamate the many insect collections that had been assembled over the years by George Spencer, forming a single composite collection, which later became the Spencer Entomological Museum (now the Spencer Entomological Collection in the Beaty Biodiversity Museum). In this way I became familiar with British Columbia insect fauna, and I was able to save some of the seventy dollars for research. However, when I ordered some stencils to label my D.Phil. research diagrams for publication, Ian vetoed this purchase as too expensive. I purchased them myself.

Each year the lumber baron H.R. MacMillan took his luxury yacht on a fishing trip to Mexico and invited a zoologist along to identify his captures; in early 1959 Ian went along as the zoologist. In his absence he assigned me to give his lectures to his first-year zoology course, which he considered to be one of the most important courses in the department. He was a very popular lecturer and had a very large class. Fortunately, at that time he was lecturing about insects, so it was appropriate for me to take on this task. But

Ian considered that the only really interesting thing to talk about regarding insects was the work of Karl von Frisch on the dance of the honeybee, and he had introduced this topic before he left. I was familiar with the research, having read von Frisch's book as part of the compulsory reading for honours zoology students at Aberystwyth. I gave the required lectures, but afterwards I found out that my account differed from the details that he had outlined before he left. His comment to me later was that details were not important.

In my first few years at UBC Ian was very involved in his CBC television program, which was very popular with students and the public. I started research on the aquatic insects in the lakes around Williams Lake in 1959, and in the early 1960s Ian visited our campsite at Westwick Lakes with his CBC camera crew, preparing material for a new TV series. The camera crew filmed some of the freshwater insects that I was asked to name and also took film footage of muskrats that Ian had trapped. I was impressed by his knowledge of the biology of those vertebrates.

Ian taught a popular course at the senior level on wildlife biology, and all the time he was associated with the Department of Zoology he had a large number of graduate students—far more than any other faculty member. These graduate students were assigned to teach in the laboratory section in various courses in zoology.

When I became head of the Department of Zoology in 1976, although Ian was no longer at UBC, he was very supportive and remained so for my fifteen years in this post. He also supported my nomination for membership on the governing board of the Nature Trust of British Columbia, and I served on the board with him for several years. I was impressed with his deep knowledge and dedication to the aims of this conservation organization.

One final memory of Ian was his ability to "nod off" during guest lectures and seminars in zoology and then "wake up" at the end and ask a very pertinent, penetrating and relevant question. I also recall that he always kept a notepad by his bedside so that at night he could record his thoughts or questions. This is one of the many habits I copied from him.

Spencer G. Sealy

B.Sc. (1964, Zoology), University of Alberta; M.Sc. (1968, Zoology), UBC; Ph.D. (1972, Zoology), University of Michigan

Spencer is a professor emeritus of biological sciences at the University of Manitoba in Winnipeg. He has conducted research on the biology of marine birds in the Bering Sea and in British Columbia and studied the social behaviour of tropical birds in Costa Rica. For more than twenty-five years, in conjunction with about fifty honours and graduate students, he conducted experiments to elucidate behavioural and evolutionary interactions between avian brood parasites and their hosts in Manitoba, Texas, Costa Rica and Italy.

He is a founding member of the Pacific Seabird Group (PSG) and the Society of Canadian Ornithologists/Société des ornithologistes du Canada (SCO) and has served on councils of several scientific societies

Spencer Sealy travelling along the north shore of St. Lawrence Island in the Bering Sea, AK. PHOTO BY LISA M. SHEFFIELD, AUGUST 2004.

and on national grant-selection panels. Spencer recently completed a term as editor of *The Auk*, the journal of the American Ornithologists' Union (AOU). His teaching and research activities have been recognized by a lifetime achievement award from the PSG, the Doris Huestis Speirs Award for contributions to Canadian ornithology, the Jamie Smith Award for student mentoring from the SCO and the William Brewster Memorial Award from the AOU in recognition of his ornithological research in 2008[207] and the Marion Jenkinson AOU Service Award in 2013.[208]

Spencer retired in 2011 and presently serves as editor of *Wildlife Afield*, a biannual natural history journal published by the Biodiversity Centre for Wildlife Studies.[209]

Spencer Sealy at an Inuit cairn near Perry River, NWT (now Nunavut), July 1965. PHOTO BY JOHN P. RYDER.

My interest in ornithology, which emerged during my boyhood days in rural Saskatchewan, led me from my high school in Battleford to the zoology program at the University of Alberta. I was particularly interested in colonial waterbirds and fortunate to meet graduate student Kees Vermeer who had recently completed a study of breeding ecology of the glaucous-winged gull at UBC[210] with Miklos Udvardy. Vermeer described the exciting atmosphere at UBC and encouraged me to approach Dr. Udvardy about pursuing a master's degree there. I arrived in the Department of Zoology at UBC in the autumn of 1965.

Ian McTaggart-Cowan's influence was everywhere—his long history of research on wildlife overlapping with ongoing studies by his current students, some of whom became my friends. Cowan did not serve on my master's committee, at least not at the beginning, but he stepped in later when the need arose. Upon my return to UBC after my first field season studying auklet breeding ecology in Alaska, I stopped by Udvardy's office only to find that over the summer he had moved to California—without telling me! I learned subsequently that he had not informed me of his impending move while I was in the field because he felt the news might interfere with my work as my project was being conducted on a remote island in the Bering Sea. I appreciated Udvardy's thoughtfulness, as I also appreciated that of Cowan who without hesitation stepped in to fill the gap in my committee. Despite his heavy schedule as dean of the Faculty of Graduate Studies, he provided advice on my progress report and preparation for my final field season and eventually commented on drafts of my thesis. This was my only personal association with Cowan, but his influence on my work has continued over the years through his vast network of publications on the fauna of British Columbia, which I continue to read and cite in my ongoing work.

Roderick Sterling Silver
B.Sc. (1971, Plant Science), M.Sc. (1976, Plant Science), UBC

Rod was fortunate to work as a field biologist for the British Columbia Ministry of Environment in the Okanagan (California bighorn sheep), Peace River (moose) and West Kootenay before moving to Victoria in 1980

From left: Dr. Geoff Scudder, Dr. Bert Brink, Rod Silver and Dr. Ian McTaggart-Cowan at the reception for Bert at Government House, Victoria, BC, February 2003. PHOTO BY VISIONS WEST.

to help create the new Habitat Conservation Fund. He retired as its administrator. He was a founding member of several successful conservation partnerships including the award-winning Pacific Estuary Conservation Program and the Okanagan-Similkameen Conservation Program. He is currently a director of the Nature Trust of British Columbia.

He has been active in establishing chairs, bursaries and professorships to honour a number of the province's conservation leaders at several British Columbia universities; these include the Ian McTaggart-Cowan Wildlife Management Scholarship at the University of Northern British Columbia (UNBC, 1994), the Ian McTaggart-Cowan Muskwa-Kechika Research Professorship (UNBC, 2000), the Ian McTaggart-Cowan Professorship of's Biodiversity Conservation and Ecological Restoration at the University of Victoria (UVic, 2008) and the Ian and Joyce McTaggart-Cowan Scholarship in Honours Biology (UVic, 2009).

Dr. Cowan was a member of Rod's committee for his M.Sc. thesis on the winter ecology of moose.

As a graduate student in plant science at UBC in 1971, I was indeed very fortunate when my supervisor, Dr. Bert Brink, arranged for me to be enrolled in a directed studies course in wildlife management. I spent the term in one-on-one sessions with Dr. Ian McTaggart-Cowan, the distinguished zoologist who was the dean of Graduate Studies at that time. It was an unprecedented and rewarding learning experience that provided a valuable foundation for my career.

Ian was a great communicator with encyclopedic knowledge, a contagious and passionate fascination with the natural world and a style that made everyone comfortable with his vast knowledge and many experiences. These exceptional qualities were never more apparent than in 1981 when he volunteered to become the first chair of the Public Advisory Board of the new Habitat Conservation Fund. His distinguished leadership spanned an incredible nineteen years, and it is safe to say that the fund survived and thrived due to his strong commitment to peer-reviewed science-based investments, transparent administration practices and deep appreciation and respect for the outdoor enthusiasts who contributed to the fund.

I was indeed fortunate to work with Ian on the fund for over eleven years. I found that every time I spoke with him I learned something new—not just about nature or science but about the world. He also had a remarkable memory and a very quick wit. I recall writer Briony Penn asking him in 2005 about the secrets to living a long life. His recipe was:

- Choose your parents carefully.
- Find yourself an excellent partner.
- Eat lots of venison.
- Maintain enthusiasm.

To have venison, he reasoned, you must get out into the woods, hike the hills and mountains and get exercise, and he continued to do that even into his ninetieth year. He told me of his last hunt for deer on a ranch west of Calgary. On the second day he was slowly working his way through a patch of timber when he saw a buck heading his way. He sat motionless as the deer approached and then, in his words, "readjusted his outlook on life." He told me he had shot a deer every year for seventy-one years.

He had an appreciation and enjoyment of nature that continued until his death. It made him such an interesting and relevant teacher to all his students and the others he touched. Thanks to Ian, we are all so much the wiser.

David (Dave) J. Spalding
B.A. (1956, Zoology), M.A. (1963, Zoology), UBC

Dave is a retired wildlife biologist and scientist. He served as an assistant scientist with the Fisheries Research Board of Canada in Nanaimo from 1957 to 1964, as a wildlife biologist with the British Columbia Ministry of Environment (MOE) from 1964 to 1973 and as an administrator with the MOE from 1964 to 1980. From 1985 to 2000, Dave worked as a wildlife consultant and between contracts found time to conduct private research.

Dr. Cowan was Dave's supervisor for his M.A. thesis on the comparative feeding habits of three species of pinnipeds. It was published as Fisheries Research Board of Canada Bulletin No. 146 in 1964.[211]

As a boy growing up in the country, I was interested in the outdoors, but I was not an aspiring young naturalist, and when I began my university education, I had not considered biology as a possible career. However, I took Dr. Cowan's

Dave Spalding worked as a federal and provincial wildlife biologist.
PHOTO BY ELAINE JACOBSON, SOUTH PENDER ISLAND, BC, MAY 14, 2014.

general zoology course during the 1953–54 session at UBC, and it was the influence of Dr. Cowan and the content of those lectures that determined my professional life. I will never forget sitting in that large lecture hall in the biological sciences building and Dr. Cowan striding into the room carrying skulls or mammal skins or bird specimens—whatever he needed to emphasize some aspect of the outdoors in his lectures. He was a joy to listen to: his enthusiasm, his knowledge and the confidence in which he approached his role as a teacher convinced me that I could find a career involving the study of animals.

My M.A. thesis was entitled "Comparative Feeding Habits of the Fur Seal, Sea Lion and Harbour Seal on the British Columbia Coast." Dr. Cowan chaired my committee; he provided the initial encouragement to proceed with the study and the follow-up to see that it was completed. The thesis was accepted during the 1962–63 session at UBC and, following some modification, was published in 1964.

Brian Starzomski

B.Sc. (1996, Geology and Biology), St. Francis Xavier University; M.Sc. (2000, Biology), Acadia University; Ph.D. (2006, Zoology), UBC

Originally from Nova Scotia, Brian is broadly trained as a community ecologist and conservation biologist and enjoys working in a variety of systems to study biodiversity questions. He joined the School of Environmental Studies at the University of Victoria as an assistant professor in 2009.

His research focusses on biodiversity structure and dynamics and seeks to link theory and empirical approaches. Recently much of his work has taken place at the treeline and in the alpine zone in Labrador, British Columbia and the southwestern Yukon. Other recent projects involve examining facilitation among species in bromeliad food webs in Costa Rica. Brian doesn't have an organismal bias to his research and is comfortable working across the taxonomic spectrum from insects to plants to birds.

Like most people, I knew of Ian McTaggart-Cowan long before I ever met him. I grew up in Nova Scotia but spent as much time in British Columbia as I could, especially after I turned eighteen. My summers of working in Vancouver and exploring the mountains of the Coast Range on days off were followed by hours of studying *The Mammals of British Columbia* by McTaggart-Cowan and Guiguet. I even made a special trip to Alta Lake to see why so much work had been done around it. Natural history in British Columbia for me was Ian McTaggart-Cowan on the animal side and Nancy Turner,[212] Jim Pojar and Andy MacKinnon on the plant side.[213]

When I finally had the chance to do my Ph.D. at UBC, Cowan's name was everywhere—from the portrait on the wall of past heads of the Department of Zoology to the Cowan Room where I endured my comprehensive exam but also where I would spend hours poring over past theses of his students.

Gordon Pike (left) and Dave Spalding tagging a northern sea lion pup. Sartine Island, in the Scott Island group off northwestern Vancouver Island, BC, June 1959. PHOTO COURTESY OF DAVID J. SPALDING.

Brian Starzomski conducting a bird survey in a mangrove forest on the Pacific coast of Mexico, south of Zihuatanejo, December 26, 2007. PHOTO BY AIMEE PELLETIER.

While at UBC I often borrowed stuffed birds and mammals from the Cowan Vertebrate Museum to bring to elementary schools where I gave talks on biodiversity and then, with the students, took apart owl pellets and put the tiny rodent skeletons back together.

I am forever grateful that I had the chance to meet the man himself on several occasions after being selected as the first Ian McTaggart-Cowan Professor of Biodiversity Conservation and Ecological Restoration in the School of Environmental Studies at the University of Victoria. It's a real mouthful but what an honour! Dr. Ian and I had tea several times at his house on Ten Mile Point, and his recollections—at age ninety-eight and then ninety-nine—amazed me on the topics on which we spoke. One afternoon we were discussing coyote ecology and I happened to mention that in 1994 I had seen a coyote on the roadside just south of Whistler. He immediately said, "You won't see many there, and I am surprised you saw even one that far west. Of course, their range runs out just about there." I thought about it for a second and wracked my brain for another sighting farther west— from Squamish or Ashlu or even on the coast. He continued, "You won't find them on the coast. They can't make it past the mountains." I was stunned, having just assumed they were there, but when I returned to my office at the University of Victoria and opened my well-worn copy of the *Mammals of BC,* I saw that he was exactly right: at that time the range ended just northwest of Whistler—although coyotes have since arrived on the south coast. He also talked of seeing eighteen mountain caribou on a mountain ridge just outside McBride in the mid-1930s, another example of how he retained his recollection of the things he loved—and knew them down to the smallest details.

Finally, I remember one afternoon when we toured his backyard rhododendron collection and watched the birds foraging through his trees. I shared with him that I had just put up a bird feeder at my office, and that all I had so far was one dark-eyed junco. He reminded me of what a gift it was that even one junco saw fit to hang around outside my office window. He had, of course, nailed it: how lucky we are to be surrounded by and experience nature in our daily lives. He was a tremendous man, well ahead of his time.

Robert Thomas (Tom) Sterling

B.Sc. (Hons.) (1950, Zoology), UBC; M.Sc. (1966, Zoology), University of Saskatchewan

Tom is a retired wildlife biologist, having worked his entire professional career with Ducks Unlimited Canada. Over a period of thirty-seven years he worked mainly with waterfowl in Alberta (1949–50), Saskatchewan (1951–69), British Columbia (1970–82) and Yukon Territory (1983–85). He officially retired in late 1985. Along with Robert D. Harris and Ernest W. Taylor of the Canadian Wildlife Service, Tom was recognized for his work in preserving wetland habitats in British Columbia and by having the landmark four-volume set of *The Birds of British Columbia* dedicated to him. In 2012 Ducks Unlimited Canada nominated Tom for an award to

Tom Sterling with a catch of eastern brook trout, Pasquia River, SK, spring 1950. PHOTO BY TOM STERLING.

recognize his contributions to wetland conservation in British Columbia, and on July 18, 2012, he was the recipient of the Premier's Conservation Award for the Province of British Columbia.

Dr. Cowan was Tom's supervisor for his B.A. (Hons.) thesis on ageing and sexing scoters.

> I consider Dr. Cowan to be the most inspiring and compelling influence on my life's career. Before encountering him, I had spent an uneventful youth on a prairie farm during the dirty thirties followed by undistinguished military service in World War II and subsequent discharge to civilian life, ill-prepared and ill-equipped for life. My search for employment in the field of natural resources met with polite rejection but kind advice, making it clear my ambitions far exceeded my level of education. I was loath to commit more years to schooling before gaining life's rewards but reluctantly applied for entrance to UBC. I have since realized this was the most pivotal point influencing my future. The gentleman who assisted me in course selection unexpectedly expressed interest in my history, my hopes and aspirations and suggested the newly available wildlife management courses as being the most suitable for me. I joyfully agreed and was further pleased when at my first biology lecture I recognized the professor, Dr. Ian McTaggart-Cowan, as the same gentleman.
>
> Dr. Cowan's lectures were most inspiring, a revelation of the real purpose of education and a calling to achieve more than the essentials of life's needs. He was a source of wisdom on life affairs to students as well. A gem I have not forgotten was slyly bestowed on a few of us bleary-eyed post-revelers at one morning lecture; he told us that when temptation struck again, we would be better served by purchasing a good book rather than a bottle. I still use this excuse when adding more precious books to a library that is already beyond what I can ever read.
>
> After graduation I had occasional contact with Dr. Cowan, but most gratifying, in retirement, I was honoured to serve on the advisory board of the Habitat Conservation Trust Fund under his able leadership. Still the naïve farm lad, I again felt the teacher-student relationship, but it affirmed Dr. Cowan's efforts and intent in his students having something to give, and it closed the circle for me.

Ward Earl Stevens

B.Sc. (1942, Forestry) Utah State University; M.Sc. (1947), Iowa State University; Ph.D. (1955, Zoology), UBC

After receiving his Ph.D., Ward took a position with the Northwest Territories government as superintendent of game, based in Fort Smith. In 1958 he joined the Canadian Wildlife Service (CWS) in Ottawa as chief mammalogist, and in 1962 he was appointed regional superintendent for western Canada based in Edmonton. In 1966 under the auspices of the Canadian International Development Agency (CIDA) he was seconded

Ward Stevens, ninety-three years old, at his home in Duncan, BC, December 2012. PHOTO BY RONALD D. JAKIMCHUK.

Ward Stevens weighing a juvenile muskrat during his Ph.D. research in the Mackenzie River Delta, NWT, summer 1949. PHOTO BY DON FLOOK.

to a project in Malaysia for two years then returned to CWS in Edmonton as research director of mammalogy for the western region, a position he occupied until his retirement in 1984. From 1975 to 1980, Ward was seconded to Kenya as head of a co-operative rangeland monitoring study under CIDA.

Dr. Cowan was Ward's supervisor for his Ph.D. dissertation on adaptations of the muskrat to a northern environment.

I had just completed my master's degree in zoology and asked my advisor at Iowa State University to see if he could get the names of Canadians whom I could contact seeking employment in the wildlife field in Canada. I had been away from the Canadian scene for many years, first in three American universities and then in the Royal Canadian Air Force in India. The name I got was Dr. I. McT.-Cowan at UBC. Our correspondence culminated in a meeting in Fort Smith, Northwest Territories, en route to the Mackenzie Delta for the summer. Our path took us to Norman Wells in a Dakota airplane and thence to the little settlement of Aklavik in the Mackenzie Delta in a Norseman float plane piloted by veteran pilot Ernie Boffa. The date was June 7, 1947, and we were the first plane to land after the ice broke up and floated out to the Arctic Ocean. As usual, many townsfolk were there to meet the plane—not to see us but to get their mail. Dr. Cowan was the first onto the aircraft float and was asked to wait until they could run a plank out so he could walk to shore. But it was not a great distance so he decided to jump ashore, which landed him halfway to his knees in Mackenzie River Delta mud, a pervasive northern medium we quickly got used to—like the mosquitoes we endured.

We had for our use a heavy old Chipewyan skiff and a ten-horsepower outboard motor for transport and arranged to meet our guide at Knud Lang's trading post about thirty miles upriver. The meeting culminated in Dr. Cowan asking our guide whether he was an Indian or an Eskimo. It was hard to tell because Henry Firth had a round face, a fringe of hair around a bald pate and a paucity of teeth that changed the contours of his face. Old Henry drew himself up and announced, "Doctor, I am a Scot." It seemed a most interesting venue for two Scots to meet. Henry's father was John Firth who had established the Hudson's Bay Company trading post at nearby Fort McPherson and his mother was the daughter of Sandy Stewart, one of the HBC clerks who had married a local girl.

Dr. Cowan taught me the importance of keeping meticulous field notes; we counted every duck on the river. We collected and prepared skins of local birds, we trapped and did likewise for small mammals, including my first lemming. We even attended the yearly reindeer roundup and watched the herders deftly corral and count the animals. On Richards Island we had our first meal of inconnu (coney), a freshwater whitefish that migrates up and down the Mackenzie River. While there, Dr. Cowan shot a glaucous gull for his collection; it fell into the Arctic Ocean and I was asked to wade out to get it. The water was far from tropical, the Indian Ocean being the last ocean I had waded into.

Dr. Cowan knew the three kinds of jaegers we encountered and he pointed out a northern [Siberian] wheatear, a bird new to me. We also saw Sabine's gulls and even one ivory gull. He was a consummate field man and I was lucky to have his company and his guidance.

Later I attended UBC as one of his students in the Department of Zoology. We returning veterans at UBC had a somewhat different outlook on life than the aspiring students just out of high school. That we were earnest in pursuing our education must have pleased the professors, though some students were just about their own age. Dr. Cowan accepted such students very well; he had his own standards, which we accepted and appreciated, even when he locked up the supply of ethyl alcohol, which was unaccountably dwindling.

I join with many others in saluting Ian Cowan for his many accomplishments, for his even-handed dealing with his students, and for the example he set for all of us.

Ian Stirling

B.Sc. (1964, Zoology), M.Sc. (1966, Zoology), UBC; Ph.D. (1969, Zoology), University of Canterbury, New Zealand

Ian is a research scientist emeritus with the wildlife research division of Environment Canada and an adjunct professor in the Department of Biological Sciences, University of Alberta in Edmonton. For forty-four years he has done research on polar bears and polar seals in the Arctic and Antarctic regions. He has won several awards for his work, including the Northern Science Award. He is an Officer of the Order of Canada and a fellow of the Royal Society of Canada. He participates in a number of national and international committees on polar bears and marine

Ian Stirling removing a satellite radio collar from a female polar bear with a cub. PHOTO BY G.W. THIEMANN, SOUTHERN BEAUFORT SEA, APRIL 2006.

237

mammals and has authored or co-authored over two hundred peer-reviewed scientific articles and three books.

Dr. Cowan was a member of Ian's supervisory committee for his M.Sc. thesis on the behaviour of captive sooty [blue] grouse.

> When I first indicated my interest in graduate studies to Ian Cowan back in 1963, he was immediately enthusiastic and supportive. Then, as in later years, that unqualified support was a significant confidence builder to a kid from small-town British Columbia. As a member of my M.Sc. committee, he was always available for discussion, to give encouragement and offer valuable insights. In the early years of my career while I worked in New Zealand, Antarctica, Australia and then back in the Canadian Arctic, he was my most significant mentor and a towering example of everything I have come to believe a scientist should be. In particular, Ian was incredibly accessible to students, always listened to their ideas and was completely unstinting in his encouragement of anyone who was genuinely interested and willing to work. I think his particular gift for making a student relax a bit in his rather awe-inspiring presence was reflected in his comment to me, once, that he didn't think there was any such thing as a dumb question if it was asked sincerely. Actually, I wondered at the time what particularly dumb question I might have asked recently. Ian led by example, and the work ethic he modelled was inspirational. His personal integrity and his drive to make the world a better place ecologically was, and always will be, a continuing legacy to us all. All of us who had the opportunity to know and work with Ian, in whatever capacity, were truly among the most fortunate environmental scientists of the last century.

Lawson G. Sugden

B.A. (1950, Zoology), UBC; M.Sc. (1957), Utah State Agricultural College; Ph.D. (1969, Ecology, Fisheries and Wildlife), Utah State University

Lawson Sugden, born June 22, 1927, passed away on November 4, 2011 in his eighty-fifth year.

Lawson spent the initial part of his professional career as a regional game biologist for the British Columbia Wildlife Branch at Williams Lake. During his seven years in the province he was credited with restoring the endangered California bighorn sheep herds to their numbers of today.[214] In 1959 he joined the Canadian Wildlife Service (CWS) in Edmonton and for nine years conducted research on migratory waterfowl in Alberta. His last twenty years were spent as a CWS research scientist at the Prairie Migratory Bird Research Centre in Saskatoon. He published at least forty articles on waterfowl and wetland birds,[215] including incidental field observations.[216]

Lawson retired in 1987 and moved to Skaha Lake in the Okanagan Valley, where he lived for the next twenty-four years and continued to enjoy his passion for nature and travel.

Lawson Sugden during a California bighorn sheep transplant near Doc English Gulch in the Chilcotin region of BC, circa 1950s. PHOTO COURTESY OF OREGON STATE GAME COMMISSION.

Dr. Cowan influenced my choice of career although he likely never realized it. Upon finishing senior matriculation, I worked for a year, after which I planned to enter studies in the UBC forestry department. I had met J.A. Munro and often thought that his line of work with migratory birds would be a nice choice for a career, but I was not aware of similar opportunities.

In 1947 while living at Francois Lake, I was appointed a delegate by the local [Burns Lake] sportsmen's group to attend the first provincial game convention at Harrison Hot Springs.[217] It was sponsored by the Game Commission and was attended by Drs. Cowan and Clemens as scientific advisors to the Commission. Through meeting Dr. Cowan and one of his first wildlife students, Jim Hatter, I discovered that there were courses in wildlife biology offered at UBC and listed in the 1946–47 university calendar. With this new information, I quickly abandoned the notion of forestry and in the fall of 1947 enrolled in an arts program, majoring in zoology.

It is high time I acknowledged Dr. Cowan for pointing a way for a successful and satisfying career in the wildlife field.

David Suzuki

B.A. (1958), Amherst College, MA; Ph.D. (1961), University of Chicago

David is professor emeritus at UBC in the Department of Zoology. He has had a long career as a broadcaster and is well known nationally and internationally for his work as an environmentalist and educator.

Wow, it never occurred to me that Ian had so closely approached his one-hundredth birthday. What a staggering achievement!

After living in the United States for eight years to get my undergraduate and graduate education, I decided I wanted to come home to Canada. It was the post-Sputnik era when the United States was lavishing money on anyone interested in science and there were jobs everywhere, but I was turned off by the racism I witnessed in Tennessee during a year of post-doctoral study there, so I took the first job I could get in Canada. It was a great job in the Department of Genetics at the University of Alberta, but that winter it dropped to minus 40°F for a week. When the job at UBC came up, I applied. When I left Edmonton for the interview, it was minus 20°F, and when I arrived in Vancouver, it was 30°F above zero and everyone was complaining about how cold it was!

Ian was head of the Zoology Department. At that time genetics was taught by a woman in the Department of Botany. I don't think Ian cared so much about genetics as he did about getting as many of the courses as possible away from Botany. Anyway, he hired me and I was ever grateful to him for that. He then gave me another great gift: he left me alone. I wasn't loaded with all kinds of administrative work that is usually given to people low on the totem pole.

Back in 1963 when I came to UBC, fisheries and wildlife ruled the department. Folks in physiology and cell biology felt like we were warts on the body of zoology. The way I dealt with the seeming disparities between genetics and wildlifers was to look down on all those folks who were counting songbirds and

David Suzuki, professor and popular environmentalist, at an old-growth Sitka spruce on the coast of BC. PHOTO COURTESY OF DAVID SUZUKI FOUNDATION.

watching elk in the woods. There was a friendly rivalry between faculty members that extended to the students, though I really enjoyed playing football with the wildlifers. Ian never tried to impose his ideas on me. I can't emphasize how much I appreciated his hands-off treatment of a young assistant professor.

I had never been a television watcher and fell into television totally by chance. It was only years after I was involved in it that I learned Ian had already used television to educate the public, and he really was a pioneer in the medium along with Hume and Ivey who pioneered physics on television from Toronto. As environmental issues occupied my interest more and more, I regretted that I hadn't taken advantage of the strong ecology group at UBC. Indeed, when I gave a keynote address to the annual meeting of the Ecological Society of America,[218] I spent the first five minutes apologizing for being so arrogant when I was younger. I wish Ian had banged me on the head about the importance of ecology.

I am truly grateful to Ian for saving me from the Siberia of Edmonton.

J. Mary Taylor

B.A. (1952, magna cum laude, Zoology) Smith College; M.A. (1953, Zoology), Ph.D. (1959, Zoology), University of California, Berkeley

When Ian Cowan was appointed dean of the Faculty of Graduate Studies at UBC, Mary Taylor came from the faculty of Wellesley College to the Department of Zoology at UBC to teach and to head the Cowan Vertebrate Museum. She was the first woman in the department to achieve the rank of full professor. Two decades later she became executive director of the Cleveland Museum of Natural History. Upon her retirement, she was made executive director emerita and a lifetime honorary trustee.

Mary's research field is mammalogy with special interest in systematics and reproductive biology of Australian mammals. She was the first woman to become president of the American Society of Mammalogists. Both this society and the Australian Mammal Society elected her an honorary member, their highest honour. She is a member of Sigma Xi, a past Fulbright scholar, a Killam Senior Research Fellow and recipient of a number of grants from the National Science Foundation and the Natural Sciences and Engineering Research Council of Canada. Mary serves on several boards of non-profit institutions.

My head is full of wonderful and often hilarious memories of happy times with Ian and Joyce. One such time was early on when they invited me to their cabin-under-construction on Mayne Island. Ian was the chief and only trench digger and Joyce and I were the plumbers assigned to lay the water pipe in the wake of the diggings. It was a wet morning that turned to pouring rain so we sought refuge under a cedar tree where not a drop could penetrate through the branches. After a hearty lunch, we finished the job. It was a good job, too, and on later visits I could not help but notice how gracefully and elegantly the water seemed to flow from the taps in the house.

J. Mary Taylor, the first female full professor in the Department of Zoology, UBC, was appointed by Ian as Director of the Cowan Vertebrate Museum, a position she held from 1965 to 1982. PHOTO BY BLYTHE OLSON, PORTLAND, OR, USA, MAY 22, 2014.

My greatest challenge was to take over from Ian the teaching of Zoology 416 when he became the very first dean of Graduate Studies at UBC. Those were huge footsteps to fill, and I felt that my whole foot was no longer than his big toe. He had already been decorated with national, regional and provincial honours to recognize his many outstanding contributions to his field and to his country, not the least of which was the lecture series in the natural sciences that was televised throughout Canada. What an act to follow! It was he who had spearheaded the origin and growth of the Vertebrate Museum in the Department of Zoology that is full of invaluable research materials, much of which were collected by his own hand. I am delighted that the museum is named for him.

Ian and Joyce were full of surprises, too. When we were about to host the fifty-second annual meeting of the American Society of Mammalogists, Joyce—Ian's conspirator on this occasion—invited me to dinner not long before the meeting commenced and served me a piece of meat that I could not identify. It looked a bit like rabbit or pork, but I could not guess by the taste. Well, after I had eaten it, Ian told me it was mountain lion! A few of them had been culled from Vancouver Island by provincial wildlife officials where the cougars had overpopulated an area, and he had arranged that they give a couple of them to us to be served at the Society's banquet. I'm sure that occasion was a "first" for many of our mammalogist colleagues and today, we would hope, would have been their "last."

I was deeply touched when Ian and Joyce came to visit me after I became executive director of the Cleveland Museum of Natural History. Not only was it then one of the ten largest in the United States, it was and still is a magnificent museum, and I was so proud to be able to take them through some of the collections and exhibits. Ian was especially interested in the fine collection of old duck decoys, some of which were meticulously covered with real feathers. It is a wonder that they ever survived the wear and tear of rough handling by the hunters.

Then there was the matter of the sourdough given to Joyce by a friend from Victoria. It had a positive effect on Ian's life because Joyce made bread, pancakes, biscuits and other delicious sourdough offerings for breakfast. That sourdough was at least ten years old when Joyce gave me some. I kept it for over thirty years, gave some away, lost mine and retrieved it once again. At Ian's ninetieth birthday party, Joyce asked if I would give her back a starter of it, but she subsequently declared that, "It wasn't the same." My reputation as a steward of sourdough was ruined!

Ian's wry and irrepressible humour kept us all on our toes. It is hereditary, too, because his dear father, whom I had the great pleasure of knowing, had a bountiful supply of good humour genes as well.

Among those of us who had the opportunity to know Ian over many years (for me it is forty-five), most of us could not keep up with him, be it in academia, elk hunting, philatelic prowess, longevity, etc. By example, he showed us that one can reach for the century mark, keep one's spark with enthusiasm, and focus forward. I'm sure he would have told us that it was easy.

John Theberge at Cowichan Station, Vancouver Island, BC, April 22, 2014.
PHOTO BY MARY THEBERGE.

John B. Theberge

B.Sc.A. (1964, Wildlife Management), University of Guelph; M.Sc. (1968, Zoology), University of Toronto; Ph.D. (1970, Zoology) UBC

John is a retired wildlife ecologist living in British Columbia's Okanagan Valley. He was a professor of ecology and conservation biology in the Faculty of Environmental Studies at the University of Waterloo in Ontario for thirty years. He and his wife Mary have specialized in research on wolves and their prey and on formulating methods of ecological evaluation of wilderness areas. He has been active in promoting the establishment of national parks and the application of ecological approaches in protected areas, serving on boards and as an executive of several conservation organizations. As a husband and wife team, they continue to lecture, conduct wildlife research and write. In addition to his scientific and magazine articles he has published five books including *The Ptarmigan's Dilemma*, which won the 2010 Lane Anderson Award for best science book written by a Canadian.[219]

Ian was on my Ph.D. dissertation committee at UBC, but he made his most momentous contribution to me in just our first meeting. To this meeting I owe a decision not to call off my candidacy as a Ph.D. student, which I came close to doing in my first weeks after moving to Vancouver. (I recounted this event in a book just published titled *The Ptarmigan's Dilemma: An Exploration of How Life Organizes and Supports Itself.*[220])

When I arrived at the University of British Columbia for Ph.D. research, knowledge on the subject of population regulation had progressed far enough for the emergence of some lively general hypotheses that divided the Department of Zoology into ideological camps: a food regulation camp, a predation regulation camp and an intrinsic or quality-of-stock regulation camp. It was disconcerting for a newcomer trying to decide where to pitch a research tent. Each camp seemed convinced that it was focussing on an underlying and universal tenet of population regulation, and I was perplexed by the various camps established around their various population theories. I went to see the dean, Ian McTaggart-Cowan, a respected and acknowledged leader in wildlife ecology in North America, to ask him if I had any future at UBC because I could not see myself fitting into any of these camps. He reassured me by saying that he, too, found himself fitting into no single camp. His thinking was that, just as individual species have evolved different mechanisms and behaviours to win at the evolutionary game, those differences must be reflected by a wide variety of ways that their populations are regulated.

At the time this was good enough for me, and after our own journey of several decades in population ecology, it still is. With this sympathetic and thoughtful comment, Ian saved a struggling student.

Donald C. Thomas

B.A. (Hons.) (1962, Biology), University of Saskatchewan; Ph.D. (1970, Zoology) UBC

Don retired from the Canadian Wildlife Service in 1998 and was adjunct research scientist with Environment Canada (EC) until 2009. He conducted research on caribou and their habitats from the high Arctic islands to Jasper National Park and near Prince Albert National Park. After retiring, he consulted on projects that included a status report for woodland caribou in Canada (2002)[221] and an advisory group advising EC on what constituted "critical habitat" for woodland caribou (2008).[222] He won several awards including the Northern Science Award.

Don was fortunate to have Dr. Cowan as a Ph.D. advisor for his dissertation on reproduction in deer.

Don Thomas (left) and Fred Zwickel, Ph.D. graduate students, UBC, Vancouver, BC, November 1963. PHOTO BY BRYAN R. GATES.

> Dr. Cowan had the rare ability to stimulate enthusiasm and a positive outlook for wildlife research. I always came out of his office ready to tackle my thesis project with great spirits. Maybe that is why he allowed me to work in his office for two or three weeks while I was writing a joint paper on reproduction in deer; he was away on an extended trip to Australia and New Zealand at the time.
>
> Dr. Cowan would introduce a seminar speaker and then appear to nod off for ten or fifteen minutes. The audience was amazed when he would get up and thank the speaker and summarize all the main points of the talk. No one will ever know if he really did catch a few winks.
>
> Graduate students learned about wildlife management from Dr. Cowan and also about life and ethics. He did not hide his views on social issues, even though some of them were not politically correct for the era. His upbeat temperament and ready laugh lifted the spirits of all. He was a great teacher, a superior leader and a wonderful mentor of graduate students.

Frank Stephen Tompa

B.Sc. (1956, Biology and Chemistry), Szeged University of Natural Sciences, Hungary; Ph.D. (1963, Zoology), UBC

Frank was born in Budapest, Hungary, in 1933 and graduated from high school there in 1951. He immediately started his university education, but in 1956 he served as co-chairman in a local revolutionary council and had to flee Hungary when the uprising was crushed by the Russians. He became a new immigrant to Canada on March 23, 1957. Shortly after arriving in this country he found work as a lab technician at Queen Mary Veterinary Hospital in Montreal but in 1960 entered UBC to study for his Ph.D.

Between 1963 and 1965, while on a National Research Council of Canada grant, Frank carried out field and laboratory research at the

Frank Tompa, Pender Island, BC, circa 2002. PHOTO BY CHRISTEL TOMPA.

University of Helsinki, Finland, on flycatchers and titmice. From there he was invited to be a guest researcher at the University of Aberdeen in Scotland to work on the social behaviour and population regulation of shelducks. From 1966 to 1968 he was an assistant professor at Simon Fraser University in Burnaby where his interests included comparative ethology and vertebrate and developmental biology.

Frank carried out ecological research in Norway, Newfoundland and Labrador between 1970 and 1972 with the International Biological Program, then between 1972 and 1974 he was guest professor at the University of Basel in Switzerland to introduce population ecology as a new subject. While there, he conducted a study for the Swiss Ornithological Institute on controlling crop damage by crows. He also spent a sabbatical research year at Stockholm University where he studied the social behaviour of roe deer. From 1975 to 1988 he served as the large carnivore management section head with the British Columbia Ministry of Recreation (now Environment) dealing mainly with problem wildlife.

Frank has been happily retired since 1988.

I can confidently claim that after my father it was Ian who had the greatest impact upon my life and career. In 1959 with a Hungarian B.Sc. degree under my belt, I worked as a lab technician in Montreal, anxious to get back to my real ambitions. Jim Bailey of the Toronto Museum [Royal Ontario Museum] suggested that I contact Ian McTaggart-Cowan. The response was swift and positive, and by the spring of 1960 I was working on Mandarte Island, an ecological goldmine, studying a song sparrow population for an M.Sc. degree.[223]

Ian, a member of my graduate committee, was keenly interested in my progress. During my second summer on the island, I had to spend a couple of days at the department, and Ian invited me for lunch at the Faculty Club where in due time I was asked to give him a progress report. At the end he said, "Frank, this exceeds the scope of a masters. I shall propose to your committee to convert your study into a Ph.D. program!" and so he did. Following my third summer of research I presented my first ever paper at the 1962 American Ornithologists' Union conference at the Smithsonian Institution in Washington, D.C. Later that paper became recommended literature at several American, European and even Japanese universities and was eventually reprinted as a "benchmark" paper in Allen W. Stokes's symposium volume *Territory*.[224]

It was also Ian who taught us the axiom in the confines of a graduate class that to succeed in research we had to spend the money first then ask for it! In the fall of 1963 the Cowans gave me a farewell party before my departure for postgraduate research at Helsinki University in Finland—a job that resulted in my marriage as well as several publications.

Thanks to his support, I was able to teach and do research at Simon Fraser University as well as at several European universities. Thus it was in Switzerland that we met again. I was a guest lecturer at the University of Basel as well as doing research with crows, while Ian was attending a World

Wildlife Fund conference at Lake Geneva. Again we had lunch together. By then I had decided to break with academic work and through him managed to end up with a wildlife biologist position with the British Columbia government. I held that post until 1988 when I took early retirement. Working for fourteen years in a politically sensitive position, trying to reconcile often-irreconcilable differences between opposing groups of the public had taken its toll. Ian honoured me by coming to my retirement party.

Following that position and several years in Europe, I returned to British Columbia and had further opportunities to explore. By then I had a new hobby, genealogical research. I could trace the roots of my clan as far as the first millennium and the court of Frederick Barbarossa—resulting in a book and a shorter essay. The Cowans came to an exhibition of paintings by my wife, Christel, during the 1990s, and one of her watercolours ended up in their Victoria home. After that, our encounters were infrequent—usually aboard a ferry between Swartz Bay and the Gulf Islands. My memories hold the warmest regards and thanks to Ian.

Kees Vermeer

B.Sc. (1959, Zoology), M.Sc. (1963, Zoology), UBC; Ph.D. (1967, Zoology), University of Alberta

Kees is a retired ornithologist. After graduation from the University of Alberta with a Ph.D. in zoology in 1967, he was employed as a research scientist with the Canadian Wildlife Service where he remained until retirement in 1994. He conducted research and published many papers on the effects of oil pollution, pesticides, heavy metals, predation and habitat destruction on aquatic birds. Kees also examined the effects of changing sea surface temperatures on the reproductive success and diet of nesting seabirds.

Dr. Cowan was a key member of Kees' M.Sc. committee, which resulted in a major publication that forty-seven years later remains the major source of breeding information for the glaucous-winged gull.[225]

Kees Vermeer (right front) with archaeology students at Port au Choix, NL, July 2008. PHOTO BY REBECCA VERMEER.

My memories of Ian McTaggart-Cowan and my years at UBC fall into four categories.

First, my university studies and Mandarte Island. I attended UBC as an undergraduate from 1956 to 1959 and as a graduate student from 1960 to 1963. The year between, I did not attend due to lack of finances. In my graduate years I began an M.Sc. program, which included a field study on the ecology of the glaucous-winged gull. This study was conducted for a total of eight months in the summers of 1961 and 1962 on Mandarte Island, a small rocky island in Haro Strait north of Victoria. My sole companion there was Frank Tompa who was studying the population ecology of song sparrows. However, many other graduate students visited the island, among them Gerry van Tets, who initiated the first seabird studies on the island,[226] and Rudi Drent, who studied the biology of pigeon guillemots there in 1959 and 1960.[227]

My first contact with Dr. Cowan was when I attended his introductory course in zoology, which I enjoyed very much. He was immaculately dressed for the occasion and radiated confidence and authority but was nevertheless very approachable for students. Dr. Cowan was a busy man because he also taught other courses and was head of the Department of Zoology. He was so busy that, when he sat down, he often fell asleep. I tested how deeply asleep he was in an advanced zoology class that I attended with three other students. When it was my turn to make a presentation, he fell asleep as usual. I stopped my talk for half a minute and just watched him. He suddenly woke up and immediately asked a relevant question and a lively conversation ensued. I concluded that not much escaped him, which later proved to be a very useful observation during my thesis defence.

Third, my thesis committee consisted of Dr. Miklos Udvardy, who was my supervisor, Dr. Cowan, Dr. Bendell and Dr. Chitty. Dr. Udvardy was a wonderful person to get along with, and we often discussed gull behaviour as observed by Dr. Niko Tinbergen of Oxford, England.[228] But Dr. Udvardy had the notion that I was studying behaviour even though I had informed him on several occasions that it was ecology I studied. It just didn't seem to register. When my draft thesis was ready in early 1963, I submitted copies to my committee for review. Not unexpectedly, Dr. Udvardy was very surprised that my thesis was on the ecology of gulls. He suggested I expand my one hundred typed pages to two hundred pages with more on the subject of behaviour. I included a few pages on behaviour but he was not satisfied with it.

Next I saw Dr. Chitty, who liked my thesis, but he suggested it should be tightened from one hundred to fifty pages. I shortened a number of paragraphs, but in the end I was back to one hundred pages. I could not sleep that night and wondered how to reconcile a thesis of two hundred pages with one of fifty pages. The next day I saw Dr. Cowan for advice and explained my dilemma to him. He listened carefully and said, "You have tried to satisfy both committee members. Now you can do it your way." I was very relieved and grateful for his advice.

In May 1963 I did my thesis defence. Besides questions on the thesis itself, I was grilled on various subjects in zoology. One course I had missed in my schooling was invertebrate zoology, but I did not expect that any of my committee members would check my course background—except for Dr. Cowan. On that hunch, I crammed on as much information on invertebrates as possible. On the day of my defence, I presented an overview of the thesis and answered questions from all the committee members except Cowan who remained silent. When the others were finished, Dr. Cowan rapidly fired one question after another on the subject of invertebrates, thus confirming my hunch. He looked surprised when I answered each question correctly and then asked, "How do you know so much about invertebrates without taking a course on the subject?" I answered, "I read a lot." That was true but it was not on invertebrates!

Fourth, Dr. Tinbergen's reaction to my thesis. I forwarded a copy of my thesis to Dr. Tinbergen, a Nobel laureate. He was impressed and called it a "first-rate study." He invited me to conduct my Ph.D. research with him at Oxford, but I did not accept his offer for practical reasons. Part of the reason my research was recognized by Dr. Tinbergen and the fact that the published thesis became a "citation classic" in 1989 was that Dr. Cowan had allowed me to do my own thing.

James (Jim) H.C. Walker

B.A. (1964), Mount Allison University; M.Sc. (1967, Zoology), University of New Brunswick

Jim was the director of the British Columbia Wildlife Branch from 1984 to 1988 and an assistant deputy minister with the British Columbia Ministry of Environment from 1988 to 2001. He is now retired and serves on the board of the Nature Trust of British Columbia and is currently the chair of the Vancouver Island Marmot Recovery Foundation.

James (Jim) H.C. Walker in Victoria, BC, 2005. While director of the British Columbia Wildlife Branch, Jim frequently called on Ian to lecture at important events to instill enthusiasm and credibility into current wildlife programs. PHOTO BY THE NATURE TRUST OF BRITISH COLUMBIA.

One of my greatest impressions of Ian was his wonderful ability to communicate with everyone at a level that was immediately meaningful to them. When I was director of the British Columbia Wildlife Branch, we asked him to speak at several functions or conferences over the years and he never disappointed.

I always remember a day in August 1986 when he and I, Rod Silver and John Elliot were touring by helicopter in the northern Rockies to look at prescribed burns funded by the Habitat Conservation Fund. We had stopped for dinner at the main lodge of Garry Vince, the prominent guide outfitter in the Upper Muskwa River area. Garry had several American sheep hunters there, preparing to go to spike camps and start their hunts, and we all ate together at a communal table. Conversation was a bit stilted as they stuck to their clique and we to ours. Then one of the hunters mentioned the Chadwick ram—the largest Stone's sheep ever recorded—that had been shot near the headwaters of the Muskwa and Prophet rivers in 1936.[229] Ian said, "You know, I remember there was something really peculiar about the annuli on those horns." It turned out that he had been asked to examine and measure that sheep, and for the next ten minutes he regaled all of us as only he could about the horn structure and how the animal's lifestyle had probably affected its horn development. The sheep hunters were absolutely spellbound and asked question after question, and by the end of the meal he had them eating out of his hand.

He was as natural and effective a communicator as they come.

Robert B. Weeden

B.Sc. (1953), University of Massachusetts; M.Sc. (1955), University of Maine; Ph.D. (1959, Zoology), UBC

Bob left UBC in 1959, married fellow Ph.D. candidate Judith Stenger and moved to Alaska as research biologist for the Alaska Department of Fish and Game. For ten years he studied ptarmigan and supervised statewide

Bob Weeden (left) leading a birding trip at Ford Lake, Salt Spring Island, BC, 2008. PHOTO COURTESY OF ROBERT B. WEEDEN.

research on grouse, waterfowl and furbearers. At that time there were few researchers studying tetraonids in the world. His pioneering field research in Alaska and northwestern British Columbia provided new information on the use of segregated habitats in summer and shared habitats in winter for willow ptarmigan, white-tailed and rock ptarmigan.

Moving in 1970 to the University of Alaska, Fairbanks, he taught in the Department of Wildlife Biology, held a joint appointment with the Institute of Social and Economic Research and helped to create the School of Agriculture and Natural Resources Management. His teaching broadened into original courses in wildlife management, resource policy, environmental law, environmental decision-making and environmental ethics. He retired in 1990 as professor emeritus of natural resources.

In 1975 Bob took leave to serve as director of Policy Development and Planning in the Office of the Governor. He also was appointed to the Alaska Environmental Advisory Council and the Alaska Power Authority. He was a member of the Federal Marine Fisheries Advisory Committee and was appointed by two presidents to the United States Marine Mammal Commission, "probably," he says, "because neither of them knew me."

For fifty-one years Bob has advocated for conservation, beginning in 1959 as a founder of the Alaska Conservation Society and continuing through today with his work as a director of the Salt Spring Island Conservancy. He was also a director of the National Audubon Society for six years. Birds and words are among his favourite things: as evidenced by two non-fiction books,[230] over eighty scientific articles and hundreds of short pieces and essays.

Bob and Judy have a small farm and orchard on Salt Spring Island.

The impulse that carried Ian through his century also fired the lives of all the great naturalists throughout history: an insatiable fascination with how living things meet the opportunities and challenges of circumstance. To Ian, every species was a unique genetic idea of how to get along, set loose on a journey through time and space. Individuals are exceedingly brief sparks but carry the possibility of morphing seamlessly into a succession of new forms surviving a billion years. Tiny stories, immense stories: Ian found absorbing interest in them all. To me and to many who were buoyed and energized by his guidance, the unbounded reach of his enthusiasm was the hallmark of the man.

While my major professor (1955–59), Ian's career was navigating several challenges. He had pulled away from research of his own, though his graduate students and faculty collaborators (I think of the physiologists in animal husbandry in the late 1950s with whom he studied the adaptive physiology of ruminant metabolism) connected him robustly to new ideas in science. He had become the head of the Department of Zoology and soon would become UBC's dean of Graduate Studies. Administrative work made it harder to retain his focus on the classes he still taught and the dozens of students who relied

Bob Weeden (left) and field assistant Harold Gibbard enjoying a break from ptarmigan thesis research at Boulder Creek, near Atlin, BC. PHOTO BY JAMES F. BENDELL, MAY 6, 1957.

on him for alert counsel. As well, he juggled an incredible schedule of public lectures, television appearances and professional advisory commitments.

He remained loyal to graduate students—Canada's last enslaved people. That loyalty helped me more than once, especially when, after I spent a field season climbing mountains to study ptarmigan ecology, James Bendell, full of a hundred ideas a minute, suggested that I catch a bunch of ptarmigan chicks and experiment to see whether the three species have different temperature tolerances. It was a perfectly good idea, but not mine, and not obviously more likely to pan out. Privately Ian had a chat with Jim, suggesting that I be allowed to run on my own track; no more was said about my conversion to physiology.

While I was being grilled during my comprehensive examination, Ian dragged out a huge skull totally unfamiliar to me and asked me what it was. I fumbled and filibustered about the sagittal crest, the expanse of masseter muscle attachment, the shape of the holes where teeth had been—but no inspiration came. And Ian moved on to something more comfortable. Afterwards he confessed that he thought I had been in his vertebrate zoology class (I had not) where he always presented this plaster cast of a sabre-toothed tiger as a kind of *pièce de résistance*. He had been confident I would impress the inquisitors with my broad knowledge.

Ian served on scores, if not hundreds, of advisory committees. I served on one with him—the United States National Research Council's advisory panel on Yellowstone Park grizzlies (1973–74). We were to weigh the evidence on numbers and distribution of grizzlies in the Yellowstone ecosystem and to advise on the contradictory management strategies pursued by state and federal agencies. As much as any other single factor, Ian's professionalism, familiarity with interplay of management and science and candour kept us focussed, fair and helpful.

Nancy Wilkin in her office as assistant deputy minister for the British Columbia Environmental Stewardship Division, Ministry of the Environment, Victoria, BC, October 2006. PHOTO COURTESY OF NANCY L. WILKIN.

Nancy L. Wilkin

B.A. (1971, Environmental Studies), Department of Geography, University of Victoria

Nancy is a retired assistant deputy minister (ADM), Environmental Stewardship Division, British Columbia Ministry of Environment. She has over thirty years of experience in the public sector, which has resulted in wide and deep roots in the fabric of British Columbia, working collaboratively with First Nations, local governments, recreation and conservation organizations and resource industries. As the ADM for Environment, she had responsibility for Fish and Wildlife, Ecosystems and British Columbia Parks. During this time she was the trustee of the Habitat Conservation Trust Fund (now Foundation) and a board member of the Freshwater Fisheries Society of BC. From 1998 to 2002 she served as a chief treaty negotiator for the Province of British Columbia. In 2008 Nancy's Environmental Stewardship Division received three Premier's Awards.

After her retirement from the British Columbia Public Service, she accepted a position as executive in residence at Royal Roads University (RRU) in Victoria; she is still at RRU and is responsible for the university's new Office of Sustainability. She was recently appointed to the British Columbia Regional Board of the Nature Conservancy of Canada and is a board member of the Child Nature Alliance.

It's funny after all these years to think that Ian McTaggart-Cowan touched my head during my graduation ceremonies at the University of Victoria when he was our chancellor, and here I am working at Royal Roads University and watching so many young people graduate and start their lives with such energy and hope! Maybe it was that touch that moved me into the field of fish and wildlife and gave me the passions I carry for all things related to the environment.

During the many years of work after that graduation ceremony I would come into contact with Ian at special occasions—sometimes at Government House, sometimes at Nature Trust events and always at Habitat Conservation Trust Foundation (HCTF) dinners. We would find each other, talk very seriously about the state of fish and wildlife and the government—I actually think that for a number of years he thought I was an elected official, and maybe I was! Ian and I would then turn to a full discussion of alpine plants—his passion. I would see him at the University of Victoria plant sale, chatting away—always teaching. I went on a garden tour in Victoria, and sure enough, it included Ian and Joyce's beautiful garden, and he was on his hands and knees showing me his latest acquisition. How such a great man found such joy in the smallest of nature's bounty!

My last dinner with Ian was truly a wonderful occasion, for on that night we raised the last dollars needed for the Ian McTaggart-Cowan chair at UVic. (Thank you, Jim Walker and Rod Silver and others!) I had attended the dinner at the HCTF in the hope of raising twenty thousand dollars of the needed eighty-five thousand dollars—we were so close to our one million dollar goal—but I think when all of the board members saw Ian again and saw how strong his mind was and how fragile his frame had become, they were overwhelmed—so overwhelmed they came through with the entire eighty-five thousand! I just wanted to cry and I did. It is occasions like that, when friends and colleagues celebrate the success of such a great man, and yet such a gentleman, that we know our fish and wildlife are in good hands.

With loving thoughts of Ian, his contributions and his legacy.

Robin Wilson
B. Com (Hons.) (1973), Faculty of Commerce, UBC

Robin Wilson in front of Canada Place, Vancouver, BC. PHOTO BY LARRY GOLDSTEIN © CANADA PLACE, JANUARY 26, 2009.

Robin is a partner in Whitewater Communications, a full-service marketing and communications company. She has an honours degree in commerce from UBC and was a Lieutenant Governor's Gold Medalist. She has an extensive background in consumer, business-to-business, non-profit and event marketing and management.

Robin has a long record of community involvement, including chair of the board of governors of Capilano University, president of the board of Ronald McDonald House British Columbia and chair of Canada Place Corporation. She is currently a member of the advisory boards of the Capilano University School of Business Administration, a director and past chair of the Nature Trust of British Columbia and a director of the Duke of Edinburgh Awards.

I have a vivid memory of my first meeting with Dr. Ian McTaggart-Cowan. It was my first Nature Trust of British Columbia board meeting at the venerable Vancouver Club. I had done research on my fellow board members prior to the meeting and was already in awe of Ian, a long-standing director. His long list of accomplishments, awards, distinctions and history of public service were daunting. I was to learn that he was incredibly approachable and had an amazing ability to make everyone feel at ease in his company. He had an engaging smile and a delightful twinkle in his eye. He was a wonderful listener and told great, entertaining stories. He could draw pictures with words as he reminisced about his many adventures as he, his wife and a myriad of friends, students and associates explored the natural world. And he had an incredible memory that went back decades and included the most amazing detail.

It was during that first board meeting that I developed an enduring admiration and respect for this truly exceptional human being. He got into a discussion about the Vancouver Island marmot—a highly opinionated and philosophical discussion, I must say, and one I will never forget. In fact, I started to take notes—notes that I still have today—and I continued to do this whenever I had the opportunity to be in Ian's presence.

Ian's love of the outdoors is legendary. I credit him with instilling in me an enduring curiosity and appreciation of the outdoors and an understanding of the resounding effects of interfering with Mother Nature. To have the opportunity of spending any time with Ian was a true gift. He was larger than life and he built an enduring legacy that will continue to impact future generations.

While enjoying retirement on Cortes Island, BC, Fred Zwickel—shown here in summer 2005—remains passionate about research on sooty and dusky grouse. PHOTO BY RUTH ZWICKEL.

Fred C. Zwickel

B.Sc. (1950, Wildlife Management), M.Sc. (1958, Wildlife Management), Washington State University, Pullman; Ph.D. (1965, Zoology), UBC

Fred retired as a professor in the Department of Zoology at the University of Alberta, Edmonton. He was born in Seattle in 1926 and attended Washington State University from 1947 to 1950 and again in 1958. In 1953 through early 1961 Fred studied blue [sooty] grouse while employed as a wildlife biologist with the state of Washington Department of Game. In 1961 he returned to university at UBC where he completed his Ph.D. in 1965. This was followed by a post-doctoral fellowship at the Nature Conservancy Unit of Grouse and Moorland Ecology in Scotland. He then spent a year teaching in the Department of Fisheries and Wildlife at Oregon State University, followed by eighteen years in the Department of Zoology at the University of Alberta in Edmonton.

Population studies of blue grouse have been the main focus of his research, which was principally carried out in British Columbia after 1961, and he has published widely on this species. In collaboration with Jim Bendell, Fred authored an award-winning monograph on the biology and natural history of blue grouse, which was published in 2004.[231]

Since his retirement in 1985 Fred and his wife Ruth have lived on six hectares of an old homestead on the shores of Manson's Lagoon on Cortes Island, BC.

Fred Zwickel and assistant recording details for a banded sooty (blue) grouse with English pointer, Kate, in a regenerating burned area west of Courtenay, BC, in the mid-1970s. PHOTO COURTESY OF FRED C. ZWICKEL.

As the teaching assistant for Ian's wildlife class in the early 1960s, I helped arrange a field trip to western Washington for the class. We went in private cars and I was driving with five other students on board. At the border crossing at Blaine, the officer on duty began with me. "Where are you from?" "United States," I replied. I explained that this was a UBC class field trip. No problem—borders were easy to cross in those days. He moved on to the student beside me. "Where are you from?" "Spain." Next: "Ecuador." Next: "England." Next: "Holland." The last student to be queried was Benny Simard who replied, "Quebec." The officer then asked, "When did you come to Canada?" Need I say more?

In the early 1960s when Ian was still head of the Department of Zoology, he got a new secretary. She was a Kiwi, perhaps around forty years old and, as with many Kiwis, a quick wit. One day I, and I believe it was Ron Jakimchuk, poked our heads into Ian's office door as Ian and she were discussing some matter. She was speaking and the discussion went something like this: "I recently had an offer to have my picture in *Playboy*," and as she thrust her chest forward, "but they couldn't get all of me on one page." Great secretary. Shortly after that, Ian moved on to become dean of Graduate Studies, and I understand that his secretary and her husband returned to New Zealand. She was sorely missed by virtually all the graduate students that I knew in that fine and fun department.

I really enjoyed my time and experiences at UBC and have fond memories of Ian and the Department of Zoology.

Part III

LEGACY

CHAPTER 9
Honours and Awards

The array of awards and honours bestowed upon Ian McTaggart-Cowan over a period of nearly seven decades reveals the astonishing diversity of his interests and accomplishments as well as the esteem in which he was held. They originated from three major sectors of society: academic institutions, peer recognition and public service organizations as represented by both private groups and governments.

In recognition of his outstanding achievements Ian was awarded honorary D.Sc. degrees by the University of British Columbia (UBC) (see Part I, Chapter 7), the University of Victoria (UVic) and the University of Northern British Columbia (UNBC). He received LL.D. degrees from the University of Alberta (U of A) and Simon Fraser University (SFU) and a Doctor of Environmental Studies degree from the University of Waterloo.

Ian's name is also associated with three permanent post-secondary scholarships to support students in his discipline. These are the Ian and Joyce McTaggart-Cowan Scholarship at UVic for outstanding students proceeding to year three or four of an honours program in biology, the Dr. Ian McTaggart-Cowan Scholarship in the School of Environmental Studies for UVic graduate students who are focussing on endangered species recovery and/or ecological restoration and the Ian McTaggart-Cowan Scholarship in wildlife management at UNBC.

In addition, two Ian McTaggart-Cowan professorships have been established at British Columbia universities. Dr. Brian M. Starzomski (see Part II) currently holds a professorship of Biodiversity, Conservation and Ecological Restoration in the School of Environmental Studies at UVic, and in 2000 UNBC created the Muskwa-Kechika research professorship presently held by Dr. Katherine L. Parker. As well, in 1998 UVic named a student residence in the Commonwealth Village in Ian's honour and dedicated a bench in front of the alpine garden in memory of Dr. Ian McTaggart-Cowan.

During his long life, Ian received numerous honours and awards from all sectors of society. PHOTO BY RONALD D. JAKIMCHUK.

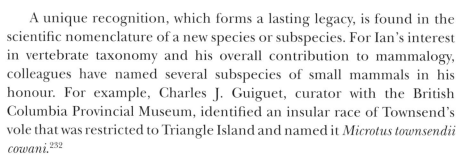

Four of the six recognized subspecies of Townsend's vole in North America occur in the southern coastal areas of BC. One very large insular race, found only on Triangle Island off the northwestern tip of Vancouver Island, was named by Charles J. Guiguet as *Microtus townsendii cowani* in Ian's honour. PHOTO BY R. WAYNE CAMPBELL.

A unique recognition, which forms a lasting legacy, is found in the scientific nomenclature of a new species or subspecies. For Ian's interest in vertebrate taxonomy and his overall contribution to mammalogy, colleagues have named several subspecies of small mammals in his honour. For example, Charles J. Guiguet, curator with the British Columbia Provincial Museum, identified an insular race of Townsend's vole that was restricted to Triangle Island and named it *Microtus townsendii cowani*.[232]

Ian also made contributions and developed lifelong friends in disciplines other than vertebrate zoology, and those colleagues have also honoured him in various ways. In their paper "The Talitroidean Amphipod Family Hyalidae Revised, with Emphasis on the North Pacific Fauna: Systematics and Distributional Ecology,"[233] invertebrate biologists E.L. Bousefield and E.A. Hendrycks identified a new species of amphipod off Vancouver Island and named it *Parallorchestes cowani;* they stated that "the patronym recognizes the outstanding career contributions of Dr. Ian McTaggart-Cowan." Roger N. Clark, a malacologist, in his paper "Two New Chitons of the Genus *Tripoplax* Berry, 1919 from the Monterey Sea Canyon"[234] commented concerning his discovery of a new species: "Etymology: It is with great pleasure that I name this species [*Tripoplax cowani*] after my friend and colleague, Dr. Ian McTaggart-Cowan of Victoria, British Columbia."

Other honours Ian received include the highest civilian honour of the governments of Canada and British Columbia and various peer-related organizations. Details of a few of those awards and their associated citations follow.

1946—Fellow of the Royal Society of Canada

The Royal Society of Canada, also known as the Academies of Arts, Humanities and Sciences of Canada, is the senior national, bilingual body of distinguished Canadian scholars, humanists, artists and scientists. The primary objective of the Royal Society of Canada is to promote learning and research in the arts, humanities and sciences. It consists of nearly two thousand fellows, men and women who are selected by their peers for outstanding contributions; to be invited to become a Fellow of the Royal Society of Canada is considered the highest honour that can be attained by scholars, artists and scientists in Canada. Ian was appointed a fellow at the age of thirty-six.

1970—Aldo Leopold Memorial Award

The Wildlife Society established this award in 1950 in honour of Aldo Leopold (1887–1948), the American ecologist, forester, environmentalist and founder of the science of wildlife management. The award is presented each year at the Society's annual conference.

In 1950–51 Ian McTaggart-Cowan served as the fourteenth president (and first from Canada) of The Wildlife Society. He received the Aldo Leopold Memorial Award in 1970.
PHOTO BY RONALD D. JAKIMCHUK.

Although they never met, Leopold was one of Ian McTaggart-Cowan's heroes. In a 1998 speech he quoted Leopold's statement that "there are some who can live without wild things, and some who cannot . . . For us of the minority, the opportunity to see geese is more important than television, and the chance to find a pasque flower is a right as inalienable as free speech."[235] Ian continued his tribute by saying:

> This simple, eloquent observation gave image to what thousands have felt deeply and with growing anger as they watched, throughout North America, the ravaging of landscapes and the destruction, in the name of progress, of private beauty spots. Half a century has elapsed since Leopold voiced his convictions in terms that caught the imagination and gave new impetus to the fledgling conservation movement. Research in the wild and active dissemination of results have been powers for change in the ways we conduct our lives. Nationwide organization and international communication were essential to the progress that was made, but knowledgeable, dedicated individuals drive conservation and identify its directions.[236]

Ian McTaggart-Cowan was the twenty-second recipient of the prestigious Aldo Leopold Memorial Award that recognizes a distinguished career dedicated to wildlife conservation. The published citation recognized him for building "his distinguished career as a research biologist by specializing in the systematics and ecology of birds and mammals, and enlarging our understanding of the wildlife of his homeland and far beyond." The citation also commended him for being "largely responsible for convincing the Canadian government to hire trained wildlife biologists to staff their wildlife management agencies." It concluded:

Cowan became dean of Graduate Studies in 1964 but continued to teach a course in wildlife biology, supervise directed studies and guide the research of zoology doctoral candidates. Cowan's findings and philosophies, presented in 179 published papers and two books, had a profound influence on focussing attention and in tempering human impact upon our world. He was among the first to use television to arouse public awareness of wildlife ecology, with educational programs that garnered international awards.

1970—Arthur S. Einarsen Award

This award was established in 1966 by the Northwest Section of the Wildlife Society, which includes five states—Alaska, Idaho, Montana, Washington and Oregon—British Columbia, Alberta and the Northwest Territories. It recognizes outstanding service to the wildlife profession by individuals residing in the area encompassed and is presented at the annual meeting of the Northwest Section whenever a worthy recipient is identified.

Arthur S. Einarsen (1897–1965) was a pioneering wildlife scientist who was best known for his books *The Pronghorn Antelope and its Management*[237] and *Black Brant: Sea Goose of the Pacific Coast.*[238]

The Right Honourable D. Roland Michener, Governor General of Canada, presenting Ian McTaggart-Cowan with the Order of Canada on March 31, 1971. PHOTO COURTESY OF ANN SCHAU.

1970—Officer of the Order of Canada

Created in 1967 to coincide with the one hundreth anniversary of the formation of Canadian Confederation, the Order of Canada has three tiers, which in order of precedence are: companion, officer and member. An Officer of the Order of Canada is a Canadian citizen who is recognized for "outstanding achievement and service to the country or to humanity at large." Up to sixty-four officers may be appointed each year with no limit on how many may be living at one time. As of July 2009 there were 1,012 living officers of the Order of Canada.

Ian became an officer of the Order of Canada on December 18, 1970—just three years after the Order was created— and was invested on March 31, 1971, for his contribution to zoology and allied sciences and his work as a conservationist.

1975—Honorary Life Fellow of the Pacific Science Association

The Pacific Science Association, founded in 1920, is a non-governmental, scholarly organization based in Honolulu that seeks to advance science and technology in support of sustainable development in the Asia-Pacific region. This includes all countries and islands within or bordering on the Pacific Ocean. The Association confers honorary life fellowships on scientists "who have given distinguished service either directly to the Association or by furthering the objectives for which the Association was founded." These fellowships are awarded every four years at Pacific Science congresses to "outstanding and distinguished leaders in Pacific science."

The honour was first conferred in 1961, and Ian became the tenth international scientist and first Canadian to be recognized. He received notification at the Thirteenth Pacific Science Congress held at UBC in Vancouver from August 18 to 30, 1975. Ian was president and his colleague Dr. W.S. Hoar was secretary-general of the Association at the time of the meeting.

1976—F.E.J. Fry Medal of the Canadian Society of Zoologists

This award, established in 1974, honours Frederick E.J. Fry, founding member and first president (1966–67) of the Canadian Society of Zoologists. It is presented to "a Canadian zoologist who has made an outstanding contribution to knowledge and understanding of an area in zoology." The recipient is expected to deliver a plenary lecture at the following annual general meeting.

Ian McTaggart-Cowan was the third recipient of this annual award and, as a requirement of accepting the honour, presented a lecture entitled "The Sociology of Carnivores Related to Their Use of Resources."

1982—J. Dewey Soper Award and Honorary Life Membership in the Alberta Society of Professional Biologists

J. Dewey Soper (1893–1982) was an Arctic explorer, zoologist and ornithologist who became the chief federal migratory bird officer for Alberta, Northwest Territories and Yukon. He was a prolific author; by the end of his career he had published over 130 research papers and articles. His books include the original *The Mammals of Alberta*.[239] He was highly regarded for his role in the development of biology in western and northern Canada.

The J. Dewey Soper Award is given periodically by the Alberta Society of Professional Biologists to "a Canadian biologist who has made significant contributions to the field of biology." In his acceptance speech on receiving the Dewey Soper Award, Ian stated: "There is no higher honour than that bestowed by one's peers."

1989—Award of Excellence by the Association of Professional Biologists of British Columbia

In 1988 the Association of Professional Biologists of British Columbia (APB) established an award of excellence to be bestowed on a member in good standing in recognition of a significant contribution to the biological sciences in this province. This award is not presented annually, though in exceptional circumstances may be given to two or three members in a single year. In 1993 it was renamed The Ian McTaggart-Cowan Award for Excellence in Biology. Ian received the award in 1989 and was made an honorary member of the APB in 2003.

Nine biologists have received the APB award over its twenty-five-year history.

Ian received an outstanding achievement award from the Foundation for North American Wild Sheep in 1990. PHOTO BY RONALD D. JAKIMCHUK.

The insignia of the Order of British Columbia consists of a stylized dogwood, the floral emblem of British Columbia. The insignia is part of a medal that also features a crowned shield of arms. It is worn with a green, gold, white and blue ribbon. In addition to the medal, members of the Order receive a lapel pin and a Certificate of Appointment. PHOTO BY MARK NYHOF.

1990 – The Foundation for North American Wild Sheep: Outstanding Achievement Award

The Foundation for North American Wild Sheep (now the Wild Sheep Foundation or WSF) was officially formed in 1977 with the purpose of "putting and keeping wild sheep on the mountain." The foundation is dedicated to "enhancing wild sheep populations, promoting professional wildlife management, educating the public and youth on sustainable use and the conservation benefits of hunting while promoting the interests of the hunter and all stakeholders." To date, the foundation has expended more than seventy million dollars on programs benefiting wild sheep, other wildlife and their critical habitats.

The WSF issues awards in three major categories: service, North American and international. In 1990 Ian became the fourteenth recipient of the "outstanding achievement award" in the service category, which recognizes outstanding contributions to wildlife conservation. Ian's Ph.D. student, Valerius Geist, had received the same award twelve years earlier.

1991—Officer of the Order of British Columbia

Instituted in 1989 by then Lieutenant Governor David Lam, the Order of British Columbia is a civilian honour for service with the greatest distinction in any field benefiting the people of British Columbia or elsewhere. It represents the highest form of recognition the province can extend to its citizens. The text from the program at the investiture of Ian McTaggart-Cowan at Government House in Victoria began by outlining his academic career and previous awards and continued:

> Dr. McTaggart-Cowan has devoted a lifetime to studying, teaching and conserving the natural resources of British Columbia. His involvement extended far beyond the UBC campus. Naturalist groups around British Columbia frequently called upon his knowledge and enthusiasm to inspire members; many of those who listened would pursue careers in biology and involve themselves in environmental conservation. Dr. McTaggart-Cowan was himself heavily involved as chairman or member of many of the lead organizations concerned with the environment, such as the National Research Council's Advisory Committee on Wildlife Research and the Environmental Council of Canada, to name only two in a long list. He has been a worldwide environmental emissary for British Columbia and Canada. Although now retired, he continues to serve on many committees, boards and organizations dedicated to ensuring the environmental integrity of British Columbia's natural resources. An internationally recognized conservationist, Dr. McTaggart-Cowan has given distinguished service to the people of British Columbia and their natural resources.

1998—Doris Huestis Speirs Award

Ian received this award from the Society of Canadian Ornithologists / Société des ornithologistes du Canada at their seventeenth annual general meeting in Vancouver in August 1998. The award is given annually "to honour any significant contribution to Canadian ornithology," a definition that is broad enough to include scientific research, contributions through art, conservation activities and the popularization of ornithology.

Doris Huestis Mills (1894–1989), an artist, naturalist and author, lived her entire life in Toronto. She is well known as an artist as she painted with the Group of Seven. She was also an avid birder, and some of her research on the evening grosbeak was published as "*Hespercphora [Hesperiphona] vespertina brooksi* Grinnell, Western Evening Grosbeak" in a volume of A.C. Bent's series of life histories of North American birds.[240] For many years she and her husband, J. Murray Speirs, maintained a regular journal of bird sightings.

The citation for Ian's presentation read in part:

The award honours Dr. Cowan's outstanding lifetime contribution to Canadian ornithology, spanning seven decades, with major achievements in avian science, research, conservation and environmental education and management. Dr. Cowan is presently active in the completion of the fourth and final volume of *The Birds of British Columbia*,[241] one of the most comprehensive regional reviews of birds and their distribution produced in North America.[242] Ian McTaggart-Cowan is distinguished for his scientific work in vertebrate zoology on mammals and birds and for his mastery of both university teaching and administration, a rare combination of talents. Although better known as a mammalogist, Dr. Cowan's contributions in ornithology are also impressive, including publications on birds, supervision and encouragement of graduate students and conservation activities.

He has been characterized as the "Dean of Vertebrate Zoologists in Canada," a fitting title. He started publishing on birds in the 1930s and is still at it. His more than 260 publications include at least 40 explicitly on birds, primarily in avian journals as well as government series and books. These works cover general biology, systematics, distribution, parasites and disease and conservation. Many other publications are concerned with conservation of wildlife and habitats and the management of environmental impacts in resource development. His Doris H. Speirs lecture entitled "Moments from the Education of an Ornithologist" gives glimpses of the range of his knowledge of birds—and the people who study them. He served on many conservation bodies in and outside government in Canada and the USA, for example, as former vice-president of IUCN and current chair of the BC Habitat Conservation Trust Fund Board.

Dr. Cowan has received many honours and awards, none previously for his work and support of ornithology alone. His influence on avian science and conservation, directly and indirectly, in this country has been immense.

Although Ian was generally considered a mammalogist, the Society of Canadian Ornithologists/ Société des ornithologistes du Canada recognized his significant contributions to ornithology by presenting him with the Doris Huestis Speirs Award in 1998. PHOTO BY RONALD D. JAKIMCHUK.

Dr. Cowan has been honoured across North America for his scientific and conservation achievements—officer of the Order of Canada 1972, fellow of the Royal Society of Canada and other scientific societies, honorary doctorates from five universities (1971–86) and various awards from wildlife associations. He served as president or chairman of many associations. Dr. Cowan stands out as a model to us as scientist, conservationist and teacher.

The Society of Canadian Ornithologists takes great pleasure in presenting the 1998 Doris Huestis Speirs Award to Ian McTaggart-Cowan for his outstanding contributions to Canadian ornithology and conservation.

1999—Barsby Trophy: Conservationist of the Year

The British Columbia Wildlife Federation (BCWF), the largest and oldest conservation organization in the province, consists of hunters, anglers and recreational shooters. One of its objectives is "to ensure the sound, long-term management of British Columbia's fish, wildlife, park and outdoor recreational resources." The BCWF presents twelve annual awards of which the (Ted) Barsby Trophy is "the greatest honour the federation can bestow on any individual for an outstanding contribution to conservation over the years."

Ian was the twenty-sixth recipient of the award, at ninety years old. The inscription read: "In recognition for your dedication to the fish & wildlife resource and your outstanding contribution to conservation in the province of British Columbia." Two other UBC professors had previously received the award: Dr. Bert Brink in 1982 and Dr. Peter Larkin in 1990.

In recognition of Ian's contributions to conservation and habitat preservation in the province, the British Columbia Wildlife Federation presented Ian with their highest honour, the Barsby Trophy, in 1999.
PHOTO BY RONALD D. JAKIMCHUK.

In addition to the foregoing awards, Ian was also honoured by the BC Field Ornithologists on July 8, 2007 (first recipient of this award for ornithology). He also received the Canadian Environmental Achievement Award (1992), the Council of College and Institute Principals of British Columbia Award (1981), the Federation of British Columbia Naturalists (now Nature BC) designation of honorary president, a British Columbia government citation for service on the public advisory committee of the Habitat Conservation Trust Fund (2001), director emeritus designation by the Nature Trust of British Columbia (2004), a lifetime membership by the Vancouver Island Rock and Alpine Garden Society, and the National Wildlife Federation award as international conservationist of the year (1978). In March 2013 the government of British Columbia announced the creation of the McTaggart-Cowan/ns k'l nim't Wildlife Management Area on the east side of Skaha Lake in the south Okanagan.

Recognition from such diverse sectors as those listed in the foregoing awards and citations attest to Ian McTaggart-Cowan's profound influence on so many aspects of Canadian society.

Awards for Hobbies

Philately (Stamp Collecting):

- The British North America Philatelic Society Gold Medal Award

- 2004 – Law Stamps of the Yukon[243]

- 2005 – Law Stamps of British Columbia Revenue and Their Uses[244]

The following review was published by the British North America Philatelic Society (BNAPS) in 2004. (see www.bnaps.org/reviews/notes2004.html).

Ian McTaggart-Cowan's National Gold award-winning exhibit, THE LAW STAMPS OF YUKON, includes proofs, cancels and many interesting documents. A fabled part of the Canadian North, the Yukon includes the Rocky Mountains [and Mackenzie Mountains] from the 60th parallel northward to the Arctic coast and most of the headwaters of the Yukon River. In scenic terms it is spectacular and has attracted the attention of many devotees of wilderness landscapes. The gold rush of the years around 1898 focussed the attention of the world on the Yukon. Due to an economic depression at the time, thousands of people flooded into central Yukon in search of instant riches. In just a few months the small settlement of Dawson found itself transformed into Dawson City, with a population of 40,000 people! The results were a much more complex society with many more aspects for historians and philatelists to study and report on.

The author first visited Yukon some 50 years ago in his capacity as a wildlife ecologist and a member of the Arctic Institute of North America. His then early interest in philately was focussed on revenue stamps and their uses, particularly on the wealth of legal cases reflected in the documents validated by law stamps. The Law Stamps of Yukon were especially fascinating because the founding arrangement involved two series of stamps. One series was attached to a Gold Court charged with adjudicating disagreements within the mining industry. This court was very active for a period of eight years, after which the Territorial Court, responsible for everyday problems, handled most legal cases. The interesting Law Stamps of Yukon offer insight into many day-to-day events of times past.

Ian McTaggart-Cowan has been involved in Canadian philately for many years. In addition to his Yukon exhibit he has also prepared a gold-award winning exhibit of British Columbia Revenues. Ian has written many articles on revenue subjects as diverse as the Weights and Measures, Gas and Light Inspection stamps of Canada, and federal, Alberta and British Columbia wildlife stamps.

In 2004 Ian's presentation of his collection *The Law Stamps of Yukon, 1902–1971: Their Development and Use* earned him a gold medal from the Northwest Federation of Stamp Clubs, a chapter of the British North America Philatelic Society. PHOTO BY RICHARD FLEET.

In 2005 Ian's well-researched collection of *The Law Stamps of British Columbia and Their Uses, 1879–1984* earned him another gold medal. PHOTO BY RICHARD FLEET.

Gardening

In retirement Ian spent more time in his garden and entering specimens and even his garden itself into competition. Between 1985 and 2001 he displayed plants at the Vancouver Island Rock and Alpine Garden Society's annual spring show. He won prizes in seven of the twenty categories in fifteen different years.

For three consecutive years, beginning in 1999, Ian won the Madge Hamilton Trophy for "Best *Sempervivum* or *Jovibarbe*" (succulent plants) in the Vancouver Island Rock and Alpine Garden Society spring show. PHOTO BY R. WAYNE CAMPBELL.

CHAPTER 10

A Legacy of Scientific and Other Publications

Ian McTaggart-Cowan was fortunate in his early development as a zoologist to have several inspiring and supportive mentors, two of which strongly influenced him to write and publish his findings. One was Kenneth Racey, his eventual father-in-law, and the other was his professor, Dr. Joseph Grinnell, founder of the Museum of Vertebrate Zoology at the University of California, Berkeley.

Kenneth Racey was a prominent bird and mammal collector whose publications included pioneering summaries of the bird life of the Alta Lake region from 1920 to 1948.[245] After he developed a friendship with Ian in the late 1920s, he gave the young man an autographed copy of his first paper on the birds of Alta Lake.[246] This inspired Ian, with Racey's help, to write and publish his first article in 1929 when he was just nineteen years old.[247] When Ian became a biologist with the Provincial Museum in Victoria, he invited his mentor to co-author two articles on mammals, their only joint papers.[248]

Prior to entering studies at Berkeley for his Ph.D., Ian received two signed books authored by his future supervisor, Joseph Grinnell.[249] In 1947 he used Grinnell's publications on California birds[250] to develop a template for a book on BC birds that he co-authored with James A. Munro.[251]

Grinnell provided guidance and mentoring that strongly influenced Ian's subsequent career as a professor at UBC. In his Doris Huestis acceptance lecture Ian recalled that Grinnell insisted "the end result of research was publication 'meticulously crafted,'" a credo Ian followed all his life.[252] During his Ph.D. studies Ian published several papers that Grinnell edited[253] and submitted his doctoral dissertation for publication in a peer-reviewed journal before returning to BC.[254]

It could be said that Ian McTaggart-Cowan was the right person at the right time in the right position, and it is certainly true that these circumstances contributed to his extraordinary productivity when it came to describing the fauna of British Columbia. Without question, by arriving on the scene when there had been so little previous investigation, he had a virtual clean slate of opportunity. It might also be said that he led a charmed life as a result of the opportunities open to him as a university professor. There is a very persuasive argument for this—witness the latitude given to him to freely collect biological specimens in Banff and Jasper national parks as the first scientific observer to conduct a biological survey of the parks.

But the real difference between Ian and others in the field was in his documentation and the publication of his observations. He had a lifelong commitment to the belief that the publication of results was the researcher's key responsibility and the underpinning of progress in advancing knowledge. His commitment to recording discoveries, large and small, was an integral part of that philosophy. He was in his early nineties when, as one of its co-authors, the final volume of *The Birds of British Columbia*[255] was published. When told that it represented an amazing seventy-year record of scientific publication for him, he still felt the need to reiterate the necessity of publishing research results, a policy well known to all of his graduate students. He frequently told them that "good writing is hard work and if you complete a manuscript page a day it has been a productive twenty-four hours."

Notwithstanding all of the above, it was the eye of a keen and motivated observer that was paramount in everything he did. His former student Jim Hatter recounts an example of luck coinciding with Ian's astute power of observation:

> On our way to Banff Park in the summer of 1944 we visited the spectacular Columbia Icefield on the Banff-Jasper highway. At a place tourists seldom reach we had a remarkable experience. Dr. Cowan found a large canine tooth from a wolf lying exposed on the top of a glacier. It was later identified by experts as the tooth of a dire wolf, a prehistoric race of wolf that lived in Canada thousands of years earlier.

A paper resulting from this discovery was published in 1954.[256]

The list of publications that follows covers the incredible range of Ian McTaggart-Cowan's interests and contributions. Topics include something for everyone—taxonomy, life history, anatomy, parasitology, animal nutrition, ethics of conservation, sustainable land use and philosophy— because the biosphere and its preservation were his overarching interest and passion. However, at the start of his career, there were virtually no field guides to ease the acquisition of knowledge, only an antiquated, incomplete literature and "keys" to identification in miscellaneous publications.

A Lifetime with Museums and Specimens

Some of Ian's scientific publications included the analysis of museum specimens. In addition to these records, his various collections of birds, mammals and invertebrates are preserved as specimens in British Columbia museums, and these are also an integral part of his scientific and educational legacy.

In his first appointment as a biologist (1936–40), he was a driving force in curating and expanding collections for the British Columbia Provincial Museum (now the Royal BC Museum). Then in his years as a professor in the Department of Zoology at UBC, he established and expanded what became known as the Cowan Vertebrate Museum. That collection, now known as the Cowan Tetrapod Collection, is housed in the renowned Beaty Biodiversity Museum at UBC. Other parts of Ian's personal collections, such as his molluscs, are housed in the Royal BC Museum in Victoria.

But his inquiring mind and prodigious memory, supplemented with diligent research, gave him the tools to develop this formidable legacy of scientific literature.

He was first a naturalist. Even small creatures and single interesting events deserved his curiosity and attention. Then, as he grew in scientific skill and intellectual breadth, he found academia an exciting place in which to practice his craft. He encouraged and, where necessary, prodded his students to publish and share their results. His efforts and those of his cadre of former students helped to lay a scientific foundation for management and conservation of our wildlife and their habitats provincially and nationally. His publications and the ideas that they generated are, therefore, a central portion of his legacy.

The following list of Ian McTaggart-Cowan's publications reveals the amazing scope of his interests and contributions in a variety of fields and disciplines. Few have been so bold as to publish beyond a narrow expertise, and fewer still have had so many of their predictions and the synthesis of their values vindicated by the passage of time.

Books

During the course of his busy career, Ian was author, co-author or contributor to nine books. He published his first book as sole author in 1939 when he was just twenty-nine. Publication of a book requires a much more comprehensive approach and organization than does a scientific paper because it takes a concerted effort to integrate a broad range of knowledge or concepts. In addition, books are generally directed toward a wider readership than technical papers. Ian's early works were largely technical in nature. Later in his career he wrote on topics pertaining to wildlife conservation and policy, attracting a wider readership. Finally, in his last years he returned to his roots, co-authoring the four volumes of *The Birds of British Columbia*.[257] The last volume in the series was published in 2001 when Ian was ninety-one years of age and twenty-six years into his retirement.[258]

Ian examining a grey wolf pelt in the Cowan Vertebrate Museum at the University of British Columbia, Vancouver, BC. COURTESY OF UNIVERSITY OF BRITISH COLUMBIA ARCHIVES, PHOTO 1.1-12670-4.

Campbell, R. Wayne, Neil K. Dawe, Ian McTaggart-Cowan, John M. Cooper, Gary W. Kaiser and Michael C.E. McNall. 1990a. *The Birds of British Columbia: Volume 1: Nonpasserines: Introduction, Loons through Waterfowl.* Royal British Columbia Museum, Victoria, BC. 514 pp.

Campbell, R. Wayne, Neil K. Dawe, Ian McTaggart-Cowan, John M. Cooper, Gary W. Kaiser and Michael C.E. McNall. 1990b. *The Birds of British Columbia: Volume 2: Nonpasserines: Diurnal Birds of Prey through Woodpeckers.* Royal British Columbia Museum, Victoria, BC. 636 pp.

Campbell, R. Wayne, Neil K. Dawe, Ian McTaggart-Cowan, John M. Cooper, Gary W., Kaiser, Michael C.E. McNall and G.E. John Smith. 1997. *The Birds of British Columbia: Volume 3: Passerines: Flycatchers through Vireos.* UBC Press, Vancouver, BC. 693 pp.

Campbell, R. Wayne, Neil K. Dawe, Ian McTaggart-Cowan, John M. Cooper, Gary W. Kaiser, Andrew C. Stewart and Michael C.E. McNall. 2001. *The Birds of British Columbia: Volume 4: Passerines: Wood-Warblers through Old World Sparrows.* UBC Press, Vancouver, BC. 739 pp.

Cowan, Ian McTaggart. 1939. "The Vertebrate Fauna of the Peace River District of British Columbia." British Columbia Provincial Museum Occasional Paper, No. 1, Victoria, BC. 102 pp.

Cowan, Ian McTaggart. 1973. *The Conservation of Australian Waterfowl.* Australian Government Publishing Service Special Publication No. 2, Canberra, Australia. 84 pp.

Cowan, Ian McTaggart and Charles J. Guiguet. 1956. *The Mammals of British Columbia.* British Columbia Provincial Museum Handbook, No. 11, Victoria, BC. 413 pp.

Wayne Campbell processed over forty-two thousand pieces of correspondence during the preparation of *The Birds of British Columbia*. In this photo, he is dealing with two weeks of correspondence that accumulated during an absence for fieldwork! Summer 1974. PHOTO BY JOHN ELLIOTT, VICTORIA, BC.

Collecting in the Peace River District: 1938

The avifauna of the south Peace River region of British Columbia remained relatively unexplored until 1938 when the British Columbia Provincial Museum organized a collecting trip into the area. It was headed by Ian McTaggart-Cowan with partner Patrick W. Martin; it was the first significant investigation of the area. In fifty-seven days of fieldwork from May 5 to June 30 between Swan Lake and Charlie Lake, they recorded 168 species of birds, of which Cape May warbler, bay-breasted warbler and Nelson's sharp-tailed sparrow were species new to the avifauna of British Columbia.

Typical boreal wetland of the Peace River District, near Taylor, BC, June 15, 1990. PHOTO BY R. WAYNE CAMPBELL.

Geist, Valerius and Ian McTaggart-Cowan (eds.). 1995. *Wildlife Conservation Policy*. Detselig Enterprises Ltd., Calgary, AB. 310 pp.

Munro, J.A. and Ian McTaggart Cowan. 1947. *A Review of the Bird Fauna of British Columbia*. British Columbia Provincial Museum Special Publication, No. 2, Victoria, BC. 285 pp.

Wildlife Publications

Invertebrates

Living on the Pacific Coast enabled Ian to expand his collecting interests to marine species. Initially he focussed on the intertidal zone, but later explorations included dredging deeper waters off British Columbia, California and Mexico. The joint father-son publication (1977) describing a new species of chiton must be unique.

Cowan, Garry I. McTaggart and Ian McTaggart Cowan. 1977. "New Chiton of the Genus *Mopalia* from the Northeast Pacific Coast." *Syesis 10:* 45–52.

Cowan, Ian McTaggart. 1962. "Molluscs of a Single Dredge Haul." *Pacific Northwest Shell News* 2: 37.

Cowan, Ian McTaggart. 1963a. "*Tonicella insignis* Reeve in British Columbia." *Pacific Northwest Shell News* 3: 53.

Cowan, Ian McTaggart. 1963b. "The Preservation of Colour in Chitons." *Pacific Northwest Shell News* 3: 65.

Cowan, Ian McTaggart. 1964a. "The Egg Capsule and Young of *Beringius eyerdami* Smith (Neptuneidae; Mollusca Gastropoda)." *The Veliger* 7: 43–45.

Cowan, Ian McTaggart. 1964b. "A New Species of the Lamellibranch Genus *Aligena* from Western Canada." *The Veliger* 7: 108–109.

Cowan, Ian McTaggart. 1964c. "New Information on the Distribution of Marine Mollusca on the Coast of British Columbia." *The Veliger* 7: 110–113.

Cowan, Ian McTaggart. 1964d. "The Egg Capsule and Young of the Gastropod *Pyrulofusus harpa* (Morch)." *The Veliger* 8: 1–2.

Cowan, Ian McTaggart. 1968. "The Interrelationships of Certain Boreal and Arctic Species of *Yoldia* Moller." *The Veliger* 11: 51–58.

Cowan, Ian McTaggart. 1969. "A New Species of Gastropod (Fissurellidae, *fissurisepta*) from the Eastern North Pacific Ocean." *The Veliger* 12: 24–26.

Cowan, Ian McTaggart. 1974a. "*Sabia conica* (Schumacher) on the Pacific Coast of North America." *The Veliger* 16: 290.

Cowan, Ian McTaggart. 1974b. "The West American Hipponicidae and the Application of *Malluvium, Antisabia,* and *Hipponix* as Generic Names." *The Veliger* 16: 377–382.

Cowan, Ian McTaggart and J.H. McLean. 1964. "A New Species of *Puncturella (cranopsis)* from the Northeastern Pacific." *The Veliger* 11: 105–108.

Sirenko, B.I. 1973. "Amphipacific Distribution of Chitons (Loricata) and Their New Species in the Northwest Section of the Pacific Ocean." *Zoological Journal* 52: 667–669. Translated for and edited by Ian McTaggart Cowan and Allyn G. Smith. Republished in *Of Sea and Shore* 5: 59–62 [Summer 1974]. Port Gamble, WA.

Smith, Allyn G. and Ian McTaggart Cowan. 1966. "A New Deep-water Chiton from the Northeastern Pacific." *Occasional Papers of the California Academy of Sciences* 56: 1–15.

Fishes

Ian was a periodic guest on H.R. MacMillan's yacht *Marijean* for Pacific Coast cruises, and he was thus afforded the rare opportunity to observe marine birds and mammals from an oceanic perspective. In addition, he was able to identify fish species taken during sport fishing on these cruises—and was probably one of the participants!

Cowan, Ian McTaggart. 1938. "Some Fish Records from the Coast of British Columbia." *Copeia* 1938: 97.

Cowan, Ian McTaggart. 1960. "Sundry Thoughts on Fishing Efficiency: How Far Can We Go?" *Western Fisheries* 59: 17–18.

Amphibians and Reptiles

From the late 1930s through the mid-1940s Ian wrote scientific and popular articles on amphibians and reptiles and carried his natural history curiosity about herpetology through to his graduate students at UBC.

Carl, G. Clifford and Ian McTaggart Cowan. 1945a. "Notes on the Salamanders of British Columbia." *Copeia* 1945: 43–44.

Carl, G. Clifford and Ian McTaggart Cowan. 1945b. "Notes on Some Frogs and Toads of British Columbia." *Copeia* 1945: 52–53.

Norman A.M. McKenzie (left), president of the University of British Columbia, and Ian McTaggart-Cowan aboard the yacht *Marijean* with a striped marlin (left) and Pacific sailfish. COURTESY OF UNIVERSITY OF BRITISH COLUMBIA ARCHIVES, MARCH 1962, PHOTO 23.1-510-1.

Cowan, Ian McTaggart. 1937. "A Review of the Reptiles and Amphibians of British Columbia." pp. 16–25 in Report of the British Columbia Provincial Museum for the year 1936, Victoria, BC.

Cowan, Ian McTaggart. 1938a. "Distribution of Turtles in Coastal British Columbia." *Copeia* 1938: 91.

Cowan, Ian McTaggart. 1938b. "Nature's Children in Our Western Gardens." *The Garden Beautiful* 7: 6–8.

Cowan, Ian McTaggart. 1941. "Longevity of the Red-legged frog." *Copeia* 1941: 48.

Cowan, Ian McTaggart and W.B.M. Hick. 1951. "A Comparative Study of the Myology of the Head Region in Three Species of *Thamnophis* (Reptilia, Ophidia)." *Proceedings and Transactions of the Royal Society of Canada.* Series 3, 45: 19-60.

Over seven decades ago Ian worked on establishing a baseline of the distribution of the western toad (*Anaxyrus boreas*) in BC. Today range contractions and decrease in numbers is a growing concern among herpetologists. PHOTO BY R. WAYNE CAMPBELL.

Birds

From his earliest days as a Boy Scout Ian had a keen interest in birds—both collecting and field identification. One of his earliest awards was a Boy Scout naturalist badge and a book prize for listing all the bird species he had observed around his home over the course of one year. The following publications encompass a wide range of ornithological topics from the distribution of birds and their habitats to diseases and population dynamics. Ian was also an impetus for the monumental undertaking of the four-volume *The Birds of British Columbia* (see books section above), participating as a co-author and motivator throughout the life of the twenty-eight-year project.

Clarke, G.H. and Ian McTaggart Cowan. 1945. "Birds of Banff National Park, Alberta." *Canadian Field-Naturalist* 59: 83-103.

Cowan, Ian McTaggart and James A. Munro. 1944-1946. "Birds and mammals of Revelstoke National Park." *Canadian Alpine Journal* 29: 100–121; 29: 237–256.

Cowan, Ian McTaggart. 1937a. "Additional Breeding Colonies of the Herring Gull in British Columbia." *The Murrelet* 18: 28.

Cowan, Ian McTaggart. 1937b. "The House Finch at Victoria, British Columbia." *The Condor* 39: 225.

Cowan, Ian McTaggart. 1938. "Distribution of the Races of the Williamson Sapsucker in British Columbia." *The Condor* 40: 128–129.

Cowan, Ian McTaggart. 1939a. "Black Phoebe in British Columbia." *The Condor* 41: 123.

Cowan, Ian McTaggart. 1939b. "The White-tailed Ptarmigan on Vancouver Island." *The Condor* 41: 82–83.

Cowan, Ian McTaggart. 1940a. "Bird Records from British Columbia." *The Murrelet* 21: 69–70.

Cowan, Ian McTaggart. 1940b. "Pentadactyly in a Spotted Sandpiper." *The Murrelet* 21: 6.

Ian McTaggart-Cowan's analysis of regurgitated barn owl pellets for prey remains was the earliest attempt to develop a diet profile for owl species in BC. His paper on their food habits motivated other students and naturalists to complement field studies, some of which led to graduate degrees. PHOTO BY R. WAYNE CAMPBELL.

A First for Canada

Just before his death in 1938, R.A. Cumming, a carpenter and amateur collector from Vancouver, BC, wrote James A. Munro in Okanagan Landing requesting that he publish a record of a black phoebe he had collected in South Vancouver in 1936. Munro passed the letter on to Ian at the British Columbia Provincial Museum, where the Cumming collection was housed, requesting that Ian "put the specimen on record." This resulted in a paper in *The Condor* in 1939.

Cowan, Ian McTaggart. 1940c. "Two Apparently Fatal Grouse Diseases." *Journal of Wildlife Management* 4: 311–312.

Cowan, Ian McTaggart. 1940d. "Winter Occurrence of Summer Birds on Vancouver Island, British Columbia." *The Condor* 42: 213–214.

Cowan, Ian McTaggart. 1942a. "Food Habits of the Barn Owl in British Columbia." *The Murrelet* 23: 48–53.

Cowan, Ian McTaggart. 1942b. "Termite Eating by Birds in British Columbia." *The Auk* 59: 451.

Cowan, Ian McTaggart. 1942c. "Some Diseases and Parasites of Game Birds and Fur-bearing Mammals in British Columbia." pp. K40–K45 in Annual Report of the British Columbia Game Commission for 1941. Victoria, BC.

Cowan, Ian McTaggart. 1942d. "Economic Status of the Pheasant on the Cultivated Lands of the Okanagan Valley, British Columbia." pp. M49–M62 in *Annual Report of the British Columbia Game Commission* for 1942. Victoria, BC.

Cowan, Ian McTaggart. 1943. "Aspergillosis in a Thayer Gull." *The Murrelet* 24: 29.

Cowan, Ian McTaggart. 1944. "The House Finch (*Carpodacus mexicanus*) in Alberta." *The Murrelet* 25: 45.

Cowan, Ian McTaggart. 1946a. "Death of a Trumpeter Swan from Multiple Parasitism." *The Auk* 63: 248–249.

Cowan, Ian McTaggart. 1946b. "Notes on the Distribution of *Spizella breweri taverneri.*" *The Condor* 48: 93–94.

Cowan, Ian McTaggart. 1948. "Waterfowl Conditions on the Mackenzie Delta: 1947." *The Murrelet* 29: 21–26.

Cowan, Ian McTaggart. 1949a. "Pheasant Study in British Columbia in 1948." pp. 112–116 in British Columbia Game Department, Proceedings of the Third Annual Game Convention, Victoria, BC.

Cowan, Ian McTaggart. 1949b. "Waterfowl Nesting Ground Studies in British Columbia, 1948." pp. 26–38 in Waterfowl Populations and Breeding Conditions in 1948. Canadian Wildlife Service, Ottawa, ON.

Cowan, Ian McTaggart. 1950. *A Pocket Check List of the Birds of Southwestern British Columbia: Land Birds.* Issued by University of British Columbia, Department of Zoology, Vancouver, BC. 8 pp.

Cowan, Ian McTaggart. 1951. "The Passenger Pigeon." *Museum and Art Notes* (Second Series) 1: 25–26.

Cowan, Ian McTaggart. 1952a. "Waterfowl at Beacon Hill Park." *Victoria Naturalist* 9: 21–22.

Cowan, Ian McTaggart. 1952b. *A Pocket Check List of the Birds of Southern Vancouver Island.* Issued by University of British Columbia, Department of Zoology, Vancouver, BC. 6 pp.

Cowan, Ian McTaggart. 1953. Book review: *Birds of Washington State* by S.G. Jewett, W.P. Taylor, W.T. Shaw and J.W. Aldrich. *Canadian Field-Naturalist* 69: 29–30.

Fifty-eight Years and Counting

In 1955 Professor Miklos D.F. Udvardy and graduate student Timothy Myres suggested that the Department of Zoology at UBC initiate a nest-card program similar to the successful venture by the British Trust for Ornithology in Great Britain. The initial response was encouraging, and in 1957 Tim prepared a manuscript for publication in the peer-reviewed journal *The Condor* and invited Ian and Miklos (his supervisor) to be co-authors. Fifty-eight years later the British Columbia Nest Record Scheme (BCNRS) is still being operated by unpaid volunteers, and in 2011 received 25,680 new breeding records. The BCNRS is currently the largest central repository for breeding information on birds in any province or state in North America. It is also the longest-running volunteer program for monitoring birds in the province.

Publications are Forever

Although Ian encouraged others to publish their findings, he also led by example. Whenever a specimen came into the BC Provincial Museum that was a new record or significant range extension, he immediately sent off a note for publication. He always said "the written word is forever." In his article on four *Bird Records from British Columbia*, the flesh-footed [pale-footed] shearwater (*Puffinus carneipes*) and south polar skua [skua] (*Stercorarius maccormicki*) were new species for the province, whereas Wilson's phalarope (*Phalaropus tricolor*) and lark bunting (*Calamospiza melanocorys*) were exciting range extensions.

Cowan, Ian McTaggart. 1954a. "An Indication of Population Mixing in Canada Geese." *The Murrelet* 35: 45.

Cowan, Ian McTaggart. 1954b. "A New Northern Record for Xanthus Murrelet, *Brachyrhamphus hypoleuca*." *The Murrelet* 35: 50.

Cowan, Ian McTaggart. 1955a. *Birds of Jasper National Park, Alberta, Canada*. Canadian Wildlife Service Wildlife Management Bulletin Series 2, No. 8, Ottawa, ON. 66 pp.

Cowan, Ian McTaggart. 1955b. "The Whooping Crane." *Bulletin of the Vancouver Natural History Society* 95: 2–3.

Cowan, Ian McTaggart. 1956. Book review: *Prairie Ducks* by L.K. Sowls. *Canadian Field-Naturalist* 70: 145.

Cowan, Ian McTaggart. 1964. "The Holotype of the Franklin Grouse (*Canachites franklinii*)." *Canadian Field-Naturalist* 78: 127–128.

Cowan, Ian McTaggart. 1965. Book review: *Geographical and Sexual Variation in the Long-tailed Jaeger (Stercorarius longicaudus Vieillot) by T.H. Manning. The Murrelet* 46: 17.

Cowan, Ian McTaggart and Mary F. Jackson. 1954. *Population Dynamics of Barrow's Golden-eye in British Columbia: Progress Report*. UBC, Department of Zoology Unpublished Report, Vancouver, BC. 7 pp.

Cowan, Ian McTaggart and Garry McT. Cowan. 1961. "The Amur Barn Swallow off British Columbia." *The Condor* 63: 419.

Cowan, Ian McTaggart and James A. Munro. 1944–1946. "Birds and mammals of Revelstoke National Park." *Canadian Alpine Journal* 29: 100–121; 29: 237–256.

Fennell, C., W.M. Wallace, J.A. Bruce, R.A. Ryder, L.A. Roper, C.A. Ely, E. Willis, W.C. Hanna, Ian McTaggart Cowan and G. McTaggart Cowan. 1961. "From Field and Study." *The Condor* 63: 417–419.

Gabrielson, Ira N., Robert P. Allen, Ian McTaggart-Cowan, Philip A. DuMont, Richard H. Pough and Gustav A. Swanson. 1950. "Report of the A.O.U. Committee on Bird Protection," 1949. *The Auk* 67: 316–324.

Grant, Peter R. and Ian McTaggart Cowan. 1964. "A Review of the Avifauna of the Tres Marías Islands, Nayarit, Mexico." *The Condor* 66: 221–228.

Hatter, James and Ian McTaggart Cowan. 1949. "Waterfowl Breeding Ground Survey in British Columbia." British Columbia Game Commission Memorandum, Victoria, BC. 2 pp.

Hatter, James and Ian McTaggart Cowan. 1950. "Waterfowl Breeding Ground Survey in British Columbia, 1949." pp. 24–29 in "Waterfowl Populations and Breeding Conditions, Summer 1949." United States Fish and Wildlife Service Special Scientific Report, Washington, DC.

Johnson, Stephen R. and Ian McTaggart Cowan. 1974. "Thermal Adaptation as a Factor Affecting Colonizing Success of Introduced Sturnidae (Aves) in North America." *Canadian Journal of Zoology* 52: 1559–1576.

Johnson, Stephen R. and Ian McTaggart Cowan. 1975. "The Energy Cycle and Thermal Tolerance of the Starlings (Aves, Sturnidae) in North America." *Canadian Journal of Zoology* 53: 55–68.

A POCKET CHECK LIST OF THE

BIRDS OF SOUTHWESTERN

BRITISH COLUMBIA

LAND BIRDS

This list is intended for local use in walks afield. A seasonal grouping is adopted as follows: (1) Resident throughout the year; (2) present through the summer only; (3) present in winter only; (4) transient, that is, migrant in spring or fall or both; (5) vagrant, that is, of irregular or sporadic appearance in this area, irrespective of season; (6) introduced species. This area includes the Fraser valley inland as far as Hope and north to the mountains fringing the valley, Grouse, Seymour, Hollyburn and Black mountains on the north shore of Burrard inlet, the waters and islands of the Gulf of Georgia, and the east coast of Vancouver Island from Victoria north to Nanaimo; the southern limit is the International Boundary.

Inasmuch as subspecies are not usually identifiable under field conditions, extended vernacular names are not used, but for the information of the observer the full scientific name applicable to local species and subspecies is given where such is known with reasonable certainty. If two or more subspecies occur in our area both have been given if they can be separated under field conditions; if they cannot, only the specific name is given followed by a statement of the number of subspecies occurring (e.g., *Passerella iliaca 6 ssp.*).

Those of uncommon occurrence are marked with an asterisk ✱.

SUMMER RESIDENTS (*Absent in Winter*)

Turkey Vulture (*Cathartes aura septentrionalis*)
Osprey (*Pandion haliaetus carolinensis*)
Band-tailed Pigeon (*Columba f. fasciata*)

As an aid to encouraging naturalists to record their observations of birds, in 1950 Ian produced the first pocket checklist for a region of BC. The list was designed to record species and numbers by date for visits to specific locations.

A Far Eastern Visitor

On July 15, 1960, while Garry McTaggart Cowan was engaged in research at sea aboard the motor vessel *Key West II*, about 145 kilometres (ninety miles) west of Tasu Sound off the west coast of the Queen Charlotte Islands, a barn swallow landed on the ship in weakened condition. It died the following day but Garry froze the carcass and gave it to his father when he returned to Vancouver. Ian sent the emaciated specimen to a colleague, Dr. Herbert Girton Deignan, an expert on Asiatic bird species, at the United States National Museum of Natural History (Smithsonian Institution) in Washington, DC, who identified it as the Amur barn swallow *Hirundo rustica gutteralis*, a subspecies that breeds from the eastern Himalayas northeast to Myanmar, Japan and Korea.

Ian then wrote a scientific article, adding his son's name as co-author, and noted that the record, the third for North America, reflected "a rather remarkable overseas crossing, even if the bird came by way of the Aleutian Island chain."[261]

In 1998 Ian received a detailed summary of a friend's sixteen years of notes recording a pair of bald eagles at their nest on BC's Gulf Islands. He was so fascinated with this record and what could be learned from such a long observation period that, at eighty-nine years of age, Ian wrote an article for a peer-reviewed publication as co-author.
PHOTO BY R. WAYNE CAMPBELL.

Kennedy, E. and Ian McTaggart Cowan. 1998. "Sixteen Years with a Bald Eagle's (*Haliaeetus leucocephalus*) Nest." *Canadian Field-Naturalist* 112: 704–706.

McTaggart-Cowan, Ian. 1989. "Birds and Mammals on the Queen Charlotte Islands." pp. 175–186 in G.G.E. Scudder and N. Gessler (eds.). *The Outer Shores*. Queen Charlotte Islands Museum Press, Queen Charlotte City, BC.

Munro, James A. and Ian McTaggart Cowan. 1944. "Preliminary Report on the Birds and Mammals of Kootenay National Park, British Columbia." *Canadian Field-Naturalist* 58: 34–51.

Myres, M.T., Ian McTaggart Cowan and M.D.F. Udvardy. 1957. "The British Columbia Nest Records Scheme." *The Condor* 59: 308–310.

Sibley, C.G., H.E. Broadbooks, W.H. Sholes, Jr., Ian McTaggart Cowan, W.P. Taylor, C. Cottam, J.G. Peterson, C.W. Quaintance, R.L. Peterson, B.P. Glass, R.R. Talmadge, H.H. Dill and L.R. Wolfe. 1946. "From Field and Study." *The Condor* 48: 92–97.

Syverton, J.T. and Ian McTaggart Cowan. 1944. "Bird Pox in the Sooty Grouse *Dendragapus fuliginosus fuliginosus* with Recovery of the Virus." *American Journal of Veterinary Research* 16: 215–222.

Mammals

Ian was most recognized for his personal and graduate student research on mammals from shrews to walruses and even lions. Most of his publications on mammals dealt with their systematics, biology, ecology, nutrition, conservation and management. Ecological investigations led to his first publication in the field of entomology: a life history and morphology of two dipterous fly species parasitic on Columbian black-tailed deer.

While most early mammal taxonomy in North America occurred in the 1700s and 1800s, Ian described fifteen subspecies new to British Columbia. These included: dusky shrew (*Sorex monticolus calvertensis* and *S. m. insularis*; American pika (*Ochotona princeps littoralis, O. p. saturatus* and *O. p. septentrionalis*); snowshoe hare (*Lepus americanus pallidus*); northern flying squirrel (*Glaucomys sabrinus reductus*); deer mouse (*Peromyscus maniculatus alpinus*); Keen's mouse (*Peromyscus keeni cancrivorous, P. k. isolatus, P. k. maritimus, P. k. pluvialis* and *P. k. rubriventer*); yellow-pine chipmunk (*Eutamias amoenus septentrionalis*; and least chipmunk (*Tamias minimus selkirki*).

Other subspecies new to North America described from specimens he collected included a meadow vole (*Microtus pennsylvanicus arcticus*) from Kidluit Bay, Northwest Territories, and the Inyo mule deer (*Odocoileus hemionus inyoensis*) from Big Pine, California.

Aleksiuk, Michael and Ian McTaggart-Cowan. 1969a. "Aspects of Seasonal Energy Expenditure in the Beaver (*Castor canadensis* Kuhl) at the Northern Limit of its Distribution. *Canadian Journal of Zoology* 47: 471–481.

Aleksiuk, Michael and Ian McTaggart-Cowan. 1969b. "The Winter Metabolic Depression in Arctic Beavers (*Castor canadensis* Kuhl) with comparisons to California Beavers." *Canadian Journal of Zoology* 47: 965–979.

Bandy, P.J., W.D. Kitts, A.J. Wood and Ian McTaggart-Cowan. 1957. "The Effect of Age and the Plane of Nutrition on the Blood Chemistry of the Columbian Black-tailed Deer (*Odocoileus hemionus columbianus*): B Blood Glucose, Non-protein Nitrogen, Total Plasma Protein, Plasma Albumin, Globulin and Fibrinogen." *Canadian Journal of Zoology* 35: 283–289.

Bandy, P.J., Ian McTaggart-Cowan, W.D. Kitts and A.J. Wood. 1956. "A Method for the Assessment of the Nutritional Status of Wild Ungulates." *Canadian Journal of Zoology* 34: 48–52.

Bandy, P.J., Ian McTaggart-Cowan and A.J. Wood. 1970. "Comparative Growth in Four Races of Black-tailed Deer. Part 1. Growth in Body Weight." *Canadian Journal of Zoology* 48: 1401–1410.

Bowen, W. Don and Ian McTaggart-Cowan. 1980. "Scent Marking in Coyotes." *Canadian Journal of Zoology* 58: 473–480.

Calaby, John Henry, Hans Henry and Ian McTaggart Cowan. 1971. "The Mountain Pygmy Possum *Burramys parvus* Broom (Marsupalia) in the Kosciuszko National Park, New South Wales." Commonwealth Scientific and Industrial Research Organization, Division of Wildlife Research Technical Paper No. 23, Melbourne, Australia. 11 pp.

Cowan, Ian McTaggart. 1932. "The Ecology and Life History of the Columbian Black-tailed Deer, *Odocoileus columbianus columbianus* (Richardson) in British Columbia." B.A. Thesis, University of British Columbia, Department of Zoology, Vancouver, BC. 98 pp.

Cowan, Ian McTaggart. 1935. "Distribution and Variation in Deer (Genus *Odocoileus*) of the Pacific Coastal Region of North America." Ph.D. dissertation, University of California, Berkley, CA. 338 pp.

The mountain pygmy possum (*Burramys parvus*) was first discovered in Australia in a fossil deposit in 1896. Although additional fossils were found, the marsupial was considered to be extinct. In 1966 a live animal was found in Mount Hotham, Victoria. Subsequently, while Ian was on sabbatical in Australia in 1970, he and his Australian colleagues in Kosciuszko National Park were the first to trap the species. Although the mammal is considered endangered, it is more widely distributed than previously thought. PHOTO COURTESY OF LINDA BROOME, OFFICE OF ENVIRONMENT AND HERITAGE, NEW SOUTH WALES, AUSTRALIA.

Cowan, Ian McTaggart. 1936a. "Distribution and Variation in Deer (Genus *Odocoileus*) of the Pacific Coastal Region of North America." *California Fish & Game* 22: 155–246.

Cowan, Ian McTaggart. 1936b. "Nesting Habits of the Flying Squirrel *Glaucomys sabrinus*." *Journal of Mammalogy* 17: 58–60.

Cowan, Ian McTaggart. 1936c. "Notes on Some Mammals in the British Columbia Provincial Museum with a List of the Type Specimens of North American Recent Mammals in the Museum." *Canadian Field-Naturalist* 50: 145–148.

Cowan, Ian McTaggart. 1937a. "The Distribution of Flying Squirrels in Western British Columbia with the Description of a New Race." *Proceedings of the Biological Society of Washington* 50: 77–82.

Cowan, Ian McTaggart. 1937b. "A New Race of *Peromyscus maniculatus* from British Columbia." *Proceedings of the Biological Society of Washington* 50: 215-216.

Cowan, Ian McTaggart. 1938a. "Geographic Distribution of Color Phases of the Red Fox and Black Bear in the Pacific Northwest." *Journal of Mammalogy* 19: 202–206.

Cowan, Ian McTaggart. 1938b. "Notes on the Hares of British Columbia with the Description of a New Race." *Journal of Mammalogy* 19: 240–243.

Cowan, Ian McTaggart. 1938c. "What Causes Freak Antlers?" *Angler and Hunter Outdoor Magazine*. 3 pp.

Cowan, Ian McTaggart. 1939. "The Sharp-headed Finner Whale of the Eastern Pacific." *Journal of Mammalogy* 20: 215–225.

Cowan, Ian McTaggart. 1940. "Distribution and Variation in the Native Sheep of North America." *American Midland Naturalist* 24: 505–580.

Cowan, Ian McTaggart. 1941a. "Insularity in the Genus *Sorex* on the North Coast of British Columbia." *Proceedings of the Biological Society of Washington* 54: 95–108.

Cowan, Ian McTaggart. 1941b. "Fossil and Subfossil Mammals from the Quaternary of British Columbia." *Transactions of the Royal Society of Canada*, Section IV, 1941: 39–50.

Cowan, Ian McTaggart. 1942a. "Report upon Some Diseases and Parasites of Game Birds and Fur-bearing Mammals in British Columbia." pp. K40-K45 in Annual Report of the British Columbia Game Commission for 1941. Victoria, BC.

Cowan, Ian McTaggart. 1942b. "Notes on the Winter Occurrence of Bats in British Columbia." *The Murrelet* 23: 61.

Cowan, Ian McTaggart. 1943a. "Notes on the Life History and Morphology of *Cephenemyia jellisoni* (Townsend) and *Lipoptena depressa* (Say), Two Dipterous Parasites of the Columbian Black-tailed deer (*Odocoileus hemionus columbianus* [Richardson])." *Canadian Journal of Research* D21: 171–187.

Cowan, Ian McTaggart. 1944a. "The Dall Porpoise, *Phocoenoides dalli* (True), of the Northern Pacific Ocean." *Journal of Mammalogy* 25: 295–306.

Ian was fascinated with abnormalities in nature, especially deer with atypical antlers. He wrote an article for a sportsmen's magazine explaining the possible reasons, including genetics, age, nutrition, injury, hormones, parasites and disease. PHOTO BY MARK NYHOF.

Cowan, Ian McTaggart. 1944b. "Further Notes on the Winter Occurrence of Bats in British Columbia." *The Murrelet* 25: 2.

Cowan, Ian McTaggart. 1944c. "Parasites, Diseases and Injuries of Game Animals in Banff, Jasper and Kootenay National Parks." National Parks Bureau, Ottawa, ON. 48 pp.

Cowan, Ian McTaggart. 1945a. "The Ecological Relationships of the Food of the Columbian Black-tailed deer *Odocoileus hemionus columbianus* (Richardson), in the Coast Forest Region of Southern Vancouver Island, British Columbia." *Ecological Monographs* 15: 109–139.

Cowan, Ian McTaggart. 1945a. "A Beaked Whale Stranding on the Coast of British Columbia." *Journal of Mammalogy* 26: 93–94.

Cowan, Ian McTaggart. 1945b. "The Free-tailed Bat *Tadarida macrotis* in British Columbia." *Canadian Field-Naturalist* 59: 149.

Cowan, Ian McTaggart. 1945c. "Report of Wildlife Studies in the Rocky Mountain Parks in 1945." Unpublished mimeographed report, National Parks Bureau, Ottawa, ON. 34 pp.

Cowan, Ian McTaggart. 1945d. "Standing Room Only: There's Plenty of Wildlife in Jasper." *Canadian National Magazine* (September). Toronto, ON.

Cowan, Ian McTaggart. 1946a. "Notes on the Distribution of the Chipmunk *Eutamias* in Southern British Columbia and the Rocky Mountain Region of Southern Alberta with Descriptions of Two New Races." *Proceedings of the Biological Society of Washington* 59: 107–118.

Cowan, Ian McTaggart. 1946b. "Parasites, Diseases, Injuries and Anomalies of the Columbian Black-tailed deer, *Odocoileus hemionus columbianus* (Richardson), in British Columbia." *Canadian Journal of Research* 24 (Section D): 71–103.

Cowan, Ian McTaggart. 1946c. "Antlered Doe Mule Deer." *Canadian Field-Naturalist* 60: 11–12.

Cowan, Ian McTaggart. 1946d. "General Report on Wildlife Conditions in the Rocky Mountain National Parks in 1946." Unpublished mimeographed report, National Parks Bureau, Ottawa, ON. 19 pp.

Cowan, Ian McTaggart. 1947a. "Range Competition Between Mule Deer, Bighorn Sheep and Elk in Jasper Park, Alberta." *Transactions of the 12th North American Wildlife Conference* 12: 223–227.

Cowan, Ian McTaggart. 1947b. "The Timber Wolf in the Rocky Mountain National Parks of Canada." *Canadian Journal of Research* 25 (Section D): 139–174.

Cowan, Ian McTaggart. 1948a. "The Occurrence of the Granular Tapeworm, *Echinococcus granulosus*, in Wild Game in North America." *Journal of Wildlife Management* 12: 105-106.

Cowan, Ian McTaggart. 1948b. "Scientific Research on Game and Game Parasites and Diseases in British Columbia." pp. 16–31 in Proceedings Second Annual Game Convention, British Columbia Game Department, Victoria, BC.

Cowan, Ian McTaggart. 1948c. Book review: *Catalogue of Canadian Recent Mammals. Canadian Field-Naturalist* 61: 200–202.

Most of BC's population of Rocky Mountain bighorn sheep occurs outside protected areas. In 1940 Ian published a major work on the taxonomy of North America's wild sheep. PHOTO BY R. WAYNE CAMPBELL.

Cowan, Ian McTaggart. 1949a. "Rabies as a Possible Population Control of Arctic Canidae." *Journal of Mammalogy* 30: 396–398.

Cowan, Ian McTaggart. 1949b. "Preliminary Report upon the Sayward Forest Deer Study, 1948–49, British Columbia." Unpublished mimeographed report, British Columbia Game Commission, Vancouver, BC. 5 pp.

Cowan, Ian McTaggart. 1950a. "Preliminary Study of the Ashnola Herd of California Bighorn Sheep." British Columbia Game Commission, Vancouver, BC. 3 pp.

Cowan, Ian McTaggart. 1950b. "Some Vital Statistics of Big Game on Overstocked Mountain Ranges." *Transactions of the 15th North American Wildlife Conference* 15: 581–588.

Cowan, Ian McTaggart. 1950c. "The Control of Wolves and Coyotes." pp. 20–28 in Convention of the International Association of Game, Fish and Conservation Commissioners. September 12 and 13, 1949. Washington, DC.

Cowan, Ian McTaggart. 1951a. "The Diseases and Parasites of Big Game Mammals of Western Canada." *Proceedings of the 5th Annual Game Convention* 5: 37–64.

Cowan, Ian McTaggart. 1951b. "Report on the Deer Population of Graham Island, Queen Charlotte Islands, British Columbia." British Columbia Game Department Unpublished Report, Victoria, BC.

Cowan, Ian McTaggart. 1951c. "A New *Microtus* from the Western Arctic of Canada." *Journal of Mammalogy* 32: 353–354.

Cowan, Ian McTaggart. 1952a. "Big Game in the Mountain Province." *Canadian Geographical Journal* XLIV: 226–241.

Cowan, Ian McTaggart. 1952b. Book review: *The Elk of North America* by O.J. Murie. *Journal of Wildlife Management* 16: 96–97.

Cowan, Ian McTaggart. 1953. "Small Mammals of the Western Mountains." *Canadian Geographical Journal* XLVII: 130–141.

Cowan, Ian McTaggart. 1954a. "The Distribution of the Pikas (*Ochotona*) in British Columbia and Alberta." *The Murrelet* 35: 20–24.

Cowan, Ian McTaggart. 1954b. Book review: *A Herd of Mule Deer* by J.M. Linsdale and P.Q. Tomich. *Journal of Wildlife Management* 18: 274–275.

Cowan, Ian McTaggart. 1954c. "The Occurrence of the Pleistocene Wolf (*Canis dirus*) in the Rocky Mountains of Central Alberta." *Canadian Field-Naturalist* 68: 44.

Cowan, Ian McTaggart. 1955. "An Instance of Scabies in the Marten *(Martes americana)*." *Journal of Wildlife Management* 19: 499.

Cowan, Ian McTaggart. 1956a. "What and Where are the Mule and Black-tailed Deer? pp 334–359 in W.T. Taylor (ed.). *The Deer of North America: The White-tailed, Mule and Black-tailed Deer, Genus Odocoileus; Their History and Management*. The Stackpole Co, Harrisburg. PA and the Wildlife Management Institute, Washington, DC.

Cowan, Ian McTaggart. 1956b. "The Life and Times of the Coast Black-tailed Deer." pp. 523–617 in W.T. Taylor (ed.). *The Deer of North America: The White-tailed, Mule and Black-tailed Deer, Genus Odocoileus; Their*

A Haven for Pikas

A new subspecies of American pika (*Ochotona princeps septentrionalis*), described by Ian McTaggart-Cowan, was collected by Kenneth Racey in the Itcha Mountains of west-central British Columbia in 1946. Of the thirty-six subspecies of American pika in North America, nine occur in British Columbia. More taxonomic work is required to confirm *O. p. septentrionalis* as a separate subspecies because it has only been described from two specimens.

History and Management. The Stackpole Co, Harrisburg. PA and the Wildlife Management Institute, Washington, DC.

Cowan, Ian McTaggart. 1956c. Book review: *The Barren Ground Caribou* by F. Harper. *Ecology* 37: 626–627.

Cowan, Ian McTaggart. 1962a. "Hybridization between the Black-tailed Deer and the White-tailed Deer." *Journal of Mammalogy* 43: 539–541.

Cowan, Ian McTaggart. 1962b. Book review: *A Revision of the Reindeer and Caribou, Genus Rangifer* by A.W.F. Banfield, National Museum Bulletin. *Canadian Field-Naturalist* 76: 168–169.

Cowan, Ian McTaggart. 1964a. Report on term research grant: T 152/I. McT. Cowan: "A Study of Mammalian Adaptation to Physical and Biotic Factors." UBC, Department of Zoology, Vancouver, BC. 25 pp.

Cowan, Ian McTaggart. 1964b. Book review: *Proceedings of the First National White-tailed Deer Disease Symposium* by M.F. Baker. *Journal of Wildlife Management* 28: 186–188.

Cowan, Ian McTaggart. 1964c. "Threatened Species of Mammals in North America." *XVI International Congress of Zoology* 8: 17-21.

Cowan, Ian McTaggart. 1970. Foreword: *Wolf: Ecology and Behavior of an Endangered Species* by L.D. Mech. United States Fish and Wildlife Service, Natural History Press, Garden City, NY. 384 pp.

Cowan, Ian McTaggart. 1971. "Summary of the Symposium on the Status of Native Cats of North America." Pages 2-8 in Proceedings of a Symposium on the Native Cats of North America, Their Status and Management. Held in conjunction with the thirty-sixth North American Wildlife and Natural Resources Conference (S. Jorgensen and D.L. Mech, eds.). United States Department of the Interior, Fish and Wildlife Service, Portland, OR.

Cowan, Ian McTaggart. 1972. "The Status and Conservation of Bears (Ursidae) of the World: 1970." pp. 343–367 in S. Herrero (ed.). *Bears: Their Biology and Conservation*. International Union for Conservation of Nature Publications New Series 23. Morges, Switzerland.

Cowan, Ian McTaggart. 1974. "Management Implications of Behaviour in the Large Herbaceous Mammals." pp. 921–934 in V. Geist and F. Walther (eds.). *The Behaviour of Ungulates and its Relation to Management. Volume 2.* International Union for Conservation of Nature New Series Publication 24. Morges, Switzerland.

Cowan, Ian McTaggart and M.G. Arsenault. 1954. "Reproduction and Growth in the Creeping Vole, *Microtus oregoni serpens* Merriam." *Canadian Journal of Zoology* 32: 198–208.

Cowan, Ian McTaggart and P.J. Bandy. 1969. "Observations on the Haematology of Several Races of Black-tailed Deer (*Odocoileus hemionus*)." *Canadian Journal of Zoology* 47: 1021–1024.

Cowan, Ian McTaggart and V.C. Brink. 1949. "Natural Game Licks in the Rocky Mountain National Parks of Canada." *Journal of Mammalogy* 30: 379–387.

Cowan, Ian McTaggart and G. Clifford Carl. 1945. "The Northern Elephant Seal in British Columbia Waters and Vicinity." *Canadian Field-Naturalist* 59: 170–172.

Cowan, Ian McTaggart and V. Geist. 1961. "Aggressive Behavior in the Deer of the Genus *Odocoileus*." *Journal of Mammalogy* 42: 522–526.

Cowan, Ian McTaggart and V. Geist. 1971. "The North American Wild Sheep." pp. 58–83 in R.C. Alberts (ed.). *North American Big Game*. The Boone and Crockett Club. Pittsburg, PA.

Cowan, Ian McTaggart and Charles J. Guiguet. 1952. "Three Cetacean Records from British Columbia." *The Murrelet* 33: 10–11.

Cowan, Ian McTaggart and James Hatter. 1940. "Two Mammals New to the Known Fauna of British Columbia, *Ziphius cavirostris* and *Sylvilagus nuttalli nuttalli*." *The Murrelet* 21: 9.

Cowan, Ian McTaggart, W.S. Hoar and J. Hatter. 1950. "The Effect of Forest Succession upon the Quantity and upon Nutritive Values of Woody Plants used as Food by Moose." *Canadian Journal of Research* 28: 249–271.

Cowan, Ian McTaggart and W. Colin Holloway. 1973a. "Threatened Deer of the World: Conservation Status." *Biological Conservation* 5: 243–250.

The "Go-To" Biologist

During his first ten years as a professor in the Department of Zoology at UBC, Ian established such renown as an author, researcher and educator that he became the one individual in the province that people went to for advice and recommendations on wildlife issues. In May 1950 he and graduate student Winston Mair visited the California bighorn sheep ranges along the Ashnola River. After four days of fieldwork he sent the following management recommendations to the British Columbia Game Commission:

- That no open season on this band of sheep be declared until biological investigations reveal it to be justified.
- That the game reserve situated south of Juniper Creek be heavily posted and its boundaries enforced. This reserve embraces the most important area of sheep winter range.
- That additional protection from illegal hunting be given these sheep during the fall and winter months.
- That coyote bait stations be established so as to remove coyotes from the winter lambing ranges.
- That application be made to have domestic livestock excluded from the game reserve area.

In 1961 Donald A. Blood completed a master's thesis on the declining Ashnola sheep population; it was followed in 1965 by Raymond A. Demarchi's master's thesis on the same important topic.

Changing Taxonomy

In 1951 Ian described a new subspecies of meadow vole (*Microtus pennsyvanicus arcticus* Cowan) collected on Richards Island in the Mackenzie Delta.[262] He based his decision on colour and size and noted that the vole was restricted to tundra habitat in the area. However, in 1975 Arthur Martell showed that a north-south gradient existed in size for taiga and tundra meadow vole (*M. p. drummondi* Audubon and Bachman) and assigned all *arcticus* to that of *drummondi*.[263]

Mountain goats are adapted to steep high-elevation terrain. PHOTO BY ALAN D. WILSON.

Cowan, Ian McTaggart and W. Colin Holloway. 1973b. "Threatened Deer of the World: Research Programs for Conservation." *Biological Conservation* 6: 112–117.

Cowan, Ian McTaggart and W. Colin Holloway. 1978a. "Geographical Location and Current Conservation Status of the Threatened Deer of the World." pp. 11–25 in *Threatened Deer* by the Deer Specialist Group of the Survival Service Commission of the International Union for Conservation of Nature and Natural Resources. Alden Press, London, England.

Cowan, Ian McTaggart and W. Colin Holloway. 1978b. "Research Towards Conservation of Threatened Deer of the World." pp. 329–337 in *Threatened Deer*. International Union for Conservation of Nature and Natural Resources, Alden Press, London, England.

Cowan, Ian McTaggart and P.A. Johnston. 1962. "Blood Serum Protein Variations at the Species and Subspecies Level in Deer of the Genus *Odocoileus*." *Systematic Zoology* 11: 131–138.

Cowan, Ian McTaggart and L. Karstad. 1969. "Postmortem Examinations." pp. 51–258 in R.H. Giles (ed.). *Wildlife Management Techniques*. 3rd edition. The Wildlife Society, Washington, DC.

Cowan, Ian McTaggart and R.H. MacKay. 1950. "Food Habits of the Marten (*Martes americana*) in the Rocky Mountain Region of Canada." *Canadian Field-Naturalist* 64: 100–104.

Cowan, Ian McTaggart and Wayne McCrory. 1970. "Variation in the Mountain Goat, *Oreamnos americanus* (Blainville)." *Journal of Mammalogy* 51: 60–73.

Cowan, Ian McTaggart, A.M. O'Riordan and J.S. McTaggart Cowan. 1974. "Energy Requirements of the Dasyurid Marsupial Mouse Antechinus swainsonii (Waterhouse)." *Canadian Journal of Zoology* 52: 269–275.

Cowan, Ian McTaggart and K. Racey. 1946. "A New Pika (genus *Ochotona*) from British Columbia." *Canadian Field-Naturalist* 60: 102–104.

Cowan, Ian McTaggart and A.G. Raddi. 1972. "Pelage and Molt in the Black-tailed deer (*Odocoileus hemionus* [Rafinesque])." *Canadian Journal of Zoology* 50: 639–647."

Cowan, Ian McTaggart and A.J. Wood. 1955a. "The Normal Temperature of the Columbian Black-tailed Deer." *Journal of Wildlife Management* 19: 154–155.

Cowan, Ian McTaggart and A.J. Wood. 1955b. "The Growth Rate of the Black-tailed Deer (*Odocoileus hemionus columbianus*)." *Journal of Wildlife Management* 19: 331–336.

Cowan, Ian McTaggart, A.J. Wood and W.D. Kitts. 1957. "Food Requirements of Deer, Beaver, Bear and Mink for Growth and Maintenance." *Transactions of the North American Wildlife Conference* 22: 179–186.

Cowan, Ian McTaggart, A.J. Wood and H.C. Nordan. 1962. "Studies in Tranquilization and Immobilization of Deer (*Odocoileus*)." *Canadian Journal of Comparative Medicine and Veterinary Science* 26: 57–61.

Currier, A., W.D. Kitts and Ian McTaggart Cowan. 1960. "Cellulose Diges-
tion in the Beaver (*Castor canadensis*)." *Canadian Journal of Zoology* 38:
1109–1116.

Edwards, R.Y. and Ian McTaggart Cowan. 1957. "Fur Production of the
Boreal Forest Region of British Columbia." *Journal of Wildlife Management* 21: 257–267.

Elliott, John P. and Ian McTaggart Cowan. 1978. "Territoriality, Density
and Prey of the Lion in Ngorongoro Crater, Tanzania." *Canadian Journal of Zoology* 56: 1726–1734.

Elliott, John P., Ian McTaggart Cowan and C. Stanley Holling. 1977. "Prey
Capture by the African Lion." *Canadian Journal of Zoology* 55: 1811–1828.

Geist, V. and Ian McTaggart Cowan. 1968. "Film E 1333. *Ovis canadensis*
(Bovidae): Social Behavior of Males." *Encyclopedia Cinematographica.*
Göttingen Institute für den Wissenschaftlichen, Germany. 12 pp.

Haber, Gordon C., Ian McTaggart Cowan and Carl J. Walters. 1976. "Sta-
bility Properties of a Wolf-ungulate System in Alaska and Management
Implications." University of British Columbia, Institute of Resource
Ecology Research Report R-5-R, Vancouver, BC. 104 pp.

Hebert, Daryll M. and Ian McTaggart Cowan. 1971a. "Natural Salt Licks
as a Part of the Ecology of the Mountain Goat." *Canadian Journal of
Zoology* 49: 605–610.

Hebert, Daryll M. and Ian McTaggart Cowan. 1971b. "White Muscle Disease in the Mountain Goat." *Journal of Wildlife Management* 35: 752–756.

Hoefs, Manfred and Ian McTaggart Cowan. 1980. "Ecological Investigation of a Population of Dall Sheep (*Ovis dalla dalli* Nelson)." *Syesis* 12
(Supplement 1): 1–81.

Hoefs, Manfred, Ian McTaggart Cowan and Vladimir T. Krajina. 1975.
"Phytosociological Analysis and Synthesis of Sheep Mountain, Southwest Yukon Territory, Canada." *Syesis* 8 (Supplement 1): 125–228.

Jonkel, C.J. and Ian McTaggart Cowan. 1971. "The Black Bear in the
Spruce-Fir forest." *The Wildlife Society Wildlife Monographs* No. 27, Lawrence, Kansas. 57 pp.

Kitts, W.D., P.J. Bandy, A.J. Wood and Ian McTaggart Cowan. 1956. "Effect
of Age and Plane of Nutrition on the Blood Chemistry of the Columbian Black-tailed Deer *(Odocoileus hemionus columbianus)*, A. Packed-
cell Volume, Sedimentation Rate and Hemoglobin." *Canadian Journal
Zoology* 34: 477–484.

Kitts, W.D., R.J. Bose, A.J. Wood and Ian McTaggart Cowan. 1957. "Preliminary Observations of the Digestive Enzyme System of the Beaver
(*Castor canadensis*)." *Canadian Journal of Zoology* 35: 449–452.

Kitts W.D., Ian McTaggart Cowan, P.J. Bandy and A.J. Wood. 1956. "The
Immediate Post-natal Growth in the Columbian Black-tailed Deer in
Relation to the Composition of the Milk of the Doe." *Journal of Wildlife
Management* 20: 212–214.

Kitts, W.D., M.C. Robertson, B. Stephenson and Ian McTaggart Cowan.
1958. "The Normal Blood Chemistry of the Beaver (*Castor canadensis*),

IAN McTAGGART-COWAN

Canada's largest population of grizzly bears (*Ursus arctos*) is found throughout coastal and mountainous areas of BC. However, the size of the population has become a polarized issue that engages government, non-governmental environmental organizations, guides, biologists, hunters and ranchers. PHOTO BY R. WAYNE CAMPBELL.

Carnivores Need Wilderness

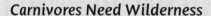

Large carnivorous mammals such as bears, wolves, cougars and wolverines are the essence of unspoiled wild places in Canada. To many, these mammals are known largely from television, from the work of skilled wildlife photographers and artists, and from the writings of naturalists who roam wilderness places, seeking to learn more about these great creatures. Nonetheless, many thousands of Canadians and visitors make pilgrimages specifically to see the great white bears of the Arctic, to view the controlled power of a grizzly bear in its alpine habitat, to catch even a fleeting glimpse of the tawny length of Canada's only great cat in its mountain habitat or to listen to a wolf chorus echoing in the northern woods.

People treasure these fascinating creatures, whether or not they have ever had direct contact with them. And they expect provincial and federal politicians and the government agencies that share responsibility for the mammals' survival to enact and enforce measures that will insure that self-perpetuating populations of all of them will persist.

—Ian McTaggart-Cowan
Foreword to *Wild Hunters: Predators in Peril,* 1991.

To support Jim Hatter in his pursuit of a Ph.D. on moose ecology, Ian formally became an adjunct professor, for a dollar a year, at the State College of Washington in Pullman. Hatter's pioneering research emphasized the importance of an interdisciplinary approach involving plant science, microbiology, animal science and ecology when appraising the value of early successional plants in moose nutrition. PHOTO BY R. WAYNE CAMPBELL.

A. Packed-cell Volume, Sedimentation Rate, Haemoglobin, Erythrocyte Diameter and Blood Cell Counts." *Canadian Journal of Zoology* 36: 279–283.

Krebs, Charles J. and Ian McTaggart Cowan. 1962. "Growth Studies of Reindeer Fawns." *Canadian Journal of Zoology* 40: 863–869.

Lewall, E.F. and Ian McTaggart-Cowan. 1963. "Age Determination in Black-tailed Deer by Degree of Ossification of the Epiphyseal Plate in the Long Bones." *Canadian Journal of Zoology* 41: 629–636.

Low, William A. and Ian McTaggart Cowan. 1963. "Age Determination of Deer by Annular Structure and Dental Cementum." *Journal of Wildlife Management* 27: 466–471.

Lykke, J. and Ian McTaggart-Cowan. 1968. "Moose Management and Population Dynamics on the Scandinavian Peninsula with Special Reference to Norway." *Proceedings of the North American Moose Workshop* 5: 1-22.

Manzer, J.I. and Ian McTaggart Cowan. 1956. "Northern Fur Seals in the Inside Coastal Waters of British Columbia." *Journal of Mammalogy* 37: 83–86.

McCabe, T.T. and Ian McTaggart Cowan. 1945. "*Peromyscus maniculatus macrorhinus* and the Problem of Insularity." *Transactions of the Royal Canadian Institute* 25: 117–216.

McTaggart-Cowan, Ian. 1929. "Note on Yellow-bellied Marmot." *The Murrelet* 10: 64.

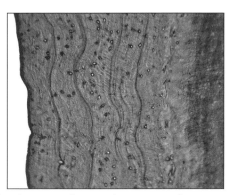

Estimating the age of a large mammal by the annual growth pattern of cementum in its teeth was first reported for northern fur seal (*Callorhinus ursinus*). The technique was later applied successfully to ungulates by examining cross sections of their incisors (left) to determine annual growth. Photo (right) indicates this deer was five and a half years old. PHOTOS BY DENNIS A. DEMARCHI (LEFT) AND COURTESY OF GARY MATSON (MATSON LAB), MONTANA, USA (RIGHT).

McTaggart-Cowan, Ian. 1930. "Mammals of Point Grey." *Canadian Field-Naturalist* 44: 133-134.

McTaggart-Cowan, Ian. 1933a. "The British Columbia Woodchuck *Marmota monax petrensis*." *Canadian Field-Naturalist* 47: 57.

McTaggart-Cowan, Ian. 1933b. "Some Notes on the Hibernation of *Lasionycteris noctivagans*." *Canadian Field-Naturalist* 47: 74–75.

McTaggart-Cowan, Ian. 1933c. "The Mule Deer of Southern California and Northern Lower California as a Recognizable Race." *Journal of Mammalogy* 14: 326–327.

McTaggart-Cowan, Ian. 1933d. "A New Race of Deer from Eastern California." *Proceedings of the Biological Society of Washington* 46: 67–70.

McTaggart-Cowan, Ian. 1934. "Two Cases of Pathologic Skin Growths in Deer of the Genus *Odocoileus*." *The Murrelet* 15: 81–82.

McTaggart-Cowan, Ian. 1935. "A Distributional Study of the *Peromyscus sitkensis* Group of White-footed Mice." *University of California Publications in Zoology* 40: 429–438.

McTaggart-Cowan, Ian. 1989. "The Marine Mammals of British Columbia: Their Status and Distribution." pp. 95–104 in Rosemary J. Fox, ed. The Wildlife of Northern British Columbia Past, Present and Future: The Proceedings of a Symposium, November 1987. Spatsizi Association for Biological Research, Smithers, BC.

McTaggart-Cowan, Ian. 1991. Foreword: *Wild Hunters: Predators in Peril* by Monte Hummel and Sherry Pettigrew. Key Porter Books, Toronto, ON. 244 pp.

McTaggart-Cowan, Ian. 1992. "Capture and Maintenance of Cetaceans in Canada." A report prepared by the Advisory Committee on Marine Mammals to the Minister of Fisheries and Oceans, Ottawa, ON.

McTaggart-Cowan, Ian. 2005. Foreword: *Grizzly Chronicles of the Dean and Kimsquit Rivers, British Columbia* by James Sirois. Skookum Press, Hagensborg, BC. 272 pages.

During fieldwork in BC, Ian frequently discovered new distributional information for mammals. In a paper published in the *Canadian Field-Naturalist* in 1933, he described the new range for a subspecies of woodchuck (*Marmota monax petrensis*) as extending from northern Idaho and extreme northeastern Washington northward to include southeastern and central BC and ranging as far north as the Stikine River. PHOTO BY R. WAYNE CAMPBELL.

McTaggart-Cowan, Ian. 2010 (updated). Badger, Marten, Mink, Otter, Sea Otter, Seal, Skunk and Walrus. *The Canadian Encyclopedia*. www.thecanadianencylopedia.com.

Nordan, H.C., Ian McTaggart Cowan and A.J. Wood. 1968. "Nutritional Requirements and Growth of Black-tailed deer, *Odocoileus hemionus columbianus*, in captivity." *Symposium of the Zoological Society of London* 21: 89–96.

Nordan, H.C., Ian McTaggart Cowan and A.J. Wood. 1970. "The Feed Intake and Heat Production of the Young Black-tailed Deer (*Odocoileus hemionus columbianus*)." *Canadian Journal of Zoology* 48: 275–282.

Nordan, H.C., A.J. Wood and Ian McTaggart Cowan. 1962. "Further Studies on Immobilization of Deer with Succinylcholine Chloride." *Canadian Journal of Comparative Medicine and Veterinary Science* 26: 246–248.

Ommundsen, Peter and Ian McTaggart Cowan. 1970. "Development of the Columbian Black-tailed Deer (*Odocoileus hemionus columbianus*) During the Fetal Period." *Canadian Journal of Zoology* 48: 123–132.

Racey, K. and Ian McTaggart Cowan. 1935. "Mammals of the Alta Lake Region of Southwestern British Columbia." pp. H15-H29 in Report of the British Columbia Provincial Museum 1935. Victoria, BC.

Robinson, D.J. and Ian McTaggart Cowan. 1954. "An Introduced Population of the Gray Squirrel (*Sciurus carolinensis* Gmelin) in British Columbia." *Canadian Journal of Zoology* 32: 261–282.

Steenson, A.B., W.D. Kitts, A.J. Wood and Ian McTaggart Cowan. 1959. "The Normal Blood Chemistry of the Beaver (*Castor canadensis*). B. Blood Glucose, Total Protein, Albumin, Globulin, Fibrinogen, Non-protein Nitrogen, Amino Acid Nitrogen, Creatine, Cholesterol and Volatile Fatty Acids." *Canadian Journal of Zoology* 37: 9–14.

Stewart, S.F., H.A. Nordan, A.J. Wood and Ian McTaggart Cowan. 1963. "Changes in the Plasma Lipids of the Black-tailed Deer throughout a Year." *XVI International Congress of Zoology* 2: 46

Thomas, D.C. and Ian McTaggart Cowan. 1975. "The Pattern of Reproduction in Female Columbian Black-tailed Deer, *Odocoileus hemionus columbianus*." *Journal of Reproduction and Fertility* 44: 261–272.

van Tets, P. and Ian McTaggart Cowan. 1966. "Some Sources of Variation in Blood Sera of Deer (*Odocoileus*) as Revealed by Starch-gel Electrophoresis." *Canadian Journal of Zoology* 44: 631-647.

van Tets, P. and Ian McTaggart Cowan. 1967. "The Starch-gel Electrophoretic Serum Lipid Fraction of Two Species of Deer in the Genus *Odocoileus*." *Canadian Journal of Zoology* 45: 579–581.

Wood A.J. and Ian McTaggart Cowan. 1968. "Post Natal Growth." pp. 106–113 in F.B. Golley and H.K. Buechner, (eds.). *A Practical Guide to the Study of the Productivity of Large Herbivores*. International Biological Program Handbook No. 7, Blackwell Scientific Publications, Oxford, England.

Wood, A.J., W.D. Kitts and Ian McTaggart Cowan. 1960. "The Interpretation of the Protein Level in the Ruminal Contents of Deer." *California Fish and Game* 46: 227–229.

The eastern grey squirrel (*Sciurus carolinensis*) was introduced to Stanley Park in Vancouver, BC, in 1914. In the early 1950s Ian directed field research on this urban squirrel population, and the resulting paper remains the only major work on the species in the province. PHOTO BY R. WAYNE CAMPBELL.

At 6.4 million hectares, the Muskwa-Ketchika Management Area of northeastern British Columbia is the largest wilderness region in the Canadian Rocky Mountains. It is designated as an integrated resource management area. PHOTO BY R. WAYNE CAMPBELL.

A large stone seat, with an embedded plaque "In Memory of Dr. Ian McTaggart-Cowan" is located in the alpine garden within the Finnerty Gardens on the campus of the University of Victoria. The alpine garden was designed by Ian's sister, Joan Zink. PHOTO BY DENNIS A. DEMARCHI, SEPTEMBER 21, 2012.

The Wild Sheep
Foundation, with
chapters across North
America, supports
research, management,
conservation and
educational activities
related to native
sheep. PHOTO BY LARRY
HALVERSON.

Ian with the Order of British
Columbia medal received
at the investiture ceremony
at Government House in
Victoria on June 13, 1991.
PHOTO COURTESY OF ANN SCHAU.

Even during a leisurely trek over the Columbia Icefields, Ian was attentive to his surroundings, looking for animals and tracks. He picked up a canine tooth from the ice and later had it identified. It turned out to be from a dire wolf (*Canis dirus*), a Pleistocene carnivore that persisted for 1.8 million years in North and South America before becoming extinct over 10,000 years ago. PHOTO BY R. WAYNE CAMPBELL.

The marine shore littered with seashells and a myriad of new plants and animals may have attracted Ian as a lad to the intertidal beaches around Vancouver, BC. His fascination with shells led to a professional interest in malacology. PHOTO BY R. WAYNE CAMPBELL.

Most chitons are intertidal molluscs and occur in greatest concentrations along the west coast of North America. Chitons may have beautifully coloured patterns, and in his article for *Pacific Northwest Shell News*, Ian, who was also recognized as a malacologist, focussed on keeping those coloured qualities intact in collections. PHOTO BY JOHN DEAL.

Ian's interest in natural history included fascinating discoveries of species longevity, skeletal structure and even diet as shown in this western terrestrial garter snake (*Thamnophis elegans*) with a recently captured clingfish (*Gobiesox maeandricus*). PHOTO BY R. WAYNE CAMPBELL.

Prior to 1936, there were three known breeding colonies of herring gull in British Columbia: Atlin Lake, Babine Lake and Bridge Lake. In the summer of 1936, incidental to other field work in northern regions of the province, Ian and his wife, Joyce, discovered small colonies on Ootsa Lake and Eutsuk Lake. PHOTO BY R. WAYNE CAMPBELL. BRIDGE LAKE, BC. JUNE 1, 2009.

Ian's 1955 wildlife management report stated that in 1917 the common nighthawk was a common species in Jasper National Park. When he visited the park in the mid-1940s, the species was seen only eight times in 69 days of field work. PHOTO BY MARK NYHOF.

The yellow-pine chipmunk is widely distributed throughout the interior of British Columbia with five recognized subspecies. The new subspecies that Ian identified occurs on the Fraser Plateau west of the Fraser River and north to the Skeena River valley. PHOTO BY R. WAYNE CAMPBELL.

Northern river otter is one of at least 17 species of fur-bearing mammals that are economically important to the fur industry in northern and northeastern British Columbia. PHOTO BY ALAN D. WILSON.

Newly born northern flying squirrels (*Glaucomys sabrinus*). The first reproductive data in British Columbia came from museum specimens and observations made by Ian McTaggart-Cowan. Even today, basic reproductive information on the species in this province is limited. PHOTO BY R. WAYNE CAMPBELL.

Columbian black-tailed deer (*Odocoileus hemionus columbianus*) can be found in almost any coastal forest in the southern half of British Columbia. Ian's early field research showed that to maintain viable populations on Vancouver Island, wildlife managers should retain a variety of forest types along with adequate old-growth forests for winter range. PHOTO BY MARK NYHOF.

For chipmunks, cheek pouches are handy places to carry extra food. PHOTOS BY ALAN DIBB (LEFT) AND LARRY HALVERSON (RIGHT).

There are two species of pika in British Columbia. The collared pika (*Ochotona collaris*) occurs in the northwestern area of the province west of Atlin Lake, whereas the American pika (*O. princeps*) [in photo] ranges throughout the mountains of the southern half of the province. Both species are absent from north-central British Columbia. Pikas are a common species in alpine communities that may be affected in the future by climate change. PHOTOS BY R. WAYNE CAMPBELL.

Ian's student, Chuck Jonkel, undertook ground-breaking research on American black bear ecology. Toward the end of his professional career, Ian focussed his decades of wildlife experience, teaching and research toward conservation issues world-wide involving wildlife and their habitats. PHOTO BY R. WAYNE CAMPBELL.

Still active in his 90s and seeking to reach a broader audience, Ian authored various popular articles including eight species accounts of mammals for *The Canadian Encyclopedia*, an on-line source of information written by experts. PHOTO BY MARK NYHOF.

Ian supervised seven masters and four doctoral students on a variety of topics on Columbian black-tailed deer, including nutritional requirements and growth. PHOTO BY MARK NYHOF.

Both scientific research and the application of the findings are essential for good management of wildlife and their habitats. In some national parks, radio collars are attached to Rocky Mountain elk to provide answers to questions such as where females calve and how to mitigate collisions with vehicles. PHOTO BY R. WAYNE CAMPBELL.

Ian provided a unique perspective for the summary chapter of the four-volume set *The Birds of British Columbia* because he had known the province's avifauna from his 1947 treatise.[264] During the 53-year span between those books, the list of birds in the province grew from 367 to 483 (a rate of about 2.2 species a year). During that period the Caspian tern slowly began moving into the province from the south and bred here for the first time in 1984. PHOTO BY R. WAYNE CAMPBELL.

Sixty-five years after he wrote it, David Aird Munro's unpublished Bachelor of Arts thesis remains the only baseline study for comparison of waterfowl populations on Burnaby Lake, BC, after decades of industrial and recreational developments. PHOTO BY MARK NYHOF.

The principal prey of Canada lynx is the snowshoe hare. However, during periods when hare numbers are low, lynx may prey upon other species or feed opportunistically on ungulate carcasses. PHOTO BY LARRY HALVERSON.

Bobcats, which are at the northern limit of their North American range in central British Columbia, are predators on a wide variety of small mammals and birds and will also consume carrion. PHOTO COURTESY OF PARKS CANADA.

Douglas's squirrel is a highly arboreal species that lives in mixed coniferous forests along the coast of British Columbia. PHOTO BY R. WAYNE CAMPBELL.

Two winter-killed adult male muskoxen. PHOTO BY RONALD D. JAKIMCHUK, KAGLORYUAK RIVER DELTA, VICTORIA ISLAND, NWT, AUGUST 1980.

Northern sea lions hauled out on rocky islet. PHOTO BY R. WAYNE CAMPBELL.

The fur trade, based primarily on the valued pelt of the beaver, stimulated early exploration and colonization of Canada. PHOTO BY R. WAYNE CAMPBELL.

In the southern United States, collared peccary or javelina breeds year-round in mesquite habitats and is an economically important species.
PHOTO BY GLEN MILLS, CHOKE CANYON, SOUTH TEXAS, USA. COURTESY OF TEXAS PARKS AND WILDLIFE DEPARTMENT, PHOTO 612.12.

The grey wolf is a widely distributed and versatile predator in North America. This photo reveals how even a butterfly can arouse the animal's curiosity.
PHOTO BY ALAN DIBB.

The Vancouver Island marmot is indigenous to the east side of Vancouver Island. It is an endangered species that has been increased in numbers by captive breeding programs.
PHOTO BY ANDREW A. BRYANT, SEPTEMBER 10, 2005.

The yellow-bellied marmot is a colonial and diurnal rodent that is active above ground for four or five months of the year. It is also prey for many top-level predators.
PHOTO BY MARK NYHOF.

Wood, A.J., Ian McTaggart Cowan and M.J. Daniel. 1965. "Organ weight-body weight relations in the family Mustelidae: the mink (*Mustela vison*)." *Canadian Journal of Zoology* 43: 55–68.

Wood, A.J., Ian McTaggart Cowan and H.C. Nordan. 1962. "Periodicity of Growth in Ungulates as Shown by Deer of the Genus *Odocoileus*." *Canadian Journal of Zoology* 40: 593–603.

Wood, A.J., H.C. Nordan and Ian McTaggart Cowan. 1961. "The Care and Management of Wild Ungulates for Experimental Purposes." *Journal of Wildlife Management* 25: 295–302.

Conservation and Wildlife Management

In addition to providing for the continuation of his publications on classical zoological topics of systematics and distribution, the early days of Ian's career at UBC marked the broadening of his interests and those of his students into studies of ecological interrelationships. He also fostered an interdisciplinary interface with other faculties that included collaborations involving plant science and nutrition. At the same time he was developing important relationships with the governmental agencies that had responsibilities for wildlife and parks, and he became a pioneer in establishing the importance of scientific research as the underpinning of wildlife management. His early work in the national parks also led him into a broader advocacy role for sound science as the basis for conservation strategies and policies.

As Ian recognized the importance of bringing together disparate groups and interests to achieve wildlife management and conservation goals, he began working tirelessly and effectively to involve the university, government agencies and private groups in a common goal. As a result, his impact on conservation and wildlife management was reflected by the adoption of scientific research as the rational basis for management decisions and policies. His influence in this regard extended beyond British Columbia to the entire country, and as an advisor to governments and a leader of conservation organizations and foundations, he became instrumental in protecting vital habitats in perpetuity. He was a pioneer and leader who straddled an era that saw wildlife emerge from a period of little knowledge and understanding to one of vital concern to society.

The Care of Captive Wild Hoofed Mammals for Research

After ten years of studying the growth and nutrient intake of mule deer (which included all three subspecies that occur in British Columbia) in captivity, Ian encouraged colleagues A.J. Wood and H.C. Nordan to summarize what they had learned about keeping wild deer under essentially laboratory conditions. The paper provided important long-term information as a background for more detailed studies and was a valuable reference for other researchers considering studies on captive wild ungulates.

Cathro, R., G. Collins, Ian McTaggart-Cowan and M. Stutter. 1971. Submission. To the Honourable Jean Chrétien, Minister of Indian Affairs and Northern Development, Ottawa, ON. *UBC Law Review* 101: 6.

Cowan, Ian McTaggart. 1938. "The Fur Trade and the Fur Cycle: 1825–1857." *British Columbia Historical Quarterly* 2: 19–30.

Cowan, Ian McTaggart. 1942. "The Preservation of Wildlife." pp. 10–12 in Special Publications of the Society for the Prevention of Cruelty to Animals, Vancouver, BC.

Cowan, Ian McTaggart. 1944. "Report on Game Conditions in Banff, Jasper and Kootenay National Parks, 1943." Canadian Wildlife Service Report C313, Ottawa. ON. 72 pp.

Cowan, Ian McTaggart. 1945. "Report of the Wildlife Studies in 1944 and Parasites, Diseases and Injuries of Game Animals in the Rocky Mountain National Parks, 1942–44." Canadian Wildlife Service unpublished report, Ottawa, ON. 147 pp.

Cowan, Ian McTaggart. 1947a. "Report of the Wildlife Studies in the Rocky Mountain National Parks, 1945." Canadian Wildlife Service unpublished report, Ottawa, ON. 34 pp.

Cowan, Ian McTaggart. 1947b. "General Report on Wildlife Conditions in the Rocky Mountain National Parks in 1946." Canadian Wildlife Service unpublished report, Ottawa, ON. 19 pp.

Cowan, Ian McTaggart. 1947c. "Predation." pp. 34–44 in Proceedings of the British Columbia Game Department Game Convention. Victoria, BC.

Cowan, Ian McTaggart. 1948. "Scientific Research on Game and Game Parasites and Diseases in British Columbia." pp. 16–31 in British Columbia Game Department, Proceedings Second Annual Game Convention, Victoria, BC.

Cowan, Ian McTaggart. 1949a. "A Study of Hunting in British Columbia." pp. 75–79 in British Columbia Game Department, Proceedings Third Annual Game Convention, Victoria, BC.

Cowan, Ian McTaggart. 1949b. "Wildlife Conservation in Canada." *The Forestry Chronicle* 1949: 315–318.

Cowan, Ian McTaggart. 1950. "Problems of Wildlife Research and Management in the Province of British Columbia." pp. 20–27 in British Columbia Game Department, Proceedings Fourth Annual Game Convention, Victoria, BC.

Cowan, Ian McTaggart. 1951. "Nature Sanctuaries in the United States and Canada." *The Living Wilderness* No. 35, Washington, DC. 45 pp.

Cowan, Ian McTaggart. 1952a. Book review: *Union Bay: The life of a City Marsh* by H.W. Higman and E.J. Larrison. *Journal of Wildlife Management* 16: 102.

Cowan, Ian McTaggart. 1952b. "Ruts and Ridges: Some Major Issues in Wildlife Conservation." pp. 63–68 in Proceedings of the 6th Annual British Columbia Big Game Convention, Victoria, BC.

Cowan, Ian McTaggart. 1952c. "The Role of Wildlife on Forest Land in Western Canada." *The Forestry Chronicle* 28: 42–49.

Cowan, Ian McTaggart. 1953a. "Getting Wise to Our Wildlife." *Canadian Industries Limited Oval*: 14–17.

Cowan, Ian McTaggart. 1953b. "*Riistanhoito Kanadassa* [Canadian beaver]." *Eripainos Sumomen Riista* 8: 84–109.

Cowan, Ian McTaggart. 1954. "Observations on Wildlife Conservation and Management in Britain and Norden." Report of Proceedings of the British Columbia Game Department Game Convention, Victoria, BC 9 pp.

A Signature for a Sanctuary

The British Columbia Waterfowl Society was created in 1961, and two years later the society took over the management of the George C. Reifel Migratory Bird Sanctuary in the Fraser River Delta, a critical estuarine wetland for migratory birds. Ian was one of the fourteen original signatories to formally establish the sanctuary. The others were Arthur Benson, Alan Best, Frank Butler, Mike Crammond, Robert D. Harris, Dr. James Hatter, Ronald Jackson, Dr. Barry Leach, Richard Littler, Ed Meade, Jim Murray, Jim Railton and Ernest W. Taylor.

Cowan, Ian McTaggart. 1955a. "Wildlife Conservation in Canada." *Journal of Wildlife Management* 19: 161–176.

Cowan, Ian McTaggart. 1955b. "Chemical Sprays and their Relation to Wildlife." Proceedings of the 9th Annual British Columbia Game Convention, Victoria, BC. 10 pp.

Cowan, Ian McTaggart. 1955c. "Getting Wise to Our Wildlife." *Canadian Nature* (May–June): 90–97.

Cowan, Ian McTaggart. 1955d. "The Challenge We Take: Appraisal of the 20th North American Wildlife Conference." *Transactions of the 20th North American Wildlife Conference* 20: 662–670.

Cowan, Ian McTaggart. 1955e. "The Wildlife Resources in Canada: A Brief to the Royal Commission on Canada's Economic Prospects." The Canadian Association for Conservation, Ottawa. ON. 34 pp.

Cowan, Ian McTaggart. 1956. "The Gamble of Game Management." *Wildlife Review* 1(5): 4–5.

Cowan, Ian McTaggart. 1957. "The Penalties of Ignorance to Man's Biological Independence." pp. 41–50 in E.G.D. Murray (ed.). *Our Debt to the Future*. Presented on the 75th Anniversary of the Royal Society of Canada, Ottawa, ON.

Cowan, Ian McTaggart. 1959. Publications review: *Survey on the Galapagos Islands* by I. Eibl-Eibesfeldt. *United Nation Educational, Scientific and Cultural Organization* 9: 40–41.

Cowan, Ian McTaggart. 1961. "A Review of Wildlife Research in Canada." *Resources for Tomorrow Conference* 2: 889–899.

Cowan, Ian McTaggart. 1963. "Report of the Standing Committee on Conservation (as Chair)." *Proceedings of the 10th Pacific Science Congress*, pp. 209-256.

Ron Jakimchuk with a Boone and Crockett Club–record white-tailed deer, November 1971. PHOTO BY MEL W. PROWSE.

Ahead of his Time

As a professor of zoology, Ian rarely passed up an opportunity to promote his environmental ethic. He was greatly concerned about the dramatic changes that were occurring in settled areas of North America during the twentieth century due to advanced technology, but he also sensed it was time to address major issues in Arctic regions where resource developments were being proposed. In 1969 he published a thought-provoking overview of the ecology in northern environments in the journal *Arctic*. This ten-page article, "Ecology and Northern Development," alerted colleagues that they must get prepared for the rapidly growing "Protection Movement" that can impact and at times hasten conservation efforts.

Cowan, Ian McTaggart. 1964a. "A Naturalist-Scientist's Attitude Toward National Parks." *Canadian Audubon* (May-June): 93–96.

Cowan, Ian McTaggart. 1964b. "Wildlife." Proceedings of the 15th British Columbia Resources Conference, Victoria, BC. 3 pp.

Cowan, Ian McTaggart. 1965. "Conservation and Man's Environment." *Nature* 208: 1145–1151.

Cowan, Ian McTaggart. 1966a. "Conservation and Man's Environment." pp. 76–81 in *Knowledge Among Men. Eleven Essays on Science, Culture and Society Commemorating the 200th Anniversary of the Birth of James Smithson.* Simon and Schuster and the Smithsonian Institution, Washington, DC.

Cowan, Ian McTaggart. 1966b. "Management, Response and Variety. pp. 55–65 in Darling, F.F. and J.P. Milton, eds. *Future Environments of North America* series, Natural History Press, Garden City, NY.

Cowan, Ian McTaggart. 1967. "Water and Wildlife." Proceedings of the 17th British Columbia Resources Conference, Victoria, BC. 6 pp.

Cowan, Ian McTaggart. 1968a. "Wilderness, Concept, Function and Management." The 8th Horace M. Albright Conservation Lectureship, Berkeley, CA. 36 pp.

Cowan, Ian McTaggart. 1968b. "The Role of Ecology in the National Parks." pp. 931–939 in J.G. Nelson and R.C. Scace (eds.). *The Canadian National Parks: Today and Tomorrow.* Studies in Landscape History and Landscape Change No. 3. National and Provincial Parks Association of Canada and the University of Calgary.

Cowan, Ian McTaggart. 1969a. "Ecology and Northern Development." *Arctic* 22: 3–12.

Cowan, Ian McTaggart. 1969b. "Ecology of the North: Knowledge is Key to Sane Development." *Science Forum* 2: 3.

Cowan, Ian McTaggart. 1973. Book review: *The Great Barrier Reef* by I. Bennett. *Pacific Affairs* 46: 180.

Cowan, Ian McTaggart. 1974. Keynote address. 1974. Annual Wildlife Diseases Conference sponsored by the Wildlife Disease Association, Pacific Grove, CA.

Cowan, Ian McTaggart. 1975. Transcript (47: 6267) of Mackenzie Valley pipeline inquiry at Yellowknife, Northwest Territories. Alwest Reporting Ltd., Burnaby, BC.

Cowan, Ian McTaggart. 1976. Foreword. pp. 10–12 in T.A. (Tommy) Walker. *Spatsizi.* Antonson Publishing Ltd., Surrey, BC. 272 pp.

Cowan, Ian McTaggart. 1977a. "Cumulative Impact of Development of the Mackenzie Estuary/ Delta, NWT." pp. 71–82 in *Mackenzie Delta: Priorities and Alternatives.* Canadian Arctic Resources Committee Conference Proceedings, December 3–4, 1975, Ottawa, ON. 193 pp.

Cowan, Ian Mctaggart. 1977b. "Natural Resources Research in Canada's National Parks: An Evaluation." Parks Canada, Ottawa, ON. 135 pp.

Cowan, Ian McTaggart. 1980a. "The Basis of Endangerment." pp. 3–20 in R. Stace-Smith, L. Johns, and P. Joslin (eds.). *Proceedings of Threatened and Endangered Species and Habitats in British Columbia and Yukon,*

Richmond, BC, March 8–9, 1980. British Columbia, Ministry of Environment, Fish and Wildlife Branch, Victoria, BC. 320 pp.

Cowan, Ian McTaggart. 1980b. "The Impact of Land Use Policy in Western Canada upon Wildlife, 1945 to 1980." pp. 133–170 in *Symposium on Environmental Management Strategies: Past, Present and Future*. Proceedings published by Alberta Society of Professional Biologists, Edmonton, AB. 308 pp.

Cowan, Ian McTaggart. 1981. "Wildlife Conservation Issues in Northern Canada." Canadian Environmental Advisory Council, Report No. 11, Ottawa, ON. 30 pp.

Cowan, Ian McTaggart. 1982. "Faunal Diversity as a Habitat Goal." pp. 20–30 in D. Day and R. Stace-Smith (eds.) *British Columbia Land for Wildlife Past, Present and Future*. Proceedings of Land for Wildlife Symposium, Simon Fraser University, Burnaby BC.

Cowan, Ian McTaggart. 1985. "Forestry and Forest Wildlife: A Conference Overview." *The Forestry Chronicle* 61: 200–202.

Dawe, N.K., I. McTaggart-Cowan, R.W. Campbell and A.C. Stewart. 2001. "What Lies Ahead for the Birds of British Columbia? New Philosophies, Concerns and Conservation Challenges." pp. 679–695 in R.Wayne Campbell, Neil K. Dawe, Ian McTaggart-Cowan, John M. Cooper, Garry W. Kaiser, Andrew C. Stewart and Michael C.E. McNall. 2001. *The Birds of British Columbia: Volume 4 – Passerines: Wood-Warblers through Old World Sparrows*. UBC Press, Vancouver, BC.

Hummel, Monte and Ian McTaggart-Cowan. 1990. "A Conservation Strategy for Large Carnivores in Canada." World Wildlife Fund Canada, Toronto, ON. 98 pp.

Kendeigh, S.C., H.I. Baldwin, V.H. Cahalane, C.H.D. Clarke, C. Cottam, Ian McTaggart Cowan, P. Dansereau, J.H. Davis, F.W. Emerson, I.T.

Ian's article "The Basis of Endangerment" (March 1980) was the opening address of the inaugural public forum held on threatened and endangered species and habitats. His synopsis was that habitat alteration is the main reason for their decline.
PHOTO BY R. WAYNE CAMPBELL.

Ian McTaggart-Cowan (third from left), founding director of the Nature Trust of British Columbia, on a field tour in the southern Okanagan Valley. After formal retirement from UBC, Ian sat on the boards of several conservation organizations. PHOTO BY THE NATURE TRUST OF BRITISH COLUMBIA, ANTLER SADDLE, CIRCA 1993. COURTESY OF ANN SCHAU.

The tops of broken, decaying trees in second-growth and old-growth forests provide nesting sites for species such as great horned owl. PHOTO BY R. WAYNE CAMPBELL.

Haig, A. Hayden, C.L. Hayward, J.M. Linsdale, J.A. MacNab and J.E. Potzger. 1950–51. "Nature Sanctuaries in the United States and Canada: A Preliminary Inventory." *The Living Wilderness* 15: 1–45.

Leopold, S. with C.C. Cottam, Ian McTaggart Cowan, I.N. Gabrielson and T.L. Kimball.1969. "The National Wildlife Refuge System." pp. 30–54 in *Transactions of the 33rd North American Wildlife Natural Resources Conference*, Washington, DC.

Lindblad, S.O. and L. Lindblad (eds.). 1987. *Baja California.* Rizzoli, NY. 184 pp. (With contributions from G. Lindsay, Ian McTaggart-Cowan and D. Cornejo.)

McTaggart-Cowan, Ian. 1984. "Some Environmental Considerations in the Planning, Construction and Maintenance of Northern Roads with Relevance to the Mackenzie Valley Highway" in J.K. Fraser and H. Bruyere (eds.). *Report on the Canadian Environmental Advisory Council,* Ottawa, ON. (Selected papers from assemblies of the environment councils of Canada, 1975–1980).

McTaggart-Cowan, Ian. 1987. "Science and the Conservation of Wildlife in British Columbia." pp. 85–106 in A. Murray (ed.). *Our Wildlife Heritage: 100 Years of Wildlife Management* [in British Columbia]. The Centennial Wildlife Society of British Columbia.

McTaggart-Cowan, Ian. 1989. "Room at the Top?" pp. 249–266 in M. Hummel (ed.). *Endangered Spaces: The Future for Canada's Wilderness.* Key Porter Books Ltd, Toronto, ON.

McTaggart-Cowan, Ian. 1996. "Conservation and Man's Environment." *Parks and Recreation* 3: 2.

McTaggart-Cowan, Ian. 1998. "Moments from the Education of an Ornithologist." *Picoides* 11: 17–22.

McTaggart-Cowan, Ian. 2006. Foreword. *The Nature Trust of British Columbia: Over 35 years of Conservation,* Victoria, BC. 96 pp.

A Legacy of Scientific and Other Publications

McTaggart-Cowan, Ian, N.K. Dawe, R.W. Campbell and A.C. Stewart. 2001. "Avian Biodiversity, Ecological Distribution and Patterns of Change. pp. 633–678 in R. Wayne Campbell, Neil K. Dawe, Ian McTaggart-Cowan, John M. Cooper, Gary W. Kaiser, Andrew C. Stewart and Michael C.E. McNall. 2001. *The Birds of British Columbia: Volume 4: Passerines: Wood-Warblers through Old World Sparrows.* UBC Press, Vancouver, BC.

Mosby, Henry S., Ian McTaggart Cowan and Lars Karstad. 1969. "Collection and Field Preservation of Biological Materials." pp. 259–276 in Robert H. Giles (ed.). *Wildlife Management Techniques* (Third edition, revised). The Wildlife Society, Washington, DC.

Taber, Richard D. and Ian McTaggart Cowan. 1969. "Capturing and Marking Wild Animals." pp. 277–318 in Robert H. Giles (ed.). *Wildlife Management Techniques* (Third edition, revised). The Wildlife Society, Washington, DC.

Educational Initiatives

Ian's duties as dean of the Faculty of Graduate Studies provided him with insight into broader issues of post-secondary education. His experience gave him an understanding of how academic institutions must adapt to changing needs.

Cowan, Ian McTaggart. 1965. "A New Necessity of the New age: the Ph.D." *University of British Columbia Alumni Chronicle* (Spring): 7-8.

Cowan, Ian McTaggart, G.C. Andrew, T.C. Byrne, J.F. Ellis, L.S. Gansner, R. Hughes, J. Patterson and E.E. Wallach. 1974. Royal Commission on Post-secondary Education in the Kootenay Region: Volumes 1 and 2. Queens Printer, Victoria, BC.

Hobbies

In his spare time Ian pursued several hobbies and, true to form, developed a recognized expertise in these other endeavours. Ever the collector and competitor, he developed an impressive reputation in philately and gardening. While travelling through the Yukon and British Columbia, he became fascinated with early history, which renewed his early interest in stamp collecting. Over time he amassed an impressive assortment of law stamps that caught the attention of the British North America Philatelic Society, and he was invited to display his collections for a public viewing as well as for judging by a panel of international philatelic judges. The rules to exhibit were formal and the collections had to physically show the stamps and covers as well as all documented research to authenticate a presentation. In Part I, Chapter 7, Richard Fleet presents a detailed account of Ian's entry into collecting revenue and law stamps and his subsequent major awards for his exhibits.

Ian's interest in gardening also included collections, notably that of

Ian's collection of Yukon and BC law and revenue stamps included new and cancelled stamps and associated material to document their use. This block of nine fifty-cent stamps (bottom) is from a centennial issue (1858–1958) in BC and shows the Kamloops courthouse of 1885.

311

the rhododendrons that occupied a major portion of his garden. He was active in garden clubs and participated in shows as well as acting as a speaker on various topics. Characteristically, he published an account on preparation of entries for a garden show (See Part I, Chapter 7). He also developed notes on topics such as the seed propagation of hardy *Cyclamen*, a group of perennial plants valued both for their variegated foliage and their flowers.

Late winter-blooming *Cyclamen coum*. In addition to his formal publications, Ian prepared many unpublished reference notes on his hobbies. PHOTO BY RONALD D. JAKIMCHUK.

Cowan, Ian McTaggart. 1979a. "Part Imperforate Stamps in British Columbia." *The Canadian Philatelist* 30: 89–95.

Cowan, Ian McTaggart. 1979b. "The Dawson Mining Court Law Stamps of Yukon Territory." *British North America Philatelic Society Topics* 36: 50–52.

Cowan, Ian McTaggart. 1979c. "New Information on the Yukon Territorial Law Stamps." *British North America Philatelic Society Topics.* 36: 43–45.

Cowan, Ian McTaggart. 1982. "A New Series of British Columbia Law Stamps." *British North America Philatelic Society Topics* 39(3): 30–31.

McTaggart-Cowan, Ian. 1983. "Canadian Revenue Study Group." *British North America Philatelic Society Topics* 40(1): 43.

McTaggart-Cowan, Ian. 1984. "Canadian Revenues Study Group." *British North America Philatelic Society Topics* 41(5): 48.

McTaggart-Cowan, Ian. 1985a. "Canadian Revenues Study Group." *British North America Philatelic Society Topics* 42(1): 50.

McTaggart-Cowan, Ian. 1985b. "Canadian Revenues Study Group." *British North America Philatelic Society Topics* 42(5): 55.

McTaggart-Cowan, Ian. 1987. "New Developments in Wildlife Revenue Stamps." *British North America Philatelic Society Topics* 44(6): 22–25.

McTaggart-Cowan, Ian. 1988a. "British Columbia 1987 Hunting Stamps and their Uses." *British North America Philatelic Society Topics* 45(2): 36–39.

McTaggart-Cowan, Ian. 1988b. "Proofs of Manitoba Law Stamps." British North America Philatelic Society Topics 45(5): 29–31.

McTaggart-Cowan, Ian. 1989. "Alberta Wildlife Certificate Stamps: Numbers Sold 1964–1985." *British North America Philatelic Society Topics* 46 (3): 44–46.

McTaggart-Cowan, Ian. 1990. "The Day before the Show." *Vancouver Island Rock and Alpine Garden Society Newsletter* (March 1990): 1–3. (See Part I, Chapter 7.)

McTaggart-Cowan, Ian. 2004. *The Law Stamps of Yukon, 1902–1971: Their Development and Use (Collection of Ian McTaggart-Cowan).* Published by the British North America Philatelic Society (BNAPS) and Auxano Philatelic Services, Calgary, AB. 104 pp.

McTaggart-Cowan, Ian. 2005. *The Law Stamps of British Columbia and their Uses, 1879-1984.* Published by the British North America Philatelic Society Ltd. as BNAPS Exhibit Series No. 36, Ottawa, ON. 162 pp.

CHAPTER 11
Student Theses and Dissertations

Ian McTaggart-Cowan's role as a graduate research supervisor and/or advisor was an extension, in part, of his own interests and contributions. In this chapter we have listed and summarized master's theses and doctor of philosophy dissertations to reveal and preserve the depth and breadth of knowledge arising from his tenure in the Department of Zoology and Faculty of Graduate Studies at UBC. We have presented the principal findings of these theses to extend the content beyond the titles and assist students who find the results relevant to their own interests. These "principal findings" summaries are not intended to be complete but are an attempt to indicate key results. However, it was often difficult to summarize complex research results or to summarize abstracts that varied enormously in the details presented. For example, some abstracts did not present actual results, whereas there were up to nine pages of detailed findings and conclusions in others! We take responsibility for the findings selected, but readers should access the actual theses and dissertations for complete details.

At present, all theses and dissertations are stored within the Department of Zoology at UBC. We were given access and selected those that involved Dr. Cowan, photographed the abstracts then reviewed them once they were converted to hard copy. In some older theses only carbon paper copies were available and legibility was a problem. Recently all UBC theses and dissertations have been scanned and are available online at https://circle.ubc.ca/advanced-search.

For all of the authors it was a great pleasure to read the research results of so many former colleagues and friends. Although we knew them for decades, we were very often unaware of the specific research topics they had chosen. In at least two cases we discovered that the research

Ronald D. Jakimchuk searching one of hundreds of theses and dissertations in the Department of Zoology collection at UBC. May 5, 2010. PHOTO BY R. WAYNE CAMPBELL.

conducted had not been about the species they originally intended, and that they had subsequently enjoyed distinguished careers specializing in the species or group studied rather than their initial interests.

Bachelor's (Hons.) Theses, Master's Theses and Doctor of Philosophy Dissertations

Ian was the senior supervisor or unofficially served in that capacity for at least 122 undergraduate and graduate students during his career as an educator. In addition, he sat on many other student advisory committees. He supported and encouraged students both in the field and in the classroom and urged them to complete their academic journey by publishing their findings, and although each student arrived with a unique set of expectations and interests, their thesis topics usually met with Ian's enthusiasm and interest.

He supervised an impressive number of graduate students, many of exceptional quality. Both he and other faculty members on supervisory committees helped to guide their scientific enquiries, and many of their findings still hold true decades after completion of their theses and dissertations. This body of research provides a significant contribution to management of wildlife and their habitats and extended into the incorporation of science into conservation programs and land management initiatives. Ian was not satisfied with simply building good scientific tools; he strived to ensure that others applied them.

Besides the contribution made by the results of all of these theses, dissertations and published papers, Ian's greater contribution was the training and mentoring of his students. When they "fledged and left the nest," many became professors, research scientists or managers

Table 1. Theses and dissertations supervised by Dr. Ian McTaggart-Cowan at the University of British Columbia, 1942–79.

THESES AND DISSERTATIONS					
Years	Bachelor's*	Master's	Doctoral	Total	%
1942–44	2	1	0	3	2.5
1945–49	10	6	0	16	13.1
1950–54	7	16	2	25	20.5
1955–59	1	12	8	21	17.2
1960–64	5	10	9	24	19.7
1965–69	3	7	8	18	14.8
1970–74	0	0	5	5	4.1
1975–79	0	6	4	10	8.2
Total	28 (23%)	58 (47.5%)	36 (29.5%)	122	

*Denotes a bachelor's thesis with honours that was usually based on empirical research. A few of those theses merited publication, some introduced students to research, and others provided a baseline for an advanced degree.

314

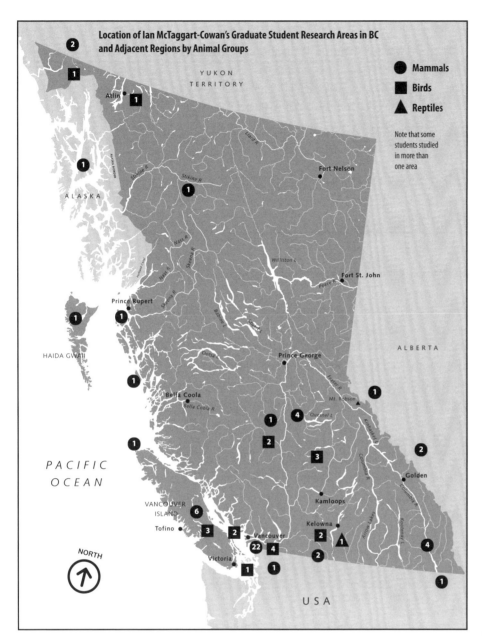

Location of Ian McTaggart-Cowan's Graduate Student Research Areas in BC and Adjacent Regions by Animal Groups

● Mammals
■ Birds
▲ Reptiles

Note that some students studied in more than one area

A complete list of students Dr. Cowan supervised was not available; hence, each graduate thesis and dissertation had to be checked. Here Dennis Demarchi searches the collection housed in Ian's former office in the Department of Zoology at UBC, May 5, 2010. PHOTO BY R. WAYNE CAMPBELL.

with universities, institutes, government agencies, private companies and public foundations. His mentoring was passed on by his successors, themselves becoming mentors to a new generation. This, then, is one of Ian's most important and enduring legacies. His fervent hope was that his students' research would lead them to careers in wildlife biology and conservation as well as contributing to a greater knowledge of natural history and ecology of wildlife and their habitats in British Columbia.

Over the years his research program, as revealed in the collective projects completed by his students, spanned a wide taxonomic range, a broad geographic extent and a breadth of biological disciplines and ecological processes. Some of his students investigated growth physiology and reproduction. Others examined relationships between species and

ANIMAL GROUPS					
Years	Reptiles	Birds	Mammals	Total	%
1942–44	0	2	1	3	2.5
1945–49	1	4	11	16	13.1
1950–54	0	9	16	25	20.5
1955–59	0	5	16	21	17.2
1960–64	1	6	17	24	19.7
1965–69	0	1	17	18	14.8
1970–74	0	1	4	5	4.1
1975–79	0	1	9	10	8.2
Total	2 (1.6%)	29 (23.8%)	91 (74.6%)	122	

Table 2. Animal groups for theses and dissertations supervised by Dr. Ian McTaggart-Cowan at the University of British Columbia, 1942–79.

Opposite:
Table 3. Distribution of Cowan's students' study areas or laboratories by jurisdiction in North America, Europe and Africa and by advanced degrees. (Note that 88 students studied in only one jurisdiction while seven students conducted field research in two or more areas.)

their environment and how habitat quality affected their productivity and survivorship. Some studies examined processes at the interspecific level such as predation and competition while others examined speciation as affected by islands and other biological and geographical factors. There was a strong representation of mammals and birds in the research, many of which were game species or species of concern to the public and management agencies in British Columbia and Canada.

Of the theses and dissertations that Ian supervised, twenty-eight (23%) were bachelor's (Hons.), fifty-eight (47.5%) were master's and thirty-six (29.5%) were doctoral. Animal groups researched in descending order were mammals ninety-one (74.6%), birds twenty-nine (23.8%) and reptiles two (2%). Most of the students he mentored went beyond documenting the natural history of a species to include an ecological component of the species' interaction with their environment, habitat or other species. Hence, besides the scientific understanding of particular

Nearly three-quarters of Ian's students completed theses on mammals. In this photo two male mule deer are fighting during the rutting period, Invermere, BC, 2012.
PHOTO BY LARRY HALVERSON.

Theses Distribution Table

Jurisdictions*	Masters Students**	Doctoral Students	Total Number of Study Areas
NORTH AMERICA			
BELIZE			
Belize		1- B***	1 - B
CANADA			
Alberta	2 - M	1 - B 2 - M	1 - B 4 - M
British Columbia	1 - R 12 - B 34 - M	5 - B 13 - M	1 - R 17 - B 47- M
Manitoba	2 - B 1 M	1 - B	3-B 1-M
Newfoundland and Labrador		1 - M	1-M
Northwest Territories (non-Nunavut)	3 - M	1 - M	4- M
Nova Scotia		1 - B	1 - B
Nunavut****	1 - M	2 - M	3- M
Ontario	1 - M	1 - M	2- M
Prince Edward Island		1 - B	1-B
Quebec		1 - B	1-B
Saskatchewan	1 - M		1-M
Yukon Territory		1 - B 2 - M	1-B 2- M
MEXICO			
Nayarit		1 - B	1-B
UNITED STATES of AMERICA			
Alaska		4 - B 3 - M	4-B 3-M
Idaho		1 - M	1-M
Louisiana		1 - B	1-B
Michigan		2 - B	2-B
Montana		1 - M	1-M
Texas		1 - M	1-M
Washington		1 - M	1-M
EUROPE			
HOLLAND			
North Holland		1 - B	1-B
South Holland		1 - B	1-B
ENGLAND			
Northumberland		1 - B	1-B
AFRICA			
UGANDA			
Western	1 - M		1-M
TANAZANIA			
Arusha		1 - M	1-M
Lindi	1 - M		1-M
TOTALS	1 - R 14 - B 45 - M	23 - B - 29 - M	1-R 37-B 74-M

* Below each country is the province, state, region or county where the students studied
** Master's degree includes, Master of Arts (prior to 1955), Master of Science (after 1955), Master of Science in Agriculture (MSA), and Master of Forestry (MF)
*** B= Bird study, M= Mammal study, R = Reptile Study
**** These studies were conducted in the Northwest Territories before Nunavut was created

species, this research program was highly relevant to land usage and the state of ecosystems. Perhaps this common theme is what led Ian in later years to be instrumental in conservation initiatives such as the Habitat Conservation Trust Foundation and the Nature Trust of British Columbia

The theses and dissertations that follow are arranged chronologically and demonstrate the changes in Ian's research interests over his thirty-eight-year tenure. Because many of the theses completed in academic institutions are never published, we have included principal findings of each student's individual research taken directly from the abstracts of all master's theses and doctoral dissertations.

1942

Fowle, Charles David. 1942. "A Preliminary Investigation of Certain Birds' Nests with Reference to their Environmental Relationships." B.A. (Hons.) thesis, University of British Columbia, Department of Zoology. 90 pp.

Note: Although Ian was never an amateur egg collector, he was interested in the structure of bird nests and where they were built. When student David Fowle arrived in Ian's office with a proposal to study bird nests, he invited him to be his first student. When the thesis was completed,[265] Ian realized he had underestimated his student's enthusiasm and intent; the work produced could have been a master's thesis. David Fowle retained his early interest in nesting birds and three decades later produced a significant publication on *Effects of Phosphamidon on Forest Birds in New Brunswick.*[266]

Morton, Betty Helen. 1942. "The Digestive, Respiratory and Urogenital Systems of the Columbian Black-tailed Deer (*Odocoileus hemionus columbianus* Rafinesque)." B.A. (Hons.) thesis, University of British Columbia, Department of Zoology, Vancouver, BC. 52 pp.

David Fowle's undergraduate thesis focussed on nest dimensions, differences in composition, diversity of nest material, nest heights and ecological placement for American robin (left), red-winged blackbird (centre) and Brewer's blackbird (right). Note the egg of the parasitic brown-headed cowbird (top) in the Brewer's blackbird nest. PHOTOS BY MARK NYHOF (L.) AND R. WAYNE CAMPBELL (C. AND R.).

1944

Fowle, Charles David. 1944. "The Sooty Grouse (*Dendragapus fuliginosus fuliginosus* Ridgway) on Its Summer Range." M.A. thesis, University of British Columbia, Department of Zoology. 79 pp.

Principal findings: This pioneering work set the stage for long-term research that continued for the next six decades on sooty grouse in coastal British Columbia. The study had 12 conclusions, many of which reported basic natural history attributes of this grouse for the first time. Some of these included reasons for an elevational migration of hens and chicks, the impact of blood parasites on clutch size, defining the breeding cycle and diet, the role of ectoparasites in the spread of epidemic diseases and the effect of predators on grouse populations.

1945

Hatter, James. 1945. "Food Habits of Coyotes in Jasper National Park." B.A. (Hons.) thesis, University of British Columbia, Department of Zoology. 76 pp.

1947

Fisher, Harold Dean. 1947. "The Biology, Economic Status and Control of the Harbour Seal (*Phoca vitulina richardii*) in British Columbia, with Particular Reference to the Skeena River Area." M.A. thesis, University of British Columbia, Department of Zoology. 104 pp.

Principal findings: Mating of the [Pacific] harbour seal (*Phoca vitulina richardii*) takes place in September and October in the Skeena River area and birth season ranges from early May to the latter half of June. Weight of pups is doubled in the first five or six weeks of life and declines by about 20% during the weaning period in the autumn. Few parasites or cases of disease were noted. Salmon (*Oncorhynchus* spp.) formed 28.5 % of total food volume of 20 stomachs analyzed, followed by Pacific herring (*Clupea pallasii*) (20%) and rockfish (Sebastidae) (19%). Seal predation on salmon approaches significant proportions only in upriver areas. The bounty system for control of harbour seals is considered to be inefficient.

Note: Even while tending to the demands of his own 122 graduate students, Ian somehow found time to help others whose research topics were timely and added to the knowledge of the natural history of an animal. For example, he was not Dean Fisher's principal advisor, but he suggested his research topic, solicited financial support, made arrangements for field accommodation and scheduled thesis progress meetings. In addition, Ian provided Dean with current pinniped literature, gave encouragement, read many drafts of his thesis and attended his thesis defence.

During the twentieth century, both sport and commercial fishermen deplored the predatory habits of harbour seals, often as a result of misinformation. This resulted in indiscriminate killing of seals under a bounty system. This situation was of growing concern to Ian, and he instilled in his students and colleagues the importance of scientific research as the basis for making informed decisions when managing predatory species. PHOTO BY ALAN D. WILSON.

Hatter, James. 1947. "Preliminary Studies on the Moose of Central British Columbia: 1946." This report was a co-operative research project in wildlife conservation conducted by the British Columbia Game Commission and the Department of Zoology of the University of British Columbia. It was originally intended as the start of a master of arts degree at UBC but was incorporated into a full Ph.D. program at Washington State University, Pullman, WA. 110 pp.

Principal findings: This was the first study of its kind on big game in British Columbia. The report is based on field studies by the student and by a questionnaire sent to big game guides, game wardens and people known to be careful observers. The study was conducted in the Cariboo from west of the North Thompson and Clearwater rivers to the Fraser River, the areas around Quesnel, between Burns Lake and Ootsa Lake, and portions of the Bulkley Valley. Fieldwork was conducted from May to November 1946. In an attempt to justify scientific research on moose populations and the setting of hunting regulations, Hatter suggested that hunters should have a say in setting regulations if they based their observations on careful, scientific observations and not mere casual observations and opinions.

Hick, William Bernard Martin. 1947. "A Comparative Study of the Myology of the Head Region in *Thamnophis sirtalis tetrataenia*, *Thamnophis ordinoides vagrans* and *Thamnophis ordinoides ordinoides*, Based on Detailed Description of the Condition Found in *Thamnophis sirtalis tetrataenia*." B.A. (Hons.) thesis, University of British Columbia, Department of Zoology, 87 pp.

Munro, David Aird. 1947. "A Preliminary Study of the Waterfowl of Burnaby Lake, British Columbia." B.A. (Hons.) thesis, University of British Columbia, Department of Zoology. 66 pp.

Musfeldt, Iola W. 1947. "The Significance of Diseases and Parasites of the Muskrat (*Ondatra zibethica*) in British Columbia." M.A. thesis, University of British Columbia, Department of Zoology. 108 pp.

Principal findings: Between October 1944 and May 1947, 202 skinned carcasses were collected from trappers in 17 areas of the province. Parasite and disease examinations were performed. Seventy-four percent of the carcasses were parasitized by 12 species of internal parasites, of which *Trichuris opaca* was a new record of infection for this host. Pathological conditions affecting the muskrat included two pulmonary conditions and a tumorous condition; there were also frequent infected wounds. Parasitism in muskrats in British Columbia is normal, but there are considerable regional differences in the prevalence and abundance of parasites. There was no apparent difference due to age in adults and juvenile muskrats, and mortality as a result of excessive parasitism is probably negligible.

Pfeiffer, E.W. 1947. "Ecology of the Winter Ranges of Jasper National Park." B.A. (Hons.) thesis, University of British Columbia, Department of Zoology. 63 pp.

Shaw, Dorothy Anne. 1947. "Skeletal and Muscular Adaptations to a Subterranean Environment of *Microtus oregoni serpens* (Mammalia, Rodentia)." M.A. thesis, University of British Columbia, Department of Zoology. 78 pp.

Principal findings: The anatomical differences between a fossorial species of vole (creeping vole—*Microtus oregoni*) and more terrestrial species (Townsend's—*M. townsendii*, long-tailed—*M. longicaudus* and water [Richardson's]—*M. richardsoni* voles) were compared. Some external features of the creeping vole have adapted it to a subterranean life, such as a soft plush-like pelage, a short tail, the arrangement of vibrissae with the longest being farthest from the snout, smaller eyes, and a modification of the oricularis oculi muscle to prevent dirt from entering the eyes. It also has shorter limbs and an inclusion of a larger part of them within the skin. Creeping voles also have stronger shoulder, chest and forelimb muscles, with the pectoral girdle showing the most marked modifications.

1948

Brooks, Allan Cecil. 1948. "A Comparative Study of the Cranial Muscles in Three Genera of North Pacific Alcidae (Aves)." B.A. (Hons.) thesis, University of British Columbia, Department of Zoology. 54 pp.

Mackay, Ronald H. 1948. "Food Habits of the Marten in Jasper, Banff and Kootenay National Parks." B.A. (Hons.) thesis, University of British Columbia, Department of Zoology. 31 pp.

Moloney, Patrick J. 1948. "A Study of the Pelages and Hairs of the Ungulate Mammals of Canada." B.A. (Hons.) thesis, University of British Columbia, Department of Zoology. 50 pp.

Roberts, Leslie Wilson. 1948. "A Survey of the Carotene and Ascorbic Acid Content of Moose Browse." M.A. thesis, University of British Columbia, Department of Zoology. 82 pp.

Principal findings: A 20-year-old burned area of new forest had the highest content of pro-vitamin A (carotene) and vitamin C (ascorbic acid) among a series of seral stages of forest from youngest to climax stage. A seasonal variation in vitamin content was established: deciduous species have a summer maximum and winter minimum, and coniferous species a summer minimum and winter maximum.

Taylor, Ernest William. 1948. "Winter Food Habits of the Ring-necked Pheasant in the Lower Fraser [River] Valley of British Columbia." B.A. (Hons.) thesis, University of British Columbia, Department of Zoology. 59 pp.

Note: A bachelor's degree with an honours thesis combined with faculty guidance is a helpful introduction to wildlife research. Two years after completing an undergraduate degree, Ernie Taylor completed a M.A. thesis examining reasons behind the decline of ring-necked pheasant populations in the Lower Mainland of British Columbia.

Two years after completing an undergraduate degree, Ernie Taylor completed an M.A. thesis examining reasons behind the decline of ring-necked pheasant populations in the Lower Mainland of BC. PHOTO BY ALAN D. WILSON.

1949

Cottle, Walter H. 1949. "A Study of the Feeding Behavior of Some Members of the Anatinae Wintering in the Lower Fraser [River] Valley of British Columbia." B.A. (Hons.) thesis, University of British Columbia, Department of Zoology. 65 pp.

Mair, William Winston. 1949. "A Preliminary Survey of the Timber Wolf (*Canis lupus*) Populations in the Northwest Mountain Region." B.A. (Hons.) thesis, University of British Columbia, Department of Zoology. 69 pp.

Merry, Margaret Gertrude. 1949. "Life History of the Creeping Vole, *Microtus oregoni serpens* Merriam." M.A. thesis, University of British Columbia, Department of Zoology. 66 pp.

Principal findings: This study was conducted at the University of British Columbia campus in Vancouver and had three components: a habitat field study, the examination of animals that were trapped and a study of the biology of captive voles. Merry found that the creeping vole (*Microtus oregoni*) was a species of the forest edge and early forest seral stages. This species has a longer gestation period and smaller litter sizes than other species of *Microtus;* in other respects the creeping vole is similar to other vole species, but this study showed many anatomical differences.

1950

Benson, Walter Arthur. 1950. "The Effect of Orchard Spraying on Pheasants in the Okanagan Valley with Observations on Bird Life in Orchard Areas." M.A. thesis, University of British Columbia, Department of Zoology. 90 pp.

Principal findings: With the growing concern of the effect of DDT and other chemicals on birds in North America in the 1940s, this study looked at the immediate and residual effect of spraying in orchards in the Okanagan Valley. Targeted species included mourning dove, mountain and western bluebird,

American robin, California quail, ring-necked pheasant, and song, chipping and white-crowned sparrows. The study involved experimental observations of birds sprayed in cages as well as those recorded in the field. The results showed that while some deaths occurred from spraying activities, there was great variability in toxic effects, suggesting that other factor(s) may have also influenced the impact on individual species.

Edwards, Roger Yorke. 1950. "Variations in the Fur Productivity of Northern British Columbia in Relation to Some Environmental Factors." M.A. thesis, University of British Columbia, Department of Zoology. 126 pp.

Principal findings: The yearly reports of 155 registered traplines in northern and northeastern British Columbia were grouped into seven distinct areas exhibiting physiographic and vegetational differences. Production figures for most species were highly variable among the seven areas. Coyote, grey wolf, weasel, red squirrel and muskrat appear to be taken in numbers inversely proportional to the size of trap lines. The size of lines, in turn, appears to be an expression of the human population density, habitat modification, depletion of populations of valuable fur species, and other factors. Red fox, American marten, fisher, mink, wolverine, Canada lynx and beaver appear to be taken in numbers proportional to their abundance. Highest production appears to result from the most favourable environmental conditions. Raccoon, river otter, striped skunk and cougar are not abundant in northern BC and the number of pelts harvested is low.

Guiguet, Charles Joseph. 1950. "An Ecological Study of Goose Island, British Columbia, with Special Reference to Terrestrial Mammals." M.A. thesis, University of British Columbia, Department of Zoology. 80 pp.

Principal findings: The Goose Island group represents a well-isolated ecological unit about 24 miles off the central mainland coast of British Columbia. The archipelago supports populations of dusky shrew (*Sorex monticolus*), long-tailed vole (*Microtus longicaudus*), Keen's [deer] mouse (*Peromyscus keeni*) and perhaps resident populations of Pacific [winter] wren (*Troglodytes pacificus*) and song sparrow (*Melospiza melodia*).

Hatter, James. 1950. "The Moose of Central British Columbia." Ph.D. dissertation, Washington State University, Pullman, WA. 360 pp.

Principal findings: It was suspected that the [American] moose (*Alces americana*) invaded the southern half of British Columbia within the early half of the 20th century. Destruction of climax forests in the latter decades of the 19th century, which previously limited moose population density, apparently made it possible for large populations of moose to become established in

Although DDT was banned in the 1970s, its residual effects on wildlife are long-lasting. Sixty-five years after Art Benson's pioneering work on orchard spraying in the Okanagan Valley, new research shows that DDT has accumulated in earthworms and is passed on to the eggs and nestlings of American robins. Despite high levels of contamination, American robins continue to reproduce successfully in orchards in the Okanagan Valley. PHOTO BY R. WAYNE CAMPBELL.

Charles Guiguet's study suggests that many large offshore islands along the BC coast with resident, non-migratory populations of birds may harbour endemic forms. The recently fledged Pacific wren in this photo is common year-round on the coast. PHOTO BY MARK NYHOF.

James Hatter's original work on moose in BC in 1950 was the first complete synthesis for this species in the province. PHOTO BY R. WAYNE CAMPBELL.

suitable sub-climax forests concomitant with human habitation. In addition to widespread deforestation, early settlers, prospectors and railroad builders altered and expanded the pre-existing fire patterns providing optimal foraging habitats for moose during their expansion into the province.

The main emphasis throughout this study was habitat change, ecology and etiology of intraspecific competition. The years 1946–48, during which the study was in progress, were characterized by unusually severe winters that resulted in high mortality in the moose population. Moose numbers had increased to such high densities by the mid-1930s that they over-browsed their winter food supply, and this, coupled with the series of severe winters, caused moose numbers to crash. Hunting of bull moose, wolf predation and parasite loads had not reduced the population sufficiently to maintain numbers within food-carrying capacity and avoid the severe crash.

Law, Cecil Ernest. 1950. "An Initial Study of the Ecology of the Muskrat (*Ondatra zibethica spatulata* Osgood) of the Slave River Delta with Particular Reference to the Physical Environment." B.A. (Hons.) thesis, University of British Columbia, Department of Zoology. 120 pp.

Macleod, Charles Franklyn. 1950. "The Productivity and Distribution of Fur-bearing Species of the Coast Forest of British Columbia in Relation to Some Environmental Factors." M.A. thesis, University of British Columbia, Department of Zoology. 105 pp.

Principal findings: The yearly fur-bearer harvest returns from 1929 to 1948 for 211 registered traplines on the coast north of Howe Sound were examined for fur-bearer species' distribution. Twenty fur-bearers occur in this region of which 18 were examined: raccoon, red fox, coyote, grey wolf, [American] marten, fisher, weasel, [American] mink, wolverine, [northern] river otter, spotted and striped skunks, cougar, [Canada] lynx, bobcat, red squirrel, beaver and muskrat. The productivity of spotted and striped skunks, bobcat, raccoon and northern river otter does not appear to be indicative of the abundance of the animals in the areas where they occur. For the latter species, the low catch is probably because of the difficulty skinning the animals and preparing the pelt. The other four species seem to be disregarded by the trappers due to the low value of those furs. For the remainder of species (13), the productivity figures are indicative of abundance, at least in accessible areas.

Red fox, coyote, fisher, Canada lynx and striped skunk appear to be confined to inland valleys with an interior forest type. Raccoon, bobcat and spotted skunk are restricted to the southern regions. The remaining species are of general distribution with American marten, weasel, mink and northern river otter the only ones present in any number. Insular conditions have not prevented the majority of the coastal species from spreading, except in the case of the Queen Charlotte Islands [Haida Gwaii] where only American marten, northern river otter and weasel are indigenous.

Sterling, Robert Thomas. 1950. "An Anatomical Study of the Cloaca of the Scoters." B.A. (Hons.) thesis, University of British Columbia, Department of Zoology. 40 pp.

Taylor, Ernest William. 1950. "A Study of Factors Affecting Reproduction and Survival of the Ring-necked Pheasant in the Lower Fraser Valley of British Columbia." M.A. thesis, University of British Columbia, Department of Zoology. 116 pp.

Principal findings: This study gathered quantitative data on population trends of ring-necked pheasant since its introduction on the southwestern mainland coast of British Columbia in 1891. By the late 1940s it was suggested that pheasant populations on the Fraser River delta had declined substantially. Results of this study suggested that increased urbanization, quality of original habitat, chemical spraying, changing agricultural practices, plant diseases and insect pests had contributed to the species' decline. One of the recommendations suggested that annual introductions of farm-reared birds as a means to increase numbers was of doubtful value.

1951

Bryant, Joseph Edward. 1951. "A Survey of the Bounty System in British Columbia from 1943–49 (exclusive of 1948)." B.A. (Hons.) thesis, University of British Columbia, Department of Zoology. 130 pp.

Cottle, Walter H. 1951. "A Study of the Ecology of Beaver in British Columbia." M.A. thesis, University of British Columbia, Department of Zoology. 58 pp.

Principal findings: This study was conducted in the Meldrum Creek watershed in the eastern Chilcotin. In 1942 a pair of beavers was released here and by 1950 they had increased to 21 colonies. Water levels of nine beaver ponds showed that beaver dams act as a regulating mechanism and tend to prolong the flow of water. Beaver consume mostly the bark of trembling aspen and willow, but other foods were also used. Beaver cut all sizes of trembling aspen without preference, the mean weight of bark and twigs made available by cutting was about 3,700 lbs/colony. Beaver in the study area occupied two somewhat distinct habitats, lakes and streams. Populations on lakes tend to be stable as there is sufficient reproduction in the large stands of trembling aspen stands to maintain the stand during use by beaver. Populations on creeks, however, eliminate their food supplies and are forced to emigrate to new habitats.

Dzubin, Alexander. 1951. "Palatability Studies on Some Foods of the Columbian Black-tailed Deer *Odocoileus hemionus columbianus* (Richardson)." B.A. (Hons.) thesis, University of British Columbia, Department of Zoology. 44 pp.

Malysheff, Andrew. 1951. "Lead Poisoning of Ducks in the Lower Fraser [River] Valley of British Columbia: A Chemical Study." M.A. thesis, University of British Columbia, Department of Zoology. 90 pp.

Principal findings: A considerable number of mallard (*Anas platyrhynchos*) and northern pintail (*Anas acuta*) were survivors of post-contamination by lead. Pintails appeared to sustain more contamination by lead than mallards and to have less resistance to the effects of lead. A lower survival rate in juvenile mallards occurred than in adults, and a lower survival rate was recorded for adult females than adult males.

Robinson, Donald Joseph. 1951. "The Inter-relations of the Introduced Gray Squirrel (*Sciurus carolinensis*) with the Ecological Conditions in Stanley Park." M.A. thesis, University of British Columbia, Department of Zoology. 99 pp.

Principal findings: The [eastern] gray squirrel (*Sciurus carolinensis*) reached saturated density in the mixed deciduous-conifer forest of 0.7 per acre (spring) and about 1.0/acre (autumn population). Two litters are produced by adult squirrels and one by yearlings. Mating occurred in March/April and June/July. Reproductive success at 1.6 per young/breeding female at weaning was considered to be very low. The gray squirrel is not territorial in Stanley Park, Vancouver, British Columbia. Males are polygamous.

The most important food plants are vine maple (*Acer circinatum*) and broad-leafed [big leaf] maple (*Acer macrophyllum*). Competition between the gray and Douglas' squirrel (*Tamiasciurus douglasii*) was reduced by differing habitat preferences of the two species. Two of 26 bird nests watched were destroyed by squirrels.

1952

Bandy, Percy John. 1952. "A Study of the Fur-bearing Mammals of the Subalpine and Columbia Forest Regions of British Columbia in Relation to the Fur Production from 1929 to 1949." B.A. (Hons.) thesis, University of British Columbia, Department of Zoology. 82 pp.

Delisle, Clement. 1952. "A Preliminary Study of the Protein Metabolism of the Coastal Deer of British Columbia, *Odocoileus heminonus columbianus* (Richardson)." M.A. thesis, University of British Columbia, Department of Zoology. 36 pp.

Principal findings: A nitrogen balance experiment was carried out using a six-month-old fawn and a two-year-old pregnant doe Columbian black-tailed deer. The necessary intake of grass for the maintenance of nitrogen balance was nine grams for the fawn and 15 grams for the doe. It was determined that the poorest area would be critical for growth of the fawn in winter, whereas the best area would enhance the chances of survival. The amount of browse that the pregnant doe would have to handle in April in the best areas is within limits of her capacity to consume that amount of forage.

Honours bachelor's theses, while seldom published, are often useful sources of information. For example, John Bandy's B.A. thesis provides the information that prior to 1934 the red squirrel was seldom trapped for the fur market in British Columbia. Over the next fifteen years (1934–49) 218,738 squirrels were trapped, forming the highest aggregate total of skins for all seventeen species of mammals considered fur-bearers.

PHOTO BY MARK NYHOF.

Hagmeier, Edwin M. 1952. "A Contribution to the Classification and Phylogeny of the Marten (Subgenus *Martes* Pinel) of North America with Special Reference to Those of British Columbia." M.A. thesis, University of British Columbia, Department of Zoology. 81 pp.

Principal findings: The genus *Martes* arose in the lower Pliocene and segregated into the subgenera of marten and fisher during that era. Only one species of marten occurs in North America and is divided into two groups, the formerly conceived *americana* and *caurina*. The *americana* group preceded *caurina* to North America, both arriving before the Kansan ice age. In the interval between the Kansan and Illinoian ice ages the American group divided into two branches, and during the Wisconsin or earlier *origenes* had separated from *caurina*. During the Wisconsin ice ages in North America marten found refuge in four regions: the lake states, the Rocky Mountains, the Coast Range and Alaska. Repopulation of North America after the glaciers retreated occurred from these refugia, during which time or later final subspeciation occurred. A study of 418 American marten skulls gives evidence for the subspecific status of *brumalis, americana, actuosa, caurina* and *nesophoila; abietinoides* is probably separable from *americana*. However, the subspecies *vancouverensis, caurina* and *origenes* cannot be differentiated. Thus, on the basis of geographic distribution, their status should not be changed at this time.

William Winston Mair concluded that the intentional introduction of large mammals, such as elk, to new locations must be done with caution. The transplant must consider the impact of competition for resources with resident wildlife. PHOTO BY R. WAYNE CAMPBELL.

George Mitchell clearly showed that twelve species of diving ducks that wintered along the inner south coast of BC used different feeding and resting habitats. For example, the ring-necked duck in this photo was only found on fresh water. PHOTO BY R. WAYNE CAMPBELL.

Jackson, Mary Fairfield. 1952. "Variation in an Isolated Population of Shrews of the *Vagrans-obscurus* Group." M.A. thesis, University of British Columbia, Department of Zoology. 73 pp.

Principal findings: Complete separation of two species of shrew, *Sorex vagrans* and *S. obscurus*, at Point Grey in Vancouver, British Columbia, was found to be impossible based on standard skull and body measurements. An arbitrary separation of 95% was achieved based on tail length and length of the maxillary tooth row. Intergradation of all morphological features was taken as evidence of considerable hybridization of the two species. Hybridization in a local population was not considered a sufficient basis to change the specific status of the two species studied.

Mair, William Winston. 1952. "The Impact of an Introduced Population of Elk upon the Biota of Banff National Park." M.A. thesis, University of British Columbia, Department of Zoology. 98 pp.

Principal findings: Elk (*Cervus elaphus*), which were introduced into Banff National Park in 1917 and 1919-1920, rapidly increased in numbers to the extent that control by removal was considered necessary. By 1949 most winter ranges were heavily over-browsed and overgrazed while summer ranges were deteriorating. Moose (*Alces alces*) entered the park in 1916, increasing to the late 1930s then stabilized about 1943. Over-browsing by elk was not considered detrimental to moose at the time of the study, but encroachment on moose habitats was occurring and predicted to be eventually detrimental to moose. Use by elk had detrimental effects on mule deer, depressing their numbers in the Bow Valley. Bighorn sheep (*Ovis canadensis canadensis*) rapidly declined from maximum levels in the 1930s, possibly as a result of an epizootic, and recovery has been adversely affected by ongoing competition from elk.

Mitchell, George Joseph. 1952. "A Study of the Distribution of Some Members of the *Nyrocinae* Wintering on the Coastal Waters of Southern British Columbia." M.A. thesis, University of British Columbia, Department of Zoology. 93 pp.

Principal findings: This study of diving ducks on the coastal waters of southern British Columbia took place during the autumn and early winter of 1951-1952. All species showed habitat preferences; both protected and unprotected coastlines were preferred over lake, bay and estuarine waters. During the winter, drakes and hens were distributed non-randomly because of the preponderance of males and their tendency to flock together. During the early spring the sexes were distributed non-randomly due to pair formation and the preponderance of males. Only a small percentage of juveniles of all species wintered.

Rye, Darrell. 1952. "Factors Affecting Orchard Pheasant Populations in the Okanagan Valley of British Columbia with Special Reference to Orchard Insecticides." M.A. thesis, University of British Columbia, Department of Zoology. 67 pp.

Principal findings: This research was an update of W.A. Benson's study in the late 1940s to evaluate the effect of several factors, including orchard spraying, upon ring-necked pheasant numbers in the Okanagan Valley. Both DDT and Parathion, although potential threats to pheasants, were not regarded as major causes of population declines. It was also concluded that sprinklers combined with more intensive cover removal within orchards was inhospitable for pheasants and one of the critical limiting factors in their numbers.

Smith, William Glen. 1952. "The Food Habits of a Population of Black Turnstones, Aleutian Sandpipers and Surf-birds Wintering in Southern British Columbia." B.A. (Hons.) thesis, University of British Columbia, Department of Zoology. 51 pp.

Note: Glen Smith's thesis remains the only detailed study in British Columbia of the diet of rock-frequenting shorebirds like the black turnstone. Rarely are bachelor theses cited in the technical literature, but the thoroughness of his research was acknowledged in *The Birds of North America* account for black turnstone.[268]

Glen Smith's thesis remains the only detailed study in BC of the diet of rock-frequenting shorebirds like the black turnstone shown in this photo.
PHOTO BY R. WAYNE CAMPBELL.

Tener, John Simpson. 1952. "A Preliminary Study of Musk-oxen at Slidre Fjord District, Fosheim Peninsula, Ellesmere Island." M.A. thesis. University of British Columbia, Department of Zoology. 91 pp.

Principal findings: Herds of musk-oxen [muskox] in the vicinity of Slidre Fiord, Ellesmere Island, NWT [now Nunavut], were studied from April 19 to August 24, 1951. The sexes and ages, the calving and breeding seasons and winter and summer ranges were examined. Movements between the winter and summer ranges were observed to determine migratory status. Food habits were observed by timed counts and examination of the stomach contents of a two-year-old bull. Wolf predation was evaluated by scat analysis, wolf stomachs, remains of dead musk-oxen and observation of attempted predation.

1954

Bendell, James F.S. 1954. "A Study of the Life History and Population Dynamics of the Sooty Grouse, *Dendragapus obscurus fuliginosus* (Ridgway)." Ph.D. dissertation, University of British Columbia, Department of Zoology. 145 pp.

Principal findings: This was a study of sooty grouse (*Dendragapus* [*obscurus*] *fuliginosus*) on its summer range from 1950 to 1953. Life history data on moult, aging, weight and behaviour were presented. The population studied was apparently stable with young birds replacing older birds that had died. Disease was an important mortality factor in the chicks and a major factor affecting population dynamics.

Note: Jim Bendell continued his research interests on sooty grouse for the rest of his career, and in retirement—fifty-one years after completing his Ph.D.— he and Fred Zwickel published the monograph *Blue Grouse: Their Biology and Natural History*. The work received The Wildlife Society's Publications Award for Outstanding Monograph for 2005.

Cooper, Ann. 1954. "A Contribution to the Anatomy of the Marten *Martes americana*." B.Sc. (Hons.) thesis, University of British Columbia, Department of Zoology. 68 pp.

Dzubin, Alexander. 1954. "An Intensive Study of Waterfowl Populations on a Small Block of Agricultural Land, Minnedosa, Manitoba: The Breeding Biology and Production of Some Diving and Dabbling Ducks of the "Pothole-Agricultural" Breeding Habitat in South-Central Manitoba." M.A. thesis, University of British Columbia, Department of Zoology. 85 pp.

Principal findings: This two-year study showed that populations of ducks rose to a peak during the first week of May on the 960-acre study area of pothole habitats in south-central Manitoba. The most common species breeding in the area were mallard (33.7% of the total composition), blue-winged teal (23.3%) and canvasback (10.1%). The remainder consisted of baldpate [American wigeon], [northern] pintail, redhead, ruddy duck, [northern] shoveler, gadwall, green-winged teal and lesser scaup. An area of one square mile (640 acres) produced 331 young in 1952 and 355 young in 1953. Average maximum brood-size for all species was 6.9. All divers nested in emergent vegetation in potholes. Slightly over 50% of dabbler nests were recorded on road allowances, fence rows, or waste upland areas, 30.6% on pothole edges and the remainder in various other habitats. The ratio of broods per pair was highly variable for dabbling ducks ranging from a high of 0.85 for blue-winged teal to a low of 0.28 for pintail. The ratio for divers was higher than for dabblers.

Predation losses were higher for dabblers (about 30% in successive years) than for divers (between six and seven percent for successive years). Predation was the principal cause of most nest destruction and had a marked effect on final production.

Breeding home ranges were highly variable by species (160 acres for blue-wing teal (*Anas discors*), 640 acres for mallard *A. platyrhynchos*) and over 2,500 acres for canvasback (*Aythya valisineria*).

1955

Bandy, Percy John. 1955. "Studies of Growth and Nutrition in the Columbian Black-tailed Deer (*Odocoileus hemionus columbianus*)." M.A. thesis, University of British Columbia, Department of Zoology. 90 pp.

Principal findings: Columbian black-tailed deer up to 18 months of age were fed a diet that was considered capable of supporting maximum growth. The resultant growth patterns showed that there was a marked seasonal influence on size-growth. A retardation of growth occurred during the winter, which was associated with a reproductive rhythm. Males voluntarily reduced their food intake when they became sexually active. However, changes in form shown by the growth of body parts relative to the weights of the animals remained constant. Animals that were on a growth-restricting diet showed that nutritional levels affected their reproductive activity and therefore modified the effect of reproductive activity on growth.

Bryant, Joseph Edward. 1955. "A Preliminary Study of the Moose (*Alces alces andersoni* Peterson) in Northern Manitoba, with Special Reference to its Management." M.A. thesis, University of British Columbia, Department of Zoology. 247 pp.

Principal findings: Utilization by humans varied between 6% and 20% of reported moose (*Alces alces*) populations in First Nation sections, and between 2% and 12% in other areas. [Grey] wolf (*Canis lupus*) poisoning programs

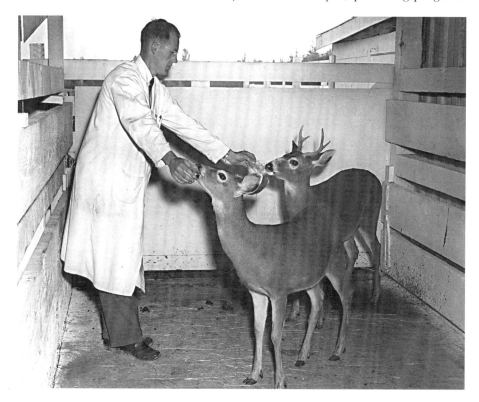

John Bandy with two Columbian black-tailed deer at the UBC animal husbandry research facility in Vancouver, circa 1965. PHOTO COURTESY OF HELEN BANDY.

eliminated wolf predation as a limiting factor on moose populations, and parasitism and disease were not considered to be important. Accidental death of moose by drowning took a fairly large annual toll. Lack of variety of browse species was considered to be a major limiting factor for moose.

Fay, Francis Hollis. 1955. "The Pacific Walrus (*Odobenus rosmarus divergens*): Spatial Ecology, Life History and Population." Ph.D. dissertation, University of British Columbia, Department of Zoology. 173 pp.

Principal findings: The Pacific walrus inhabits the Bering Sea during winter and the Chukchee [Chukchi] Sea (between far northeastern Siberia and northwestern Alaska) in summer, generally near sea ice. The animals frequent waters of less than 50 fathoms [91 m] deep where their preferred food, the bivalve molluscs *Mya, Saxicava, Astarte, Macoma,* and *Clinocardium* occur.

The bull Pacific walrus reaches sexual maturity at six to eight years of age, the cow at four to five years of age. Breeding takes place from April to June as the animals migrate northward. There is no evidence of any organized polygamy or "harem breeding." Gestation is one year, and twinning is unknown. An individual cow rarely conceives in successive years, the first three pregnancies generally being at two-year intervals and later ones three or more years apart. Males become senile at about 15 years of age. Full adult body size is achieved at four to six years of age by both sexes. The tusks and other teeth grow at a relatively high rate throughout their life span. The population of Pacific walrus, upwards of 40,000 animals in 1954, had declined slightly over the previous 15 years. The birth rate and death rate are about equal with human predation accounting for most of the latter.

Pacific walrus spend much of their lives on sea ice in the Arctic Ocean and feed in shallow waters on benthic molluscs. PHOTO BY JOEL GARLICH-MILLER, COURTESY OF UNITED STATES FISH & WILDLIFE SERVICE (ALASKA REGION), ANCHORAGE, AK.

Hagmeier, Edwin M. 1955. "The Genus *Martes* (Mustelidae) in North America: Its Distribution, Variation, Classification, Phylogeny and Relationship to Old World Forms." Ph.D. dissertation, University of British Columbia, Department of Zoology. 469 pp.

Principal findings: The concept of the subspecies proves in many respects to be unsatisfactory. Among other failings, it lacks reality, it involves the arbitrary partitioning of continua, it possesses no lower limit and it is determined deductively. This together with the clinal nature of variation in the [American] marten (*Martes americana*) and fisher (*M. pennanti*) leads to the conclusion that marten of the new world should be represented by only two subspecies (*M. a. americana* and *M. a. caurina*, both formerly considered species), the fisher by one species, and no named subspecies. Fossils referable to the genus *Martes* are first recorded from the Miocene of both the old and new worlds. Modern martens and fishers arrived in the new world (or evolved there) late in the Pliocene or early in the Pleistocene.

McAllister, Nancy Mahoney. 1955. "Reproductive Behaviour of the Eared Grebe, *Podiceps caspicus nigricollis*." M.A. thesis, University of British Columbia, Department of Zoology. 68 pp.

Principal findings: The behaviour of the eared grebe (*Podiceps nigricollis* [*caspicus*] *californicus* [*nigricollis*]) was compared to published accounts of the great crested grebe (*P. cristatus*). While threat and escape behaviour have been seen in the courtship of many birds, for the two grebe species this does not seem to be important. After courtship, nesting behaviour takes place, the timing of which is caused by a general climatic stimulus; egg-laying takes place only in warm, dry weather and females stop laying eggs during periods of inclement weather. Thus these two species are on the borderline between determinate and indeterminate egg layers.

Stevens, Ward Earl. 1955. "Adjustments of the Northwestern Muskrat (*Ondatra zibethicus spatulatus*) to a Northern Environment." Ph.D. dissertation, University of British Columbia, Department of Zoology. 196 pp.

Principal findings: This study investigated what adjustments the northwestern muskrat (*Ondatra zibethicus spatulatus*) has made in occupying the Arctic environment of the Mackenzie River Delta in northern Canada. Depressed survival is indicated in shallow summer habitats for those animals that do not leave before ice forms. Only deeper lakes with adequate submerged food plants constituted a satisfactory wintering environment. Normal movement of muskrats in the Mackenzie River Delta is an average of 300 yards in summer and 100 yards in winter. Winter activity is supported by an extensive system of feeding stations or "push-ups" constructed on lake ice. The number of muskrats using each push-up varies from 3 to 13 with an average of 6.

Because of the short breeding season, primaparous females probably

An important management application to Nancy McAllister's thesis was to document times when eared grebe colonies should be surveyed to minimize disturbance and allow full clutches of eggs to be completed. PHOTO BY R. WAYNE CAMPBELL.

Muskrats are widely distributed in North America and are an important species in the trapping economy. Dome-like piles of coarse vegetation and other marsh debris in a wetland are an indication that a muskrat is present. In summer these "push-ups" or lodges are used mainly for feeding but later in the year become over-wintering lodges. PHOTO BY R. WAYNE CAMPBELL.

produce only one litter of young in their first year of life. However, they can produce two litters in their second year. The delay in breeding induced by the late removal of ice on lakes and channels significantly reduces the rate of population increase. The restrictive effects of climate on breeding are compensated for by larger litters (8.3 young). There are few losses of young from depredations of adults, as has been reported in other areas, and there is a very satisfactory survival of young through the first year. Most muskrats do not survive long past their second year of life.

The Mackenzie River Delta provides marginal habitat for muskrats; densities per unit area are low when compared with races of muskrats from other regions, and body size is small. The physical factors induced by the severity of climate represent the major influences limiting population growth. There is no tendency for muskrat numbers to fluctuate in a cyclical manner as has been reported for other parts of North America.

1956

Baynes, Raymond Arthur. 1956. "The Use of Aerial Photographs and Sub-sampling in the Identification and Assessment of Moose Ranges in Southern British Columbia." M.A. thesis, University of British Columbia, Department of Zoology. 111 pp.

Principal findings: Cover types for a 500-square-mile area between the North Thompson and Fraser rivers were mapped from air photos. Cover types were sampled on the ground for available food and degree of utilization by moose (*Alces alces*). Dense, mature forests received more use than open forest stands. Based on indices derived for available browse and utilization, it was concluded that moose ranges in the remainder of a sample district may be assessed solely from aerial photographs thereby eliminating the need for extensive ground survey.

Sandilands, Keith M. 1956. "The Effect of Age on the Teeth of Columbian Black-tailed Deer *Odocoileus hemionus columbianus*." B.A. (Hons.) thesis, University of British Columbia, Department of Zoology. 28 pp.

Stephenson, Arthur B. 1956. "Preliminary Studies on Growth, Nutrition and Blood Chemistry of Beavers." M.A. thesis, University of British Columbia, Department of Zoology. 135 pp.

Principal findings: This study examined the optimal and maximal growth rates in beavers held in captivity to determine the caloric requirements necessary for maintenance, growth and reproduction and thus to establish normal values for various blood constituents and correlate variations in those constituents with growth and nutrition. Results indicated that beavers grow relatively fast and can efficiently use foods high in fiber content, which is similar to other herbivores, especially those with large caeca, the site of extensive cellulose degradation.

1957

Holling, Crawford Stanley. 1957. "The Components of Predation as Revealed by a Study of Predation by Small Mammals of *Neodiprion sertifer* (Geoff.)." Ph.D. dissertation, University of British Columbia, Department of Zoology. 143 pp.

Principal findings: Field and laboratory studies investigated the predation by small mammals on the cocoon stage of the European pine sawfly (*Neodiprion sertifer* Geoff.). Only three species of small mammals were important predators: [common shrew] *Sorex cinereus cinereus* (Kerr), [short-tailed shrew] *Blarina brevicauda talpoides* (Gapper) and [deer mouse] *Peromyscus maniculatus bairdii* (Hoy and Kennicott). Prey density and predator density were the only variables affecting predation. There were two basic responses to changes in prey density: where the number of cocoons consumed per predator changed (functional response) and where the density of predators changed (numerical response). These responses differed for the three predators. Predation increased initially with increase in prey density and thereafter decreased. Laboratory experiments showed that subsidiary factors can exert an effect. The strength of stimulus from prey can change both the functional and numerical responses. Similarly, increase in the number or palatability of alternate foods may decrease the functional response and increase the numerical response. A hypothetical predator-prey model showed that under certain conditions the peaked type of predation can regulate the numbers of prey and can dampen oscillations of prey numbers.

Myres, Miles Timothy. 1957. "An Introduction to the Behaviour of the Goldeneyes: *Bucephala islandica* and *B. clangula* (Class Aves, Family Anatidae)." M.A. thesis, University of British Columbia, Department of Zoology. 254 pp.

Principal findings: In goldeneyes, comfort movements (drinking, wing and leg stretching) give rise to courtship display. Preening and splash bathing occur frequently under conditions of stress such as a territorial encounter or coition. The upwards stretch, wing flap and tail wag complex of movements also occur under stress and at the end of a (coital) encounter. Diving ducks tend to use underwater diving as their major aggressive tactic. Interspecific aggression is frequent and Aythyini are more of an irritant to goldeneyes than are Anatini. Barrow's goldeneye (*Bucephala islandica*) and common goldeneye (*B. clangula*) have similar courtship displays, with more extreme movements in head throw shown by *B. clangula*. The coition sequence is similar in both species. There is a marked post-coition display. A special call

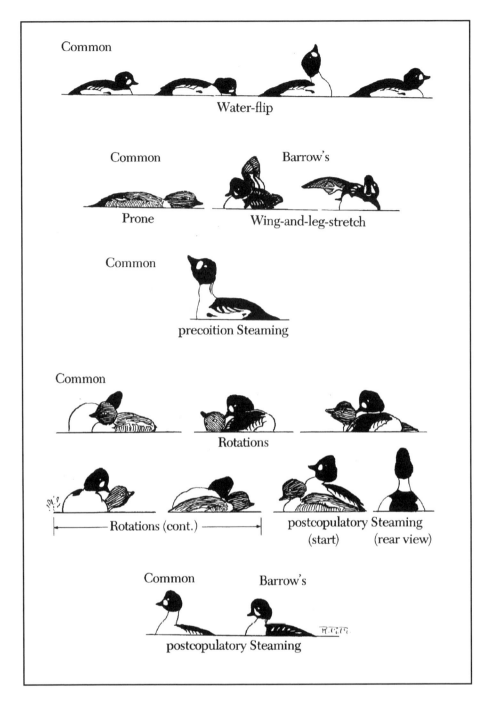

These illustrations from Palmer[269] are based on Timothy Myres's thesis and show various poses of courting behaviour for common and Barrow's goldeneye.

by the female is used to call all downy young from the nest and to gather them on the lake. Females are poor guardians of broods but are hostile toward other females during the brood-rearing period. Rotary pumping by downies is a "greeting" movement.

O'Keefe, James John. 1957. "Dry-matter Intake During Early Phases of Growth for Subspecies of Deer (*Odocoileus hemionus*)." M.A. thesis, University of British Columbia, Department of Zoology. 63 pp.

Principal findings: Dry matter intake reflected the net energy demands of maintenance and growth of 45 fawns of three subspecies of *Odocoileus* (*hemionus*, *columbianus* and *sitkensis*). Dry matter intake was also influenced by plane of nutrition, composition, digestibility of the ration and condition of the animal. Some subspecific differences in growth and nutritional efficiencies were observed.

1958

Francis, George Reid. 1958. "Ecological Studies of Marten (*Martes americana*) in Algonquin Park, Ontario." M.Sc. thesis, University of British Columbia, Department of Zoology. 74 pp.

Principal findings: Foraging ranges of male [American] marten (*Martes americana*) averaged 0.74 square miles, and males irregularly shifted ranges over summer. Females occupied discrete ranges for months or even years averaging 0.29 square miles. One nest den was found among boulders and another in a hollow log. Summer trapping showed no significant difference among captures in different forest types. Winter tracking showed that American marten preferred conifer forests that coincided with shallower snow and the greatest occurrence of voles (*Clethrionomys* spp.). Small mammals formed the major part of the diet, but no species preference was evident. The diet was heavily supplemented with nestling birds and ripe berries during their seasonal abundance.

Note: While Ian was not directly involved in supervising, planning or conducting George Francis's research on American marten in Algonquin Park, Ontario, he played a significant role in providing advice on the approach and content for his thesis. He also provided editorial comments and encouragement.

Jolicoeur, Pierre. 1958. "Geographical Variation in Wolves (*Canis lupus* L.) of Northwestern North America." M.A. thesis, University of British Columbia, Department of Zoology. 337 pp.

Principal findings: Pale [grey] wolves (*Canis lupus*) are more numerous and dark wolves are less numerous towards the tundra between Great Slave Lake and Great Bear Lake. There are no discrete colour phases. Divergence in 12 skull dimensions is approximately proportional to geographic separation. Male wolves are larger than females by approximately four percent in linear skull dimensions.

Scheppe, Walter A. 1958. "Systematic and Ecological Relations of *Peromyscus oreas* and *P. maniculatus*." Ph.D. dissertation, University of British Columbia, Department of Zoology. 228 pp.

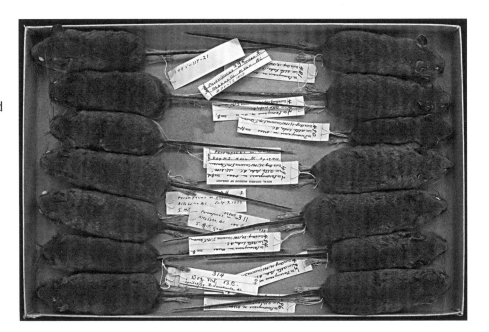

A long-tailed form of *Peromyscus* had been recognized by Ian McTaggart-Cowan and other taxonomists for years as occurring along the coast of BC. Analysis of specimens by Walter Scheppe suggested that P. *maniculatus oreas* be elevated to full species status as P. *keeni*. PHOTO BY R. WAYNE CAMPBELL.

Principal findings: Analysis of 2,500 specimens of *Peromyscus* from Puget Sound in Washington and the Lower Mainland of British Columbia show that *P. m. oreas* [Keen's mouse *P. m. keeni*] is largely reproductively isolated from [deer mouse] *P. m. maniculatus*, and it is raised to specific status. These species maintain their identities over a large area in which they are sympatric. *P. oreas* has remained distinct from *P. maniculatus* through a combination of geographical, ecological, temporal, psychological and genetic isolation.

1959

Daniel, Michael J. 1959. "Organ Weight-Body Weight Interrelationships in the Family Mustelidae: (Order Carnivora)." M.Sc. thesis, University of British Columbia, Department of Zoology. 67 pp.

Principal findings: The main objective of this study was to draw up prediction tables of presumably "normal" organ weights from the computed regression equations for three species of the family Mustelidae: mink (*Mustela vison*), American marten (*Martes americana*) and fisher (*Martes pennanti*). Mink had relatively lighter hearts and lungs than both of the other two species. The adrenal glands of the mink were also well below those of the marten and fisher. The regression of organ weight and body weight gave high correlations in the three species studied for the heart, lungs, kidney, liver and stomach. Low correlation coefficients were found for the spleen, adrenal glands, thyroid and parathyroid glands and testes. Heart weight, being the organ least affected by changing physiological conditions in an animal, is proposed as a new baseline against which to express the other organ systems.

Krebs, Charles J. 1959. "Growth Studies in the Reindeer (*Rangifer tarandus*) with an Analysis of Population Changes in the Mackenzie Delta

Herd over the Period 1938–1958." M.A. thesis, University of British Columbia, Department of Zoology. 164 pp.

Principal findings: A study of the growth rates of four reindeer fawns, under natural conditions, was carried out during the spring and summer of 1958 in the Mackenzie River Delta, NWT. The rate of growth of reindeer fawns is slightly less than that of Columbian black-tailed deer fawns and does not differ greatly in pattern from reindeer in Russia.

Myres, Miles Timothy. 1959. "The Behaviour of the Sea-duck and its Value in the Systematics of the Tribes Mergini and Somateriini of the Family Anatidae." Ph.D. dissertation, University of British Columbia, Department of Zoology. 506 pp.

Principal findings: The purpose of this study, which was conducted in British Columbia and Alaska, was to describe unique display characteristics in the behavior of sea-ducks and use these to suggest systematic relationships among different genera and species. In ducks, pre-copulatory displays of male and female and the general displays particular to the female are highly conservative. They may be used as taxonomic characters at the generic and tribal levels of classification. The general "courtship" characters of the male are of little value at any taxonomic level, except within a very large genus (*e.g., Anas*). In female and pre-copulatory behavior characteristics, both Somateriini and Mergini are shown to be quite distinct from the Anatini. In female courtship behaviour, *Somateria* resembles some of the Aythyini and *Melanitta*. On the behavioural evidence, the Mergini appear to consist of two unrelated lines (*Melanitta – Clangula* and *Bucephala – Mergus*). It is suggested that the paucity of visual displays is an indication of isolation from related groups due to ancestral divergence so that the generic rankings of *Clangula* and *Histrionicus* should perhaps stand.

Radvanyi, Andrew. 1959. "Inherent Rhythms of Activity of the Northern Flying Squirrel in Relation to Illumination and to Lunar and Solar Photoperiodism." Ph.D. dissertation, University of British Columbia, Department of Zoology. 191 pp.

Although double-crested cormorants build stick nests on flat rock outcroppings (top) and pelagic cormorants build seaweed nests on vertical rock cliff ledges (bottom), Gerry van Tets determined that the methods of incubating the eggs and raising the chicks were identical for the two species. PHOTOS BY R. WAYNE CAMPBELL.

Principal findings: All of the northern flying squirrels (*Glaucomys sabrinus*) in this study were live-trapped in the wooded area beside the University of British Columbia. Twenty-two experiments were set up and direct observations were made from the roof of the biology building and a small storage room nearby to determine the mammal's periods of activity. Hours of direct observation, the use of activity wheels, treadle-boards connected electrically to clock and tape mechanisms, and/or three vibration apparati were used to record the hours and intensity of individual or groups of caged flying squirrels outdoors as well as under controlled light conditions indoors. Based on 1,285 observations over 16 months, the time at which individually caged flying squirrels became active each night averaged 35.4 minutes after sunset.

The peak of activity usually occurred between 2200 hours and 0100 hours, after which it steadily declined with a second but much smaller peak an hour or two before sunrise. A marked reduction in activity was noted during nights of full moon or shortly thereafter with a return to high activity during the last quarter and new moon conditions. A similar negative response occurred in most experiments involving artificial lunar conditions.

Van Tets, Gerrard Frederick. 1959. "A Comparative Study of the Reproductive Behaviour and Natural History of Three Sympatric Species of Cormorants, (*Phalacrocorax auritus, P. penicillatus* and *P. pelagicus)* at Mandarte Island, B.C." M.A. thesis, University of British Columbia, Department of Zoology. 86 pp.

Principal findings: Three sympatric species of cormorants (*Phalacrocorax auritus, P. pelagicus* and *P. penicillatus*) on Mandarte Island, eight kilometres east of Sidney, British Columbia, were found to select different sites for perching and nesting and to use different habitats for feeding. *P. auritus* and *P. pelagicus* are polymorphic prior to breeding and almost monomorphic after the breeding season and have several distinct calls. No polymorphism was found in *P. pennicillatus*, which has only one call, but it can flash its gular pouch. The method of incubating eggs and raising chicks was identical in *P. auritus* and *P. pelagicus*. Specificity of signals during courtship and social contact prevents hybridization and preserves the divergent ecological specialization of the three species.

Weeden, Robert Barton. 1959. "The Ecology and Distribution of Ptarmigan in Western North America." Ph.D. dissertation, University of British Columbia, Department of Zoology. 247 pp.

Principal findings: This study summarized and compared the life history and habitats of three species of ptarmigan in western North America: *Lagopus lagopus* [willow ptarmigan], *L. mutus* [rock ptarmigan] and *L. leucurus* [white-tailed ptarmigan]. All known populations of *leucurus* and many populations of *lagopus* and *mutus* are non-migratory although seasonal vertical movements may occur. Male ptarmigan defend areas of ground in the breeding season. Ptarmigan are monogamous and produce only one brood each year. Where the three species are present on the same mountain, the ranges of *lagopus, mutus* and *leucurus* are progressively farther above timberline. The segregation seems to be based primarily on features of vegetation form and terrain. *L. lagopus* established territories and nested where clusters of shrubs three to six feet high alternated with openings and where vegetation was relatively luxuriant with a wide variety of species. *L. mutus* occupied a zone of tundra with lower shrubs and a greater proportion of herbaceous vegetation, whereas *L. leucurus* preferred shrubless alpine areas. It is proposed that each ptarmigan species responds to a set of visual cues that is peculiar to that species in choosing habitat to which it is best adapted, thus establishing range boundaries of a particular population.

Female rock ptarmigan on nest (lower centre) blends with surrounding habitat. Bob Weeden's Ph.D. dissertation led directly to a ten-year study (1959–69) of rock ptarmigan ecology and population dynamics in central Alaska, which he carried out as a biologist for the Alaska Department of Fish and Game.
PHOTO BY R. WAYNE CAMPBELL.

1960

Erskine, Anthony John. 1960. "A Discussion of the Distributional Ecology of the Bufflehead (*Bucephala albeola*; Anatidae; Aves) Based upon Breeding Biology Studies in British Columbia." M.A. thesis, University of British Columbia, Department of Zoology. 240 pp.

Principal findings: Climate is of major importance in limiting the breeding distribution of bufflehead (*Bucephala albeola*). Climate limits the distribution of trees and thus nest sites. Dense growth of shrubs may limit the numbers of young reaching water. Adverse weather may cause mortality of young.

Holsworth, William Norton. 1960. "Interactions between Moose, Elk and Buffalo in Elk Island National Park, Alberta." M.Sc. thesis, University of British Columbia, Department of Zoology. 92 pp.

Principal findings: The high incidence of *brucellosis* in buffalo [bison] (*Bison bison*), indicates that they are the source of the organism infecting moose (*Alces alces*) and elk (*Cervus canadensis*) in Elk Island National Park, Alberta. Buffalo are dominant over moose and elk in the park.

Pearson, Arthur M. 1960. "A Study of the Growth and Reproduction of the Beaver (*Castor canadensis* Kuhl) Correlated with the Quality and Quantity of Some Habitat Factors." M.Sc. thesis, University of British Columbia, Department of Zoology. 103 pp.

Principal findings: The growth rates of beaver on two different habitat types in Prince Albert National Park, Saskatchewan, were compared. Beaver were also raised under experimental conditions at the University of British Columbia, and the growth rates and food consumption were recorded. Differences in the condition of beaver occurred most prominently during the winter as a result of the strict limitations in the quality and quantity of available food. Fourteen beaver livers were analyzed to determine whether a chemical change of liver tissue accompanies a change in the condition of the animal; over the period studied, May 2 to October 15, no progressive change could be found. Beaver from the Elk Island National Park, Alberta, showed a significantly higher reproductive rate than beaver from Prince Albert National Park, Saskatchewan. This was correlated with habitat differences between the two areas, indicating that the reproductive rate is another attribute of the animal that will reflect the adequacy of the environment.

Tener, John Simpson. 1960. "A Study of the Muskox (*Ovibos moschatus*) in Relation to its Environment." Ph.D. dissertation, University of British Columbia, Department of Zoology. 259 pp.

Although the bufflehead was not valued as a game bird, Ian McTaggart-Cowan expected that logging activities in the interior of British Columbia would soon affect all cavity-nesting species. Graduate student Tony Erskine's pioneering work on the breeding biology of the bufflehead in the late 1950s was a big factor in drawing the attention of industry and wildlife managers to this species. PHOTO BY R. WAYNE CAMPBELL.

Principal findings: A study of the muskox (*Ovibos moschatus*) in relation to its environment was carried out in the Canadian Arctic. Range studies at the southern and northern limits of muskox distribution in Canada revealed major differences in plant species occurrence, annual production and chemistry. The summer ranges in the Thelon Game Sanctuary, NWT, (now Nunavut) produced more woody food species than Lake Hazen ranges and were calculated to support as many as 7 times the number of muskoxen. Thelon Game Sanctuary winter ranges may support up to 10 times as many muskoxen as Lake Hazen winter ranges of comparable size. Chemical analyses of the important foods revealed that adequate amounts of protein, carbohydrates, calcium and phosphorous were available on Thelon Game Sanctuary summer ranges although less fat was available than was perhaps desirable. Thelon Game Sanctuary winter range foods contain less phosphorous than recommended for range cattle. Lake Hazen summer and winter range foods appeared to be nutritionally adequate although low forage production may affect population growth adversely. Calf production is low by most ungulate standards. Lactation is prolonged, up to 15 months at least, which would assist calf survival during winter. Adaptations by muskoxen to Arctic living include short limbs, dense inner and outer hair and generally slow movements, all of which contribute to heat conservation. The late age of sexual maturity, low productivity of calves in the populations studied, and low productivity of range and nutritional constraints indicate that muskoxen will not reach densities that will support intensive utilization.

1961

Blood, Donald A. 1961. "An Ecological Study of California Bighorn Sheep *Ovis canadensis californiana* in Southern British Columbia." M.Sc. thesis, University of British Columbia, Department of Zoology. 127 pp.

A decade after Ian visited the California bighorn sheep band in the Ashnola River Valley and made recommendations on management of the population, graduate student Don Blood completed a two-year ecological study of the species. Similkameen Valley. PHOTO BY R. WAYNE CAMPBELL.

Principal findings: There have been alarming declines in the numbers of California bighorn sheep, *Ovis canadensis californiana*, in the Similkameen region of British Columbia since the late nineteenth century. In May 1960 a two-year study of the Ashnola bighorn herd was initiated that was broad in scope and designed to provide a background for future, more intensive investigations. Major objectives were merely to gather sound range and population data on which to base management and conservation practices for the herd. The herd consisted of 250 to 300 sheep in 1962 and its maximum range was about 200 square miles. During mid-winter most of the herd may be concentrated on less than five square miles of key winter range. Age structure was determined by collecting remains of sheep that died of natural causes and by field observations. Natality and mortality rates indicate that the herd is relatively stable. Predation, accidents and hunting are not considered to be presently limiting herd increase. No deaths directly attributable to parasitism were noted. Grazing by cattle appears to be the primary land use threatening the welfare of the herd. Bighorn sheep/cattle competition involves spring and fall utilization by cattle of sheep winter ranges. Forage shortages resulting from cattle grazing and occasional severe snow conditions are suggested as the factor limiting the bighorn herd.

Whitehead, Philip Edward. 1961. "The Digestible Energy Content of UBC Fawn Ration # 15-5-59." B.Sc. (Hons.) thesis, University of British Columbia, Department of Zoology. 16 pp.

1962

Krebs, Charles J. 1962. "The Lemming Cycle at Baker Lake, N.W.T., During 1959–61." Ph.D. dissertation, University of British Columbia, Department of Zoology, Vancouver, BC. 183 pp.

Principal findings: Lemmings of the central Canadian Arctic showed changes in reproduction, mortality and individual variation in properties during a four-year study. These changes were not due to starvation or malnutrition, nor were there any obvious symptoms of stress. They may have been associated with changes in the behaviour of the animals.

Low, William Alec. 1962. "Age Determination of Deer by Annular Structure of Dental Cementum." B.Sc. (Hons.) thesis, University of British Columbia, Department of Zoology. 55 pp.

Perret, Nolan G. 1962. "The Spring and Summer Foods of the Common Mallard (*Anas platyrhynchos platyrhynchos* L.) in South Central Manitoba." M.Sc. thesis, University of British Columbia, Department of Zoology. 82 pp.

Principal findings: The spring and summer food of adult mallards (*Anas*

Although numerous studies of mallards have been completed, at the time of Nolan Perret's thesis, few had dealt with regional food habits during the non-hunting seasons.
PHOTO BY R. WAYNE CAMPBELL.

platyrhynchos) consisted of 45.7% plant material and 54.3% animal material. By contrast, young mallards consumed 9.0% plant and 91.0% animal foods. Insects provided the main source of animal foods. Male adult mallards consumed more plant and less animal foods than did adult females. The proportion of plant versus animal foods in the diet of adult mallards varied with the seasonal availability of the major food sources.

Terins, Edite Edith. 1962. "The Investigation of Five Methods of 17-Ketosteroid Extraction from Urine as Applied to Deer of the Genus *Odocoileus*." B.Sc. (Hons.) thesis, University of British Columbia, Department of Zoology. 24 pp.

1963

Addison, Ralor Blendle. 1963. "Food and Water Requirements of Four Races of *Peromyscus*." B.Sc. (Hons.) thesis, University of British Columbia, Department of Zoology. 30 pp.

Foster, J. Bristol. 1963. "The Evolution of the Native Land Mammals of the Queen Charlotte Islands and the Problem of Insularity." Ph.D. dissertation, University of British Columbia, Department of Zoology. 210 pp.

Principal findings: The isolated archipelago of the Queen Charlotte Islands [Haida Gwaii], British Columbia, has only eight extant indigenous land mammals, all except one of which are represented by endemic forms. Geological and botanical evidence suggest that these islands formed a refuge to most of these mammals during the last (Vachon) glaciation. The unique mammal fauna here could be the product of insular evolution or it may be a geographical relict. The absence of fossil material precluded a final conclusion.

Horvath, Otto. 1963. "Contributions to Nesting Ecology of Forest Birds." M.F. thesis, University of British Columbia, Faculty of Forestry. 181 pp.

Ten species of mammals have been introduced to Haida Gwaii; all of them have had some degree of ecological impact. In the late 1800s and early 1900s Sitka black-tailed deer (*Odocoileus hemionus sitkensis*) were introduced to the islands by the BC government. Without major predators, the deer increased dramatically and they have had a significant negative impact on forest ecology. PHOTO BY R. WAYNE CAMPBELL.

The Indigenous Mammals of Haida Gwaii

The isolated archipelago of Haida Gwaii is recognized internationally for its endemic subspecies of flora and fauna. In 1963, when Bristol Foster completed his Ph.D. research there, the mammals included Keen's mouse (*Peromyscus keeni keeni* and *P. k. prevostensis*), dusky shrew (*Sorex monticolus elassodon* and *S. m. prevostensis*), ermine (*Mustella erminea haidarum*), northern river otter (*Lontra canadensis periclyzomae*), black bear (*Ursus americanus carlottae*) and the extinct Dawson caribou (*Rangifer tarandus dawsonii*).

Principal findings: The nesting of eight common bird species in a 228-acre forest plot adjacent to Hope, British Columbia, was found to be a function of present vegetation, physical environment and the adaptive range of the species. The results indicate that microclimate strongly influences the site, height, position and material of the nests, and ultimately the selection of nesting habitat of the species studied.

Klein, David Robert. 1963. "Physiological Response of Deer on Ranges of Varying Quality." Ph.D. dissertation, University of British Columbia, Department of Zoology. 167 pp.

Principal findings: This study in southeast Alaska was conducted to identify factors of the environment that alter the plane of nutrition of [Sitka black-tailed] deer (*Odocoileus hemionus sitkensis*) and result in variations in body size. Two islands suspected to produce deer of wide contrast in body size were chosen as study areas. Qualitative and quantitative measurements were made of both the deer and the range on the two islands.

Woronkofski Island outranked Coronation Island in a number of vegetation parameters including plant density and species abundance in the forest, total area of subalpine and alpine, total area of forest type on an equal density basis, and total vegetated area on an equal density basis. Chemical analyses of forage did not show significant differences between islands in comparisons of similar species under comparable site conditions. The physiological stage of plant growth appeared to be the most important factor in determining nutritive quality of vegetation. Nitrogen content of rumen samples was consistently higher in the Woronkofski Island group than the Coronation Island samples. An inverse relationship existed with respect to fiber content.

Weights and skeletal measurements showed growth differences, which are apparently attributable to differing levels in the annual nutritional regimen of these deer. The larger size of deer on Woronkofski Island than on Coronation Island is the product of nutritional rather than genetic causes. No significant differences that could be related to nutritional factors were found in levels of parasitism among the deer of the two islands.

The larger size and more rapid rate of growth of deer on Woronkofski Island than Coronation Island are the result of pronounced differences in the nutritive quality and quantity of forage present on the ranges. These differences are primarily a result of the degree of altitudinal and topographic variation between the islands and in the relative proportions of alpine and subalpine areas.

McAllister, Nancy Mahoney. 1963. "Ontogeny of Behaviour in Five Species of Grebes." Ph.D. dissertation, University of British Columbia, Department of Zoology. 135 pp.

Principal findings: The resting postures, locomotion, feeding behaviour and comfort movements of pied-billed grebe (*Podilymbus podiceps*), horned grebe

Of the species of passerines studied by Otto Horvath in 1963, the American robin showed the strongest nest fidelity to sites where the light ranged between forty and fifty percent of the light intensity in the open. PHOTO BY R. WAYNE CAMPBELL.

One of a number of orphaned Sitka black-tailed deer fawns transferred to the Ian McTaggart-Cowan and A.J. Wood deer nutrition and growth studies at UBC. PHOTO BY DAVID R. KLEIN, PETERSBURG, AK, 1950S.

Nancy McAllister studied the behaviour of five species of grebes, including eared grebe. PHOTO BY ALAN D. WILSON.

(*Podiceps auritus*), red-necked grebe (*P. grisegena*), eared grebe (*P. [caspicus] nigricollis*) and western grebe (*Aechmophorus occidentalis*) are described, compared and their development traced to the adult form. The birds hatch at the beginning of stage two, the first appearance of comfort movements, and pass into stage three, the maturation of comfort movements, within a few hours. They remain in stage three until the adult sleep posture is assumed, functional preening and oiling are established and swimming appears at eight days. Stage four includes the appearance of simple bathing, diving and the substitution of following for riding on the parent's back. Stage five, which begin on about the sixteenth day, includes matured bathing, alarm calls, self-feeding and finally flight.

Because of the increase of the length of stage three over that of precocial birds, it is suggested that the grebes be considered semi-precocial birds along with the gulls. The grebe nest is unsuitable for prolonged brooding; very young chicks leave the nest and climb onto the backs of parents where they sleep, beg and are often fed during the first week of their lives.

Spalding, David J. 1963. "Comparative Feeding Habits of the Fur Seal (*Callorhinus ursinus*), Sea Lion (*Eumetopias jubata*) and Harbour Seal (*Phoca vitulina*) on the British Columbia Coast." M.A. thesis, University of British Columbia, Department of Zoology. 113 pp.

Principal findings: Notable differences were found in that the digestive tract of [Steller] sea lion (*Eumetopias jubata*) was longer and the eruption of permanent teeth later than the other species studied. There is little evidence of [northern] fur seal (*Callhorinus ursinus*) feeding while on rookeries. The majority of a [Steller] sea lion rookery population fasts for a few days only, during pupping, whereas harbour seals (*Phoca vitulina*) fast for at least part of June. No evidence of interspecific competition was found between harbour seals, [Steller] sea lions and [northern] fur seals on the British Columbia coast. Predation by seals and [Steller] sea lions on the annual commercial salmon and Pacific herring (*Clupea pallisi*) catch (1.6% and 2.7%, respectively) was negligible in reducing salmon and herring stocks.

Stewart, Sheila Frances. 1963. "The Interrelationship of Growth, Sexual Development, Feed Intake and Plasma Lipids in the Black-tailed Deer (*Odocoileus hemionus columbianus*), and the Wistar rat." M.Sc. thesis, University of British Columbia, Department of Zoology, Vancouver, BC. 192 pages.

Principal Findings: Based upon the premise that growth (weight change) is of a seasonally cyclical nature in the deer (*Odocoileus*), and that this change is primarily manifested in the fat compartments of the body, a study of the plasma lipids was undertaken to ascertain whether they reflect the seasonal changes. Preliminary studies were carried out on the laboratory albino Wistar [Norway] rat (*Rattus norvegicus*) to develop a technique. In the deer study six-year old Columbian black-tailed deer were observed for a period of 12 months. In both sexes weight increases from March to October when a decrease in feed intake and weight gain occurs. At the point of maximum gain, in October, a difference between the sexes occurs. The males decrease their feed intake further and the plasma "fats" fall, whereas the females increase their feed intake and the plasma "fats" rise. Both sexes show a marked increase in the plasma cholesterol level. After October, the rut period ensues and is characterized by a loss of weight and a low feed intake in both sexes. Weight and plasma lipid changes are closely allied to fluctuations in gonadal activity. The plasma "fat" levels rise to augment the caloric requirements of the animal if the feed intake is not adequate, both when weight is being gained and lost. The plasma cholesterol appears to reflect the state of sexual activity, that is, the level is raised in the "rut" period; otherwise it is low.

Van Tets, Gerrard Frederick. 1963. "A Comparative Study of Some of the Social Communication Patterns of Cormorants and Related Birds in the Pelecaniformes." Ph.D. dissertation, University of British Columbia, Department of Zoology. 226 pp.

Principal findings: A comparative study was made of the social communication patterns of seventeen species of Pelecaniformes: four species of *Pelecanus* [pelicans], *Morus bassanus* [northern gannet], *Sula sula* [red-footed booby], *Anhinga anhinga* [Anhinga], seven species of *Phalacrocorax* [cormorants], and *Fregata magnificens* [magnificent frigatebird]. It was found that signal patterns are combinations of a limited number of discrete postures, movements and sounds, and that they are mainly derivatives from four main sources: locomotion, fighting, nest building and begging. From a comparison of the taxonomic distribution of the form, function and derivation of the social communication patterns in the Pelecaniformes, it was concluded that these reflect the phylogenetic implications of the current systematic classifications of the Order.

Watney, Muriel J. 1963. "The Prevention of a Genetically Determined Eye Anomaly in the Mouse by the Administration of Cortisone During Pregnancy." B.Sc. (Hons.) thesis, University of British Columbia, Department of Zoology. 15 pp.

1964

Barkley, William Donald. 1964. "Preliminary Studies on the Suitability of Trilafon (Perphenazine) as a Tranquillizer for Black-tailed deer (*Odocoileus hemionus columbianus*)." B.Sc. (Hons.) thesis, University of British Columbia, Department of Zoology. 76 pp.

Grant, Peter R. 1964. "The Significance of Some Insular Characteristics in Birds." Ph.D. dissertation, University of British Columbia, Department of Zoology. 215 pp.

Principal findings: In this study of passerine birds of the Tres Marias Islands, an archipelago of nine islands northwest of Puerto Vallarta, Mexico, several species showed an expected trend for larger wings, especially larger tarsal bones, and bills. On the other hand, there was no apparent tendency for body sizes of the island birds to be larger. The island birds tended to be drabber and one species even had a reduced vocal repertoire. Although the climate was similar to the Mainland, there were habitat differences between the islands and the mainland; in addition, there were fewer passerine species on the islands. Thus the island birds had a wider choice of food. In view of the value of distinctive plumages and songs as specific recognition characteristics, the features displayed by the Tres Marias birds may be attributed to the absence of closely related species.

Hayward, John Stanley. 1964. "Aspects of Temperature Adaptation in *Peromyscus*." Ph.D. dissertation, University of British Columbia, Department of Zoology. 110 pp.

Principal findings: The metabolic rate characteristics of six subspecies of *Peromyscus* were measured over a temperature range 0°C to 35°C. Metabolic responses to temperatures below thermoneutrality was primarily related to body size. They show no evidence of racial metabolic rate adaptation or significant insulative differences. The basal metabolic rates of each race showed no temperature adaptive differences especially when considered in relation to body composition. It is concluded that metabolic rate is adaptive to climate in these races of *Peromyscus* and consequently has played no important role in their distribution and speciation. The major temperature-adaptive feature of these small mammals is the use of a suitable microclimate. There is no significant differential selective pressure for temperature adaptation among the six races.

The two reptile studies by Ian McTaggart-Cowan's students dealt with structural aspects of the head region of snakes, including the western rattlesnake. PHOTO BY R. WAYNE CAMPBELL.

Preston, William Burton. 1964. "The Importance of the Facial Pit of the Northern Pacific Rattlesnake (*Crotalus viridis oerganus*) under Natural Conditions in southern British Columbia." M.Sc. thesis, University of British Columbia, Department of Zoology. 64 pp.

Principal findings: Forty western rattlesnakes (*Crotalus viridis oreganus*) were captured in the southern Okanagan Valley and 20 had their facial pits destroyed by electrical cautery and then all 40 snakes were released back to where they had been captured. Subsequent recapture of those snakes showed that the growth rate of cauterized females was slower compared with the non-cauterized females. There was no difference between cauterized and non-cauterized males. There was no difference, however, in the survival between rattlesnakes that were or were not cauterized.

Van Tets, Patricia Anne. 1964. "A Starch-gel Electrophoretic Study of Some of the Sources of Variation in the Blood Sera of Deer of the

Genus *Odocoileus.*" M.Sc. thesis, University of British Columbia, Department of Zoology. 108 pp.

Principal findings: Using captive deer (*Odocoileus*) held at the University of British Columbia in Vancouver, large individual variation was found in both the mobility and the percent composition of blood serum proteins. Percent composition was affected by sex, age and season, whereas mobility was affected by sex but not by age or season. Comparisons of mobility in three groups of adult female deer indicated greater intra-specific differences than inter-specific ones. The technique of starch-gel electrophoresis may be useful in recognizing individuals or even herds of the same species but not in the recognition of subspecies or species of deer.

Wasylyk, Gerald M. 1964. "Age Determination of Wolves by Annular Structure of Dental Cemetum." B.Sc. (Hons.) thesis, University of British Columbia, Department of Zoology. 23 pp.

1965

Bandy, Percy John. 1965. "Study of Comparative Growth in Four Races of Black-tailed Deer." Ph.D. dissertation, University of British Columbia, Department of Zoology. 189 pp.

Principal findings: Fawns of four racial stocks of black-tailed deer were captured and reared in laboratory conditions for over 1,000 days. Of the initial 66 fawns, 29 were measured for the duration of the study: 6 Columbian black-tailed fawns of the 20 captured; 8 Columbian black-tailed deer from the east coast of Vancouver Island of the 16 captured; 8 of the Sitka black-tailed deer from Juneau, Alaska, of the 9 captured; and 7 mule deer fawns of the 21 captured.

Weight curves fluctuated seasonally in response to physiological conditions associated with reproduction. In addition, growth in both sexes was suppressed by the winter environment in spite of constancy in the type and availability of the daily diet. However, deer fed a low plane nutritional diet actually showed positive growth responses during winter, indicating that growth is not suppressed in animals that have not attained their seasonal maximum weights. Parameters derived from growth patterns demonstrated racial differences in one or more aspects of their growth responses. Mule deer were the largest and fastest growing, followed in turn by Sitka black-tailed deer, California stock and the Vancouver Island stock of Columbian black-tailed deer. Differences in growth characteristics indicated that the two races of Columbian black-tailed deer may be separable at the sub-specific level. No racial differences were shown in the efficiencies of their growth processes.

Demarchi, Raymond A. 1965. "An Ecological Study of the Ashnola Bighorn Winter Ranges." M.S.A. (Agriculture) thesis, University of British Columbia, Department of Plant Science. 103 pp. (Co-chaired with Dr. Vernon C. Brink).

Principal findings: An ecological study of the important winter ranges of California bighorn sheep (*Ovis canadensis californiana*) in the Ashnola River Valley was conducted from May 1963 through August 1964. Emphasis was placed upon the floristic composition, productivity and soils as well as the use by cattle, mule deer and bighorn sheep. The use by domestic cattle and, on some areas the combined use by cattle and mule deer, were the principal factors presently maintaining the plant communities in seral stage. Bighorn sheep were shown to have an affinity for the climax *Agropyron – Koeleria* and *Agropyron – Festuca* communities and used them three times more than seral communities.

Chemical analysis revealed that the seven forage species that comprised more than 95 percent of the bighorn sheep winter diet contained sufficient crude protein, fat, fibre, ash, nitrogen and calcium for maintenance. However, by the same standards, all plant species and notably the grasses were deficient in phosphorus. Low phosphorus and moderate calcium levels produced unfavourable calcium-phosphorus ratios by mid-winter. The retrogression of *Agropyron spicatum* dominated climax communities caused by past overgrazing by domestic stock, present forage competition with domestic stock, and possible phosphorus deficiencies were believed to be the principal factors limiting the population.

McCrory, Wayne. 1965. "Variation in the Mountain Goat (*Oreamnos americanus*)." B.Sc. (Hons.) thesis, University of British Columbia, Department of Zoology. 44 pp.

Raymond Demarchi—shown here at Ashnola River, BC, in September 1963—followed Ian McTaggart-Cowan's practice of using horses for field research. PHOTO BY DENNIS A. DEMARCHI.

1966

Addison, Ralor Blendle. 1966. "Skeletal Development in the Black-tailed Deer (*Odocoileus hemionus columbianus*)." M.Sc. thesis, University of British Columbia, Department of Zoology. 81 pp.

Principal findings: The growth gradients described in the literature as a typical mammalian pattern were confirmed for [Columbian] black-tailed deer (*Odocoileus hemionus columbianus*) and were quantified graphically.

DeBock, Elmer A. 1966. "A Comparative Study of the Skull Variation in Captive and Wild Black-tailed Deer." B.Sc. (Hons.) thesis, University of British Columbia, Department of Zoology. 43 pp.

Geist, Valerius. 1966. "On the Behaviour and Evolution of American Mountain Sheep." Ph.D. dissertation, University of British Columbia, Department of Zoology. 251 pp.

Principal findings: Three populations of wild sheep (*Ovis dalli stonei*, *O.d. dalli* and *O. canadensis*) were studied in all seasons. Sheep evolved from a rupicaprid ancestor that established a new defense system against hornblows of conspecifics. Hornblows were caught with the horned head, which led to the evolution of pneumated skulls, thick facial skin, and heavy horn bases. The damaging combat form of rupicaprids was thus replaced by a ritualized fight in which opponents clash head on with minimal damage. Thus horns became not only weapons but also shields and ultimately display organs and symbols of rank. Rams remain juvenile in character for five to six years past sexual maturity with a prolonged behavioural and bodily maturation and increased sexual dimorphism. Females are paedogenic in that they only reach a developmental stage in appearance and behaviour similar to yearling rams. Rams have no distinct behaviour shown only to females; rather, they treat females and subordinate rams in an almost identical manner. Conversely, subordinate rams may behave like females towards dominants. Non-estrous females act like sexually immature juveniles, whereas estrous females exhibit the behaviour of young subordinate males. Non-estrous females form unisexual bands and are more gregarious than rams. Sheep evolved to specialize in clashing and replaced broadside blows with a horn display. This was adaptive in colonizing and expanding populations in which rams had a relatively short life expectancy. In their evolution, sheep changed primarily in social adaptations.

Stone's sheep (*Ovis dalli stonei*) was one of the species of wild North American sheep studied by Valerius Geist. PHOTO BY R. WAYNE CAMPBELL.

Whitehead, Philip Edward. 1966. "Some Factors Influencing the Level of Reducing Sugar in the Blood of Black-tailed Deer." M.Sc. thesis, University of British Columbia, Department of Zoology. 73 pp.

Principal findings: Some factors that influence the blood-reducing sugar level in the black-tailed deer (*Odocoileus heminonus columbianus*, Richardson;

Vancouver Island genotype) were investigated. It was found that: feed intake during the hour preceding bloodletting, short periods of fast, nature of the feed and sex of the animal have no effect on the level of blood-reducing sugars. At the same time, blood-reducing sugar increased with means of restraint (physical force versus drug immobilization); the length of time to draw the blood sample, and the longer the time the higher the blood sugar level. The results indicate that the degree of excitement, fear and pain experienced by the animals preceding and during bloodletting was the principal cause in the level of blood-reducing sugar.

1967

Bédard, Jean H. 1967. "Ecological Segregation Among Plankton-feeding Alcidae (*Aethia* and *Cyclorrhynchus*)." Ph.D. dissertation, University of British Columbia, Department of Zoology. 177 pp.

Principal findings: This research studied the differences in feeding and nesting habits of three species of Alcidae—crested auklet (*Aethia cristatella*), least auklet (*A. pusilla*), and parakeet auklet (*Cyclorrynhynchus psittacula,* now *Aethia*) on St. Lawrence Island, Alaska, in the northern Bering Sea.

The two congeneric *Aethia* species differ markedly in size. Least auklet is 90 g and crested auklet is 300 g. The parakeet auklet is similar in body size to the crested auklet. All three species are diurnal. Crested and least auklets are active on the nesting colonies during the late morning and the evening and feed at sea in early morning and early afternoon. Parakeet auklets are present on the colonies in the morning and early afternoon and feed at sea the rest of the day. Crested and least auklets have a diversified diet from May to July but restrict themselves to one dominant prey item during the chick-rearing period in August and September. They share the same feeding grounds but differ in the size of the prey organisms used. Slightly over half of the diet of parakeet auklets was made of carnivorous macroplankton such as large hyperiids and fishes. The parakeet auklet differs from the crested auklet by occupying a slightly higher trophic level and by devoting more of its time to feeding. The two species, however, are found on the same feeding grounds and are presumed to utilize the same feeding depth-range. Differences in diet between the two can be attributed to differences in bill structure and bill shape. Crested and least auklets depend upon prey organisms that oscillate widely in abundance and availability. Parakeet auklets depend on organisms whose supply is more or less constant throughout the year.

Segregation in nesting is complete between the two genera. Parakeet auklets are cliff-nesters, whereas both the crested and least auklets occupy talus slopes. In the latter habitat, crested auklets prefer the larger boulders, while least auklets prefer small stones. Feeding adaptations (degree of tongue cornification, palatal breadth, number and arrangement of palatal papillae) follow a gradient or a regular modification throughout the family.

Among the auklets studied, the overlap in requirements is very small and no sign of competition for food or for nesting was found.

Hebert, Daryll M. 1967. "Natural Salt Licks as a Part of the Ecology of the Mountain Goat." M.Sc. thesis, University of British Columbia, Department of Zoology. 138 pp.

Principal findings: Use of natural earth licks by mountain goats (*Oreamnos americanus*) occurred mainly in the afternoon. Average time-period of use by an individual ranged from one to three weeks. Animals select certain licks over others and certain sites within a lick. High-licking sites had higher sodium content, and newly established licks had higher sodium content than old licks. Highly preferred sites were not always higher in calcium, phosphorous or cobalt. The level of sodium deficiency to cause craving is not sufficient to show up in serum analysis.

Hornocker, Maurice G. 1967. "An Analysis of Mountain Lion Predation upon Mule Deer and Elk in the Idaho Primitive Area." Ph.D. dissertation, University of British Columbia, Department of Zoology. 115 pp.

Principal findings: A study in the Idaho Primitive Area in central Idaho [declared a wilderness area in 1931] was conducted to investigate the dynamics of the cougar [mountain lion] (*Felis concolor*) population and its impact on populations of big game animals. Territoriality acted to limit lion numbers and maintain population stability. Dispersal and mortality, particularly of young individuals, appeared to be important limiting mechanisms. The population was centered around a nucleus of mature individuals well established on territories. Transient segments of the population were composed predominantly of young animals.

Maurice Hornocker's pioneering study on cougars changed attitudes of wildlife managers toward this top-level predator. PHOTO BY ALAN D. WILSON.

Strife appeared to be minimized by a "mutual avoidance" behavioural mechanism. This is advanced as an important factor in the maintenance of lion populations by avoiding costly fighting and appears to facilitate success in securing large prey animals. Hunting territories were shared but appeared never to be used by more than one lion or family of lions at a time. Lion predation on bighorn sheep (*Ovis canadensis*) appeared insignificant. Seventy-five percent of elk (*Cervus canadensis*) and 57 percent of mule deer (*Odocoileus hemionus*) killed by lions were one-and-a-half years old or younger or nine-and-a-half years or older. More young than old animals were killed. Lions exhibited "negative selectivity" in the case of mature bull elk.

Elk and deer populations were limited by the winter food supply, and predation was inconsequential in determining ultimate numbers of deer and elk. However, lion predation is a powerful force acting to dampen and protract severe prey oscillations and to distribute ungulates on restricted critical range and is considered of great significance in maintaining ecological stability in wilderness environments.

Jonkel, Charles Joseph. 1967. "Ecology, Population Dynamics and Management of the Black Bear in the Spruce-fir Forest of Northwestern Montana." Ph.D. dissertation, University of British Columbia, Department of Zoology. 170 pp.

Principal findings: Seral and climax stands of the [spruce-fir/Oregon boxwood] *Picea-Abies/Pachistima myrsinities* association are used most extensively by American black bears (*Ursus americanus*), but other vegetative types are important seasonally for bears. The home ranges of adult bears are small and remain the same size from year to year. Bears congregate but do not form compact groups, maintaining a distance of at least 50 yards between individuals. Many adult females do not have young, apparently because of failure to ovulate, prenatal mortality or early mortality of young. Inadequate nutrition of some bears as a result of weather may delay sexual maturity or inhibit estrus. The nutritional condition of adult male bears and many adult female bears is excellent. The survival of cubs is high (95%) from ½ to 1½ years of age while they are with their mothers, but mortality is higher among sub-adults from 1½ to 3½ years old. Many sub-adult bears disperse from the area. The number of adults on the area remains relatively constant from year to year. A form of territoriality spaces the bears and ultimately exerts a control over density. The density on the Big Creek study area is relatively high and probably results in more social interaction and territoriality than in bears elsewhere. Both extrinsic and intrinsic forces govern population regulation.

Ommundsen, Peter D. 1967. "Development of the Columbian Black-tailed deer (*Odocoileus hemionus columbianus*) During the Fetal Period." M.Sc. thesis, University of British Columbia, Department of Zoology. 142 pp.

Principal findings: Describes a baseline sequence of morphological changes in fetal Columbian black-tailed deer (*Odocoileus hemionus columbianus*) and compares this with mule deer and white-tailed deer. There was variation among black-tails in the rate at which various body regions developed, and males were larger than females at a given stage of development. Greater differences in relative growth were observed between black-tails and white-tails than between black-tails and mule deer.

Raddi, Arvind Govind. 1967. "The Pelage of the Black-tailed Deer *Ododoileus hemionus columbianus* (Richardson)." Ph.D. dissertation, University of British Columbia, Department of Zoology. 215 pp.

Principal findings: Morphogenesis of follicles and developmental stages of the hair in the Columbian black-tailed deer (*Ododoileus hemionus columbianus*) follow the general mammalian pattern. Large guard hair follicles have been recorded for the first time in ungulates. Hairs of the adult winter coat differ from that of the adult summer coat in colouration, length, and diameter. A well-developed wooly undercoat is present, which is functionally lacking in the summer coat. The winter guard hairs stand more erect because of the padding provided by the wooly undercoat. Hair length increases in adults in summer but decreases in the winter coat. The overcoat hairs are moulted twice, whereas the undercoat hairs are shed only once. Hair length and diameter were reduced in underfed animals and initiation of new hair growth was delayed. The medulla is an important insulator, as can be seen from its greater extent in Alaskan forms compared with those from southern California, which inhabit hot, dry habitats. In underfed animals, although actual hair diameter was less, relative increase in diameter for a unit of increase of length was greater than that in well-fed animals. Thus when nutrients are limited, growth in the diameter of hair enjoys a priority over growth in length.

Russell, Lorne J. 1967. "The Parasites of the White-tailed Deer (*Odocoileus virginianus ochrourus*) of British Columbia." M.Sc. thesis, University of British Columbia, Department of Zoology. 70 pp.

Principal findings: Ectoparasites and endoparasites in 69 white-tailed deer (*Odocoileus virginianus*) and 7 mule deer (*O. hemionus*) were studied from July 1964 to May 1966. White-tailed deer were hosts to 25 species of parasites: 3 species of lice, 2 species of ticks, 2 louse flies, 1 bot fly, 4 cestodes, 1 trematode and 11 nematodes. The maximum number of species infesting a single deer was 11 and the average number per animal was 5.9. Mule deer were host to 22 parasite species. The maximum of a single species was 13 and the average number of species per deer was 10.6. Mule deer have the same ecotoparasites as the white-tailed deer but harboured much heavier infections of intestinal nematodes and cestodes. The bot fly, liver fluke and larval lungworms were the only parasites found to have any appreciable effect on host tissues.

1968

Aleksiuk, Michael. 1968. "The Metabolic Adaptation of the Beaver (*Castor canadensis* Kuhl) to the Arctic Energy Regime." Ph.D. dissertation, University of British Columbia, Department of Zoology. 124 pp.

Principal findings: This study compared the physiological response of beaver (*Castor canadensis*) from the Mackenzie River Delta, Northwest Territories, to those from California. In animals from the Mackenzie Delta, growth was found to be rapid in the summer and absent in the winter. Fat was deposited in the autumn, maintained during the winter and mobilized in the spring. Animals were lean during the summer, thus metabolic energy expenditure is high during the summer and low in the winter. While no seasonal changes were found in thyroid activity, food intake or growth in California beavers was found in those maintained under similar Vancouver, BC, climatic conditions. Manipulation of light exposure had no detectable effects on California beavers but did affect Arctic beavers when they were exposed to constant darkness. It was concluded that in nature decreasing light intensity in autumn induces a metabolic depression in the northern beaver and that increasing light intensity in spring releases it.

Gates, Bryan Rodd. 1968. "Deer Food Production in Certain Seral Stages of a Coast Forest." M.Sc. thesis, University of British Columbia, Department of Zoology. 105 pp.

Principal findings: The study involved an examination of the relationships between forest harvesting practices and Columbian black-tailed deer populations on eastern Vancouver Island. Seasonal forage preferences of Columbian black-tailed deer (*Odocoileus hemionus columbianus*) were determined through rumen content analysis. The salal-cat's-ear (*Gaultheria-Hypochaeris*) association was preferred by deer in spring and summer. Herbaceous plants formed 60% of the diet. This seral stage produced more available forage than any other. A seral *Gaultheria-Pseudotsuga* association was preferred by deer during autumn and winter and produced more available forage in this seral stage than in any other for this period. The number of deer is affected by the efficiency at which food is produced, and this is related to season and successional stages.

West, Nels O. 1968. "The Length of the Estrous Cycle in the Columbian Black-tailed Deer or Coast Deer (*Odocoileus hemionus columbianus*)." B.Sc. (Hons.) thesis, University of British Columbia, Department of Zoology. 31 pp.

1969

Bergerud, Arthur Thompson. 1969. "Population Dynamics of Newfoundland Caribou." Ph.D. dissertation, University of British Columbia, Department of Zoology. 140 pp.

Principal findings: The woodland [Newfoundland] caribou (*Rangifer tarandus caribou*) on the island of Newfoundland occur in four herds: the Northern Peninsula, the Avalon Peninsula, the Humber River and the Interior. The two major factors limiting populations of woodland caribou appeared to be predation by Canada lynx (*Lynx canadensis*) and the shooting of adults. The major cause of mortality of calves was predation by Canada lynx. As early as two weeks after calving 27% of the calves had died.

1970

Low, William Alec. 1970. "Influence of Aridity on Reproduction of the Collared Peccary (*Dicotyles tajacu* (Linneaus) in Texas." Ph.D. dissertation, University of British Columbia, Department of Zoology. 169 pp.

Principal findings: Collared peccary (*Dicotyles tajacu angulatus*), commonly known as javelina, is an economically important species, which lives primarily in mesquite habitats with prickly pear cacti. This study examined the reproduction and productivity of populations in southwest Texas under natural moist (south Texas) and drought (west Texas) conditions as well as in captivity where conditions were presumed to be optimal. The condition of the south Texas peccaries under good range conditions was almost as high as that of pen-reared animals, and under drought conditions was almost as low as the west Texas peccaries under good conditions. Good range conditions arising from favourable rainfall patterns result in early winter breeding and strong spring breeding activity in south Texas. Drought conditions retard the winter breeding season and almost eliminate late spring breeding. During good range conditions, gross productivity was 288 young/100 adult sows and during the drought 151 young/100 adult sows. Net productivity in south Texas during the study was 81 under-1-year olds/100 adult sows and 53 (yearlings)/100 adult sows. In west Texas, there were 45 (yearlings)/100 adult sows.

Life expectancy at one year of age was estimated at 3.0 years in south Texas peccaries, and the average annual mortality rate was 21.5%. The mortality rate for west Texas peccaries was calculated at 27.5%. Animal condition based on kidney fat and carcass weight was highest in the late fall and was significantly better in the year of high rainfall and good range conditions than during the drought year. Males mature sexually at just under a year. Females also appear to be sexually mature at just under a year, but in wild populations they do not become pregnant until 16 to 20 months. Pen-raised animals have fertile post-partum and lactation oestruses and generally produce two litters a year. In south Texas, 33% of the adult sows showed ovarian evidence of consecutive pregnancies. There was no apparent decrease in reproduction in 15-year-old south Texas and 9-year-old west Texas females. In south Texas there was a major breeding period in mid-winter and a minor one in late spring; most conceptions occur in late winter.

Predation and parasitism are probably of minor importance to the populations. Combined cold weather and drought resulted in a decrease of 29% in two herds; these could function as a factor controlling populations. Drought, through its effect on food availability, appears to be the primary controlling factor of peccary populations in Texas.

Thomas, Donald Charles. 1970. "Ovary, Reproduction and Productivity of Female Columbian Black-tailed Deer." Ph.D. dissertation, University of British Columbia, Department of Zoology. 211 pp.

Principal Findings: Ovarian changes, patterns of reproduction and age-specific productivity of female Columbian black-tailed deer (*Odocoileus hemionus columbianus*) on Vancouver Island were elucidated largely by examination of serial, stained sections of ovaries from 444 females. Well-defined, eight or nine-day follicular cycles occur during the breeding season in November and early December. Many follicles rupturing at first ovulation are asynchronous and of extreme size. Twelve females provided criteria for estimating ovulation dates in other females. In each cycle about 50% of the adult females ovulated within an eight-day period. The mean date of first ovulation in each of the five years of this study was approximately November 16; the second ovulation followed after a remarkably short period of eight to nine days. About 96% of the females conceived at second ovulation and 4% on subsequent ovulations. A high proportion of "silent heats" accompany first ovulation, as indicated by lack of sperm on four of six ova. Females may cycle at least five times if pregnancy does not occur. The average number of viable fetuses per doe increased progressively from 0.91 in yearlings to 1.81 in the 5.5 to 6.5 age classes and thereafter decreased. These changes in fertility with age were mirrored by changes in weight and girth. One hundred females of reproductive age produced 137 fawns.

1972

Elliott, John Patrick. 1972. "Prey Capture by the Larger Fissipeds: the African Lion." Ph.D. dissertation, University of British Columbia, Department of Zoology. 203 pp.

Principal findings: It was found that the East African lion (*Panthera leonubica*), studied in Ngorongoro Crater in Tanzania, is able to adjust its strategy and tactics at each phase of prey capture (search, stalk, attack and subdue) so as to achieve a consistently high overall capture success with different prey and conditions.

Johnson, Stephen Robert. 1972. "Thermal Adaptation in North American Sturnidae." Ph.D. dissertation, University of British Columbia, Department of Zoology. 129 pp.

Principal findings: An important reason for the difference in success of colonization by North American Sturnidae—crested myna (*Acridotheres cristatellus*) and European starling (*Sturnus vulgaris*)—has been the relative difference in thermal adaptability. Mynas are of subtropical origin and non-migratory and starlings originate in temperate areas and migrate to warmer areas during cold months. The low hatching success of mynas was due to chilling of the eggs and subsequent embryonic death as a result of poor nest attentiveness of adult mynas. Mynas were less eurythermal than starlings and myna plumage, compared to that of starlings, was approximately half as efficient as an insulator against cold. The mynas reproductive traits are of tropical origin and do not exhibit adaptation to British Columbian climatic conditions.

1973

Hebert, Daryll M. 1973. "Altitudinal Migration as a Factor in the Nutrition of Bighorn Sheep." Ph.D. dissertation, University of British Columbia, Department of Zoology. 356 pp.

Two introduced sturnids were studied in the Lower Mainland region of BC to determine why the European starling has more successfully colonized North America than the crested myna. An important reason for the difference in success was the lack of thermal adaptability in the myna. PHOTO BY R. WAYNE CAMPBELL.

Principal findings: Range studies in the East Kootenay region of British Columbia were conducted to complement measurements of the nutritional status of various groups of captive [Rocky Mountain] bighorn sheep (*Ovis canadensis canadensis*). Between-year differences influenced availability of spring growth, nutrient intake and apparent digestibility. Animal trials used diet to simulate varying forage quality on a natural range from early spring to late winter to emulate a normal altitudinal migratory pattern, and a control group was maintained on forage from the winter range year-round. The response of each group was measured through changes in body weight. The summer range forage was assessed for nutrients in the feed, feed intake, digestibility and its influence on digestible nutrients and nitrogen retention. It proved to be superior to the corresponding winter range forage for all methods of evaluation.

A series of predictive linear equations was established for each forage type to estimate various nutritive parameters. These allowed a quantitative assessment of the effect of changes in forage quality on feed and nutrient intake. It was found that minimum ambient temperature during the critical winter period increased feed intake even though forage quality appeared to restrict the amount of feed ingested. The kidney regulated nitrogen loss via the urine during periods of nitrogen shortage.

Daryll Hebert showed that forage in the winter range for Rocky Mountain bighorn sheep was inferior to forage on the summer range. Minimum temperatures at critical periods in winter increased feeding activity.

PHOTO BY LARRY HALVERSON.

1975

Hoefs, Manfred Ernest Gustav. 1975. "Ecological Investigation of Dall Sheep (*Ovis dalli dalli* Nelson) and their Habitats on Sheep Mountain, Kluane National Park, Yukon Territory, Canada." Ph.D. dissertation, University of British Columbia, Department of Zoology. 373 pp. (Parts 1 and 2.)

Principal findings: An investigation was carried out on a population of Dall sheep (*Ovis dalli dalli*) and their range in southwestern Yukon Territory. Part 1 of the study dealt with the physical environment and a detailed analysis of vegetation. Part 2 covered the sheep population, which during the study remained fairly constant at a level of about 200 adults. Detailed population statistics were determined and historical information on the herd was reviewed. Range use patterns and forages selected by this population were described on a monthly basis. The response of Dall sheep to temperature, wind and snow thickness were analyzed. A model of the population structure is presented.

Melton, Derek Arthur. 1975. "Environmental Heterogeneity Produced by *Termitaria* in Western Uganda with Special Reference to Mound Usage by Vertebrates." M.Sc. thesis, University of British Columbia, Department of Zoology. 494 pp. (Volumes 1 and 2.)

Principal findings: Termite (Order Isoptera) mounds were studied in Ruwenzori National Park in western Uganda. The high percentages of

Dall's Sheep (*Ovis dalli dalli*) on Mount Wallace, Kluane National Park, YT. PHOTO BY MANFRED HOEFS, SUMMER 1971.

ground surface covered by termite mounds are likely to be significant to herbivores. Mounds are used as ungulate wallows, they provide a complex area for small and medium-sized vertebrates, they are concentrated sources of minerals available for geophagy or indirectly from the vegetation on the mounds, and they increase the nutritive value of grasses. Mounds are used as raised platforms by many vertebrates or as territorial markers by others. They are also used as refugia during floods or fires by small vertebrates. Aardvark, however, was the only vertebrate to regularly dig in mounds.

1976

Hatler, David Francis. 1976. "The Coastal Mink on Vancouver Island, British Columbia." Ph.D. dissertation, University of British Columbia, Department of Zoology, Vancouver, BC. 360 pp.

Principal findings: [American] Mink (*Mustela* [Neovison] *vison evagor*) found along the shores of Vancouver Island forage primarily in the marine intertidal zone, feeding mostly upon small crustaceans and fish. Water depth, substrate particle size and the degree of protection from heavy wave action are important factors influencing hunting success. Along food-rich shores, hunting success rates for most mink would have provided their daily requirements in less than two hours of hunting activity. However, accessibility to food varies with place and time, especially relative to tide level.

Males outnumbered females in all areas studied, and the proportion of juveniles was lower than expected, averaging less than two young per adult female in all seasons. The peak mating period in late May and the first half of June is two months or more later than has been recorded for mink elsewhere. A short (10- to 15-day) delayed implantation apparently has been retained.

A *Student's* Appreciation

Taking on a graduate student is an investment in time, money, energy and considerable emotional stress. Graduate students come with different aspirations; some are single, and some start families while completing their studies. A professor must adapt to each situation and remain partly aloof. Ian's graduate students, however, were more like extended family.

Two years into his Ph.D. research, Dave Hatler's wife had a daughter, Mareca, who later said, "My daddy studies the mink . . . poor ol' mink." In the acknowledgements section of his thesis, Dave best echoed a student's appreciation of having Ian as his supervisor.

> Among those who cannot be forgotten, Dr. Ian McTaggart-Cowan is at the top of the list. He was always available to direct and assist when direction and assistance were needed, but he patiently gave me the reins at other times. One could not ask more of a supervisor. His professionalism, though often beyond my capacity to understand, let alone emulate, was a stimulant, and the breadth of his experience a constant inspiration. But, perhaps most important was the revelation: once, as I floundered on a side-track of my life, I discovered in Dr. Cowan a warm, understanding human being.

Population densities ranged from about 1.5 to more than 3 animals per km of shoreline. Turnover was rapid with losses of 50% or more between successive (four-month) seasons. Most individuals were relatively sedentary. Males had larger ranges (mean 0.72 km of shoreline) than females (mean 0.41 km). Juvenile males emerged as the most mobile class, owing to dispersal movements. Range size was inversely related to the quality of local hunting habitat. Due to the dominance and higher numbers of adult males, female mink sustain increased mortality and decreased productivity as a result of intense competition for limited resources. Harvest systems designed to select males are the most likely to enhance productivity.

1977

Cuthbert, James T. 1977. "The Bald Eagle (*Haliaeetus leucocephalus alascanus* [Townsend]) as an Aircraft Hazard at Port Hardy Airport." M.Sc. thesis, University of British Columbia, Department of Zoology. 320 pp.

Principal findings: Hazards to eagles and aircraft were studied at Port Hardy, BC, on northeastern Vancouver Island. The airport is located close to the lower reaches of the Keogh River salmon spawning ground, which is a bald eagle feeding site. As a result, bald eagles regularly fly over the airspace used by landing and departing aircraft. It was recommended that an extension to

Over 10,000 bird strikes with airplanes occur in North America each year, resulting in human deaths and hundreds of millions of dollars in damage. Jim Cuthbert's research on bald eagle/aircraft conflict at a small airport on northeastern Vancouver Island, BC, was timely as bald eagle populations have increased over the years as has air traffic in this region. PHOTO BY MARK NYHOF.

the existing runway be built northwest to the existing runway and that during the period of September through November aircraft avoid flying over the Keogh River.

Haber, Gordon C. 1977. "Socio-ecological Dynamics of Wolves and Prey in a Subarctic Ecosystem." Ph.D. dissertation, University of British Columbia, Department of Zoology. 786 pp.

Principal findings: Two adjacent [grey] wolf (*Canis lupus*) packs in the Denali region of Alaska were studied over an eight-year period. Normal late winter pack sizes were about 12 to 15 animals for each pack and were apparently stable in size and home range size for at least 30 to 40 years. Moose (*Alces alces*) densities were less than half (0.26/sq. mile) in the smaller home range of the "Toklat Pack" than in the larger range of the "Savage Pack" (0.70/sq. mile). Densities of moose were thought to be relatively stable over a 30- to 40-year period, whereas Dall's sheep (*Ovis dalli*) densities fluctuated widely. Caribou (*Rangifer tarandus*) of the Denali herd, which overlapped both wolf home ranges to some degree—mostly in summer—showed a major decline in numbers from an estimated 20,000 to 30,000 in the 1940s to 1,500 in 1972.

The Savage Pack was a kin-selected family group with a strong, relatively stable dominance hierarchy, with males generally dominant over females except when a female was older. Many of the high ranks were determined by two to three months of age. Leadership was distinguished from dominance and was usually assumed by a high-ranking male, most often the beta male. The alpha male asserted his dominance role in only a few apparently "critical" activities such as scent marking, courtship, mating and encounters with wolves outside the pack. The Savage Pack appeared to have only one litter a year produced by the alpha pair.

The Toklat Pack had a less stable, multi-family social structure, which was attributed to pronounced seasonal changes in prey densities. The pack split and adopted a savage-type single family social structure co-incident with the marked decline of caribou. For both packs summer activities were based around long-established home sites.

A computer simulation model of the Denali grey wolf/moose/Dall's sheep interaction incorporating environmental (snowfall) and biological parameters was developed from field data. Under natural conditions there is resilience in prey productivity to sustain both predation and the added impact of severe winters. However, a population of moose in decline from heavy harvests can lead to further decline from predation and severe winters even if harvest is stopped. A methodology is proposed to address means to achieve sustainable harvests of moose and caribou.

Heard, Douglas C. 1977. "The Behaviour of Vancouver Island Marmots," *Marmota vancouverensis*. M.Sc. thesis, University of British Columbia, Department of Zoology. 129 pp.

Principal findings: Vancouver Island marmots live in small colonies in the subalpine parkland. Social groups consisted of one adult male, one adult female and variable numbers of two-year-olds, yearlings and infants. Social groups were highly integrated with a large amount of communication occurring among members. All age-sex classes engaged in greetings and nose touching behaviour. Alarm calls were given in response to potential predators. Short whistles were given in response to aerial predators (e.g., eagles); long calls were given in response to terrestrial predators (e.g., black bears). Both types of calls are narrow band-width sounds, which makes them difficult to locate. The degree of social tolerance is positively correlated with the length of time required to reach maturity.

Smith, Christian Arthur. 1977. "The Habitat use Patterns and Associated Movements of White-tailed Deer in Southeastern British Columbia." M.Sc. thesis, University of British Columbia, Department of Zoology. 139 pp.

Principal findings: White-tailed deer (*Odocoileus virginianus*) feeding activity was concentrated in open habitat types, which provided maximum quantity and qualities of forage. Concentration in winter shelter types of habitat as a result of snow depth, with a consequent reduction in available food compared to a mild winter, resulted in an apparent 30% reduction in the ratio of juveniles to adults the following spring. Deer density was low on summer range and habitat preferences for open areas were maintained. Summer home ranges were relatively small. Home range loyalty was relatively high on winter ranges.

Population fluctuations and declines in the white-tailed deer (*Odocoileus virginianus*) in BC prompted Chris Smith's study of movements related to habitats. PHOTO BY R. WAYNE CAMPBELL.

1978

Bowen, William Donald. 1978. "Social Organization of the Coyote in Relation to Prey Size." Ph.D. dissertation, University of British Columbia Department of Zoology. 230 pp.

Principal findings: In a study of social structure of coyote (*Canis latrans*) during winter in Jasper National Park, Alberta, between 1974 and 1977, it was found that 59% of the coyotes were in packs, 17% were resident pairs, 10% were solitary residents and 15% were transients. In coyote packs there was a clear division of labour in initiation of territorial defence, scent marking and control of group travel. Males and females scent marked throughout the year. The density of scent marks at the edge of a territory was twice that of the centre. In the winter coyote diets consisted of primarily ungulates (67%) and small rodents (23%). In the summer both young elk (*Cervus elaphus*) and old ungulates of other species comprised 50% of their diets. Columbian ground squirrel (*Spermophilus columbianus*) and small rodents were the other principal summer foods. Compared with 15 other studies, the mean size of coyote prey was larger in Jasper than elsewhere. The percentage of mule deer (*Odocoileus hemionus*) in the winter diet varied directly with pack size and mule deer density. However, pack size accounted for more of the variation in the amount of deer in the diet than did mule deer density. By contrast, the percentage of elk in the winter diet was dependent on pack size, primarily as a function of the number of elk dying within each coyote territory and the size of the pack and their ability to defend a carcass.

The coyote is an opportunistic and versatile predator that feeds on prey ranging from insects and lizards to deer and elk. They readily scavenge road-killed animals. PHOTO BY LARRY HALVERSON.

Donaldson, Judith Lee. 1978. "Population Ecology of Yellow-bellied Marmots in British Columbia." M.Sc. thesis, University of British Columbia, Department of Zoology. 183 pp.

Principal findings: Population dynamics of yellow-bellied marmots (*Marmota flaviventris*) were studied at Watch Lake, BC (24 km southeast of 100 Mile House) at the northern extension of their range. Watch Lake colonies were generally larger and denser than those reported in other studies. Individuals began breeding at a younger age, allocated relatively more energy to reproduction, produced larger litters of smaller young and grew to smaller adult size. Ninety-three percent of adult females and 8% percent of yearling females had litters of mean size of 6.1 +/- 0.38. The annual mortality rate was 62% of yearlings and 33% of adults; most yearling males and a few yearling females emigrated. Experiments indicated that adult males caused yearling males to emigrate and that adult females inhibited the reproduction of yearling females. Adult males were territorial throughout the active, above-ground season. Adult females defended territories during pregnancy and lactation, which is the first report of female territoriality in this species.

1979

Gainer, Robert Stewart. 1979. "The Role of Anthrax in the Population Biology of Wildebeest in the Selous Game Reserve." M.Sc. thesis, University of British Columbia, Department of Zoology. 203 pp.

Principal findings: Even though anthrax was responsible for the death of 10% of the blue [Nyasa, brindled, white-bearded] wildebeest (*Connochaetes taurinus*) in the Selous Game Reserve in Tanzania, it was considered an asset to the population as mortality was associated with animals "that appeared to be a disadvantage to the wildebeest population." It is suggested that to reduce the occurrence of anthrax the number of animals older than calves should be reduced.

Acknowledgements

The McTaggart-Cowan Family

We gratefully acknowledge the generous assistance of Ian's daughter, Ann Schau, in providing details of Ian's early family life, access to his collection of awards and family photographs, and reviewing parts of the text for accuracy. We also appreciate her permission to publish family photographs and excerpts from her father's field notes. Ian's grandchildren, Mariana Cowan and Robert McTaggart-Cowan, enthusiastically provided information on their grandfather as well as the McTaggart-Cowan family in general.

Ian had three siblings, Patrick, Joan and Pamela, and the children of both Joan and Pamela assisted us with their knowledge of the McTaggart-Cowan family history. Diana Bickford, daughter of Joan and Leonard Zink, provided information on her parents as well as the McTaggart Cowan and Mackenzie ancestors; Brian Charlesworth supplied information on his parents Pamela and Harold Charlesworth. Alison Apps provided information on her grandparents, Kenneth Racey and Kathleen (Stewart) Racey.

Peer-reviewers

This book has benefited greatly from three talented and accomplished external reviewers whose biographical sketches follow. These gentlemen brought their own experience and knowledge of Dr. Cowan to bear on the task of carefully reviewing and commenting on various drafts of the manuscript. They contributed their time voluntarily, and each brought a perspective which enhanced the final product. We are enormously grateful to all three individuals.

Peter Ommundsen studied wildlife biology as a student of Dr. Cowan and later served on the faculty of the wildlife and environmental science programs at Selkirk College in the West Kootenay. He now resides on Salt Spring Island, BC. Peter gave his first natural history lecture at age seven, a presentation to his school class regarding a skull that he found on the beach at Spanish Banks. His early collecting included all manner of insects, mammals and reptiles, and his parents were supportive despite his mother's aversion to snakes.

Peter also contributed material based on findings of his personal research on the early family history of the McTaggart-Cowan's, early issues of UBC calendars and the campus student newspaper *Ubyssey.*

Spencer G. Sealy is an ornithologist and professor emeritus at the University of Manitoba. At age 5, in the hamlet of Wiseton, Saskatchewan, Spencer brought home a cocoon from which soon emerged a big, beautiful moth, spreading its wings. This might have been the beginning of a career in entomology, but it was the discovery of a pair of Killdeers defending their nest on a tennis court that sparked an interest in birds that has carried him through his long career. A stop along the way as a graduate student in zoology at UBC brought him under the boundless influence of Dr. Cowan.

Alton S. Harestad is a wildlife biologist and professor emeritus at Simon Fraser University. When five years old, Alton spent a month at his grandparents farm in Bella Coola. His "gramma" occasionally hit bats with a rake as they emerged from a colony in the porch roof of the farmhouse. Alton recalls gathering the bats and laying them, wings spread, on cedar shakes in the wood shed. He regards this as his first specimen collection and his beginnings as a mammalogist. Later as a graduate student in Zoology at UBC, Alton shared a common interest in skulls and specimen skins with Dr. Cowan.

Contributors

We especially thank the ninety-one contributors to the chapter *Celebrating 100 Years with a 100 Memories.* Undoubtedly others may have been overlooked in our initial call for submissions, but this memorial of appreciation represents a rich cross-section of former students, colleagues and friends from all walks of life with a common link to Ian.

During the four-year life of the project, eight contributors to this chapter passed away, others were unable to complete a review of their submissions for health reasons, and a few could not be reached at critical times during the review process. We appreciate the efforts of the following family members and friends who expedited our requests: the late Helen Bandy (wife of the late P. John Bandy), Joe Bryant (husband of the late Mary Bryant), Audie DeBock (wife of Elmer DeBock), Colleen Cahoon (daughter of Bill Barkley), Mark Guiguet (son of Muriel and the late Charles Guiguet), Ian and Bruce Hatter (sons of the late Jim Hatter),

Peter Ommundsen, Salt Spring Island, BC, April 9, 2014. PHOTO BY ARLENE OMMUNDSEN.

Professor Spencer Sealy at his research site at Delta Marsh, MB, June 2008. PHOTO BY MÉLANIE F. GUIGUENO.

Professor Alton Harestad at his retirement bush party in the Pasayten Valley, BC, August 23, 2009. PHOTO BY KRISTIE STEWART.

Kristine Junck (daughter of Andrew Radvanyi), Patricia Ann Johnston (friend of Joyce Elliot), Elsie and Jonathan Kuyt (wife and son of the late Ernie Kuyt), Daniel and Carole Otway (son and wife of the late Bill Otway), Stella Stirling (wife of Ian Stirling) and Carolyn S. Sugden (wife of the late Lawson Sugden).

Supporters

Major support for publication of this book was provided via the Biodiversity Centre for Wildlife Studies. Although we did not conduct a formal fund raising campaign, we received additional financial contributions toward the cost of producing this book from several organizations. These include the British Columbia Conservation Foundation, British Columbia Habitat Conservation Trust Foundation and Ducks Unlimited Canada.

We have also received unsolicited donations from a number of individuals, and their moral support was appreciated as much as their financial contributions. They are Joe and Mary Bryant, Eileen C. and R. Wayne Campbell, Clifford Day, Raymond A. Demarchi and Carol L. Hartwig, Alexander Dzubin, Bryan R. Gates, J.E. Victor and Margaret (Peggy) Goodwill, Jude and Al Grass, Alton S. Harestad, Werner H. and Hilde Hesse, Patricia Huet, Ronald D. Jakimchuk, Stephen R. Johnson, Betty Keller, Sharon Laughlin, Douglas Leighton, Ron Mayo, James W. McCammon, R. Wayne Nelson, Mark Nyhof, Lowell Orcut family, Heidi M. Regehr, Michael S. Rodway, Dave Shutz, Spencer G. and Noreen Sealy, Howard A. Telosky, John B. and Mary Theberge and Harvey Thommasen.

Harbour Publishing

We are especially grateful to Harbour Publishing for preserving the legacy of Dr. Cowan.

We also express our gratitude to Betty Keller, a seasoned editor associated with Harbour Publishing, for her major contributions in skillfully restructuring the original manuscript. She was a delight to work with.

Sources of Information

This book, which began as a supplement to the journal *Wildlife Afield* in February 2010 to celebrate Ian's 100th birthday, evolved into a major reference book on his life and accomplishments. Our early research included compiling a comprehensive list of his publications as well as published articles on his life. A useful early reference was a six-page article, *Ian McTaggart-Cowan: Renaissance Man,* written by R.S. Silver and published in *Discovery* in 2004.[270] In addition, the many obituaries that were published in newspapers and magazines and posted on web pages throughout 2013 were the source of additional information. Three formal tributes also appeared in scientific journals.[271]

Over the four years of preparing the book, we communicated with hundreds of people, most of whom were supportive and encouraging. Those listed below, however, made our task much more enjoyable as each responded with enthusiasm to our requests for time-sensitive information and advice.

The following institutions or individuals provided assistance on various aspects of the project, from obtaining archival material to permission to reproduce previously published material. Archival material, usually photographs, was received from the American Association for the Advancement of Science (Norma Rosado-Blake); Barkerville Historic Town Museum (W.G. Quackenbush); Bear River Mercantile (Sandy Phillips); Beaty Biodiversity Museum (Ildiko Szabo, Christopher M. Stinson and Darren E. Irwin); Edinburgh Central Library (Alison Stoddart); Greater Vernon Museum & Archives (Ron Candy, Barbara Bell and Liz Ellison); Greater Victoria Public Library (Lucie Larivière); Harvard University Museum of Comparative Zoology (Judith M. Chupasko); Harvard University Herbaria and Botanical Museum (Lisa DeCesare); Harvard University Museum of Comparative Zoology (Dana Fisher and Linda S. Ford); Okanagan College, Penticton (Anne Cossentine); Royal British Columbia Museum/ BC Archives (Don Bourdon, Kelly-Ann Turkington and Diane Wardle); Smithsonian Institution (John J. Ososky); University of British Columbia Ceremonies Office (Eilis Courtney); University of British Columbia Irving K. Barber Learning Centre (Candice Bjur); University of California, Berkeley, Doe/Moffitt Libraries (Steve Mendoza); University of California Museum of Paleontology (Patricia A. Holroyd); University of California, Berkeley, Museum of Vertebrate Zoology (Kira Dodd, Christina V. Fidler, Anna Ippolito, Michelle Koo and Carol Spences); University of Northern British Columbia Library (Mary Bertulli); and Whyte Museum of the Canadian Rockies (Jennifer Rutkair and Edward J. Hart).

We also acknowledge the following individuals for their assistance during the development of this book: Emma Bennett, Dave Birrell, Eileen C. Campbell, Bruce Falls, Richard Fleet, Mark Fraker, Bryan R. Gates, Doug Gordon, Edythe Grant, Larry Halverson, Margaret Harney, Brian Harris, Edward J. Hart, David F. Hatler, Keith Hebert, Agnes Lacombe, Robert Lemire, Gary Matson, Bob Morris, Aaron Reid, Gretchen Roffler, Gray Scrimgeour, Brian Springinotic, Linda Stordeur and Mike Street.

We are thankful to the following individuals for permission to reproduce text from previously published articles: Bruce Falls (Society of Canadian Ornithologists/Société des Ornithologistes du Canada, *Moments from the Education of an Ornithologist*),[272] Edward J. Hart (quotes from *Jimmy Simpson: Legend of the Rockies*),[273] Ian Hatter and Bruce Hatter for quotes and photographs from their father's book *Politically Incorrect : The life and times of British Columbia's First Game Biologist: An Autobiography*,[274] Bill Otway (British Columbia Wildlife Federation, *Wild Values for the Future: Wild Land and the Sportsmen's Federation*), Linda Verbeek (Vancouver Island Rock and Alpine Garden Society, *The Day Before the Show*)[275] and Lisa Moore (The Wildlife Society for the cover art for *Pioneering professionals: Sharing a Passion for Wildlife Conservation*).[276]

Photographs

We have been fortunate in obtaining outstanding wildlife photographs to illustrate this volume, and at the end of each photo caption we have acknowledged the photographer or source. However, there were a few special images we wanted to include in the book to show the diversity of animals that Ian's graduate students studied, the environments they worked in or the exotic animals Ian wrote about. These photographs were provided for collared peccary (Glen Mills and Chase Fountain, Texas Parks and Wildlife Department), mountain pygmy possum (Linda Broome, Department of Premier and Cabinet, New South Wales), Spatsizi Plateau Wilderness Park (Tory Stevens, BC Parks) and walrus (Joel Garlich-Miller, United States Fish & Wildlife Service - Alaska region).

All photographs, images, and scanned material have been processed by Mark Nyhof for publication. Each item presented a challenge because of the varied media in which they were submitted; some were old faded prints, many were 35 mm colour slides, and the quality of digital material varied greatly. We are grateful to Mark for painstakingly processing them and for his personal commitment to the book.

Authors' Appreciation

We three authors are part of the dwindling group of ageing biologists who formed the vanguard for wildlife studies in western Canada since the mid-20th century. Wildlife was in our blood, but it took many experiences, much support, good timing and constructive mentoring to steer our passion into careers. Family, faithful friends and selfless colleagues helped along the way. The following sketches acknowledge a few of the many people who influenced our lives and careers.

Ronald D. Jakimchuk. One of my earliest experiences at UBC was my meeting with Ian McTaggart-Cowan, a man I came to admire, and over the next fifty years I crossed paths with him many times. My colleagues and fellow biologists also played an important part in my continuing education by expanding my understanding of natural history and approaches to biological study.

My friendship with Wayne Campbell started a mere five years ago when I donated my library of wildlife journals to the Biodiversity Centre for Wildlife Studies. Subsequently, we developed a close friendship during the four years that we worked on this book, which benefited immensely from his deep knowledge of natural history and the history of natural history.

Ron Jakimchuk at Beacon Hill Park, Victoria, BC, July 2013. PHOTO BY LYN MARIE BULL.

Throughout the preparation of the book, my partner Xisa, my family and friends have expressed continuing support, interest and motivation!

R. Wayne Campbell. This book is the culmination of 60 years of pursuing a passion for wildlife so I think it is the appropriate venue and time to thank special people who have supported, encouraged and discouraged me along the way. My pre-teen years of fishing and hunting with my grandfather and father introduced me to fresh air and wildlife discovery. After some time my mother, Mildred (now 93 years old), accepted having a freezer full of dead animals, allowed me to commandeer a room in our home for a work station and library, and understood that a new bird book for a birthday and or at Christmas was the ultimate gift. My sister Judy still reports bird records from her feeders in Maple Ridge and passes on the latest online wildlife videos.

Every aspiring wildlife biologist needs a mentor when thinking about a career. The late Dr. Rudolph H. Drent, a young faculty member in the Department of Zoology at UBC in the late 1960s and early 1970s, embraced this keen high-school graduate and unselfishly guided me toward a university education, instilling in me the value of writing for publication and acknowledging the people who helped me.

I am also fortunate to have had a unique rapport and long-term support and encouragement from Dennis Demarchi, Bristol Foster, the late Brian Goodacre, Larry Halverson, Alton Harestad, the late Werner and Hilde Hesse, Ken Kennedy, the late Ian and Joyce McTaggart-Cowan, Mark Nyhof, Michael Rodway, the late Glenn Ryder, Chris Siddle, Tom Stevens, David Stirling and Linda Van Damme.

The core of my life is my wife, Eileen, and son, Sean, and daughter, Tessa. They have shared and endured the joys and challenges of my passion and career and have always provided insightful advice and support.

Wayne Campbell during a respite while surveying marsh-nesting birds near Tunkwa Lake, BC. PHOTO BY EILEEN C. CAMPBELL, JUNE, 2012.

Dennis A. Demarchi. Support and mentoring are important in the development of a career. I have been very fortunate in having both from family, friends and colleagues. My parents encouraged and supported a university education and Len Marchand, the late Dr. Bert Brink and my brother Ray guided me towards a career in plant ecology. After graduation Glen Smith, Don Robinson and Art Benson offered advice and direction in wildlife habitat inventory while I was employed by the provincial government. Later, while developing the ecoregion classification system I was encouraged and inspired by colleagues Bruce Pendergast, Ted Lea, Bob Maxwell, Rick Thomas and Tony Button.

My friendship with Wayne Campbell began in 1988 with the integration of the ecoregion classification in the four-volume set The Birds of BC project. It has continued as we are both currently directors of the Biodiversity Centre for Wildlife Studies.

My life partner Marilyn Robbins, children Diana and Chris and brother Leonard provided unconditional support throughout the life of this project.

Dennis Demarchi at Royal Roads, BC, March 2014. PHOTO BY MARILYN ROBBINS.

References Cited

Allen, G.M. 1925. *Birds and Their Attributes.* Marshall Jones Company, Boston, MA. 338 pp.

Anonymous. 1941. "Professor Identifies Beastie." *Ubyssey* 23(33): 1.

Anonymous. 1954. "Kuyt Back." *Ubyssey* 27(5): 12.

Anonymous. 1955. "Who Laid a Penguin? Gender and Parents of Egg Still a Mystery." *Ubyssey*, Vancouver, BC. Friday, October 7, 1955, 4.

Anonymous. 1997. Obituary: Dr. Garry Cowan. *Memorial University of Newfoundland Gazette*, St Johns, NL. January 23, 1997.

Anonymous. 1998. "1998 Doris Huestis Speirs Award for Outstanding Contributions in Canadian Ornithology." *Picoides* 11(2): 15–17.

Anonymous. 2009. "The American Ornithologists' Union: William Brewster Memorial Award, for Significant Body of Research." *The Auk* 126: 220–221.

Anonymous. 2013. "Marion A. Jenkinson AOU Service Award, 2013 Spencer G. Sealy." *The Auk* 130: 827.

Banks, R.C., J.W. Fitzpatrick, T.R. Howell, N.K. Johnson, B.L. Monroe, H. Ouellet, J.V. Remsen, Jr. and R.W. Storer. 1998. *Check-list of North American Birds: The Species of Birds of North America from the Arctic through Panama, Including the West Indies and Hawaiian Islands, Seventh Edition.* The American Ornithologists' Union, Washington, DC. 829 pp.

Barkley, W.D. 1964. "Preliminary Studies on the Suitability of Trilafon (Perphenazine) as a Tranquillizer for Black-tailed deer (*Odocoileus hemionus columbianus*)." B.Sc. (Hons.) thesis, University of British Columbia, Department of Zoology. 76 pp.

Barkley, W.D. 1972. "The Design and Evaluation of a Land Use Simulation Game." University of British Columbia, Department of Adult Education, Vancouver, BC. 118 pp.

Bent, A.C. 1968. *Life Histories of North American Cardinals, Grosbeaks, Buntings, Towhees, Finches, Sparrows, and Allies.* Part 1. United States National Museum Bulletin 237, Washington, DC. 602 pp.

Bergerud, A.T. 1971. "Population Dynamics of Newfoundland Caribou." *Wildlife Monographs* 25: 1–66, Bethesda, MD.

Bergerud, A.T. 1974. "Decline of Caribou in North America Following Settlement." *Journal of Wildlife Management* 38: 757–770.

Bergerud, A.T. 1983. "Prey Switching in a Simple Ecosystem on an Island in Newfoundland." *Scientific American* 249: 130–141.

Bergerud, A.T., W.J. Dalton, H. Butler and L. Camps. 2007. "Woodland Caribou Persistence and Extirpation in Relic Populations on Lake Superior, 2007." *Rangifer Special Issue* 17: 57–78.

Boag, D.A. and M.A. Schroeder. 1992. "Spruce Grouse" in *The Birds of North America,* No. 5 (A. Poole, P. Stettenheim, and F. Gill, eds.). Philadelphia: The Academy of Natural Sciences; Washington, DC.: The American Ornithologists' Union. 27 pp.

Boonstra, R. and A.R.E. Sinclair. 1984. "Distribution and Habitat use of Caribou, *Rangifer tarandus caribou,* and Moose, *Alces alces andersoni,* in the Spatsizi Plateau Wilderness Area," British Columbia. *Canadian Field-Naturalist* 98: 12–21.

Bousfield, E.L. and E.A. Hendricks. 2002. "The Talitroidean Amphipod Family Hyalidae Revised, with Emphasis on the North Pacific Fauna: Systematics and Distributional Ecology." *Amphipacifica* 3: 17–134.

Brooks, A. and H.S. Swarth. 1925. "A Distributional List of the Birds of British Columbia." *Pacific Coast Avifauna* No. 17, Berkeley, CA. 158 pp.

Bryant, A.A. 1998. "Metapopulation Ecology of Vancouver Island Marmot (*Marmota vancouverensis*)." Ph.D. dissertation, University of Victoria, Victoria, BC. 125 pp.

Buckner, E.L. and J. Reneau. 2005. *Boone and Crockett Club's Records of North American Big Game* (12th edition). Boone and Crockett Club, Missoula, MT. 928 pp.

Burnett, J.A. 2003. *A Passion for Wildlife: The History of the Canadian Wildlife Service.* University of British Columbia Press, Vancouver, BC. 331 pp.

Butler, F.R. and J.G. Cunningham. 1947. Report of Proceedings of the Game Convention, Harrison Hot Springs, May 29th and 30th, 1947. First annual convention. British Columbia Game Commission, Vancouver, BC. 170 pp.

Cade, T.J., J.H. Enderson, C.G. Thelander and C.M. White. 1988. *Peregrine Falcon Populations: Their Management and Recovery.* The Peregrine Fund, Inc., Boise, ID. 949 pp.

Campbell, R.W. 1970. "Prospectus for an Annual Bird Report." *Vancouver Natural History Society Discovery* 148: 9–11.

Campbell, R.W. 1973a. "Baseline Study of Selected Nesting Waterbirds on the Northwestern Mackenzie Delta, Northwest and Yukon Territories, 1972." Section 3: 1-32 in Towards An Environmental Impact Assessment of the Portion of the Mackenzie Gas Pipeline from Alaska to Alberta. Environment Protection Board, Winnipeg, MB. 32 pp.

Campbell, R.W. 1973b. "Fall migration of Birds in the Mackenzie Delta and Lower Mackenzie River, 1972." Section 5: 1-28 in Towards An

Environmental Impact Assessment of the Portion of the Mackenzie Gas Pipeline from Alaska to Alberta. Environment Protection Board, Winnipeg, MB. 28 pp.

Campbell, R.W. 1976. "Seabirds Breeding on the Canadian West Coast." pp. 39–65 in H. Hosford, editor. Mountains and Seas: Selected Papers from a Conference. British Columbia Provincial Museum Heritage Record No. 1, Victoria, BC.

Campbell, R.W. 1977. "Sea-bird Colonies of Vancouver Island Area." British Columbia Provincial Museum, Victoria, BC. Map.

Campbell, R.W. 1983. "Feeding Ecology of the Common Barn-owl in North America." M.Sc. thesis, University of Washington, Seattle, WA. 87 pp.

Campbell, R.W. (senior editor). 1994a. *Know Your Waterfowl (Swans, Geese, and Ducks of North America)*. Axia International Wildlife Series, Calgary, AB. 137 pp. (CD-ROM).

Campbell, R.W. (senior editor). 1994b. *Know Your Owls (of North America)*. Axia International Wildlife Series, Calgary, AB. (CD-ROM).

 Campbell, R.W. (senior editor) 1994c. *Know Your Common Bird Songs (of North America)*. Axia International Wildlife Series, Calgary, AB. (CD-ROM).

Campbell, R.W. 1995 (senior editor). *Know Your Birds of Prey—Vultures to Falcons (of North America)*. Axia International Wildlife Series, Calgary, AB. (CD-ROM).

Campbell, R.W. and B. Davies. 1973. "Nesting Raptor Survey in the Western Canadian Arctic, 1972." Section 1: 1-60 in Towards an Environmental Impact Assessment of the Portion of the Mackenzie Gas Pipeline from Alaska to Alberta. Environment Protection Board, Winnipeg, MB. 60 pp.

Campbell, R.W. and H.M. Garrioch. 1979. "Sea-bird Colonies of the Queen Charlotte Islands. British Columbia." British Columbia Provincial Museum, Victoria, BC. Map.

Campbell, R.W. and V. Gibbard. 1971. "British Columbia Nest Records Scheme—Sixteenth Annual Report, 1970." *Federation of British Columbia Naturalists Newsletter* 9 (1): 3–5.

Campbell, R.W. and P.T. Gregory. 1976. "The Buff-breasted Sandpiper in British Columbia with Notes on its Migration in North America." *Syesis* 9: 123–130.

Campbell, R.W. and M.C.E. McNall. 1982. "Field Report of the Provincial Museum Expedition in the Vicinity of Kotcho Lake, Northeastern British Columbia, June 11 to July 9, 1982." Report for British Columbia Provincial Museum, Vertebrate Zoology Division, Victoria, BC. 307 pp.

Campbell, R.W. and S.G. Sealy. 2011. "Meet the New Editor of *Wildlife Afield*." *Wildlife Afield* 8: 2.

Campbell, R.W. and M.G. Shepard. 1973. "Spring Waterfowl Migration in the Mackenzie River from Norman Wells to Arctic Red River,

Northwest Territories, 1972." Section 2: 1-48 in Towards An Environmental Impact Assessment of the Portion of the Mackenzie Gas Pipeline from Alaska to Alberta. Environment Protection Board, Winnipeg, MB. 48 pp.

Campbell, R.W. and D. Stirling. 1968. "Notes on the Natural History of Cleland Island, British Columbia, with Emphasis on the Breeding Bird Fauna." pp. HH25–HH43 in *Report of the Provincial Museum of Natural History and Anthropology for the Year 1967*, Victoria, British Columbia.

Campbell, R.W. and D. Stirling. 1971. "A Photoduplicate File for British Columbia Vertebrate Records." *Syesis* 4: 217–222.

Campbell, R.W. and W.C. Weber. 1973. "Abundance and Species Composition of Birds in Selected Areas Along the Pipeline Route, 1972." Section 4: 1–39 in Towards an Environmental Impact Assessment of the Mackenzie Gas Pipeline from Alaska to Alberta. Environment Protection Board, Winnipeg, MB. 39 pp.

Campbell, R.W., H.R. Carter, C.D. Shepard and C.J. Guiguet. 1979. "A Bibliography of British Columbia Ornithology." *British Columbia Provincial Museum Heritage Record*, No. 7, Victoria, B.C. 185 pp.

Campbell, R.W., N.K. Dawe, I. McTaggart-Cowan, J.M. Cooper, Gary W. Kaiser and Michael C.E. McNall. 1990a. *The Birds of British Columbia, Vol. 1: Nonpasserines: Introduction, Loons through Waterfowl*. Royal British Columbia Museum, Victoria, BC. 514 pp.

Campbell, R.W., N.K. Dawe, Ian McTaggart-Cowan, J.M. Cooper, G.W. Kaiser and M.C.E. McNall. 1990b. *The Birds of British Columbia, Vol. 2: Nonpasserines: Diurnal Birds of Prey through Woodpeckers*. Royal British Columbia Museum, Victoria, BC. 636 pp.

Campbell, R.W., N.K. Dawe, Ian McTaggart-Cowan, J.M. Cooper, G.W., Kaiser, M.C.E. McNall and G.E.J. Smith. 1997. *The Birds of British Columbia, Vol. 3: Passerines: Flycatchers through Vireos*. University of British Columbia Press, Vancouver, BC. 693 pp.

Campbell, R.W., N.K. Dawe, Ian McTaggart-Cowan, J.M. Cooper, G.W. Kaiser, A.C. Stewart and M.C.E. McNall. 2001. *The Birds of British Columbia, Vol. 4: Passerines: Wood-Warblers through Old World Sparrows*. University of British Columbia Press, Vancouver, BC. 739 pp.

Campbell, R.W., M.L. Funk and L. Davis. 1998. "British Columbia Nest Record Scheme: 43rd Annual Report—1997 Nesting Season." *WBT Wild Bird Trust of British Columbia Wildlife Report*, No. 3, West Vancouver, BC. 22 pp.

Campbell, R.W., F.J.E. Hillary and L.M. Van Damme. 2009. "Featured Species—Clark's Grebe." *Wildlife Afield* 6: 40–105.

Campbell, R.W., T.D. Hooper and N.K. Dawe. 1988. "A Bibliography of British Columbia ornithology." *Royal British Columbia Museum Heritage Record*, No. 19, Victoria, B.C. 591 pp.

Campbell, R.W., R.D. Jakimchuk and D.A. Demarchi. 2011. "Ian McTaggart-Cowan (1910–2010): A Century with Wildlife." *Wildlife Afield* 8: 222–232.

Campbell, R.W., R.D. Jakimchuk, and D.A. Demarchi. 2013. "In Memoriam: Ian McTaggart-Cowan, 1910–2010." *The Auk* 130: 4–6.

Campbell, R.W., D.A. Manuwal and A.S. Harestad. 1987. "Food Habits of the Common Barn-owl in British Columbia." *Canadian Journal of Zoology* 65: 578–586.

Campbell, R.W, L.M. Van Damme, M. Nyhof and M.I. Preston. 2010. "British Columbia Nest Record Scheme 56th Annual Report—2010 Nesting Season." *Biodiversity Centre for Wildlife Studies Report*, No. 13, Victoria, BC. 104 pp.

Campbell, R.W., L.M. Van Damme, M. Nyhof and P. Huet. 2013. "British Columbia Nest Record Scheme 58th Annual Report—2012 Nesting Season." *Biodiversity Centre for Wildlife Studies Report*, No. 16, Victoria, BC. 112 pp.

Campbell, R.W., M.G. Shepard and R.H. Drent. 1972a. "Status of Birds in the Vancouver Area in 1970." *Syesis* 5: 180–220.

Campbell, R.W., M.G. Shepard, B.M. Van Der Raay and P.T. Gregory. 1982. "A Bibliography of Pacific Northwest Herpetology." *British Columbia Provincial Museum Heritage Record*, No. 14, Victoria, BC. 151 pp.

Campbell, R.W., M.G. Shepard and W.C. Weber. 1972b. *Vancouver Birds in 1971. Vancouver Natural History Society Special Publication*, No. 2, Vancouver, BC. 88 pp.

Campbell, R.W., M.G. Shepard, B.A, MacDonald and W.C. Weber. 1974. *Vancouver Birds in 1972. Vancouver Natural History Society Special Publication*, No. 5, Vancouver, BC. 96 pp.

Campbell, R.W., J.G. Ward and M.G. Shepard. 1975. "A New Common Murre Colony in British Columbia." *Canadian Field-Naturalist* 89(3): 244–248.

Candy, R. and R.W. Campbell. 2012. "From the Archives—Allan Brooks: Naturalist and Wildlife Illustrator (1869–1946)." *Wildlife Afield* 9: 88–106.

Carl, G.C. and C.J. Guiguet. 1957. *Alien Animals in British Columbia. British Columbia Provincial Museum Handbook*, No.14, Victoria, BC. 103 pp.

Carson, R. 1962. *Silent Spring*. Houghton Mifflin Co., Boston, MA. 153 pp.

Chitty, D. 1960. "Population Processes in the Vole and Their Relevance to General Theory." *Canadian Journal of Zoology* 38: 99-113.

Clark, R.N. 2008. "Two New Chitons of the Genus *Tripoplax* Berry, 1919 from the Monterey Sea Canyon." *American Malacological Bulletin* 25: 77–86.

Cohen, M.P. 1988. *The History of the Sierra Club, 1892–1970*. Sierra Club Books, San Francisco, CA. 550 pp.

Cowan, G.I. McTaggart. 1968. "Comparative Analysis of Separate Data Sources in a Systematic Study of the Genus *Myoxocephalus* (Pisces: Cottidae)." Ph.D. dissertation, University of British Columbia, Vancouver, BC. 226 pp.

Cowan, G.I. McTaggart and I. McTaggart-Cowan. 1977. "New Chiton of the Genus *Mopalia* from the Northeast Pacific Coast." Syesis 10: 45–52.

Cowan, I. McTaggart. 1933a. "The Mule Deer of Southern California and Northern Lower California as a Recognizable Race." *Journal of Mammalogy* 14: 326–327.

Cowan, I. McTaggart. 1933b. "A New Race of Deer from Eastern California." *Proceedings of the Biological Society of Washington* 46: 67–70.

Cowan, I. McTaggart. 1934. "Two Cases of Pathologic Skin Growths in Deer of the Genus *Odocoileus*." *The Murrelet* 15: 81-82.

Cowan, I. McTaggart. 1935a. "Distribution and Variation in Deer (Genus *Odocoileus*) of the Pacific Coastal Region of North America." Ph.D. dissertation, University of California, Berkley, CA. 338 pp.

Cowan, I. McTaggart. 1935b. "A Distributional Study of the *Peromyscus sitkensis* Group of White-footed Mice." *University of California Publications in Zoology* 40: 429–438.

Cowan, I. McTaggart. 1936. "Distribution and Variation in Deer (Genus *Odocoileus*) of the Pacific Coastal Region of North America." *California Fish and Game* 22: 155–246.

Cowan, I. McTaggart. 1939. "The Vertebrate Fauna of the Peace River District of British Columbia." British Columbia Provincial Museum Occasional Paper, No. 1, Victoria, BC. 102 pp.

Cowan, I. McTaggart. 1940a. "Winter Occurrence of Summer Birds on Vancouver Island, British Columbia." *The Condor* 42: 213–214.

Cowan, I. McTaggart. 1940b. "Distribution and Variation of the Native Sheep of North America." *American Midland Naturalist* 24: 505–580.

Cowan, I. McTaggart. 1941. "Longevity of the Red-legged Frog." *Copeia* 1941: 48.

Cowan, I. McTaggart. 1942. "Food Habits of the Barn Owl in British Columbia." *The Murrelet* 23: 48–53.

Cowan, I. McTaggart 1944b. "Report on Game Conditions in Banff, Jasper and Kootenay National Parks, 1943." Canadian Wildlife Service Report C3131, Ottawa, ON. 72 pp.

Cowan, I. McTaggart 1945a. "The Ecological Relationships of the Food of the Columbian Black-tailed Deer, *Odocoileus hemionus columbianus* (Richardson), in the Coast Forest Region of Southern Vancouver Island, British Columbia." *Ecological Monographs* 15: 109–139.

Cowan, I. McTaggart 1945b. "Report of the Wildlife Studies in 1944 and Parasites, Diseases and Injuries of Game Animals in the Rocky Mountain National Parks, 1942–44." Canadian Wildlife Service unpublished report, Ottawa, ON. 147 pp.

Cowan, I. McTaggart. 1946a. "Notes on the Distribution of *Spizella breweri taverneri*." *The Condor* 48: 93–94.

Cowan, I. McTaggart. 1946b. "Notes on the Distribution of the Chipmunks *Eutamias* in Southern British Columbia and the Rocky Mountain Region of Southern Alberta with Descriptions of Two New Races." *Proceedings of the Biological Society of Washington* 59: 107–118.

Cowan, I. McTaggart. 1951. "A New *Microtus* from the Western Arctic of Canada." *Journal of Mammalogy* 32: 353–354.

Cowan, I. McTaggart. 1954. "The Occurrence of the Pleistocene Wolf (*Canis dirus*) in the Rocky Mountains of Central Alberta." *Canadian Field-Naturalist* 68: 44.

Cowan, I. McTaggart. 1955. *Birds of Jasper National Park, Alberta, Canada. Canadian Wildlife Service Wildlife Management Bulletin* Series 2, No. 8, Ottawa, ON. 66 pp.

Cowan, I. McTaggart. 1964. "The Holotype of the Franklin Grouse (*Canachites franklinii*)." *Canadian Field-Naturalist* 78: 127–128.

Cowan, I. McTaggart. 1976. "Foreword." pp. 10–12 in T.A. (Tommy) Walker. *Spatsizi.* Antonson Publishing Ltd., Surrey, BC. 272 pp.

Cowan, I. McTaggart. 1990. "The Day Before the Show." *Vancouver Island Rock and Alpine Garden Society Newsletter* (March 1990): 1–3.

Cowan, I. McTaggart. and P.J. Bandy. 1969. "Observations on the Haematology of Several Races of Black-tailed deer (*Odocoileus hemionus*)." *Canadian Journal of Zoology* 47: 1021–1024.

Cowan, I. McTaggart. and C.J. Guiguet. 1956. *The Mammals of British Columbia. British Columbia Provincial Museum Handbook*, No. 11, Victoria, BC. 413 pp.

Cowan, I. McTaggart. and J. Hatter. 1940. "Two Mammals New to the Known Fauna of British Columbia, *Ziphius cavirostris* and *Sylvilagus nuttalli nuttalli.*" *The Murrelet* 21: 9.

Cowan, I. McTaggart. and W. McCrory. 1970. "Variation in the Mountain Goat, *Oreamnos americanus* (Blainville)." *Journal of Mammalogy* 51: 60–73.

Cowan, I.M. and K. Racey. 1946. "A New Pika (Genus *Ochotona*) from British Columbia." *Canadian Field-Naturalist* 60: 102–104.

Darling, F.F. and J.P. Milton (eds.). 1966. *Future Environments of North America: Being the Record of a Conference Convened by the Conservation Foundation in April, 1965, at Airlie House, Warrenton, Virginia.* Natural History Press, Garden City, NY. 767 pp.

Daubenmire, R.F. 1968. "Ecology of Fire in Grasslands." pp. 209–266 in J.B. Cragg (ed.). *Advances in Ecological Research.* Academic Press, New York, NY.

Demarchi, D.A., R.D. Marsh, A.P. Harcombe and E.C. Lea. 1990. "The Environment— Ecoregions of British Columbia." pp. 55–142 in R.W. Campbell, N.K. Dawe, I. McTaggart-Cowan, J.M. Cooper, G.W. Kaiser and M.C.E. McNall. 1990a. *The Birds of British Columbia, Vol. 1: Nonpasserines: Introduction, Loons through Waterfowl.* Royal British Columbia Museum, Victoria, BC. 514 pp.

Demarchi, R.A., C.L. Hartwig and D.A. Demarchi. 2000. "Status of California Bighorn Sheep in British Columbia." *British Columbia Ministry of Environment, Lands and Parks, Wildlife Branch, Wildlife Bulletin* No. B-98, Victoria, BC. 53 pp.

Dickinson, J.C. 1953. "Report on the McCabe Collection of British Columbia Birds." *Bulletin of the Museum of Comparative Zoology* 109: 123-205.

Douglas, D. 1833. "Observations of Some Species of the Genera *Tetrao* and *Ortyx*, Natives of North America; with Descriptions of Four New Species of the Former, and Two of the Latter Genus." *Transactions of the Linnean Society of London* 16: 133–149.

Douglas, D. 1914. Journal kept by David Douglas during his travels in North America, 1823–1827: Together with a particular description of thirty-three species of American oaks and eighteen species of *Pinus*. William Wesley & Son, London, England. 349 pp.

Drent, R.H. 1965. "Breeding Biology of the Pigeon Guillemot, *Cepphus columba*." *Ardea* 53: 99–160.

Drent, R.H. and C.J. Guiguet. 1961. "A Catalogue of British Columbia Sea-bird Colonies." *British Columbia Provincial Museum Occasional Paper*, No. 12, Victoria, BC. 173 pp.

Ecological Society of America. 2002. "One Scientist's Odyssey: Dr. David Suzuki to Speak at ESA Annual Meeting." Accessed at ScienceBlog. com/community/older/2002/F/20022360.html.

Edwards, R.Y. and R.W. Ritcey. 1967. *The Birds of Wells Gray Park: An Annotated List*. British Columbia Parks Branch Report, Victoria, BC. 36 pp.

Ehrenreich, J.H. and J.M. Aikman. 1963. "An Ecological Study of the Effect of Certain Management Practices on Native Prairie in Iowa." *Ecological Monographs* 33: 113–130.

Ehrlich, P.R. and A.H. Ehrlich. 1968. *The Population Bomb*. Ballantine Books, New York, NY. 201 pp.

Einarsen, A.S. 1948. *The Pronghorn Antelope and its Management*. The Wildlife Institute, Washington, DC. 238 pp.

Einarsen, A.S. 1965. *Black Brant: Sea Goose of the Pacific Coast*. University of Washington Press, Seattle, WA. 142 pp.

Environment Canada. 2008. *Scientific Review for the Identification of Critical Habitat for Woodland Caribou (Rangifer tarandus caribou), Boreal Population, in Canada*. Environment Canada, Ottawa, ON. 72 pp.

Errington, P.L. 1967. *Of Predation and Life*. Iowa State University Press, Ames, IA. 277 pp.

Erskine, A.J. 1971. *Buffleheads. Canadian Wildlife Service Monograph Series*, No. 4, Ottawa, ON. 240 pp.

Erskine, A.J. 1992. *Atlas of Breeding Birds of the Maritime Provinces*. Co-published by Nimbus Publishing Ltd. and the Nova Scotia Museum, Halifax, NS. 270 pp.

Fannin, J. 1891. *Check List of British Columbia Birds*. Province of British Columbia, Victoria, BC. 49 pp.

Fay, F.H. 1982. "Ecology and Biology of the Pacific walrus, *Odobenus rosmarus divergens* Illiger." United States Department of the Interior, Fish and Wildlife Service North American Fauna No. 74, Washington, DC. 279 pp.

Foster, J.B. 1965. "The Evolution of the Mammals of the Queen Charlotte Islands, British Columbia." *British Columbia Provincial Museum Occasional Paper*, No, 14, Victoria, BC. 130 pp.

Fowle, C.D. 1942. "A Preliminary Investigation of Certain Bird's Nests with Reference to Their Environmental Relationships." B.A. (Hons.) thesis, University of British Columbia, Department of Zoology, Vancouver, BC. 90 pp.

Fowle, C.D. 1944. "The Sooty Grouse (*Dendragapus fuliginosus fuliginosus* Ridgway) on its Summer Range." M.A. thesis, University of British Columbia, Department of Zoology, Vancouver, BC. 79 pp.

Fowle, C.D. 1972. "Effects of Phosphamidon on Forest Birds in New Brunswick." *Canadian Wildlife Service Report Series*, No. 16, Ottawa, ON. 25 pp.

Galton, F. 1872. *Statistical Inquiries into the Efficacy of Prayer.* Chapman and Hall, London, UK. 135 pp.

Geist, V. 1978. *Life Strategies, Human Evolution, Environmental Design: Toward a Biological Theory of Health.* Springer-Verlag, New York, NY. 495 pp.

Grant, P.R. and I. McTaggart-Cowan. 1964. "A Review of the Avifauna of the Tres Marías Islands, Nayarit, Mexico. " *The Condor* 66: 221–228.

Green, D.M. and R.W. Campbell. 1984. *The Amphibians of British Columbia. British Columbia Provincial Museum Handbook*, No. 45, Victoria, BC. 101 pp.

Gregory, P.T. and R.W. Campbell. 1984. *The Reptiles of British Columbia. British Columbia Provincial Museum Handbook*, No. 44, Victoria, BC. 103 pp.

Grinnell, J. 1910. "The Methods and Uses of a Research Museum." *Popular Science Monthly* 77: 163–169.

Grinnell, J. 1915. "A Distributional List of the Birds of California." *Pacific Coast Avifauna* No. 11: 1–217.

Grinnell, J. and A.H. Miller. 1944. "The Distribution and Abundance of the Birds of California." *Pacific Coast Avifauna* No. 27: 1–615.

Grinnell, J. and T.I. Storer. 1924. *Animal Life in the Yosemite: An Account of the Mammals, Birds, Reptiles, and Amphibians in a Cross-section of the Sierra Nevada.* University of California Press, Berkeley, CA. 752 pp.

GSGislason & Associates Ltd. 2009. *Freshwater Sport Fishing in British Columbia: Sending Ripples through the Provincial Economy.* Freshwater Fisheries Society of British Columbia, Victoria, BC. 63 pp.

Guiguet, C.J. 1953. "An Ecological Study of Goose Island, British Columbia, with special reference to mammals and birds." *British Columbia Provincial Museum Occasional Paper,* No. 10, Victoria, BC. 78 pp.

Guiguet, C.J. 1955. "Undescribed Mammals (*Peromyscus* and *Microtus*) from the Islands of British Columbia." pp. B64–B76 in *Report for the British Columbia Provincial Museum 1955*, Victoria, BC.

Hahn, B. 2000. *Kootenay National Park.* Rocky Mountain Books, Calgary, AB. 153 pp.

Hamilton, W.J. 1939. *American Mammals: Their Lives, Habits, and Economic Relations.* McGraw-Hill Book Company, New York, NY. 434 pp.

Handel, C.M. and R.E. Gill. 2001. "Black Turnstone (*Arenaria melanocephala*)" in A. Poole and F. Gill (eds.). *The Birds of North America*, No. 585. The Birds of North America, Inc., Philadelphia, PA. 28 pp.

Hardin, G. 1968. "Tragedy of the Commons." *Science* 162(3859): 1243–1248.

Haroldson, M.A., C.C. Schwartz and K.A. Gunther. 2008. "From Garbage, Controversy and Decline to Recovery." *Yellowstone Science* 16: 13–24.

Hart, E.J. 2009. *Jimmy Simpson Legend of the Rockies.* Rocky Mountain Books, Surrey, BC. 219 pp.

Hartman, G.F. and J.C. Scrivener. 1990. "Impacts of Forestry Practices on a Coastal Stream Ecosystem, Carnation Creek, British Columbia." *Canadian Bulletin of Fisheries and Aquatic Sciences* 223, Ottawa, ON, 85 pp.

Hatler, D.F., R.W. Campbell and A. Dorst. 1973. "Birds of Pacific Rim National Park, British Columbia." Unpublished report for Canadian Wildlife Service, Edmonton, AB. 383 pp.

Hatler, D.F., D.W. Nagorsen and A.M. Beal. 2008. *Carnivores of British Columbia. Royal British Columbia Museum Handbook,* Victoria, BC. 407 pp.

Hatter, J. 1950. "The Moose of Central British Columbia." Ph.D. dissertation, Washington State University, Pullman, WA. 360 pp.

Hatter, J. 1997. *Politically Incorrect: The Life and Times of British Columbia's First Game Biologist: An Autobiography.* O & L Enterprises, Victoria, BC. 220 pp.

Hatter, J. 2005. *Wolves and People: The Management Imperative and Mythology of Animal Rights.* Trafford Publishing, Bloomington, IN. 126 pp.

Heard, D.C. 1977. "The Behaviour of Vancouver Island Marmots, *Marmota vancouverensis.*" M.Sc. thesis, University of British Columbia, Department of Zoology, Vancouver, BC. 129 pp.

Hegel, G.W.F. and J.B. Baillie. 2009. *Phenomenology of Spirit (Phenomenology of Mind).* Digireads.com Publishing, Lawrence, KS. 368 pp.

Heming, A.H.H. 1921. *The Drama of the Forests.* McLelland & Stewart, Toronto, ON. 296 pp.

Herman, S.G., R.L. Garrett and R.L. Rudd. 1969. "Pesticides and the Western Grebe: A Study of Pesticide Survival and Trophic Concentration at Clear Lake, Lake County, California." pp 24–53 in M.W. Miller and G.G. Berg (eds.). Chemical Fallout: Current Research on Persistent Pesticides. C.C. Thomas Publishers, Springfield, IL.

Hewitt, C.G. 1921. *The Conservation of Wildlife in Canada.* C. Scribner's Sons, New York, NY. 336 pp.

Hickey, J.J. (ed.). 1969. *Peregrine Falcon Populations: Their Biology and Decline.* University of Wisconsin Press, Madison, WI. 596 pp.

Hornocker, M. 1997. *Track of the Tiger: Legend and Lore of the Great Cat.* Sierra Club Books, San Francisco, CA. 120 pp.

Hornocker, M. and S. Negri (eds.). 2009. *Cougar: Ecology and Conservation.* University of Chicago Press, Chicago, IL. 304 pp.

Hudson, R.J., W.D. Kitts and P.J. Bandy. 1970. "Monitoring Parasite Activity and Disease in the Rocky Mountain Bighorn by Electrophoresis of Seromucoids." *Journal of Wildlife Diseases* 6: 104–106.

Hudson, R.J., W.D. Kitts and P.J. Bandy. 1971. "Immunoglobulin Response of the Rocky Mountain Bighorn Sheep." *Journal of Wildlife Diseases* 7: 171–174.

Hudson, R.J., W.D. Kitts and P.J. Bandy. 1972. "Cell Adherence Reactions in Lungworm (*Protostrongylus*) Infections of the Rocky Mountain Bighorn Sheep." *Canadian Journal of Comparative Medicine* 36: 69–73.

Hunt, E.G. and A.I. Bischoff. 1960. "Inimical Effects on Wildlife of Periodic DDD Applications to Clear Lake." *California Fish and Game* 46: 91–106.

Ivey, G.A. 2004. "Conservation Assessment and Management Plan for Breeding Western and Clark's Grebes in California." Final report to American Trader Trustee Council, June 2004, Corvallis, OR. 80 pp.

Jakimchuk, R.D. 1977. "The Porcupine Caribou Herd—Management Needs for an International Resource." pp 240–241 [Abstract] in Resources Development – Processes and Problems, Vol. 1. Proceedings of the Alaska Science Conference 27, August 4 to August 7, 1976, Fairbanks, AK. 6 pp.

Johnson, S.R. and D.R. Herter. 1989. *The Birds of the Beaufort Sea.* BP Exploration (Alaska) Inc., Anchorage, AK. 372 pp.

Kermode, F. 1904. *Catalogue of British Columbia Birds.* British Columbia Provincial Museum, Victoria, BC. 69 pp.

Kermode, F. and E.M. Anderson. 1914. pp. 19–20 in "Report on Birds Collected and Observed during September, 1913, on Atlin Lake, from Atlin to South End of the Lake." *Report of the Provincial Museum of Natural History*, 1913, Victoria, BC.

Kessel, B. and D.D. Gibson. 1978. "Status and Distribution of Alaskan Birds." *Studies in Avian Biology*, No. 1, Lawrence, KS. 100 pp.

Kingston, W.H.G. 1891. *On the Banks of the Amazon.* Thomas Nelson and Sons, Ltd., New York, NY. 512 pp.

Klein, D.R., L.M. Baskin, L.S. Boogslovskaya, K. Danell, A. Gunn, D.B. Irons, G.P. Kofinas, K.M. Kovacs, M. Magomedova, R.H. Meehan, D.E. Russell and P. Valkenburg. 2005. "Management and Conservation of Wildlife in a Changing Arctic Environment." pp 598–648 in C. Symon, L. Arris, and B. Heal (eds.). Arctic Climate Impact Assessment—Scientific Report. Cambridge University Press, New York, NY.

Krajina, V.J. 1978. *Ecological Reserves in British Columbia.* British Columbia Ministry of Environment, Victoria, BC. 269 pp.

Krebs, C.J. 2008. *The Ecological World View.* University of California Press, Berkeley, CA. 592 pp.

Krebs, C.J. 2009. *Ecology: The Experimental Analysis of Distribution and Abundance* (6th edition). Benjamin Cummings Publishing Company, San Francisco, CA. 688 pp.

Krebs, C.J. and I. McTaggart Cowan. 1962. "Growth Studies of Reindeer Fawns." *Canadian Journal of Zoology* 40: 863-869.

Leopold, A. 1925. "Wilderness as a Form of Land Use." *Journal of Land & Public Utility Economics* 1(4): 398-404.

Leopold, A. 1933. *Game Management*. Charles Scribner's Sons, New York, NY. 481 pp.

Leopold, A. 1949. *A Sand County Almanac and Sketches Here and There*. Oxford University Press, New York, NY. 226 pp.

Lloyd, W.F. 1833. *Two Lectures on the Checks to Population*. Oxford University Press, Oxford, England.

Manuwal, D.A. and R.W. Campbell. 1979. "Status and Distribution of Breeding Seabirds of Southeastern Alaska, British Columbia and Washington." pp. 73–91 in J.C. Bartonek and D.N. Nettleship, (eds.). Conservation of Marine Birds in Northern North America. United States Department of the Interior Fish and Wildlife Service Wildlife Research Report Number 11, Washington, DC.

Martell, A.M. 1975. "Taxonomic Status of *Microtus pennsylvanicus arcticus* Cowan." *Journal of Mammalogy* 56: 255–257.

McTaggart-Cowan, Ian. 1929. "Note on Yellow-Bellied Marmot." *The Murrelet* 10: 64.

McTaggart-Cowan, Ian. 1930. "Mammals of Point Grey." *Canadian Field-Naturalist* 44: 133–134.

McTaggart-Cowan, Ian. 1933a. "The British Columbia Woodchuck *Marmota monax petrensis*." *Canadian Field-Naturalist* 47: 57.

McTaggart-Cowan, Ian. 1933b. "Some Notes on the Hibernation of *Lasionycteris noctivagans*." *Canadian Field-Naturalist* 47: 74–75.

McTaggart-Cowan, Ian. 1998. "Moments from the Education of an Ornithologist." *Picoides* 11 (2): 17–22.

McTaggart-Cowan, Ian. 2004. *The Law Stamps of Yukon, 1902–1971: Their Development and Use (Collection of Ian McTaggart-Cowan)*. Published by the British North America Philatelic Society (BNAPS) and Auxano Philatelic Services, Calgary, AB. 104 pp.

McTaggart-Cowan, Ian. 2005. *The Law Stamps of British Columbia and Their Uses, 1879–1984*. Published by the British North America Philatelic Society Ltd. as BNAPS Exhibit Series No. 36, Ottawa, ON. 162 pp.

McTaggart-Cowan, I., N.K. Dawe, R.W. Campbell and A.C. Stewart. 2001. "Avian Biodiversity, Ecological Distribution and Patterns of Change." pp. 633–678 in R. Wayne Campbell, Neil K. Dawe, I. McTaggart.-Cowan, John M. Cooper, Gary W. Kaiser, Andrew C. Stewart, and Michael C.E. McNall. 2001. *The Birds of British Columbia, Vol. 4: Passerines: Wood-Warblers through Old World Sparrows*. University of British Columbia Press, Vancouver, BC.

Meagher, M. 2008. "Bears in transition, 1959–1970s." *Yellowstone Science* 16: 5–11.

Medley, M. 2011. "Ptarmigan Dilemma and Evolution Win Lane Anderson Award." *National Post*, Toronto, ON. September 15, 2011.

Michelutti, N., A. Simonetti, J.P. Briner, S. Funder, R.A. Creaser and A.P. Wolfe. 2009. "Temporal Trends of Pollution Pb and Other Metals in East-central Baffin Island Inferred from Lake Sediment Geochemistry." *Science of the Total Environment* 407: 5653–5662.

Miles, J.R.W. and C.R. Harris. 1978. "Insecticide Residues in Water, Sediment, and Fish of the Drainage System of the Holland Marsh, Ontario, Canada, 1972–75." *Journal of Economic Entomology* 71: 125-131.

Munro, J.A. 1917. "Report on Field-work in Okanagan and Shuswap District." Provincial Museum of Natural History Report for 1916, Victoria, BC.

Munro, J.A. 1937. "The American Merganser in British Columbia and Its Relation to the Fish Population." *Biological Board of Canada Bulletin* LV, Ottawa, ON. 50 pp.

Munro, J.A. 1939. "Studies of Waterfowl in British Columbia No. 9—Barrow's Golden-eye, American Golden-eye. pp. 259–318 in *Transactions of the Royal Canadian Institute* No. 48, Vol. XXII (Part 2), Toronto, ON.

Munro, J.A. 1941. "Studies of Waterfowl in British Columbia—Greater Scaup Duck, Lesser Scaup Duck." *Canadian Journal of Research* 19: 113–138.

Munro, J.A. 1942. "Studies of Waterfowl in British Columbia: Bufflehead." *Canadian Journal of Research* 20: 133–160.

Munro, J.A. 1944. "Studies of Waterfowl in British Columbia: Pintail." *Canadian Journal of Research* 22: 60–86.

Munro, J.A. and I. McTaggart Cowan. 1947. *A Review of the Bird Fauna of British Columbia.* British Columbia Provincial Museum Special Publication, No. 2, Victoria, BC. 285 pp.

Munro, W.T. and R.W. Campbell. 1979. "Programs and Authorities of the Province of British Columbia Related to Marine Bird Conservation." pp. 247–250 in J.C. Bartonek and D.N. Nettleship, (eds.). Conservation of Marine Birds in Northern North America. United States Department of the Interior Fish and Wildlife Service Wildlife Research Report Number 11, Washington, D.C.

Murie, A. 1944. *The Wolves of Mount McKinley.* United States National Park Service Fauna Series No. 5, Washington. DC. 238 pp.

Northcote, T.G. and G.F. Hartman (eds.). 2004. *Fisheries & Forestry: World-wide watershed interactions and management.* Blackwell Publishing Co., Oxford, UK. 800 pp.

Osmond-Jones, E.J., M. Sather, W.G. Hazelwood and B. Ford. 1977. *Spatsizi and Tatlatui Wilderness Parks: An Inventory of Wildlife, Fisheries & Recreational Values in a Northern Wilderness.* British Columbia Parks Branch, Victoria, BC. 292 pp.

Palmer, R.S. (ed.). 1976. *Handbook of North American Birds.* Volume 3 Waterfowl concluded. Yale University Press, New Haven, CT. 560 pp.

Paul, W.A.B. 1959. "The Birds of Kleena Kleene, Chilcotin District, British Columbia, 1947–1958." *Canadian Field-Naturalist* 73: 83–93.

Perrault, E.G. 1952. "His Wild Life has Brought Honors." *The Vancouver Sun,* June 28, 1952, p. 15, Vancouver, BC.

Pojar, J. and A. MacKinnon (eds.). 1994. *Plants of the Pacific Northwest Coast: Washington, Oregon, British Columbia & Alaska.* Lone Pine Publishing, Edmonton, AB. 527 pp.

Poole, A.F. 1989. *Ospreys: A Natural and Unnatural History.* Cambridge University Press, Cambridge, UK. 270 pp.

Racey, K. 1926. "Notes on the Birds Observed in the Alta Lake Region, British Columbia." *The Auk* 43: 319–325.

Racey, K. 1933. "White Pelican (*Pelecanus erythrorhynchos*) in British Columbia." *The Auk* 50: 205.

Racey, K. 1948. "Birds of the Alta Lake Region, British Columbia." *The Auk* 63: 383–401.

Racey, K. and I. McTaggart Cowan. 1935. "Mammals of the Alta Lake Region of Southwestern British Columbia." pp. H15–H29 in *Report of the British Columbia Provincial Museum 1935*. Victoria, BC.

Reed, C.A. 1914. *The Canadian Bird Book Illustrating in Natural Colors More Than Seven Hundred North American Birds, Also Several Hundred Photographs of Their Nests and Eggs.* Musson Book Co., Toronto, ON. 472 pp.

Rhoads, S.N. 1893. "The Birds Observed in British Columbia and Washington During Spring and Summer, 1892." *Proceedings of the Academy of Natural Sciences of Philadelphia* 45: 21–65.

Ritcey, R. 1995. "Status of the Sharp-tailed Grouse in British Columbia." *British Columbia Ministry of Environment, Lands and Parks Wildlife Working Report* No. WR-70, Victoria, BC. 40 pp.

Roessingh, K. and B. Penn. 2012. "Sandhill Cranes of Coastal British Columbia: Results of Helicopter Surveys and Preliminary Observations of Habitat Use." *Proceedings of the North American Crane Workshop* 11: 1–8.

Siddle, C. 2010a. "Birds of North Peace River (Fort St. John and vicinity), British Columbia, 1975–1999: Part 1 (Introduction and Nonpasserines: Waterfowl through Woodpeckers)." *Wildlife Afield* 7: 12–123.

Siddle, C. 2010b. "Birds of North Peace River (Fort St. John and Vicinity), British Columbia, 1975–1999: Part 2 (Flycatchers through Old World Sparrows)." *Wildlife Afield* 7: 143-280.

Silver, R.S. 2004. "Vancouver Natural History Society profile—Ian McTaggart-Cowan: Renaissance Man." *Discovery* 33: 10–15.

Silver, R.S., N.K. Dawe, B.M. Starzomski, K.L. Parker, and D.W. Nagorsen. 2010. "A Tribute to Ian McTaggart-Cowan, 1910–2010, O.C., O.B.C., Ph.D., LL.D, F.R.S.C." *Canadian Field-Naturalist* 124: 367–383.

Sladen, W.J.L. 1965. "Ornithological Research in Antarctica." *BioScience* 15: 264–268.

Sladen, W.J.L., C.M. Menzie and W.L. Reichel. 1966. "DDT Residues in Adelie Penguins and a Crabeater Seal from Antarctica." *Nature* 210: 670-673.

Smith, L.K. 2004. "The Effects of *in ovo* and Early Post-hatch DDT Exposure of American Robins from the Okanagan Valley, British Columbia." Ph.D. dissertation, University of British Columbia, Faculty of Animal Science, Vancouver, BC. 161 pp.

Soper, J.D. 1964. *The Mammals of Alberta.* The Hamley Press, Edmonton, AB. 402 pp.

Spalding, D.J. 1964. "Comparative Feeding Habits of the Fur Seal, Sea Lion and Harbour Seal." *Fisheries Research Board of Canada Bulletin* No. 146, Ottawa, ON. 52 pp.

Stenhouse, J.H. 1929–30. "Bird-types in the Royal Scottish Museum." *Novitates Zoologicae* 35: 270–276.

Stokes, A.W. 1974. *Territory.* Volume 3 of benchmark papers in animal behavior series. John Wiley & Sons, Toronto, ON. 410 pp.

Sugden, L.G. 1961. "The California Big Horn in British Columbia with Particular Reference to the Churn Creek Herd." British Columbia Department of Recreation and Conservation report, Victoria, BC. 58 pp.

Sugden, L.G. 1963. "Barrow Golden-eye Using Crow Nests." *The Condor* 65: 330.

Sugden, L.G. 1973. "Feeding Ecology of Pintail, Gadwall, American Widgeon and Lesser Scaup Ducklings in Southern Alberta." *Canadian Wildlife Service Occasional Report Series,* No. 24, Ottawa, ON. 43 pp.

Sugden, L.G. 1978. "Canvasback Habitat Use and Production in Saskatchewan Parklands." *Canadian Wildlife Service Occasional Report Series,* No. 34, Ottawa, ON. 32 pp.

Sugden, L.G. 1979. "Habitat Use by Nesting American Coots in Saskatchewan Parklands." *Wilson Bulletin* 91: 599–607.

Swarth, H.S. 1912. "Report on a Collection of Birds and Mammals from Vancouver Island." *University of California Publications in Zoology* 10: 1–124.

Swarth, H.S. 1922. "Birds and Mammals of the Stikine River Region of Northern British Columbia and Southeastern Alaska." *University of California Publications in Zoology* 24: 125–314.

Swarth, H.S. 1924. "Birds and Mammals of the Skeena River Region of Northern British Columbia." *University of California Publications in Zoology* 24: 315–394.

Swarth, H.S. 1926. "Report on a Collection of Birds and Mammals from the Atlin Region, Northern British Columbia." *University of California Publications in Zoology* 30: 51–162.

Taverner, P.A. 1919. *Birds of Eastern Canada. Canada Department of Mines Memoir* 104, No. 3, Biological Series. Ottawa, ON. 297 pp.

Taverner, P.A. 1926. *Birds of Western Canada. Canada Department of Mines Museum Bulletin,* No. 41. Ottawa, ON. 380 pp.

Theberge, J.B. and M.T. Theberge. 2010. *The Ptarmigan's Dilemma: An Ecological Exploration into the Mysteries of Life.* McClelland and Stewart, Toronto, ON. 401 pp.

Tinbergen, N. 1953. *The Herring Gull's World: A Study of the Social Behaviour of Birds.* Collins, London, UK. 255 pp.

Thomas, D.C. and D.R. Gray. 2002. "Update COSEWIC Status Report on the Woodland Caribou *Rangifer tarandus caribou* in Canada."

Committee on the Status of Endangered Wildlife in Canada, Ottawa, ON. 98 pp.

Thommasen, H., K. Hutchings, R.W. Campbell and M. Hume. 2004. *Birds of the Raincoast: Habits and Habitat.* Harbour Publishing, Madeira Park, BC. 222 pp.

Tompa, F.S. 1962. "Territorial Behavior: The Main Controlling Factor of a Local Song Sparrow Population." *The Auk* 79: 687–697.

Trauger, D.L. and P.L. Kennedy. 2012. "Pioneering Professionals: Sharing a Passion for Wildlife Conservation." *The Wildlife Professional* 6: 32–37.

Tremblay-Boyer, L., D. Gascuel, R. Watson, V. Christensen and D. Pauly. 2011. "Modelling the Effects of Fishing on the Biomass of the World's Oceans from 1950 to 2006." *Marine Ecology Progress Series* 442: 169-185.

Turner, N.J. 1975. *Food Plants of British Columbia Indians: Part 1—Coastal Peoples. British Columbia Provincial Museum Handbook*, No. 34, Victoria, BC. 264 pp.

Turner, T. 1993. *Sierra Club: 100 Years of Protecting Nature.* Harry N. Abrams, Inc., New York, NY. 288 pp.

Udvardy, M.D.F. 1969. *Dynamic Zoogeography: With Special Reference to Land Animals.* Van Nostrand Reinhold Co., New York, NY. 445 pp.

University of British Columbia. 1932. "The University of British Columbia calendar: Eighteenth session (1932–1933)." University of British Columbia, Vancouver, BC. 348 pp.

Van Tets, G.F. 1959. "A Comparative Study of the Reproductive Behaviour and Natural History of Three Sympatric Species of Cormorants, (*Phalacrocorax auritus, P. penicullatus* and *P. pelagicus*) at Mandarte Island, B.C." M.A. thesis, University of British Columbia, Vancouver, B.C. 86 pp.

Vermeer, K. 1963. *The Breeding Ecology of the Glaucous-winged Gull* (Larus glaucescens) *on Mandarte Island, B.C. British Columbia Provincial Museum Occasional Papers*, No. 13, Victoria, BC. 104 pp.

Walker, T.A. 1976. *Spatsizi.* Nunga Publishing Co., Ltd., Surrey, BC. 272 pp.

Weeden, R.B. 1978. *Alaska: Promises to Keep.* Houghton Mifflin Company, Boston, MA. 254 pp.

Weeden, R.B. 1992. *Message from Earth: Nature and the Human Prospect in Alaska.* University of Alaska Press, Fairbanks, AK. 189 pp.

Wildlife Society. 2006. *Following Leopold's Footsteps—The Wildlife Society's Aldo Leopold Medal Winners, 1950–2005.* The Wildlife Society, Bethesda, MD. 68 pp.

Zwickel, F.C. and J.F. Bendell. 2004. *Blue Grouse: Their Biology and Natural History.* National Research Council of Canada Press, Ottawa, ON. 284 pp.

Chapter References

1. Campbell et al. (1990a), Campbell et al. (1990b), Campbell et al. (1997), Campbell et al. (2001)
2. McTaggart-Cowan (1929)
3. University of British Columbia (1932)
4. McTaggart-Cowan (1933c)
5. Perrault (1952)
6. Kingston (1891)
7. Heming (1921)
8. McTaggart-Cowan (1998)
9. Hewitt (1921)
10. Reed (1914)
11. Munro and Cowan (1947)
12. Munro (1937)
13. Munro (1939, 1941, 1942)
14. Brooks and Swarth (1925)
15. Munro and Cowan (1947)
16. Candy and Campbell (2012)
17. Taverner (1919)
18. Taverner (1926)
19. Swarth (1912)
20. Swarth (1922)
21. Swarth (1924)
22. Swarth (1926)
23. Foster (1965)
24. Carson (1962)
25. Poole (1989)
26. Hickey (1969)
27. Grinnell (1910)
28. Ehrenreich and Aikman (1963)
29. McTaggart-Cowan (1998)
30. Cowan (1955)
31. Cowan (1946a)
32. McTaggart-Cowan (1998)
33. Campbell and Stirling (1968)
34. Campbell et al. (1975)
35. McTaggart-Cowan (1998)
36. Munro (1944)
37. Dickinson (1953)
38. McTaggart-Cowan (1998)
39. McTaggart-Cowan (1929)
40. McTaggart-Cowan (1930)
41. University of British Columbia (1932)
42. Swarth (1922)
43. Swarth (1924)
44. Swarth (1926)
45. McTaggart-Cowan (1933)
46. McTaggart-Cowan (1933b)
47. McTaggart-Cowan (1934)
48. McTaggart-Cowan (1935)
49. Cowan (1936),
50. Cowan (1935a)
51. Fannin (1891)
52. Kermode and Anderson (1914)
53. Munro (1917)
54. Rhoads (1893)
55. McTaggart-Cowan (1998)
56. Kermode (1904)
57. Cowan (1939)
58. Kermode (1904)
59. Brooks and Swarth (1925)
60. Munro and Cowan (1947)
61. McTaggart-Cowan (1998)
62. Munro and Cowan (1947)
63. McTaggart-Cowan (1998)
64. Dickinson (1953)

65. Hatler et al. (2008)
66. McTaggart-Cowan (1998)
67. Ibid.
68. Cowan, G. (1968)
69. Anonymous (1997)
70. Allen (1925)
71. Hamilton (1939)
72. Leopold (1933)
73. Udvardy (1969)
74. Anonymous (1941)
75. Anonymous (1955)
76. Meagher (2008), Haroldson et al. (2008)
77. Cowan (1944), Cowan (1945b)
78. Cowan (1940a), Cowan (1941)
79. Cowan (1942), Cowan (1944)
80. Cowan (1945a)
81. Fowle (1944)
82. Hatter (1950)
83. Cowan (1940b)
84. Hart (2009)
85. Ibid.
86. Ibid.
87. Cowan (1964)
88. Stenhouse (1929–30)
89. Douglas (1914)
90. Douglas (1833)
91. Campbell and Gregory (1976)
92. Guiguet (1953)
93. Cowan and Guiguet (1956)
94. Drent and Guiguet (1961)
95. Campbell and Stirling (1971)
96. Campbell and Gibbard (1971), Campbell at al. (2010)
97. Campbell et al. (1972a), Campbell et al. (1972b), Campbell et al. (1974),
98. Campbell et al. (1982)
99. Campbell et al. (1979), Campbell et al. (1988)
100. Green and Campbell (1984)
101. Gregory and Campbell (1984)
102. Campbell et al. (1990a), Campbell et al. (1990b), Campbell et al. (1997), Campbell et al. (2001)
103. Campbell (1994a), Campbell (1994b), Campbell (1994c), Campbell (1995)
104. Campbell et al. (2013)
105. Campbell (1973a), Campbell (1973b), Campbell and Davies (1973), Campbell and Shepard (1973), Campbell and Weber (1973)
106. Ibid.
107. Carson (1962)
108. Ehrlich and Ehrlich (1968)
109. Hardin (1968)
110. GSGislason & Associates (2009)
111. Lloyd (1833)
112. Tremblay-Boyer et al. (2011)
113. Sladen (1965)
114. Sladen et al. (1966)
115. Michelutti et al. (2009)
116. Hunt and Bischoff (1960), Ivey (2004), Campbell et al. (2009)
117. Hardin (1968)
118. Ehrenreich and Aikman (1963), Daubenmire (1968)
119. Ibid.
120. Trudeau, Pierre Elliot. A response to the introduction of Omnibus Bill C-150, which amended the Criminal Code of Canada. December 21, 1967.
121. Miles and Harris (1978)
122. Hickey (1969)
123. Cade at al. (1988)
124. Leopold (1925)
125. Hahn (2000)
126. Hegel and Baillie (2009)
127. Cohen (1988), Turner, T. (1993)
128. Text courtesy of the University of British Columbia Archives, Vancouver, BC.
129. Walker (1976)
130. Cowan (1976)
131. Osmond-Jones et al. (1977)
132. Boonstra and Sinclair (1984)
133. Carl and Guiguet (1957)
134. McTaggart-Cowan (2001)
135. McTaggart-Cowan (1998)
136. Campbell (1970)
137. Campbell et al. (1979), Campbell et al. (1982), Campbell et al. (1988)
138. Campbell (1976), Campbell (1977), Campbell and Garrioch (1979), Manuwal and Campbell (1979)
139. Campbell and McNall (1982)
140. Campbell and Gibbard (1971), Campbell et al. (2010), Campbell et al. (2013)
141. McTaggart-Cowan (1998)
142. Campbell and McNall (1982)
143. Siddle (2010a), Siddle (2010b)

144. McTaggart-Cowan (1990)
145. McTaggart-Cowan (2004)
146. McTaggart-Cowan (2005)
147. Cowan and Cowan (1977)
148. Trauger and Kennedy (2012)
149. Hudson et al. (1970), Hudson et al. (1971), Hudson et al. (1972)
150. Cowan and Bandy (1969)
151. Barkley (1972)
152. Zwickel and Bendell (2004)
153. Bergerud (1971)
154. Bergerud (1983)
155. Bergerud (1974)
156. Errington (1967)
157. Bergerud et al. (2007)
158. Krebs (2009)
159. Heard (1977)
160. Bryant (1998)
161. Cade et al. (1988)
162. Kessel and Gibson (1978)
163. Murie (1944)
164. Campbell et al. (1990a), Demarchi et al. (1990), Campbell et al. (1990b), Campbell et al. (1997), Campbell et al. (2001)
165. Thommasen et al. (2004)
166. Munro and Cowan (1947)
167. Campbell (1976), Manuwal and Campbell (1979), Munro and Campbell (1979)
168. Hatler et al. (1973)
169. Walker (1976)
170. Erskine (1992)
171. Burnett (2003)
172. Erskine (1971)
173. Leopold (1933)
174. Darling and Milton (1966)
175. Anonymous (1998)
176. McTaggart-Cowan (1998)
177. McTaggart-Cowan (2001)
178. Krajina (1978)
179. Geist (1978)
180. Grant and Cowan (1964)
181. Cowan and Guiguet (1956)
182. Guiguet (1953)
183. Hartman and Scrivener (1990)
184. Northcote and Hartman (2004)
185. Hatler et al. (2008)
186. Hatter (1997)
187. Hatter (2005)
188. Cowan and Hatter (1940)
189. Leopold (1933)
190. Cowan and Guiguet (1956)
191. Cowan (1946b)
192. Hornocker and Negri (2009)
193. Hornocker (1997)
194. Jakimchuk (1976)
195. Johnson and Herter (1979)
196. Klein et al. (2005)
197. Fay (1982)
198. Krebs (2008)
199. Krebs and Cowan (1962)
200. Chitty (1960)
201. Anonymous (1954)
202. Cowan and McCrory (1970)
203. Roessingh and Penn (2012)
204. Ritcey (1995)
205. Edwards and Ritcey (1967)
206. Galton (1872)
207. Anonymous (2009)
208. Anonymous (2013)
209. Campbell and Sealy (2011)
210. Vermeer (1963)
211. Spalding (1964)
212. Turner (1975)
213. Pojar and MacKinnon (1994)
214. Sugden (1961), Demarchi et al. (2000)
215. Sugden (1973), Sugden (1978), Sugden (1979)
216. Sugden (1963)
217. Butler and Cunningham (1947)
218. Ecological Society of America (2002)
219. Medley (2011)
220. Theberge and Theberge (2010)
221. Thomas and Gray (2002)
222. Environment Canada (2008)
223. Tompa (1962)
224. Stokes (1974)
225. Vermeer (1963)
226. Van Tets (1959)
227. Drent (1965)
228. Tinbergen (1953)
229. Buckner and Reneau (2005)
230. Weeden (1978), Weeden (1992)
231. Zwickel (2004)
232. Guiguet (1955)
233. Bousfield and Hendricks (2002)
234. Clark (2008)
235. Leopold (1949)
236. McTaggart-Cowan (1998)
237. Einarson (1948)
238. Einarson (1965)
239. Soper (1964)
240. Bent (1968)

241. McTaggart-Cowan (2001)
242. Campbell et al. (1990a), Campbell et al. (1990b), Campbell et al. (1997), Campbell et al. (2001)
243. McTaggart-Cowan (2004)
244. McTaggart-Cowan (2005)
245. Racey (1926), Racey (1948)
246. Racey (1926)
247. McTaggart-Cowan (1929)
248. Racey and Cowan (1935), Cowan and Racey (1946)
249. Grinnell (1915), Grinnell and Storer (1924)
250. Grinnell and Miller (1944)
251. Munro and Cowan (1947)
252. McTaggart-Cowan (1998)
253. McTaggart-Cowan (1933c), McTaggart-Cowan (1933d), McTaggart-Cowan (1934)
254. McTaggart-Cowan (1936)
255. McTaggart-Cowan (2001)
256. Cowan (1954)
257. Campbell et al. (1990a), Campbell et al. (1990b), Campbell et al. (1997), Campbell et al. (2001)
258. McTaggart-Cowan (2001)
259. Munro and Cowan (1947)
260. Campbell (1983), Campbell et al. (1987)
261. Cowan and Cowan (1961)
262. Cowan (1951)
263. Martell (1975)
264. Munro and Cowan (1947)
265. Fowle (1942)
266. Fowle (1972)
267. Smith (2004)
268. Handel and Gill (2001)
269. Palmer (1976)
270. Silver (2004)
271. Silver et al. (2010), Campbell et al. (2011), Campbell et al. (2013)
272. McTaggart-Cowan (1998)
273. Hart (2009)
274. Hatter (1997)
275. McTaggart-Cowan (1990)
276. Trauger and Kennedy (2012)

Index

Photographs indicated in italics